Lecture Notes in Computer Science 15759

Founding Editors

Gerhard Goos
Juris Hartmanis

AF848478

The series Lecture Notes in Computer Science (LNCS), including its subseries Lecture Notes in Artificial Intelligence (LNAI) and Lecture Notes in Bioinformatics (LNBI), has established itself as a medium for the publication of new developments in computer science and information technology research, teaching, and education.

LNCS enjoys close cooperation with the computer science R & D community, the series counts many renowned academics among its volume editors and paper authors, and collaborates with prestigious societies. Its mission is to serve this international community by providing an invaluable service, mainly focused on the publication of conference and workshop proceedings and postproceedings. LNCS commenced publication in 1973.

Andreas Malcher · Luca Prigioniero
Editors

Descriptional Complexity of Formal Systems

26th IFIP WG 1.02 International Conference, DCFS 2025
Loughborough, UK, July 22–24, 2025
Proceedings

Springer

Editors
Andreas Malcher
Universität Giessen
Giessen, Germany

Luca Prigioniero
Loughborough University
Loughborough, UK

ISSN 0302-9743 ISSN 1611-3349 (electronic)
Lecture Notes in Computer Science
ISBN 978-3-031-97099-3 ISBN 978-3-031-97100-6 (eBook)
https://doi.org/10.1007/978-3-031-97100-6

This Springer imprint is published by the registered company Springer Nature Switzerland AG
The registered company address is: Gewerbestrasse 11, 6330 Cham, Switzerland

Preface

The 26th International Conference on Descriptional Complexity of Formal Systems (DCFS 2025) was held in Loughborough, UK, on July 22–24, 2025 and was organized by the Department of Computer Science at Loughborough University, in association with the IFIP Working Group 1.02 "Descriptional Complexity". DCFS is an annual international conference concerning the descriptional complexity of formal systems and structures (and its applications). Topics of interest are related to all aspects of descriptional complexity, including but not limited to the following

- Automata, grammars, languages and other formal systems; various modes of operation and complexity measures
- Succinctness of description of objects, state-explosion-like phenomena
- Circuit complexity of Boolean functions and related measures
- Size complexity of formal systems
- Structural complexity of formal systems
- Trade-offs between computational models and mode of operation
- Applications of formal systems—for instance in software and hardware testing, in dialogue systems, in systems modeling or in modeling natural languages—and their complexity constraints
- Co-operating formal systems
- Size or structural complexity of formal systems for modeling natural languages
- Complexity aspects related to the combinatorics of words
- Complexity in resource-bounded or structure-bounded environments
- Structural complexity as related to descriptional complexity
- Frontiers between decidability and undecidability
- Universality and reversibility
- Nature-motivated (bio-inspired) architectures and unconventional models of computing
- Blum Static (Kolmogorov/Chaitin) complexity, algorithmic information.

DCFS became an IFIP working conference in 2016, and is continuing the former Workshop on Descriptional Complexity of Formal Systems, which was the merger of two related workshops, namely, Descriptional Complexity of Automata, Grammars and Related Structures (DCAGRS) and Formal Descriptions and Software Reliability (FDSR). The DCAGRS workshop took place in Magdeburg, Germany (1999), London, Ontario, Canada (2000), and Vienna, Austria (2001), while the FDSR workshop took place in Paderborn, Germany (1998), Boca Raton, Florida, USA (1999), and San Jose, California, USA (2000). The DCFS workshop has previously been held in London, Ontario, Canada (2002), Budapest, Hungary (2003), London, Ontario, Canada (2004), Como, Italy (2005), Las Cruces, New Mexico, USA (2006), Nový Smokovec, Slovakia (2007), Charlottetown, Prince Edward Island, Canada (2008), Magdeburg, Germany (2009), Saskatoon, Saskatchewan, Canada (2010), Limburg/Giessen, Germany (2011), Braga, Portugal (2012), London, Ontario, Canada (2013), Turku, Finland (2014), and

Waterloo, Ontario, Canada (2015). The DCFS working conference has previously been held in Bucharest, Romania (2016), Milan, Italy (2017), Halifax, Nova Scotia, Canada (2018), and Košice, Slovakia (2019). Due to the COVID-19 pandemic the conferences planned to be held in Vienna, Austria (2020) and Seoul, South Korea (2021) were canceled as in-person meetings, but the accepted papers appeared in conference proceedings. The conference series was resumed as an on-site event in 2022 and took place in Debrecen, Hungary (2022) and Potsdam, Germany (2023).

This volume of *Lecture Notes in Computer Science* contains the invited contributions and the accepted papers presented at DCFS 2025. Special thanks go to the invited speakers

- Giuseppa Castiglione (Palermo, Italy),
- Ian McQuillan (Saskatoon, Canada), and
- Irek Ulidowski (Leicester, UK)

for accepting our invitation and presenting their recent results at DCFS 2025. In addition, we were very proud to have an honorary lecture in our program given by

- Erzsébet Csuhaj-Varjú (Budapest, Hungary)

Erzsébet has been a key figure in our research community, a mentor to many, and a respected member of the DCFS steering committee for years. Her contributions have had a lasting impact, and the honorary lecture aims to recognize her distinguished work and to celebrate her retirement and appointment as Professor Emerita.

Twenty papers were submitted to DCFS 2025 by a total of 51 authors from 14 different countries, from all over the world, Canada, Colombia, Czech Republic, France, Germany, Hungary, India, Italy, Japan, Portugal, Russia, Switzerland, Turkey, and the UK. From these submissions, on the basis of three referee reports each, the Program Committee selected 15 papers—the submission and single-blind refereeing process was supported by the EasyChair conference management system. We warmly thank the members of the Program Committee for their excellent work in making this selection. Moreover we also thank the additional external reviewers for their careful evaluation. All these efforts were the basis for the success of the workshop.

We are grateful to all the members of the Organizing Committee for their commitment in the preparation of the scientific sessions and social events.

We would also like to thank the editorial staff at Springer for their efficient collaboration in making this volume available before the conference. Their timely instructions were very helpful to our preparation for this volume.

Finally, we would like to thank all the participants for attending the DCFS conference. We hope that this year's meeting has stimulated new research and scientific co-operations in the field of descriptional complexity, as in previous years. We hope to see you at DCFS in 2026!

July 2025

Andreas Malcher
Luca Prigioniero

Organization

Program Committee Chairs

Andreas Malcher	Universität Giessen, Germany
Luca Prigioniero	Loughborough University, UK

Steering Committee

Cezar Câmpeanu	University of Prince Edward Island, Canada
Stavros Konstantinidis	Saint Mary's University, Canada
Martin Kutrib	Universität Giessen, Germany
Giovanni Pighizzini	Università degli Studi di Milano, Italy
Rogério Reis (Chair)	Universidade do Porto, Portugal
Kai Salomaa	Queen's University, Canada
György Vaszil	University of Debrecen, Hungary

Program Committee

Henning Bordihn	Universität Potsdam, Germany
Pascal Caron	Université de Rouen, France
Szilárd Fazekas	Akita University, Japan
Dora Giammarresi	Università degli Studi di Roma Tor Vergata, Italy
Yo-Sub Han	Yonsei University, South Korea
Galina Jirásková	Slovak Academy of Sciences, Slovakia
Stavros Konstantinidis	Saint Mary's University, Canada
Martin Kutrib	Universität Giessen, Germany
Sylvain Lombardy	Université de Bordeaux, France
Dana Pardubská	Comenius University Bratislava, Slovakia
Rogério Reis	Universidade do Porto, Portugal
Kai Salomaa	Queen's University, Canada
Marinella Sciortino	Università degli Studi di Palermo, Italy
Shinnosuke Seki	University of Electro-Communications, Japan
Taylor Smith	St. Francis Xavier University, Canada
Nicholas Tran	Santa Clara University, USA
György Vaszil	University of Debrecen, Hungary
Hsu-Chun Yen	National Taiwan University, Taiwan

Additional Reviewers

Katrin Casel
Guilherme Duarte
Yusuke Inoue
Daihei Ise
Sungmin Kim
Sang-Ki Ko
Peter Kostolányi
Zsuzsanna Liptak
Oliver Lyon
Ian McQuillan
Takuya Mieno
Nelma Moreira
Timothy Ng
Florent Nicart
Priscilla Raucci
Christian Rauch
Silas Cato Sacher
Jana Schulz
Carla Selmi
Ryoma Sin'ya
Di-De Yen
Takao Yuyama
Mohammad Zakzok

Organizing Committee

Robert Mercaş	Loughborough University, UK
Luca Prigioniero	Loughborough University, UK

Sponsors

Abstracts of Invited Talks

Wheeler Automata in Formal Language Theory (Extended Abstract)

Giuseppa Castiglione

Dipartimento di Matematica e Informatica, Università di Palermo, Via Archirafi, 34, 90123 Italy
giuseppa.castiglione@unipa.it

1 Introduction

Many significant techniques in string algorithms leverage the co-lexicographically sorted prefixes of a string as a fundamental tool for various pattern matching and compression methods [21, 24]. The Burrows-Wheeler transform [13] exemplifies a powerful tool that has profoundly influenced research on indexing and text compression in recent years. Consequently, it has been natural to extend this perspective to more complex combinatorial structures, such as labeled trees [20], sets of strings [25], and de Bruijn graphs [11].

In 2017, the concept of *Wheeler graph* [22] was introduced, providing a theoretical unification of all the previously mentioned tools. Within Wheeler graphs, a total order on the alphabet establishes an order among the nodes, which then propagates forward by traversing pairs of edges that share the same label.

Automata whose transition graph is a Wheeler graph are known as *Wheeler automata*, in which the states are ordered according to the order on the alphabet. These automata support efficient data structures for path queries and pattern matching on their languages; furthermore, they enable innovative compression techniques [4, 27]. It is noteworthy that membership and pattern matching problems on regular languages are generally challenging [7].

In addition to the extensive and productive research on the practical applications of Wheeler automata, recent years have seen a thorough exploration of their theoretical aspects. This includes investigations into the complexity of the automata and the properties of the accepted languages, known as *Wheeler languages* [3, 9, 17].

In other contexts, automata equipped with an order on the set of states that is compatible with the transition function, have been studied in connection with the synchronization of automata, as well as to the combinatorial and algebraic characterization of languages [5, 12, 29].

In what follows, we shall present some of the main known properties and theoretical challenges on Wheeler automata and Wheeler languages. This is not a complete summary of all existing knowledge, as the topic has led to a significant amount of research. Instead, we highlight some important theoretical aspects that have motivated and continue to motivate certain themes in our research.

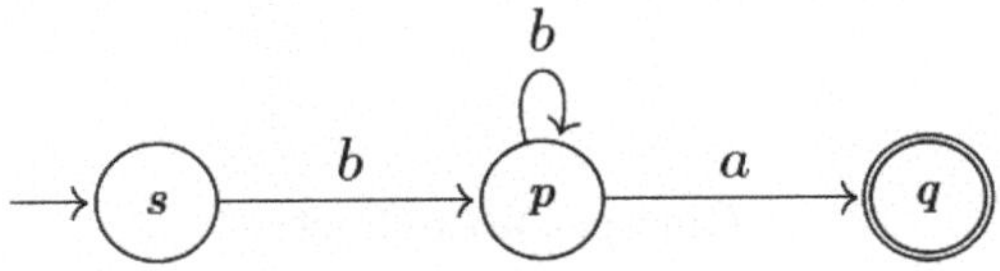

Fig. 1. An incomplete WDFA (with $a \prec b$ and $s < q < p$) accepting the language b^+a.

2 Wheeler Automata

If Σ is a finite alphabet, with Σ^* we denote the set of finite words on Σ. A *deterministic finite automaton* (DFA) is a quintuple $\mathcal{A} = (Q, \Sigma, \delta, s, F)$ where Q is a finite set of states, Σ is a finite alphabet, $\delta : Q \times \Sigma \to Q$ is the transition function, possibly a partial function, s is the initial state and $F \subseteq Q$ is the set of final states. We denote by δ^* the generalized transition function defined in the words of Σ^*. If δ is a total function, the automaton is *complete* while, if δ is a partial function, the automaton is *incomplete.* If we denote $L_p(\mathcal{A}) = \{w \in \Sigma^* | \ \delta^*(p, w) \in F\}$, a state p is an *empty state* if $L_p(\mathcal{A}) = \emptyset$ and is a *coaccesible state* if $L_p(\mathcal{A}) \neq \emptyset$. For any $p \in Q$ we define $In(p) = \{a \in \Sigma | \ \delta(q, a) = p, \text{ for some } q \in Q\}$. An automaton is said *input-consistent* if $|In(p)| = 1$, for each $p \in Q$. If Σ is ordered with $\prec$ we can define the *co-lexicograhic order* $\prec$ among words of Σ^*. If $u = u_1 \ldots u_n$ and $v = v_1 \ldots v_m$ then

$$u \prec v \Leftrightarrow (u \text{ is a suffix of } v) \text{ or } (\exists i : u_{n-i} \prec v_{m-i} \text{ and } \forall j < i, \quad u_{n-j} = v_{m-j})$$

A *Wheeler DFA* (WDFA) is an input consistent DFA $\mathcal{A} = (Q, \Sigma, \delta, s, F)$, $In(s) = \emptyset$ and there exists a total order $\leq$ on Q such that

- the initial state is the minimum;
- for $q_1 = \delta(p_1, \sigma_1)$ and $q_2 = \delta(p_2, \sigma_2)$, $p_1, p_2, q_1, q_2 \in Q$ and $\sigma_1, \sigma_2 \in \Sigma$;
  if $\sigma_1 \prec \sigma_2$ then $q_1 < q_2$;
  if $\sigma_1 = \sigma_2$ and $p_1 \leq p_2$ then $q_1 \leq q_2$.

See in Fig. 1 an example of Wheeler automaton.

The previous definition can also be given in the non-deterministic version (WNFA). It is known [3] that WNFA and WDFA have the same expressive power in terms of accepted languages. Unlike the general case and other subregular cases [10], the determinization of WNFA is polynomial.

A WDFA admits a unique order of its states that makes it Wheeler, and this order is uniquely determined by the co-lexicographic order of the strings that label the paths from the initial state to any state [2]. This provides a Myhill-Nerode Theorem for Wheeler languages, ensuring the existence of a unique minimal WDFA (with respect to the number of states) that recognizes the language. It also makes it possible to efficiently decide whether a DFA is Wheeler [3, 9]. Note that the problem of deciding whether an automaton is a Wheeler automaton is, in general, NP-complete [23].

In [1] a linear-time procedure is given to determine the minimal WDFA equivalent to a given input WDFA. If we compare the number of states of the minimal WDFA and the minimal DFA, the minimal WDFA for a Wheeler language can have a number of states that is exponentially larger than the number of states of the minimal non-Wheeler DFA [3].

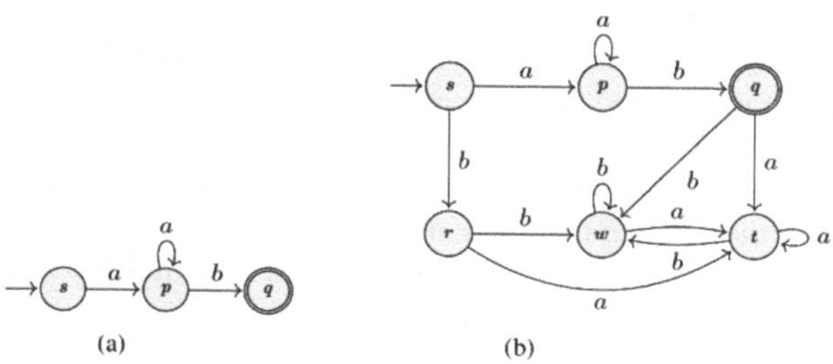

Fig. 2. (a) A WDFA (with $a \prec b$ and $s < p < q$) accepting the language a^+b; (b) an equivalent complete WDFA (with $a \prec b$ and $s < p < t < r < q < w$).

3 Completion and Boolean Operations

The problem of embedding a finite automaton into a complete one while preserving some specific properties is an old problem in automata theory [6, 14, 19, 26, 28]. It is called the *Completion Problem*.

The completion problem is of particular interest for the class of WDFA since, in general, WDFAs are not complete, and there exist some Wheeler languages that cannot be accepted by any complete Wheeler automaton [3]; for example, the language b^+a (with $a \prec b$). In this context, the problem is to embed, when possible, a WDFA $\mathcal{A}$ into an equivalent complete WDFA whose (total) order on the states is an extension of the order on the states of $\mathcal{A}$.

In the original definition, all states of a Wheeler DFA are supposed to be coaccessible. However, since we are interested in completing a WDFA, it is natural to admit some empty states while maintaining the Wheeler property regarding the order.

The classical procedure of completing an automaton by adding a unique empty state to define all missing transitions can result in a DFA that is no longer a WDFA. However, in some cases, the automaton can be completed by adding multiple empty states while still preserving the Wheeler property. See, for example, Fig. 2 for the language a^+b.

Conversely, there are instances where this problem is unsolvable, as some WDFAs cannot be embedded into any equivalent complete WDFA.

We say that a WDFA is *Wheeler-complete* if it cannot be properly embedded into another equivalent WDFA. Hence, even if a WDFA $\mathcal{A}$ cannot be completed, there always exists a Wheeler-complete DFA in which $\mathcal{A}$ can be embedded; we call it a *Wheeler-completion* of $\mathcal{A}$. We have shown in [15] that, among all the Wheeler-completions of $\mathcal{A}$, the one with the minimum number of empty states is unique. In the same paper, a completion algorithm is given that, having as input a WDFA $\mathcal{A}$, returns its minimal Wheeler-completion. The automaton in Fig. 3 is the minimal Wheeler-completion of the automaton in Fig. 1; it is Wheeler-complete but not complete.

The class of Wheeler languages is closed under intersection, but it is neither closed under complement nor union. A relevant application of this completion algorithm is the construction, under suitable conditions, of a WDFA that recognizes the complement of a Wheeler language and a WDFA that recognizes the union of two Wheeler languages. This approach is an alternative to the one proposed in [18]. Since there exist some Wheeler languages that do not admit any complete WDFA, it is not always possible to find a WDFA for the complement by simply switching final and non-final states in a complete WDFA recognizing them. Note that the complement of such Wheeler languages could be itself a Wheeler language. These considerations reveal that the matter of Boolean operations remains to be thoroughly explored.

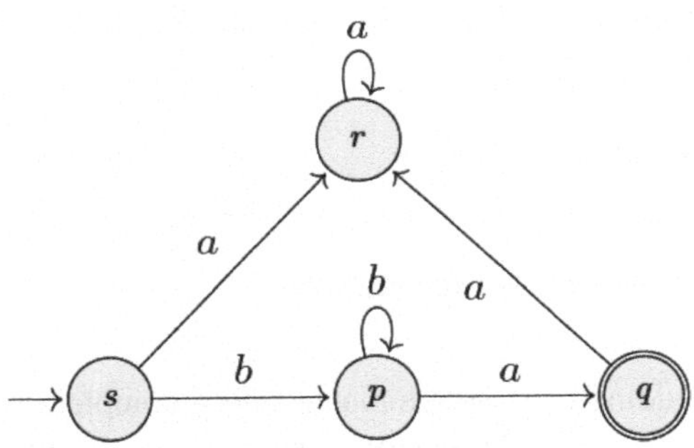

Fig. 3. The Wheeler-completion (with $a \prec b$ and $s < r < q < p$) of the automaton in Fig. 1.

4 Universally Wheeler Languages

Wheeler languages form a subclass of star-free languages [3], which means they can be generated from finite languages by Boolean operations and compositions. One of the further goals of the language-theoretic study of Wheeler languages is to establish connections with other classes of regular languages. The absence of closure under Boolean operations poses a significant challenge in characterizing Wheeler languages using Boolean operations and compositions involving some elementary Wheeler languages.

Moreover, it is important to note that the definition of Wheeler languages depends on a fixed total order of the alphabet. Given a totally ordered alphabet, a language is classified as a Wheeler language if there exists an automaton that accepts the language, which is a WDFA with respect to this order. This dependency on the alphabet order is unsatisfactory because, in the studied applications, the order of the alphabet is irrelevant. In fact, the alphabet can be changed by a mapping. Furthermore, from a theoretical point of view, if we aim to position Wheeler languages within a hierarchy of regular language classes, these classes never depend on the order of the alphabet.

For this reason, D'Agostino et al. introduced in [16] the class of *Existentially Wheeler languages* (*EW*). A language is in *EW* if there is an order in the alphabet that makes it Wheeler. However, the problem of verifying whether a language is a Wheeler language, given a DFA that accepts it, can be solved in quadratic time (w.r.t. the size of the DFA) [9]. In contrast, determining whether a language belongs to *EW* is NP-complete [16].

In [8] the class of *Universally Wheeler languages* (*UW*), i.e., those languages that are Wheeler with respect to every order of the alphabet, are defined. The authors relate *UW* to some very well-known classes of regular languages, namely the *Definite* (*DEF*), *Reverse Definite* (*RDEF*), and the *Strictly Locally Testable* (*SLT*) *languages*.

In particular, they have shown that *SLT* is strictly included in *UW*. Moreover, since *UW* is not closed under complement, they considered the class of languages $\mathcal{L}$ such that both $\mathcal{L}$ and $\overline{\mathcal{L}}$ belong to *UW* and proved that this class coincides with $DEF \cup RDEF$.

From a computational perspective, they established that verifying whether the language accepted by a given DFA belongs to *UW* can be accomplished in quadratic time with respect to the size of the DFA.

References

1. Alanko, J., Cotumaccio, N., Prezza, N.: Linear-time minimization of wheeler DFAs. In: DCC 2022, pp. 53–62. IEEE (2022). https://doi.org/10.1109/DCC52660.2022.00013
2. Alanko, J., D'Agostino, G., Policriti, A., Prezza, N.: Regular languages meet prefix sorting. In: Chawla, S. (ed.) Proceedings of the 2020 ACM-SIAM Symposium on Discrete Algorithms, SODA 2020, pp. 911–930. SIAM (2020). https://doi.org/10.1137/1.9781611975994.55
3. Alanko, J., D'Agostino, G., Policriti, A., Prezza, N.: Wheeler languages. Inf. Comput. **281**, 104820 (2021). https://doi.org/10.1016/J.IC.2021.104820
4. Alanko, J.N., Gagie, T., Navarro, G., Benkner, L.S.: Tunneling on wheeler graphs. In: Bilgin, A., Marcellin, M.W., Serra-Sagrist'a, J., Storer, J.A. (eds.) Data Compression Conference, DCC 2019, pp. 122–131. IEEE (2019). https://doi.org/10.1109/DCC.2019.00020
5. Ananichev, D.S., Volkov, M.V.: Synchronizing monotonic automata. Theor. Comput. Sci. **327**(3), 225–239 (2004). https://doi.org/10.1016/J.TCS.2004.03.068
6. Ashley, J.J., Marcus, B.H., Perrin, D., Tuncel, S.: Surjective extensions of sliding-block codes. SIAM J. Discret. Math. **6**(4), 582–611 (1993). https://doi.org/10.1137/0406046
7. Backurs, A., Indyk, P.: Which regular expression patterns are hard to match? In: Dinur, I. (ed.) FOCS 2016, pp. 457–466. IEEE Computer Society (2016). https://doi.org/10.1109/FOCS.2016.56

8. Becker, R., et al.: Universally Wheeler Languages (2025). https://arxiv.org/abs/2504.19537
9. Becker, R., et al.: Optimal wheeler language recognition. In: Nardini, F.M., Pisanti, N., Venturini, R. (eds.) SPIRE 2023. LNCS, vol. 14240, pp. 62–74. Springer, Cham (2023). https://doi.org/10.1007/978-3-031-43980-3_6
10. Bordihn, H., Holzer, M., Kutrib, M.: Determination of finite automata accepting subregular languages. Theor. Comput. Sci. **410**(35), 3209–3222 (2009). https://doi.org/10.1016/J.TCS.2009.05.019
11. Bowe, A., Onodera, T., Sadakane, K., Shibuya, T.: Succinct de Bruijn graphs. In: Raphael, B., Tang, J. (eds.) WABI 2012L. LNCS, vol. 7534, pp. 225–235. Springer, Heidelberg (2012). https://doi.org/10.1007/978-3-642-33122-0_18
12. Brzozowski, J.A., Li, B., Liu, D.: Syntactic complexities of six classes of star-free languages. J. Autom. Lang. Comb. **17**(2–4), 83–105 (2012). https://doi.org/10.25596/JALC-2012-083
13. Burrows, M., Wheeler, D.J.: A block-sorting lossless data compression algorithm. Techical report, 124, Digital Equipment Corporation (1994). https://api.semanticscholar.org/CorpusID:2167441
14. Béal, M.P., Lombardy, S., Perrin, D.: Embeddings of local automata. Ill. J. Math. **54**(1), 155–174 (2010). https://doi.org/10.1109/ISIT.2008.4595411
15. Castiglione, G., Restivo, A.: Completing wheeler automata. In: Proceedings of the 25th Italian Conference on Theoretical Computer Science, 2024. CEUR Workshop Proceedings, vol. 3811, pp. 120–132. CEUR-WS.org (2024). https://ceur-ws.org/Vol-3811/paper060.pdf
16. D'Agostino, G., Martincigh, D., Policriti, A.: Ordering regular languages: a danger zone. In: Coen, C.S., Salvo, I. (eds.) Proceedings of the 22nd Italian Conference on Theoretical Computer Science, 2021. CEUR Workshop Proceedings, vol. 3072, pp. 46–69. CEURWS. org (2021). https://ceur-ws.org/Vol-3072/paper5.pdf
17. D'Agostino, G., Martincigh, D., Policriti, A.: Ordering regular languages and automata: complexity. Theor. Comput. Sci. **949**, 113709 (2023). https://doi.org/10.1016/J.TCS.2023.113709
18. Egidi, L., Louza, F.A., Manzini, G.: Space efficient merging of de Bruijn graphs and wheeler graphs. Algorithmica **84**(3), 639–669 (2022). https://doi.org/10.1007/S00453-021-00855-2
19. Ehrenfeucht, A., Rozenberg, G.: Each regular code is included in a maximal regular code. RAIRO Theor. Inform. Appl. **20**(1), 89–96 (1986). https://doi.org/10.1051/ITA/1986200100891
20. Ferragina, P., Luccio, F., Manzini, G., Muthukrishnan, S.: Structuring labeled trees for optimal succinctness, and beyond. In: 46th Annual IEEE Symposium on Foundations of Computer Science (FOCS 2005), pp. 184–196. IEEE Computer Society (2005).https://doi.org/10.1109/SFCS.2005.69
21. Ferragina, P., Manzini, G.: Opportunistic data structures with applications. In: 41st Annual Symposium on Foundations of Computer Science, FOCS 2000, pp. 390–398. IEEE Computer Society (2000). https://doi.org/10.1109/SFCS.2000.892127
22. Gagie, T., Manzini, G., Sirén, J.: Wheeler graphs: a framework for BWT-based data structures. Theor. Comput. Sci. **698**, 67–78 (2017). https://doi.org/10.1016/J.TCS.2017.06.016

23. Gibney, D., Thankachan, S.V.: On the complexity of recognizing wheeler graphs. Algorithmica **84**(3), 784–814 (2022). https://doi.org/10.1007/S00453-021-00917-5
24. Grossi, R., Vitter, J.S.: Compressed suffix arrays and suffix trees with applications to text indexing and string matching (extended abstract). In: Proceedings of the Thirty-Second Annual ACM Symposium on Theory of Computing, pp. 397–406. ACM (2000). https://doi.org/10.1145/335305.335351
25. Mantaci, S., Restivo, A., Rosone, G., Sciortino, M.: An extension of the burrows-wheeler transform. Theor. Comput. Sci. **387**(3), 298–312 (2007). https://doi.org/10.1016/J.TCS.2007.07.014
26. Montalbano, R.: Local automata and completion. In: STACS 1993. LNCS, vol. 665, pp. 333–342. Springer, Heidelberg (1993). https://doi.org/10.1007/3-540-56503-5
27. Prezza, N.: On locating paths in compressed tries. In: Marx, D. (ed.) Proceedings of the 2021 ACM-SIAM Symposium on Discrete Algorithms, SODA 2021, pp. 744–760. SIAM (2021). https://doi.org/10.1137/1.9781611976465.47
28. Schützenberger, M.P.: A remark on incompletely specified automata. Inf. Control. **8**(4), 373–376 (1965). https://doi.org/10.1016/S0019-9958(65)90308-6
29. Shyr, H.J., Thierrin, G.: Ordered automata and associated languages. Tamkang J. Math. **5**, 9–20 (1974)

Descriptional Complexity in Natural Computing: the Case of P Systems

Erzsébet Csuhaj-Varjú

Department of Algorithms and Their Applications, Faculty of Informatics, ELTE Eötvös Loránd University, Budapest, Hungary
csuhaj@inf.elte.hu

The technological and societal challenges of our time are increasingly demanding computational models and methods that go beyond the limitations of Turing machines and are novel in their architecture and operation.

Natural computing attempts to address this challenge [18]. It is defined by L. Kari and G. Rozenberg as "a field of research that investigates models and computational techniques inspired by nature, and in parallel attempts to understand the world around us from the perspective of information processing" [14].

In natural computing, models are motivated by various natural phenomena, such as self-reproduction, group behavior, cell membranes, and the organization and functioning of cells and tissues. Evolutionary computing, swarm intelligence, artificial life, DNA computing, and membrane computing are all subfields of natural computing.

As in all areas of computer science, the need for concise descriptions of the models, i.e. low descriptional complexity, arises in the above areas. Many descriptional complexity notions of classical computational models can be defined analogously to models in natural computing. But natural computing models may also have properties that require the development of new concepts. This is because, in addition to computational aspects, the appropriate definition of descriptional complexity concepts and metrics must take into account the characteristics of natural processes.

In this presentation, we discuss the problems outlined above. After a general formulation of the questions for natural computing and a discussion of possible answers, we present descriptional complexity notions and results of a specific model, the membrane system, also known as the P system.

Membrane systems are distributed parallel computing devices. The notion of the membrane system was introduced by Gh. Păun with the aim of providing an unconventional computational model which mimics the structure and function of living cells [15]. Later, the concept was extended to modeling living tissues, neural systems, and higher organizations such as groups of bacteria. Over the years, the theory of membrane systems and its applications have become a vivid, well-established scientific field [13, 16, 17].

The original variant of P systems (the symbol-object membrane system) consists of the membrane structure (a tree), multisets of objects that are located in the compartments or also called regions of the membrane structure (in the nodes of the tree), and the rules that describe the change of the objects in the compartments. In the case of tissue (or tissue-like) P systems, where the membrane structure is an arbitrary virtual graph, we use the term cell instead of region. The current configuration (the current state) of a P system consists of its current membrane structure and the current multiset of objects in its compartments.

The P system can change its configuration by using its rules and the prescribed way of rule application. Usually, the rules are applied in the so-called maximally parallel manner (roughly speaking, a non-extendable multiset of rules is applied to the current multiset of objects in the region).

A computation is a sequence of configurations directly following each other. It starts from the so-called initial configuration and ends with a halting configuration. A configuration is halting if no rule of the P system can be applied. The result of the computation is the number of objects in a distinguished compartment, the output region, but the number of objects that leave the system in the course of the computation can also be defined as a result.

Thus, the model can be considered a distributed system of multiset rewriting systems that operate with a massively parallel derivation mode.

The original model has been extended or modified in various manner; the reader may find a lot of variants in the literature [13, 17].

For example, most P system variants apply the rules in the maximally parallel mode, but other rule application modes exist, such as minimal parallelism, limited parallelism, or sequential rule application. The rules may be multiset rewriting rules, purely communication rules, and/or rules that induce membrane creation, division, or dissolution. Distinguished objects, priorities, promoters and/or inhibitors, or so-called channels may control the application of the rules.

Over the years, P systems have been studied from several perspectives. Many studies have addressed the computational power and efficiency of different versions of P systems, especially in cases where the models are limited in some size parameters. Most membrane systems, even those that are limited in some size parameters, are Turing-complete. These results have usually been proved by simulating the register machine, the counter automaton, or certain variant thereof. The size parameters considered have been the number of cells (or compartments), the number and type of rules, the size of the rules, and the number of special objects (such as catalysts) in the P system or its components.

The studies and results on some well-known variants of P systems, such as catalytic P systems, [1–3, 11], symport/antiport P systems [4, 7], communication P systems [6, 12], generalized communicating P systems [10, 8, 19], and P colonies [5, 9] are examples of these investigations.

In this presentation, we discuss the descriptional complexity of the above variants of P systems, depending on their constituents and computation mode. We compare their descriptional complexity with the descriptional complexities of those classical computational models to which they are equivalent in computational power. Furthermore, we discuss whether there are descriptional complexity concepts for P systems that can be considered novel compared to the standard concepts of classical computational models.

Finally, we ask some open problems and make suggestions for future investigations.

References

1. Alhazov, A., Freund, R., Ivanov, S.: When catalytic P systems with one catalyst can be computationally complete. J. Membr. Comput. **3**(3), 170–181 (2021). https://doi.org/10.1007/S41965-021-00079-X
2. Alhazov, A., Freund, R., Ivanov, S., Oswald, M.: Variants of derivation modes for which purely catalytic P systems are computationally complete. Theor. Comput. Sci. **920**, 95–112 (2022). https://doi.org/10.1016/J.TCS.2022.03.007
3. Alhazov, A., Freund, R., Ivanov, S., Verlan, S.: Variants of derivation modes for which catalytic P systems with one catalyst are computationally complete. J. Membr. Comput. **3**(4), 233–245 (2021). https://doi.org/10.1007/S41965-021-00085-Z
4. Alhazov, A., Verlan, S.: Minimization strategies for maximally parallel multiset rewriting systems. Theor. Comput. Sci. **412**(17), 1581–1591 (2011). https://doi.org/10.1016/J.TCS.2010.10.033
5. Ciencialová, L., Csuhaj-Varjsú, E., Cienciala, L., Sosík, P.: P colonies. J. Membr. Comput. **1**(3), 178–197 (2019). https://doi.org/10.1007/S41965-019-00019-W
6. Csuhaj-Varjú, E.: Communicating P systems: bio-inspired computational models for complex systems. In: Holena, M., et al. (eds.) Proceedings of the 20th Conference Information Technologies - Applications and Theory (ITAT 2020), Hotel Tyrapol, Oravská Lesná, Slovakia, 18–22 September 2020. CEUR Workshop Proceedings, vol. 2718, pp. 3–8. CEUR-WS.org (2020). https://ceur-ws.org/Vol-2718/invited2.pdf
7. Csuhaj-Varjú, E., Margenstern, M., Vaszil, G., Verlan, S.: On small universal antiport P systems. Theor. Comput. Sci. **372**(2–3), 152–164 (2007). https://doi.org/10.1016/J.TCS.2006.11.023
8. Csuhaj-Varjú, E., Verlan, S.: On generalized communicating P systems with minimal interaction rules. Theor. Comput. Sci. **412**(1–2), 124–135 (2011). https://doi.org/10.1016/J.TCS.2010.08.020
9. Csuhaj-Varjú, E., Verlan, S.: Bi-simulation between P colonies and P systems with multi-stable catalysts. In: Gheorghe, M., Rozenberg, G., Salomaa, A., Zandron, C. (eds.) CMC 2017. LNCS, vol. 10725, pp. 105–117. Springer, Cham (2018). https://doi.org/10.1007/978-3-319-73359-3_7
10. Csuhaj-Varjú, E., Verlan, S.: Computationally complete generalized communicating P systems with three cells. In: Gheorghe, M., Rozenberg, G., Salomaa, A., Zandron, C. (eds.) CMC 2017. LNCS, vol. 10725, pp. 118–128. Springer, Cham (2018). https://doi.org/10.1007/978-3-319-73359-3_8
11. Freund, R.: The power of parallelism in membrane computing. In: Brejová, B., (eds.) Proceedings of the 21st Conference Information Technologies - Applications and Theory (ITAT 2021), Hotel Heľpa, Nízke Tatry and Muránska planina, Slovakia, 24–28 September 2021. CEUR Workshop Proceedings, vol. 2962, pp. 1–16. CEURWS.org (2021). https://ceur-ws.org/Vol-2962/invited01.pdf
12. Freund, R., Alhazov, A., Rogozhin, Y., Verlan, S.: Communication P systems. In: Păun, G., Rozenberg, G., Salomaa, A. (eds.) The Oxford Handbook of Membrane Computing, pp. 118–143. Oxford University Press (2009)

13. Gheorghe, M., Păun, G., Pérez-Jiménez, M.J., Rozenberg, G.: Research frontiers of membrane computing: open problems and research topics. Int. J. Found. Comput. Sci. **24**(5), 547–624 (2013). https://doi.org/10.1142/S0129054113500202
14. Kari, L., Rozenberg, G.: The many facets of natural computing. Commun. ACM **51**(10), 72–83 (2008). https://doi.org/10.1145/1400181.1400200
15. Păun, G.: Computing with membranes. J. Comput. Syst. Sci. **61**(1), 108–143 (2000). https://doi.org/10.1006/JCSS.1999.1693
16. Păun, G.: Membrane Computing: An Introduction. Natural Computing Series, Springer, Heidelberg (2002). https://doi.org/10.1007/978-3-642-56196-2
17. Păun Gh., Rozenberg, G., Salomaa, A. (eds.) The Oxford Handbook of Membrane Computing. Oxford University Press, Oxford (2010)
18. Rozenberg, G., Bäck, T., Kok, J.N. (eds.) Handbook of Natural Computing. Springer, Heidelberg (2012). https://doi.org/10.1007/978-3-540-92910-9
19. Verlan, S., Bernardini, F., Gheorghe, M., Margenstern, M.: Generalized communicating P systems. Theor. Comput. Sci. **404**(1–2), 170–184 (2008). https://doi.org/10.1016/J.TCS.2008.04.008

Inductive Inference of Lindenmayer Systems: Computational and Descriptional Complexity

Ian McQuillan

Department of Computer Science, University of Saskatchewan, Saskatoon, SK S7N 5A9 Canada
mcquillan@cs.usask.ca

Abstract. Grammatical inference involves the learning of formal grammars from data, and inductive inference involves the learning of grammars from positive examples of words that are generated.

Here, we will study inductive inference of different types of Lindenmayer systems (L-systems). L-systems are particularly useful for creating simulations of plants and other processes with inherent parallelism. We mostly analyze the problem of being given one or more sequences of strings initially generated by an (unknown) L-system and attempting to infer an L-system that indeed can initially generate those sequences. This includes different restrictions on L-systems such as deterministic, nondeterministic, tabled, non-tabled, erasing, non-erasing, context-free, context-sensitive, or parametric. We will survey older results on decidability of inference, and newer results on complexity. Computational complexity will go hand-in-hand with descriptional complexity as we will strive to inductively infer L-systems with the smallest number of rewriting rules and/or the smallest number of tables. Computational complexity will also vary depending upon whether certain parameters of the L-system are taken to be fixed or not, leading to fixed-parameter tractable algorithms. We also discuss more experimental results with implementations of inductive inference. Finally, we describe preliminary work on learning and matching L-systems to images.

There are many interesting open problems and future directions that remain in this area, which will be discussed.

The research of I. McQuillan was supported, in part, by Natural Sciences and Engineering Research Council of Canada.

Can We Efficiently Compute Concurrency and Causality Relations in the Reversible Setting?

Irek Ulidowski[1,2]

[1] University of Leicester, Leicester, UK
[2] AGH University of Science and Technology, Kraków, Poland

Keywords: Concurrency · Causality · Process Algebras · Reversibility · Labelled Transition Systems · Reachability · Polynomial Time Computability

Reversible computation is a paradigm of computation where programs can execute not only in the standard, forward direction, but also in reverse, recovering past states and data. Although it is still a young research area reversible computation [5, 17, 15, 23} has promising applications such as debugging [6, 12], robotics [10, 11], the modelling of biochemical reactions [1, 7, 20], and parallel discrete event simulation [2, 3, 22]. In many such applications programs or systems are concurrent or parallel, for example, debugging of concurrent programs or parallel event simulation. Therefore, understanding reversibility simply as "iteratively undo the last action", as is commonly done for sequential systems, is not suitable. Such view obscures and distorts causal dependence or concurrency between actions–information which is vital in applications. In debugging, for example, knowing causal dependence between actions allows us to reduce search space for origins of misbehaviour.

An accepted notion of reversibility for concurrent systems is *causal-consistent* reversibility [4]. It postulates that any action can be undone provided that all its consequences, if any, are undone first. A successful theory was developed to reason about causal-consistent reversible systems [8, 9], allowing one to prove many properties of interest from a small set of easily verifiable simple axioms. Within this theory one can work with relations between transitions such as core independence, which is a form of concurrency, causal dependence and conflict. We call concurrency, causality and conflict "true concurrency relations", since versions of these relations are studied in true concurrency models, such as event structures [16,19,24] and Petri nets [13, 16, 21].

Since it is beneficial to know in many applications which past actions are causally dependant and which are concurrent, one may wonder how costly it is to compute true concurrency relations. We answer this question in the setting of a labelled transition system with independence (LTSI), which combines both forward and backward transition relations. We equip this LTSI with a notion of input size for states, labels of transitions, and transitions, and propose suitable **complexity axioms**. We show that for any LTSI satisfying those axioms, all the true concurrency relations and problems, such as connectivity and reachability, are **polynomial-time computable** in the axiomatic input size. Some of these problems may be decision problems, such as deciding causality between transitions, or search problems, such as computing the backward transitions from a given process term. In accordance with the axiomatic approach [8, 9], the rationale for this research is that showing polynomial-time computability in a reversible calculus can be done more easily by verifying the axioms (in the LTSI of the calculus), rather than by writing down ad hoc proofs from scratch. We note that our axioms allow systems with infinitely many states and transitions.

We shall apply our results to a reversible process calculus, which extends a process calculus CCS [14] with *Communication Keys* (CCSK [18]), and with guarded recursion. We show that all complexity axioms and properties hold, providing the first complexity bounds on deciding all the true concurrency notions for CCSK.

This is a joint work with Clément Aubert (Augusta University), Ivan Lanese (University of Bologna) and Iain Phillips (Imperial College London).

References

1. Cardelli, L., Laneve, C.: Reversible structures. In: CMSB, pp. 131–140. ACM (2011). https://doi.org/10.1145/2037509.2037529
2. Carothers, C.D., Perumalla, K.S., Fujimoto, R.: Efficient optimistic parallel simulations using reverse computation. ACM Trans. Model. Comput. Simul. **9**(3), 224–253 (1999)
3. Cingolani, D., Pellegrini, A., Quaglia, F.: Transparently mixing undo logs and software reversibility for state recovery in optimistic PDES. ACM Trans. Model. Comput. Simul. **27**(2), 11:1–11:26 (2017). https://doi.org/10.1145/3077583
4. Danos, V., Krivine, J.: Reversible communicating systems. In: Gardner, P., Yoshida, N. (eds.) CONCUR 2004. LNCS, vol. 3170, pp. 292–307. Springer, Heidelberg (2004). https://doi.org/10.1007/978-3-540-28644-8_19
5. De Vos, A.: Reversible Computing: Fundamentals, Quantum Computing, and Applications. Wiley (2011). https://books.google.co.uk/books?id=sOywHUPur8gC
6. Hoey, J., Lanese, I., Nishida, N., Ulidowski, I., Vidal, G.: A case study for reversible computing: reversible debugging of concurrent programs. In: Ulidowski, I., Lanese, I., Schultz, U.P., Ferreira, C. (eds.) Reversible Computation: Extending Horizons of Computing. LNCS, vol. 12070, pp. 108–127. Springer, Cham (2020). https://doi.org/10.1007/978-3-030-47361-7_5
7. Kuhn, S., et al.: Reversibility in chemical reactions. In: Ulidowski, I., Lanese, I., Schultz, U.P., Ferreira, C. (eds.) Reversible Computation: Extending Horizons of Computing. LNCS, vol. 12070, pp. 151–176. Springer, Cham (2020). https://doi.org/10.1007/978-3-030-47361-7_7
8. Lanese, I., Phillips, I., Ulidowski, I.: An axiomatic approach to reversible computation. In: Goubault-Larrecq, J., König, B. (eds.) FoSSaCS 2020. LNCS, vol. 12077, pp. 442–461. Springer, Cham (2020). https://doi.org/10.1007/978-3-030-45231-5_23
9. Lanese, I., Phillips, I.C. C., Ulidowski, I.: An axiomatic theory for reversible computation. ACM Trans. Comput. Logic **25**(2), 1–40 (2024). https://doi.org/10.1145/3648474

10. Lanese, I., Schultz, U.P., Ulidowski, I.: Reversible execution for robustness in embodied AI and industrial robots. IT Prof. **23**(3), 12–17 (2021). https://doi.org/10.1109/MITP.2021.3073757
11. Laursen, J.S., Schultz, U.P., Ellekilde, L-P.: Automatic error recovery in robot assembly operations using reverse execution. In IROS, pp. 1785–1792. IEEE (2015)
12. McNellis, J., Mola, J., Sykes, K.: Time travel debugging: Root causing bugs in commercial scale software. CppCon talk (2017). https://www.youtube.com/watch?v=l1YJTg_A914
13. Melgratti, H.C., Mezzina, C.A., Ulidowski, I.: Reversing place transition nets. LMCS, **16**(4) (2020). https://doi.org/10.23638/LMCS-16(4:5)2020
14. Milner, R.: Communication and Concurrency. Prentice Hall (1989)
15. Morita, K.: Theory of Reversible Computing. Monographs in Theoretical Computer Science. An EATCS Series. Springer, Tokyo (2017). https://doi.org/10.1007/978-4-431-56606-9
16. Nielsen, M., Plotkin, G., Winskel, G.: Petri nets, event structures and domains, part I. Theor. Comput. Sci. **13**, 85–108 (1981). https://doi.org/10.1016/0304-3975(81)90112-2
17. Perumalla, K.S.: Introduction to Reversible Computing. Chapman & Hall/CRC Computational Science. Taylor & Francis (2013)
18. Phillips, I.C.C., Ulidowski, I.: Reversing algebraic process calculi. J. Logic Algebraic Program. **73**(1–2), 70–96 (2007). https://doi.org/10.1016/j.jlap.2006.11.002
19. Phillips, I.C. C., Ulidowski, I.: Reversibility and asymmetric conflict in event structures. J. Log. Algebraic Methods Program. **84**, 781–805 (2015). https://doi.org/10.1016/j.jlamp.2015.07.004
20. Phillips, I., Ulidowski, I., Yuen, S.: A reversible process calculus and the modelling of the ERK signalling pathway. In: Glück, R., Yokoyama, T. (eds.) RC 2012. LNCS, vol. 7581, pp. 218–232. Springer, Heidelberg (2013). https://doi.org/10.1007/978-3-642-36315-3_18
21. Wolfgang Reisig. Petri Nets, An Introduction. Springer, Heidelberg (1985). https://doi.org/10.1007/978-3-642-69968-9
22. Schordan, M., Oppelstrup, T., Jefferson, D.R., Barnes, P.D., Jr.: Generation of reversible C++ code for optimistic parallel discrete event simulation. New Gener. Comput. **36**(3), 257–280 (2018). https://doi.org/10.1007/s00354-018-0038-2
23. Ulidowski, I., Lanese, I., Schultz, U.P., Ferreira, C., (eds.) Reversible Computation: Extending Horizons of Computing - Selected Results of the COST Action IC1405. LNCS, vol. 12070. Springer, Cham (2020). https://doi.org/10.1007/978-3-030-47361-7
24. Ulidowski, I., Phillips, I.C. C., Yuen, S.: Reversing event structures. New Gener. Comput. **36**(3), 281–306 (2018). https://doi.org/10.1007/s00354-018-0040-8

Contents

Fibonacci Pictures on a Binary Alphabet

Marcella Anselmo[1], Dora Giammarresi[2], Maria Madonia[3](✉), and Carla Selmi[4]

[1] Dipartimento di Informatica, Università di Salerno, Fisciano, Italy
manselmo@unisa.it

[2] Dipartimento di Matematica, Università di Roma "Tor Vergata", Rome, Italy
giammarr@mat.uniroma2.it

[3] Dipartimento di Matematica e Informatica, Università di Catania, Catania, Italy
madonia@dmi.unict.it

[4] LITIS, Université de Rouen Normandie, Rouen, France
carla.selmi@univ-rouen.fr

Abstract. We introduce a family of finite pictures (i.e. two-dimensional words) by means of a recursive definition based on a Fibonacci-like scheme and using combined row and column concatenation operations between pictures. The resulting picture sizes are pairs of Fibonacci numbers. The limit of these pictures when growing their sizes is an infinite picture, we call $F_{\infty,\infty}$, which includes all such pictures as top-left prefixes. Moreover, $F_{\infty,\infty}$ constitutes an interlacing of the infinite Fibonacci word, that can be read along every path originating from the top-left corner and proceeding right and down. We study some interesting properties of the factors of $F_{\infty,\infty}$ such as balancing and some kind of repetitions.

Keywords: Fibonacci Words · Pictures · Two-dimensional Arrays · Repetitions

1 Introduction

Fibonacci words are both beautiful and important and, like Fibonacci numbers, they are very fascinating. They are defined over a binary alphabet and form a sequence described by a recurrence relation, this time based on the operation of word concatenation, similar to that of Fibonacci numbers [4,15]. As a result, the lengths of these words correspond to Fibonacci numbers. Moreover, the limit of this sequence is an infinite word f_∞, which possesses many remarkable properties. It is a Sturmian word, meaning it has low complexity and exhibits balanced combinatorial properties. All finite Fibonacci words appear as prefixes of f_∞. The number of distinct factors of length n is exactly $n+1$, a characteristic

Partially supported by INdAM-GNCS 2025 - CUP E53C24001950001, FARB Project ORSA240597 of University of Salerno, TEAMS Project and PNRR MUR Project PE0000013-FAIR University of Catania, MUR Excellence Department Project MatMod@TOV, CUP E83C23000330006, Department of Mathematics, University of Rome Tor Vergata.

Published by Springer Nature Switzerland AG 2025
A. Malcher and L. Prigioniero (Eds.): DCFS 2025, LNCS 15759, pp. 1–16, 2025.
https://doi.org/10.1007/978-3-031-97100-6_1

that highlights its structured complexity. Additionally, squares and cubes within Fibonacci words can be precisely counted [9,10,12,13]. Fibonacci words are also balanced, meaning that the number of occurrences of each letter does not vary too much between factors of the same length. Due to their well-structured nature, they frequently appear as edge cases in algorithmic studies, particularly in complexity analysis and combinatorial properties of words. Their unique properties make them a fundamental object in theoretical computer science and discrete mathematics.

In 2000, within the context of extending certain algorithmic techniques on strings to two dimensions, Apostolico and Brimkov introduced a special sequence of pictures called Fibonacci arrays. These arrays are defined by a recurrence relation based on row and column concatenation operations, following the same structural scheme as Fibonacci numbers but using a four-letter alphabet $\{\alpha, \beta, \gamma, \delta\}$ [3].

It is worth noting that the recurrence rules never apply both concatenation operations simultaneously. Instead, at each step, the pictures grow either horizontally (rightward) or vertically (downward).

In some possible mappings to binary pictures, the structure may include alternations between Fibonacci word-based rows (or columns) and uniform rows (or columns) consisting of only one symbol. The authors also propose a classification of two-dimensional pattern repetitions within the Fibonacci arrays.

Building on this work, in 2023 [18], the infinite two-dimensional Fibonacci word was introduced as the limit of the sequence of Fibonacci arrays defined by Apostolico and Brimkov. It is defined over the first quadrant of the plane, meaning it is a mapping from $\mathbb{N} \times \mathbb{N}$ to a four-letter alphabet.

All finite Fibonacci arrays appear as prefixes of this infinite picture. Following from the finite case, this infinite structure consists of only two distinct types of rows, corresponding to infinite copies of Fibonacci words over the alphabets $\{a, b\}$ and $\{c, d\}$, respectively. Their alternation follows the Fibonacci sequence of symbols in the first column. However, despite this regularity, the study remains within the framework of four distinct alphabet symbols, without distinguishing between different possible mappings to a binary alphabet.

Some other related literature concerns two-dimensional Sturmian words defined on the entire plane.

See for example, the papers by Berthé and Vuillon [6,7] and by Berthé and Tijdeman [5] which refer to two-dimensional infinite words as double sequences and investigate their factor complexity and balancing properties.

In this paper, we revisit the classical definition of Fibonacci words with the aim of formulating a new definition that fully captures the flexibility of two dimensions. We propose a recursive construction that follows the Fibonacci number scheme, allowing both row- and column-concatenation in defining the same picture. This approach also ensures consistency: in the special case of a single row (or column), our definition coincides with the standard one-dimensional Fibonacci word. As a result, we obtain a sequence of finite Fibonacci pictures, denoted as $F_{h,k}$, whose dimensions are the pairs of Fibonacci numbers

$(Fib(h), Fib(k))$. Moreover, each Fibonacci picture $F_{h,k}$ uniquely corresponds to a prefix of the Fibonacci word of length $Fib(h) + Fib(k) - 1$.

Building upon this, we define the infinite Fibonacci picture $F_{\infty,\infty}$ as the limit of this sequence of finite pictures, constructed according to our recursive rules. As in the one-dimensional case, all finite Fibonacci pictures appear as top-left prefixes of $F_{\infty,\infty}$. Similarly to the infinite array introduced in [18], $F_{\infty,\infty}$ contains infinite copies of Fibonacci words; but interestingly, these words are not simply replicated in horizontal and vertical stripes. They are instead interwoven in a truly two-dimensional structure, blending into each other.

Specifically, any path originating from the top-left corner, following any sequence of right and down moves, will trace out the (infinite) Fibonacci word.

As a consequence, the first row/column of $F_{\infty,\infty}$ is f_∞. Note that focusing on the first row of a picture has been the subject of study in [1,14,19]. Furthermore, the entire infinite array exhibits symmetry with respect to the main diagonal.

It appears to retain many of the properties of the Fibonacci word. It is recurrent and, in a sense, balanced (with respect to blocks of Fibonacci size). Moreover, like the Fibonacci word, $F_{\infty,\infty}$ does not contain the block 11, neither horizontally nor vertically, which makes it a suitable generalization. It is worth noting that pictures avoiding blocks are also studied in the context of isometries and generalized Fibonacci cubes [2].

Finally, $F_{\infty,\infty}$ is an intriguing structure, since it provides new insights into the combinatorial properties of two-dimensional Fibonacci-like structures.

2 Preliminaries

We use standard notation for words that will be always defined on the binary alphabet $\{0, 1\}$ [15]. Given a word $w = w(0), w(1), \ldots, w(n-1)$, its length n will be denoted by $|w|$. A *prefix* of w is a string $v = w(0)w(1)\ldots w(h)$, with $0 \leq h \leq n-1$. In this case we write $v \leq_p w$. More generally, a *factor* of w is a string $u = w(i)w(i+1)\ldots w(j)$ with $0 \leq i \leq j \leq n-1$. A factor of the form $u = xx$ i.e. the concatenation of the same string x is called a *square*. In general, a *repetition* in a word is a factor u of the form u^t where $t \geq 2$ is a rational number.

The *period* of a word w is the smallest positive integer p such that $w(i) = w(i+p)$, for all $i \geq 0, i+p \leq n-1$. If there is not such a p the words is called *aperiodic*.

We now introduce the definitions of Fibonacci strings together with some related known properties we investigate later in two dimensions.

Fibonacci numbers are defined by the famous recurrence scheme: $Fib(0) = 1$, $Fib(1) = 1$, $Fib(n) = Fib(n-1) + Fib(n-2)$ for $n \geq 2$. The same scheme, now using the string concatenation operation, defines the Fibonacci strings. Hence given by: $f_0 = 1$, $f_1 = 0$, $f_n = f_{n-1}f_{n-2}$. Then, $f_2 = 01$, $f_3 = 010$, $f_4 = 01001$, $f_5 = 01001010$, ... Note that, for each $n \geq 0$, the length of the word f_n, denoted by $|f_n|$ is the n-th Fibonacci number $Fib(n)$. The *infinite Fibonacci word*, indicated by f_∞, is the limit of this sequence and it contains f_n as a prefix for every $n \geq 1$.

$$f_\infty = 0100101001001010010100100101 0\ldots$$

The infinite Fibonacci word is probably the most studied infinite word due to its magnitude of interesting properties. To list some: it is a Sturmian word and therefore it is aperiodic with *factor complexity* $p(n) = n + 1$. This means that, for each n, there are only $n + 1$ distinct factors of length n, the minimal possible factor complexity for an aperiodic word. Furthermore, it is a *balanced* word. This means that, when taking two factors of the same length anywhere in the word, the difference between their number of 1's never exceeds one. It is recurrent; that is, every factor occurs infinitely often.

We conclude the section by recalling some basic notations on pictures in [11].

A *picture* over a finite alphabet Σ is the counterpart in two dimensions of a string and it is represented by a two-dimensional rectangular array of elements of Σ. Given a picture P with m rows and n columns, let $P(i, j)$ denote the symbol in P with coordinates (i, j), being $P(0, 0)$ and $P(m-1, n-1)$ the top left and the bottom right positions of the picture, referred to as the *tl-corner* and the *br-corner*, respectively. The *size* of the picture P is the pair (m, n). The role of a factor in strings is played by the so-called *block*, that is a picture B that is equal to a rectangular portion of P. If (i, j) and (i', j') are the tl- and the br- corner of the rectangle, with $1 \leq i \leq i' \leq m$, $1 \leq j \leq j' \leq n$, we say that B *occurs* at position (i, j) and we denote it by $P[(i, j), (i', j')]$.

A *tl-prefix* of a picture is a block that occurs at position $(0, 0)$.

A picture P is *periodic* with *periodicity vector* $(x, y), x, y \in \mathbb{Z}$, if $P(i + x, j + y) = p(i, j)$. The periodicity vector is *negative* if at least one of its coordinates is negative.

Moreover, for our results, we need to refer to the edges of the pictures. In particular, we consider two strings, the one that covers the positions in the top row and the rightmost column and the one that covers the positions in the leftmost column and in the bottom row. the two strings that cover the positions in the top row and the rightmost column and also the positions in the leftmost column and in the bottom row, respectively.

Definition 1. *Let P be a picture of size (m, n). The* top-right frame *(*tr-frame, *for short) and the* left-bottom frame *(*lb-frame, *for short) are the strings defined as follows:*

$$tr\text{-}frame(P) = P(0,0)P(0,1)\ldots P(0,n-1)P(1,n-1)\ldots P(m-1,n-1)$$
$$lb\text{-}frame(P) = P(0,0)P(1,0)\ldots P(m-1,0)P(m-1,1)\ldots P(m-1,n-1).$$

Pictures can be concatenated in the two dimensions. Let P and Q be pictures of size (m, n) and (m', n'), respectively. The *column concatenation* of P and Q (denoted by $P \oplus Q$) is the picture of size $(m, n + n')$ and the *row concatenation* of P and Q (denoted by $P \ominus Q$) is the picture of size $(m + m', n)$ described as follows. These operations are defined only if $m = m'$ for column concatenation and $n = n'$ for row concatenation, respectively.

$$P \mathbin{⦶} Q = \begin{array}{|c|c|}\hline P & Q \\ \hline \end{array} \qquad\qquad P \ominus Q = \begin{array}{|c|}\hline P \\ \hline Q \\ \hline \end{array}.$$

We consider also infinite pictures only in the case where the coordinates belong to $\mathbb{N}^2$; so the pictures are infinite only downwards and rightwards. The notion of a block occurring at position (i, j) is extended to these infinite pictures.

3 A Two-Dimensional Fibonacci Recursion

We propose a two-dimensional version of the recursive formula for Fibonacci strings to produce the finite Fibonacci pictures $F_{h,k}$ of size $(Fib(h), Fib(k))$ of corresponding Fibonacci numbers. As expected, the recursion starts from small pictures. Then, the column and row concatenations are applied in order to define the bigger ones.

Base of the Recurrence:

$$F_{0,0} = \begin{array}{|c|}\hline 1 \\ \hline \end{array} \quad F_{0,1} = F_{1,0} = F_{1,1} = \begin{array}{|c|}\hline 0 \\ \hline \end{array} \quad F_{1,2} = \begin{array}{|c|c|}\hline 0 & 1 \\ \hline \end{array} \quad F_{2,1} = \begin{array}{|c|}\hline 0 \\ \hline 1 \\ \hline \end{array} \quad F_{2,2} = \begin{array}{|c|c|}\hline 0 & 1 \\ \hline 1 & 0 \\ \hline \end{array}$$

Note that $F_{0,0}, F_{0,1}, F_{1,0}$ are dummy pictures introduced for technical reasons.

As usual, when extending a theory from strings to pictures, one of the main expectations is that "thin" pictures work as strings. In particular, everything should coincide when restricting to one-row (one-column) pictures. On the other hand, we wish that square pictures, or almost square pictures, present some two-dimensional peculiarity. For this purpose, the recursive construction proceeds through three cases, guided by the following main principles:

1. There is a Fibonacci-like recursion scheme (the new index come from the *two* previous smaller ones) applied to the *bigger* dimension (Case 1) of the picture by means of row or column concatenation operations.
2. If the two dimensions are consecutive (Case 2) or equal Fibonacci numbers (Case 3), then the Fibonacci-like recursion scheme is applied to *both* dimensions using square pictures first. This will ensure an intrinsic bidimensionality.

For better clarity, the recursion will be described using both the picture concatenation operations and a pictorial representation. The recursion is applied at the index k.

Recursion steps:

– Case 1. $h \leq k-2$. Then: $F_{h,k} = F_{h,k-1} \oplus F_{h,k-2}$ and $F_{k,h} = F_{k-1,h} \ominus F_{k-2,h}$

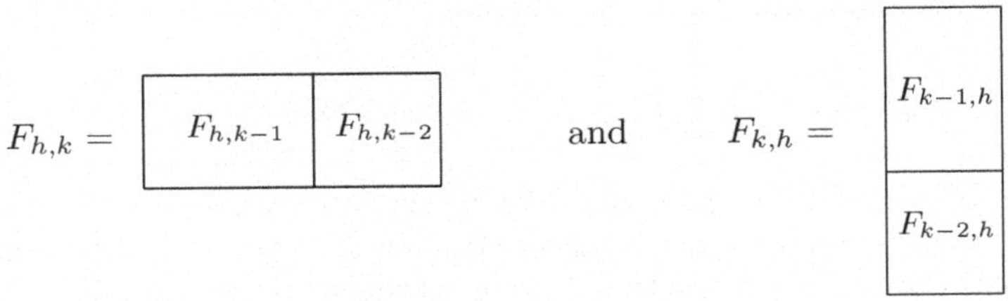

– Case 2. $h = k-1$. Then: $F_{k-1,k} = F_{k-1,k-1} \oplus (F_{k-2,k-2} \ominus F_{k-3,k-2})$ and $F_{k,k-1} = F_{k-1,k-1} \ominus (F_{k-2,k-2} \oplus F_{k-2,k-3})$

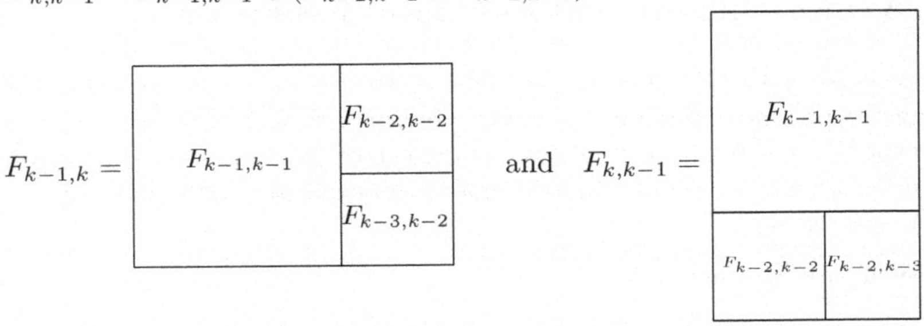

– Case 3. $h = k$. Then: $F_{k,k} = F_{k-1,k} \ominus (F_{k-2,k-2} \oplus F_{k-2,k-1})$

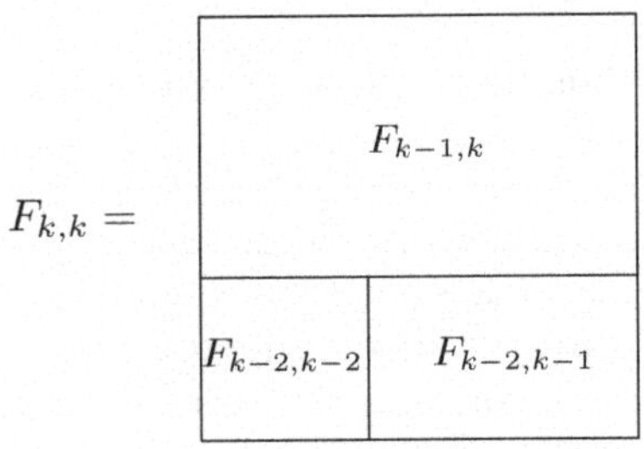

It is important to note that in the definition of $F_{k-1,k}$, in Case 2, the picture $F_{k-2,k-2} \ominus F_{k-3,k-2}$ cannot be replaced by $F_{k-1,k-2}$ since $F_{k-1,k-2}$ does not fall in Case 1 (the difference between the number of rows and columns is not greater than or equal to 2). Moreover, observe that if, in the definition of Case 3, we substitute the decomposition of $F_{k-1,k}$ as in Case 2, we get a decomposition of $F_{k,k}$ in which square pictures $F_{k-1,k-1}$ and $F_{k-2,k-2}$ are firstly placed and then the rest of the picture is properly filled. More precisely, $F_{k-1,k-1}$ occurs at the top-left corner and is followed by one occurrence of $F_{k-2,k-2}$ at its right and another one at its bottom.

Some Fibonacci pictures are given below as examples.

$$F_{3,3} = \begin{array}{|c|cc|}\hline 0 & 1 & 0 \\ 1 & 0 & 0 \\ \hline 0 & 0 & 1 \\ \hline\end{array} \quad F_{3,4} = \begin{array}{|ccc|cc|}\hline 0 & 1 & 0 & 0 & 1 \\ 1 & 0 & 0 & 1 & 0 \\ 0 & 0 & 1 & 0 & 1 \\ \hline\end{array} \quad F_{3,5} = \begin{array}{|ccccc|ccc|}\hline 0 & 1 & 0 & 0 & 1 & 0 & 1 & 0 \\ 1 & 0 & 0 & 1 & 0 & 1 & 0 & 0 \\ 0 & 0 & 1 & 0 & 1 & 0 & 0 & 1 \\ \hline\end{array}$$

Remark 2. From the definition of $F_{h,k}$, it follows that, for all $h, k \geq 1$, the first row of $F_{h,k}$ is f_k.

Remark 3. From the definitions of Fibonacci strings, it follows that, for all $h, k \geq 3$, with $h \leq k$, the prefix of f_∞ of length $Fib(k) + Fib(h)$ is equal to $f_k f_h$. Further, for $k > 3$, $f_k f_{k-1} g_{k-2}$ and $f_{k-1} f_{k-2} f_{k-2} f_{k-3}$ are prefixes of f_∞, where g_k denotes the word obtained from f_k by removing its last symbol.

The following proposition states some properties of the Fibonacci pictures $F_{h,k}$, in the case $h \leq k$. More exactly, it shows that the tr-frame of $F_{h,k}$ is a prefix of f_∞ and that all its symbols propagate spread along the bottom-left direction.

Proposition 4. *For any $h, k \geq 1$, $h \leq k$, the Fibonacci picture $F_{h,k}$ satisfies the following properties.*

1. *$tr\text{-}frame(F_{h,k})$ is the prefix of f_∞ of length $Fib(k) + Fib(h) - 1$, that is $tr\text{-}frame(F_{h,k}) = f_k g_h$*
2. *For any $i, i' \in \{0, 1, \ldots, Fib(h) - 1\}$ and $j, j' \in \{0, 1, \ldots, Fib(k) - 1\}$, if $i + j = i' + j'$, then $F_{h,k}(i, j) = F_{h,k}(i', j')$.*

Proof. We prove the property by induction on the pairs (h, k), with $h, k \geq 1$.

Case 1. Let us prove by induction that, for any pair (h, k), with $h, k \geq 1$ and $h \leq k$, $F_{h,k}$ satisfies the property that $tr\text{-}frame(F_{h,k})$ is the prefix of length $Fib(k) + Fib(h) - 1$ of f_∞. Then, $tr\text{-}frame(F_{h,k}) = f_k g_h$ from Remark 3.

The property can be easily checked for any pair (h, k), with $1 \leq h, k \leq 3$.

Let now $h, k > 3$ and assume, by inductive hypothesis, that for any $F_{h',k'}$ satisfies the property.

Assume $h \leq k - 2$. Let s_1 be the first row of $F_{h,k-1}$ and let $s_2 = tr\text{-}frame(F_{h,k-2})$. Then, $tr\text{-}frame(F_{h,k}) = s_1 s_2$. From Remark 2, $s_1 = f_{k-1}$ and, from the inductive hypothesis, s_2 is the prefix of length $Fib(k-2) + Fib(h) - 1$ of f_∞. Hence, since $h \leq k - 2$, from Remark 3, $s_2 = f_{k-2} g_h$. Altogether, $tr\text{-}frame(F_{h,k}) = s_1 s_2 = f_{k-1} f_{k-2} g_h$ and the thesis follows from Remark 3 noting that f_h is a prefix of f_{k-2}.

Suppose now that $h = k - 1$. Let s_1 be the first row of $F_{k-1,k-1}$, $s_2 = tr\text{-}frame(F_{k-2,k-2})$ and s_3 be the last column of $F_{k-3,k-2}$.
Then, $tr\text{-}frame(F_{k-1,k}) = s_1 s_2 s_3$. From Remark 2, $s_1 = f_{k-1}$. By inductive hypothesis, s_2 and $tr\text{-}frame(F_{k-3,k-2})$ are the prefixes of f_∞ of length $Fib(k-2) + Fib(k-2) - 1$ and $Fib(k-3) + Fib(k-2) - 1$, respectively. From Remark 3, $s_2 = f_{k-2} g_{k-2}$ and $tr\text{-}frame(F_{k-3,k-2}) = f_{k-2} g_{k-3}$. From $tr\text{-}frame(F_{k-3,k-2}) = f_{k-2} g_{k-3}$, the symbol a in the tr-corner of $F_{k-3,k-2}$ is the last symbol of f_{k-2} and then $s_3 = a g_{k-3}$. Altogether, $tr\text{-}frame(F_{k-1,k}) = s_1 s_2 s_3 = f_{k-1} f_{k-2} f_{k-2} g_{k-3}$ and the thesis follows from Remark 3.

If $h = k$, similar arguments show that $tr\text{-}frame(F_{k,k}) = f_k f_{k-1} g_{k-2}$ and the thesis follows from Remark 3.

Case 2. We proceed as for Case 1. The basis is again immediate to verify.

Consider now $F_{h,k}$, with $h, k > 3$ and suppose, by inductive hypothesis, that for any $h' \leq h$, $k' \leq k$ with $h' \neq h$ or $k' \neq k$, $F_{h',k'}$ satisfies the property.

Suppose $h \leq k-2$. From the inductive hypothesis, $F_{h,k-1}$ and $F_{h,k-2}$ satisfy the property. Then, it suffices to show that the last column of $F_{h,k-1}$ from its second position onwards, say c, is equal to the prefix of length $Fib(h)-1$ of the first row of $F_{h,k-2}$, say r. From Case 1. of the statement, c is equal to g_h and, from Remark 2, r coincides with f_{k-2}. Since $h \leq k-2$, $f_h \leq_p f_{k-2}$ and, hence, $c = g_h \leq_p f_{k-2} = r$.

Suppose, now, $h = k-1$. From the inductive hypothesis, $F_{k-1,k-1}$, $F_{k-2,k-2}$ and $F_{k-3,k-2}$ satisfy the property. Then, it suffices to show that the last column of $F_{k-2,k-2}$ from the second position onwards, say c, is equal to the first row of $F_{k-3,k-2}$ without the last symbol, say r, and that the last column of $F_{k-1,k-1}$ from the second position onwards, say c_1, is equal to the prefix of length $Fib(k-1)-1$ of $tr\text{-}frame(F_{k-2,k-2})$. From Case 1., $c = g_{k-2}$ and the first row of $F_{k-3,k-2}$ is f_{k-2}; hence $c = r$. Moreover, from Case 1., $c_1 = g_{k-1}$ and $tr\text{-}frame(F_U) = f_{k-2}g_{k-2}$. Therefore, the thesis follows by noting that $g_{k-1} = f_{k-2}g_{k-3}$ and $f_{k-2}g_{k-2} = f_{k-2}f_{k-3}x$ for some word x on Σ.

The case $h = k$ can be proved similarly. □

The case of Fibonacci pictures $F_{h,k}$ with $h \geq k$ can be handled similarly providing results on their lb-frames. In fact, one can show that if $h \geq k$, then $lb\text{-}frame(F_{h,k})$ is the prefix of f_∞ of length $Fib(k) + Fib(h) - 1$, that is $lb\text{-}frame(F_{h,k}) = f_h g_k$, and that the symbols on the lb-frame spread along the top-right direction. The proof is omitted since it is analogous to that of Proposition 4, once observed that, as an application of Proposition 4, for any $k \geq 1$, $lb\text{-}frame(F_{k,k}) = tr\text{-}frame(F_{k,k}) = f_k g_k$.

Such considerations, together with Proposition 4, lead to the following remark.

Remark 5. The tr- and the lb- frames of any Fibonacci picture coincide and their symbols spread along the counter-diagonal direction.

For any picture P of size (m, n), let us denote by P^T the transpose of P, i.e., the picture of size (n, m), obtained by exchanging rows and columns in P. The following result can be proved observing that, for any pictures P and Q of proper size, $(P \oplus Q)^T = P^T \ominus Q^T$ and $(P \ominus Q)^T = P^T \oplus Q^T$.

Corollary 6. *For any $h, k \geq 1$, $F^T_{h,k} = F_{k,h}$. In particular, Case 3. of the recurrence definition is equivalent to $F_{k,k} = F_{k,k-1} \oplus (F_{k-2,k-2} \ominus F_{k-2,k-2})$.*

Proposition 7. *For any $h, k, h', k' \geq 0$, such that $h' \leq h$ and $k' \leq k$, the picture $F_{h',k'}$ is a tl-prefix of $F_{h,k}$.*

Proof. Let $F_{h',k'}$ and $F_{h,k}$ as in the hypothesis. Propositions 4 and Remark 5 ensure that $tr\text{-}frame(F_{h',k'})$ and $tr\text{-}frame(F_{h,k})$ are the prefixes of f_∞ of length $Fib(h') + Fib(k') - 1$ and $Fib(h) + Fib(k) - 1$, respectively. Hence, the $tr\text{-}frame(F_{h',k'})$ is a prefix of the $tr\text{-}frame(F_{h,k})$. Therefore, the statement follows from Remark 5. □

4 The Infinite Fibonacci Picture

Using the recursion introduced in the previous section and in light of Proposition 7, we proceed as for strings and define the *infinite Fibonacci picture* as the limit $F_{\infty,\infty}$ of the pictures $F_{h,k}$ when h, k grow to infinity, that is, the (unique) infinite array that contains, for each finite pair $(Fib(h), Fib(k))$ of Fibonacci numbers, the corresponding Fibonacci picture $F_{h,k}$ as a tl-prefix. The picture $F_{\infty,\infty}$ will be simply denoted by F when ambiguity cannot arise.

Here below, it is shown a prefix of $F_{\infty,\infty}$ where it is possible to check all the properties listed in the rest of the section.

	0	1	2	3	4	5	6	7	8	9	10	11	12	13	14	15	16	17	18	19	20	...
0	0	1	0	0	1	0	1	0	0	1	0	0	1	0	1	0	0	1	0	1	0	...
1	1	0	0	1	0	1	0	0	1	0	0	1	0	1	0	0	1	0	1	0	0	...
2	0	0	1	0	1	0	0	1	0	0	1	0	1	0	0	1	0	1	0	0	1	...
3	0	1	0	1	0	0	1	0	0	1	0	1	0	0	1	0	1	0	0	1	0	...
4	1	0	1	0	0	1	0	0	1	0	1	0	0	1	0	1	0	0	1	0	0	...
5	0	1	0	0	1	0	0	1	0	1	0	0	1	0	1	0	0	1	0	0	1	...
6	1	0	0	1	0	0	1	0	1	0	0	1	0	1	0	0	1	0	0	1	0	...
7	0	0	1	0	0	1	0	1	0	0	1	0	1	0	0	1	0	0	1	0	1	...
8	0	1	0	0	1	0	1	0	0	1	0	1	0	0	1	0	0	1	0	1	0	...
9	1	0	0	1	0	1	0	0	1	0	1	0	0	1	0	0	1	0	1	0	0	...
10	0	0	1	0	1	0	0	1	0	1	0	0	1	0	0	1	0	1	0	0	1	...
11	0	1	0	1	0	0	1	0	1	0	0	1	0	0	1	0	1	0	0	1	0	...
12	1	0	1	0	0	1	0	1	0	0	1	0	0	1	0	1	0	0	1	0	0	...
13	0	1	0	0	1	0	1	0	0	1	0	0	1	0	1	0	0	1	0	0	1	...
14	1	0	0	1	0	1	0	0	1	0	0	1	0	1	0	0	1	0	0	1	0	...
15	0	0	1	0	1	0	0	1	0	0	1	0	1	0	0	1	0	0	1	0	1	...
16	0	1	0	1	0	0	1	0	0	1	0	1	0	0	1	0	0	1	0	1	0	...
⋮	⋮	⋮	⋮	⋮	⋮	⋮	⋮	⋮	⋮	⋮	⋮	⋮	⋮	⋮	⋮	⋮	⋮	⋮	⋮	⋮	⋮	⋱

Fig. 1. The prefix of size (17×21) of $F_{\infty,\infty}$.

Note that $F_{\infty,\infty}$ results in an interlacement of Fibonacci words. Each infinite path that starts in the top-left corner and at each step proceeds only right and/or down moves along the Fibonacci word f_∞. Some of such paths are highlighted. In particular, the first row and the first column contain the infinite Fibonacci word.

Proposition 8. *For any $i \geq 0$, the i-th row (column) of $F_{\infty,\infty}$ is the infinite Fibonacci word shifted by i positions to the left.*

Proof. From Propositions 4 and Remark 5, for any $h, k \geq 1$, the first row and the first column of $F_{h,k}$ are prefixes of the infinite Fibonacci word and, moreover, all the symbols on the first row (column) of $F_{h,k}$ spread along the bottom-left (top-right) direction. Hence, since for any $h, k \geq 1$, $F_{h,k}$ is a tl-prefix of $F_{\infty,\infty}$, then, the first row and the first column of $F_{\infty,\infty}$ are equal to f_∞ and, for any $i \geq 0$, the i-th row (column) of $F_{\infty,\infty}$ is equal to the first row (column), from its i-th position onwards. □

The proofs of the following propositions are not given in this version.

Proposition 9. *The infinite Fibonacci picture $F_{\infty,\infty}$ verifies the following properties.*

1. *$F_{\infty,\infty}$ is periodic with periodicity vector $(1,-1)$. Moreover, for any i, j, i', j' such that $i + j = i' + j'$, $F(i, j) = F(i' + j') = f_\infty(i + j)$.*
2. *$F_{\infty,\infty}$ is symmetric with respect to the main diagonal.*
3. *For any i, j, ℓ, the word read on any path in $F_{\infty,\infty}$ of length ℓ starting at position (i, j) and proceeding rightward and/or downward only is the same.*
4. *The sequence of symbols read on any infinite path in $F_{\infty,\infty}$ starting at position $(0,0)$ and proceeding rightward and/or downward only is f_∞.*

Proposition 10. *The blocks in the infinite Fibonacci picture $F_{\infty,\infty}$ verify the following properties.*

1. *For any i, j, i', j', h, k such that $i+j = i'+j'$, the blocks of dimensions (h, k) that occur at positions (i, j) and (i', j') are equal.*
2. *For any i, j, m such that $i + j = Fib(m)$, then (i, j) is the tl-corner of the block $F_{m,m}$ and of every block $F_{h,k}$ with $h, k \leq m$.*
3. *The tr-frame of a block is a factor of f_∞.*
4. *A block of size (h, k) is uniquely defined by its tr-frame.*

Uniform recurrence, where every factor appears infinitely often, is guaranteed for periodic sequences but also holds for special aperiodic ones like Fibonacci strings. On the other hand, note that the periodicity of $F_{\infty,\infty}$, since it has a negative vector, does not directly imply that every block appears infinitely many times. Using the properties in the proposition above, we can state the following.

Corollary 11. *The infinite picture $F_{\infty,\infty}$ is uniformly recurrent.*

5 Factor Complexity and Balancing

Properties and characterizations of the infinite strings are given by studying the properties of their finite factors. Following this approach, in this section, we analyze the sets of finite blocks of $F_{\infty,\infty}$ of given size (h, k).

In the case of strings, the Morse-Hedlund Theorem states that a word is aperiodic if and only if its factor complexity is $p(n) \geq n + 1$. Interestingly, also the property of being balanced is connected to periodicity. If a word is balanced, then its factor complexity $p(n) \leq n + 1$. Sturmian words, hence the Fibonacci word, are both aperiodic and balanced and therefore they have factor complexity $n + 1$ [15].

Going to two dimensions, Nivat's Conjecture sets to $mn+1$ the minimum number of different blocks of size (m,n) of an aperiodic infinite picture, while Berthé *et al.* in [5] characterize the infinite pictures (on $\mathbb{Z}^2$) that are balanced. We now study these properties in the picture $F_{\infty,\infty}$. Recall that $F_{\infty,\infty}$ is periodic with periodicity vector $(1,-1)$.

Proposition 12. *For any $h,k \geq 1$, the number of distinct blocks of size (h,k) of the infinite Fibonacci picture $F_{\infty,\infty}$ is $p(h,k) = h+k$.*

Proof. There is a bijection between the distinct blocks of size (h,k) and the distinct factors of length $h+k-1$ of the infinite Fibonacci word. The bijection maps a block to its tr-frame. Such a word uniquely defines the entire block as stated in item 4 of Proposition 10. Finally, the number of factors of length $h+k-1$ of the infinite Fibonacci word is $h+k$. □

The first occurrences of the $h+k$ distinct blocks of size (h,k) on the first row of $F_{\infty,\infty}$ can be obtained by applying results in [8].

Proposition 13. *For any $h,k \geq 1$, the $h+k$ distinct blocks of size (h,k) of the infinite Fibonacci picture $F_{\infty,\infty}$ occur (the first time in the first row) at positions $(0,j)$ with $j \in \{0,1,\ldots,Fib(n)-1\} \cup \{Fib(n+2)-h-k, Fib(n+2)-h-k,+1,\ldots,Fib(n+1)-1\}$, where n is such that $Fib(n) \leq h+k-1 \leq Fib(n+1)$.*

We now focus on the property of balancing. In [5], the following more general definition is given. An infinite binary string (picture) is called *C-balanced*, for some $C > 0$, if, for any pair of same-sized factors (blocks) the number of occurrences of 1 differ by C at most. It is also pointed out that not many strings are 1-balanced, while being C-balanced for some integer C is relatively common, especially for periodic structures. Then the authors characterize the infinite pictures on $\mathbb{Z}^2$ that are 1-balanced and prove that the infinite pictures whose rows are Sturmian words shifted by one position are not C-balanced for any C. We adapt this result to our case and prove that $F_{\infty,\infty}$ is not C-balanced either. Nevertheless, we prove an unexpected result regarding the 1-balancing property of some special size factors that encourages the study of this Fibonacci picture.

Proposition 14. *The infinite Fibonacci picture $F_{\infty,\infty}$ is not C-balanced for any $C \geq 1$.*

Proof. Consider the infinite picture $p : Z \times Z \to \{0,1\}$ where the 0-th row is obtained by mirroring f_∞ to its left side, and the other ones are such that p has a periodicity vector $(1,-1)$. A result in [5] shows that p is not balanced. Hence, $F_{\infty,\infty}$ is not balanced since its factors coincide with the factors of p. □

We prove that the blocks whose largest dimension is a Fibonacci number are 1-balanced. An example is given after the proof. We start with a remark on the Fibonacci word that will be applied in the proof, where, for any $n \geq 2$, $f_n^{\sim 2}$ denotes the Fibonacci word f_n in which the last two letters are commuted. If $n \in \{0,1\}$ then $f_n^{\sim 2} = f_n$.

Remark 15. For any $n \geq 3$, the two words $f_n f_n f_{n-1}^{\sim 2}$ and $f_{n+1} f_n f_n f_n$ are prefixes of f_∞.

Proposition 16. *Let $n \geq 2$, $h(n) = Fib(n+2) + Fib(n) - 1$ and let r_0, r_1, $\ldots$, $r_{h(n)-1}$ be the rows of the tl-prefix of $F_{\infty,\infty}$ of size $(h(n), Fib(n))$. Then, the sequence $(r_0, r_1, \ldots, r_{h(n)-1})$ equals the sequence*
$(r_0, r_1, \ldots, r_{Fib(n+1)-1}, r_0, r_1, \ldots, r_{Fib(n)-1}, r_0, r_1, \ldots, r_{Fib(n)-2})$.
Moreover, each row r_i has $Fib(n-1)$ occurrences of 0 and $Fib(n-2)$ occurrences of 1, except for row $r_{Fib(n+1)-1}$ which has one more, or one fewer, occurrence of 1.

Proof. The statement can be easily checked for $n = 2$. For $n \geq 3$, the proof follows from Remark 15. The fact that $f_n f_n f_{n-1}^{\sim 2}$ is a prefix of f_∞ implies that the rows $(r_0, r_1, \ldots, r_{Fib(n+1)-2})$ are cyclic rotations of f_n and thus preserve the same number of 0 and 1. On the other hand, row $r_{Fib(n+1)-1}$ is not a cyclic rotation on f_n because its last symbol comes from $f_{n-1}^{\sim 2}$ (and not from f_{n-1}). The fact that $f_{n+1} f_n f_n f_n$ is a prefix of f_∞ implies that the rows from $r_{Fib(n+1)}$ on are a repetition of the first rows and therefore preserve the same number of 0 and 1 as r_0.
Finally, recall that the Fibonacci word f_n has $Fib(n-1)$ occurrences of 0 and $Fib(n-2)$ occurrences of 1. □

Proposition 17. *For any $n \geq 2$, the number of occurrences of 1 in any two blocks of size $(Fib(n), Fib(n))$ in $F_{\infty,\infty}$ differ by 1 at most.*
Furthermore, there are $Fib(n)$ blocks with $Fib(n)Fib(n-2)$ occurrences of 1 and $Fib(n)$ blocks with $Fib(n)Fib(n-2) + 1$ or $Fib(n)Fib(n-2) - 1$ occurrences of 1.

Proof. There are $2Fib(n)$ different blocks of size $(Fib(n), Fib(n))$ (Proposition 12). Following Proposition 13, the blocks occur at positions $(0, j)$ with $j \in \{0, 1, \ldots, Fib(n+1)-1\} \cup \{Fib(n+3)-h-k, Fib(n+3)-h-k, +1, \ldots, Fib(n+2)-1\}$, because $Fib(n+1) \leq Fib(n) + Fib(n) - 1 < Fib(n+2)$. From item 1 in Proposition 10, they also occur at positions $(j, 0)$, with j ranging as above and thus from 0 to $Fib(n+2) - 1$. Therefore, the blocks involve rows from 0 to $Fib(n+2) + Fib(n) - 2$ and columns from 0 to $Fib(n) - 1$.

Proposition 16 states that the rows of the tl-prefix of $F_{\infty,\infty}$ of size $(Fib(n+2) + Fib(n) - 1, Fib(n))$ all have the same number of 1 unless for one of them, row $Fib(n+1) - 1$. Hence, there are $Fib(n)$ blocks that contain row $Fib(n+1) - 1$, whereas the other ones do not. The blocks that do not contain row $Fib(n+1) - 1$ are composed by $Fib(n)$ rows containing some cyclic rotation of f_n and thus $Fib(n-1)$ occurrences of 0 and $Fib(n-2)$ occurrences of 1 and the statement is proved. □

The previous propositions are the ingredients of the proof of our main result.

Theorem 18. *For any $h, k \geq 2$, such that the largest between h and k is a Fibonacci number, the number of occurrences of 1 in any two blocks of size (h, k) in $F_{\infty,\infty}$ differ by 1 at most.*

We omit the proof in this version, but we propose an example.

Example 19. Let $n = 4$, $Fib(n) = 5$, and consider the blocks of size $(5, 5)$ in $F_{\infty,\infty}$. There are *ten* different blocks of size $(5, 5)$ (by Proposition 12) and they occur at positions $(0, j)$ in row 0 such that $j = 0, 1, \ldots, 7, 11, 12$, as stated in Proposition 13. We report them here below:

$$\begin{array}{|ccccc|}\hline 0&1&0&0&1\\ 1&0&0&1&0\\ 0&0&1&0&1\\ 0&1&0&1&0\\ 1&0&1&0&0\\ \hline\end{array},\ \begin{array}{|ccccc|}\hline 1&0&0&1&0\\ 0&0&1&0&1\\ 0&1&0&1&0\\ 1&0&1&0&0\\ 0&1&0&0&1\\ \hline\end{array},\ \begin{array}{|ccccc|}\hline 0&0&1&0&1\\ 0&1&0&1&0\\ 1&0&1&0&0\\ 0&1&0&0&1\\ 1&0&0&1&0\\ \hline\end{array},\ \begin{array}{|ccccc|}\hline 0&1&0&1&0\\ 1&0&1&0&0\\ 0&1&0&0&1\\ 1&0&0&1&0\\ 0&0&1&0&0\\ \hline\end{array},\ \begin{array}{|ccccc|}\hline 1&0&1&0&0\\ 0&1&0&0&1\\ 1&0&0&1&0\\ 0&0&1&0&0\\ 0&1&0&0&1\\ \hline\end{array},$$

$$\begin{array}{|ccccc|}\hline 0&1&0&0&1\\ 1&0&0&1&0\\ 0&0&1&0&0\\ 0&1&0&0&1\\ 1&0&0&1&0\\ \hline\end{array},\ \begin{array}{|ccccc|}\hline 1&0&0&1&0\\ 0&0&1&0&0\\ 0&1&0&0&1\\ 1&0&0&1&0\\ 0&0&1&0&1\\ \hline\end{array},\ \begin{array}{|ccccc|}\hline 0&0&1&0&0\\ 0&1&0&0&1\\ 1&0&0&1&0\\ 0&0&1&0&1\\ 0&1&0&1&0\\ \hline\end{array},\ \begin{array}{|ccccc|}\hline 1&0&1&0&0\\ 0&1&0&0&1\\ 1&0&0&1&0\\ 0&0&1&0&1\\ 0&1&0&1&0\\ \hline\end{array},\ \begin{array}{|ccccc|}\hline 0&1&0&0&1\\ 1&0&0&1&0\\ 0&0&1&0&1\\ 0&1&0&1&0\\ 1&0&1&0&0\\ \hline\end{array}.$$

Applying Proposition 10, item 1, the blocks also occur at positions $(j, 0)$ in column 0 such that $j = 0, 1, \ldots, 7, 11, 12$, thus involving rows from 0 to 16 and columns from 0 to 4. We use now Proposition 16 and consider the rows of the tl-prefix of $F_{\infty,\infty}$ of size $(17, 5)$; refer to Fig. 1. These rows contain *three* occurrences of 0 and *two* occurrences of 1, except for the 7th row which has *four* occurrences of 0 and *one* occurrences of 1. Among the ten different blocks, five contain the 7th row and the other five do not.

Note that Theorem 18 implies that, although $F_{\infty,\infty}$ is not balanced, the difference in occurrences of 1 between two blocks of the same size grows slowly as the size increases, since it is somehow *reset* each time a Fibonacci number is reached in the size.

6 Repetitions

Repetitions in strings are a very well-studied matter both because they are connected with the notion of periodicity and because they can be exploited in pattern matching and data compression algorithms. The square detection problem consists of identifying all squares positioned in a given string. The counterparts of squares in two dimensions are named *tandems* and classified with respect to the edges or corners they share [3,16]. Let us consider repetitions in the Fibonacci picture $F_{\infty,\infty}$.

Definition 20. *A* (horizontal) tandem T *is a block composed of two equal column concatenated blocks, i.e.,* $T = B \oplus B$.

A (horizontal) tridem R is a block composed of three equal column concatenated blocks, i.e., $T = B \oplus B \oplus B$.
A diagonal tandem *D is a pattern composed of two equal blocks B such that the br-corner of the first block touches the tl-corner of the second one, denoted $D = B \oslash B$. It occurs at the position where the first block occurs.*

Example 21. The following figure shows a tandem, a tridem and a diagonal tandem occurring at positions $(0,5)$, $(0,8)$ and $(0,1)$, respectively, of $F_{\infty,\infty}$.

0 1 0	0 1 0
1 0 0	1 0 0
0 0 1	0 0 1
0 1 0	0 1 0

0 1 0 0 1	0 1 0 0 1	0 1 0 0 1
1 0 0 1 0	1 0 0 1 0	1 0 0 1 0

1 0 0	
0 0 1	
	1 0 0
	0 0 1

Similarly to Definition 20, other types of tandems, such as vertical and counter-diagonal tandems, can be defined. By Proposition 9, the symmetry property allows us to focus on horizontal tandems, as a vertical tandem $B \ominus B$ of size $(2h, k)$ occurs if and only if the horizontal tandem $B^T \oplus B^T$ of size $B^T \oplus B^T$ occurs at the same position. Moreover, the periodicity property ensures the presence of counter-diagonal tandems, composed of two square blocks of any size, at any position in $F_{\infty,\infty}$. In the following, $F = F_{\infty,\infty}$ and ϕ denotes the golden ratio.

Proposition 22. *Let $T = B \oplus B$ be a horizontal tandem, with B of size (h,k), and let w be the first row of B. The tr-frame of T is a word y such that $w^2 \leq_p y \leq_p w^3 z$, with $z \leq_p w$ and $|z| \leq (\phi - 1)|w|$. Vice versa, for any factor y of f_∞ such that $w^2 \leq_p y \leq_p w^3 z$, for some w with $z \leq_p w$, there is a tandem in F of size $(|y| - 2|w| + 1, 2|w|)$.*

Proof. Let $y = tr\text{-}frame(T)$. The fact that $w^2 \leq_p y \leq_p w^3 z$ follows from the propagation rule in Proposition 10 and from the definition of T as the concatenation of two equal blocks. Further, by Proposition 10, y is a factor of f_∞ and, hence, $|z| \leq (\phi - 1)|w|$ since the infinite Fibonacci word contains no power with an exponent greater than $2 + \phi$ [17]. The vice versa follows from the propagation rule in Proposition 10. □

Similarly, the following results can be proved for tridems and diagonal tandems.

Proposition 23. *Let $R = B \oplus B \oplus B$ be a horizontal tridem, with B of size (h,k), and let w be the first row of B. Then $tr\text{-}frame(R) = yz$ where $w^3 \leq_p y \leq_p w^3 z$, with $z \leq_p w$ and $|z| \leq (\phi - 1)|w|$. Vice versa, for any factor y of f_∞ such that $w^3 \leq_p y \leq_p w^3 z$, for some w with $z \leq_p w$ there is a tandem in F of size $(|z| + 1, 3|w|)$.*

Corollary 24. *Any tandem in F of size $(h, 2k)$ is such that $1 \leq h \leq \phi k + 1$. Any tridem in F of size $(h, 3k)$ is such that $1 \leq h \leq (\phi - 1)k + 1$.*

Proposition 25. *Let $D = B \oslash B$ be a diagonal tandem with B of size (h,k) and $w = tr\text{-}frame(B)$. If D occurs at position (i,j) in F then waw occurs at position $i + j$ in f_∞, where $a = F(i, j + k + h - 1)$. Vice versa, for any factor $y = waw$ of f_∞, with $w \in \Sigma^*$, $a \in \Sigma$, there is a diagonal tandem of size $(2, |w| - 1)$.*

References

1. Anselmo, M., Giammarresi, D., Madonia, M.: Classification of string languages via tiling recognizable picture languages. In: Dediu, A.-H., Inenaga, S., Martín-Vide, C. (eds.) LATA 2011. LNCS, vol. 6638, pp. 105–116. Springer, Heidelberg (2011). https://doi.org/10.1007/978-3-642-21254-3_7
2. Anselmo, M., Giammarresi, D., Madonia, M., Selmi, C.: Bad pictures: some structural properties related to overlaps. In: Jirásková, G., Pighizzini, G. (eds.) DCFS 2020. LNCS, vol. 12442, pp. 13–25. Springer, Cham (2020). https://doi.org/10.1007/978-3-030-62536-8_2
3. Apostolico, A., Brimkov, V.E.: Fibonacci arrays and their two-dimensional repetitions. Theor. Comput. Sci. **237**(1–2), 263–273 (2000)
4. Berstel, J.: Fibonacci Words — A Survey, pp. 13–27. Springer Berlin Heidelberg, Berlin, Heidelberg (1986)
5. Berthé, V., Tijdeman, R.: Balance properties of multi-dimensional words. Theor. Comput. Sci. **273**(1–2), 197–224 (2002). https://doi.org/10.1016/S0304-3975(00)00441-2
6. Berthé, V., Vuillon, L.: Suites doubles de basse complexité. Journal de Théorie des Nombres de Bordeaux **12**(1), 179–208 (2000)
7. Berthé, V., Vuillon, L.: Palindromes and two-dimensional sturmian sequences. J. Autom. Lang. Comb. **6**(2), 121–138 (2001). https://doi.org/10.25596/JALC-2001-121
8. Chuan, W., Ho, H.: Locating factors of the infinite Fibonacci word. Theor. Comput. Sci. **349**(3), 429–442 (2005)
9. Crochemore, M., Iliopoulos, C.S., Kubica, M., Radoszewski, J., Rytter, W., Walen, T.: The maximal number of cubic runs in a word. J. Comput. Syst. Sci. **78**, 1828–1836 (2012)
10. Crochemore, M., Iliopoulos, C.S., Kubica, M., Radoszewski, J., Rytter, W., Walen, T.: Extracting powers and periods in a word from its runs structure. Theor. Comput. Sci. **521**, 29–41 (2014)
11. Giammarresi, D., Restivo, A.: Two-dimensional languages. In: Rozenberg, G., Salomaa, A. (eds.) Handbook of Formal Languages, Volume 3: Beyond Words, pp. 215–267. Springer (1997)
12. Kolpakov, R., Kucherov, G.: Finding maximal repetitions in a word in linear time. In: 40th Annual Symposium on Foundations of Computer Science FOCS '99, pp. 596–604. IEEE Computer Society, New York, NY, USA (1999)
13. Kolpakov, R.M., Kucherov, G.: On maximal repetitions in words. In: Ciobanu, G., Paun, G. (eds.) Fundamentals of Computation Theory, 12th International Symposium, FCT '99, Proceedings. Lecture Notes in Computer Science, vol. 1684, pp. 374–385. Springer (1999)
14. Latteux, M., Simplot, D.: Context-sensitive string languages and recognizable picture languages. Inf. Comput. **138**(2), 160–169 (1997)
15. Lothaire, M.: Combinatorics on words, 2nd edn. Cambridge University Press, Cambridge mathematical library (1997)
16. Marcus, S., Sokol, D., Zelikovitz, S.: Exact and inexact search for 2D side-sharing tandems. Theor. Comput. Sci. **1026**, 115005 (2025)
17. Mignosi, F., Pirillo, G.: Repetitions in the Fibonacci infinite word. RAIRO-Inf. Theor. et Applic. **26–n.3**, 199–204 (1992)

18. Mohankumar, S., Raghavan, R.: Two-dimensional Fibonacci words: tandem repeats and factor complexity. Adv. Appl. Math. **149**, 102553 (2023)
19. Smith, T.J., Salomaa, K.: Recognition and complexity results for projection languages of two-dimensional automata. J. Autom. Lang. Comb. **28**(1–3), 201–220 (2023)

A Close Analysis of the Subset Construction

Ivan Baburin and Ryan Cotterell(✉)

Department of Computer Science, ETH Zürich, Zürich, Switzerland
{ivan.baburin,ryan.cotterell}@inf.ethz.ch

Abstract. Given a nondeterministic finite-state automaton (NFA), we aim to estimate the size of an equivalent deterministic finite-state automaton (DFA). We demonstrate that computing the state complexity of an NFA within polynomial precision is PSPACE-hard. Furthermore, we also demonstrate that it is PSPACE-hard to decide whether the classical subset construction will yield an equivalent DFA with an exponential increase in the number of states. This result implies that making any *a priori* estimate of the running time of the subset construction is inherently difficult. To address this, and to enable forecasting of such exponential blow-up in certain special cases, we introduce the notion of subset complexity, which provides an upper bound on the size of the DFA produced by the subset construction. We show that the subset complexity can be efficiently bounded above using the cyclicity and rank of the transition matrices of the NFA. This yields a sufficient condition for identifying NFAs that can be efficiently determinized via the subset construction.

Keywords: Subset construction · Determinization · State complexity

1 Introduction

The equivalence in expressivity between nondeterministic finite-state automata (NFAs) and deterministic finite-state automata (DFAs) was one of the first foundational results in the theory of finite-state automata. The original proof by Rabin and Scott [20] introduced the powerset construction, a general algorithm for converting an arbitrary NFA into an equivalent DFA. Despite its simplicity and pedagogical value, a major drawback of the powerset construction is that it yields a DFA with exactly 2^n states, where n is the number of states in the original NFA. In general, the equivalent DFA produced by the powers construction is *not* minimal and can, thus, often be reduced using standard finite-state minimization techniques [5]. Moreover, in certain pathological cases, the minimal DFA is *exponentially* smaller than the DFA returned by the powerset construction—meaning the algorithm may perform an exponential amount of unnecessary computation. A trivial example illustrates this phenomenon: consider an arbitrary n-state NFA with *no* final states. In this case, the minimal DFA is the 1-state automaton that accepts the empty language. However, the

A. Malcher and L. Prigioniero (Eds.): DCFS 2025, LNCS 15759, pp. 17–33, 2025.
https://doi.org/10.1007/978-3-031-97100-6_2

exponential blow-up is unavoidable in the worst case. Specifically, [17] showed the existence of an n-state NFA, known as the Moore automaton,[1] for which the *minimal* equivalent DFA requires *exactly* 2^n states, i.e., the exponentially large DFA output by the powerset construction is already minimal. Subsequent research identified other examples of NFAs for which the powerset construction yields the minimal DFA [4].

A complete theory of determinization for finite-state automata ought to provide a principled understanding of precisely when the minimal DFA equivalent to an NFA incurs an exponential blow-up in the number of states, and when it does not. To this end, several alternative determinization algorithms have been proposed, such as the classic subset construction [1] and Brzozowski's algorithm [6]. In addition, it has been shown that certain properties of NFAs can be decided *without* performing explicit determinization despite the fact that many naive algorithms for those tasks construct an equivalent DFA. For example, NFA equivalence and universality can be tested directly [3]. Although these problems are often PSPACE-hard to decide—universality being a prime example—modern techniques frequently outperform approaches that rely on full determinization [10]. Nevertheless, our overall understanding remains fragmented, and a comprehensive, unifying theory of determinization continues to elude us.

In this paper, we present new results on forecasting the size of an NFA's equivalent DFA. Our primary focus is a novel analysis of the subset construction, a dynamic modification of the powerset construction, which only keeps accessible states. The subset construction is the most basic and widely used determinization procedure, implemented in many automata toolkits [1]. It is also relatively well understood—the cases where it results in the minimal DFA were fully characterized by Brzozowski [5]. However, Brzozowski's characterization still does not tell us whether an NFA's equivalent minimal DFA blows up exponentially. In that context, as our first contribution, in Sect. 3, we prove that no algorithm can efficiently predict whether the minimal DFA equivalent to a given NFA will exhibit an exponential increase in the number of states. Moreover, even approximating such a forecast in a coarse-grained manner is PSPACE-hard (Proposition 1). More interestingly, we also show that the same holds when forecasting whether the subset construction will produce an equivalent DFA, non-minimal in general, with exponentially more states (Proposition 2). As our second contribution, we turn to analyzing the size of the DFA produced by the subset construction. Simply restricting nondeterminism does not prevent exponential blow-up when performing the subset construction: unambiguous NFAs and automata with multiple initial states (but otherwise deterministic structure) can still yield exponentially larger DFAs [16]. Prior attempts to bound the blow-up have examined special classes such as homogeneous NFAs [8] and employed algebraic tools like monoid complexity [2], but no general bound for subset construction has emerged. Thus, in Sect. 4, we introduce a simple yet general measure called subset complexity, which provides an upper bound on the size of the DFA produced by the subset construction (Theorem 3), and thereby a

[1] See Sect. 3 for further exposition.

bound on the size of the minimal DFA. Finally, in Sect. 5, we propose an efficient estimate for computing the subset complexity in practice (Proposition 3). Taken together, we hope these results contribute to a deeper theoretical understanding of the efficiency of determininizing NFAs.

2 Background: Automata, Determinization and Monoids

We start the technical portion of the paper by briefly reciting necessary definitions concerning finite-state automata; for a more comprehensive introduction, we refer to [13]. An **alphabet** Σ is a finite, non-empty set of symbols. With Σ^*, we denote the set of all finite words over Σ. The symbol $\varepsilon \in \Sigma^*$ denotes the empty word, i.e., the unique word of length 0. Two words are placed adjacent to one another, e.g., $\boldsymbol{xy}$, denotes the concatenation of those words.

Definition 1. *A* ***finite-state automaton (FSA)*** $\mathcal{A} = (\Sigma, Q, I, F, \delta)$ *is a quintuple where* Σ *is an alphabet,* Q *is a finite set of states,* $I \subseteq Q$ *is a set of the initial states,* $F \subseteq Q$ *is a set of accepting states and* $\delta \subseteq Q \times (\Sigma \cup \{\varepsilon\}) \times Q$ *is a finite multiset of transitions.*

Note that a transition labeled with ε can be performed at any point. The **size** of a finite-state automaton $\mathcal{A} = (\Sigma, Q, I, F, \delta)$ is its number of states; we use the cardinality operator $|\mathcal{A}| = |Q|$ to denote the size. For the remainder of this article, we assume that all automata are ε-free. This assumption is without loss of generality as there exist efficient procedures for removing ε-transitions [1].

Definition 2. *A* ***path*** $\boldsymbol{\pi} = q_0 \xrightarrow{w_1} q_1 \xrightarrow{w_2} \cdots \xrightarrow{w_N} q_N$ *is a labeled sequence of states where each label* $w_n \in \Sigma \cup \{\varepsilon\}$ *is a symbol from the alphabet and each* $q_n \in Q$ *is a state in the FSA. We will refer to the concatenation of symbols along the path* $w_1 \cdots w_N$ *as the path's* ***yield****.*

We say that a word $\boldsymbol{w} \in \Sigma^*$ is **recognized** by the FSA $\mathcal{A}$ if there exists a path from some initial state $q_I \in I$ to some final state $q_F \in F$ with yield $\boldsymbol{w}$. Moreover, we denote with $\mathcal{L}(\mathcal{A}) \subseteq \Sigma^*$ the **language** (set of all words) recognized by $\mathcal{A}$. Two FSA $\mathcal{A}$ and $\mathcal{A}'$ are called **equivalent** if they accept the same language, i.e., if $\mathcal{L}(\mathcal{A}) = \mathcal{L}(\mathcal{A}')$.

Definition 3. *An FSA* $\mathcal{A} = (\Sigma, Q, I, F, \delta)$ *is* ***deterministic*** *if and only if the initial state is unique, i.e.,* $|I| = 1$*, and for every* $(q, w) \in Q \times \Sigma$ *there is exactly one* $q' \in Q$ *such that* $(q, w, q') \in \delta$*, i.e., the relation corresponds to a total function of type* $Q \times \Sigma \to Q$*. An FSA that is not deterministic is called* ***nondeterministic****.*

As a shorthand, for any $\boldsymbol{w} \in \Sigma^*$, we write $\delta(q, \boldsymbol{w}) = \delta(\cdots \delta(\delta(q, w_1), w_2) \cdots, w_N)$ to denote an iterative application of the transition function to the word $\boldsymbol{w} = w_1 \cdots w_N$. In general, DFAs are both easier to implement and to use—many properties, e.g., equivalence to another DFA, are hard to decide for general NFAs, but can be decided for deterministic automata in polynomial time [12].

Algorithm 1. (Subset construction)

Ensure: $\mathcal{A} = (\Sigma, Q, I, F, \delta)$
  $\mathcal{Q}_I \leftarrow \{q \mid q \in I\}$
  $\mathcal{A}_{\text{DET}} \leftarrow (\Sigma, Q_{\text{DET}}, \mathcal{Q}_I, F_{\text{DET}}, \delta_{\text{DET}})$
  $\mathsf{stack} \leftarrow \mathcal{Q}_I$
  $Q_{\text{DET}} \leftarrow \{\mathcal{Q}_I\}$
  while $|\mathsf{stack}| > 0$ **do**
    pop $\mathcal{Q}$ from the stack
    for all $w \in \Sigma$ **do**
      $\mathcal{Q}' \leftarrow \{q' \mid (q, w, q') \in \delta,\ q \in \mathcal{Q}\}$
      $\delta_{\text{DET}} \leftarrow \delta_{\text{DET}} \cup \{\mathcal{Q} \xrightarrow{w} \mathcal{Q}'\}$
      if $\mathcal{Q}' \notin Q_{\text{DET}}$ **then**
        $Q_{\text{DET}} \leftarrow Q_{\text{DET}} \cup \{\mathcal{Q}'\}$
        push $\mathcal{Q}'$ on the stack
  $F_{\text{DET}} \leftarrow \{\mathcal{Q} \in Q_{\text{DET}} \mid \mathcal{Q} \cap F \neq \emptyset\}$
  return $\leftarrow \mathcal{A}_{\text{DET}}$

Definition 4. *The* ***reverse*** *FSA of an automaton $\mathcal{A}$, marked by $\mathcal{A}^R$, is an FSA obtained by reversing the direction of all transitions in $\mathcal{A}$ and swapping the initial and final states. We call FSA $\mathcal{A}$* ***co-deterministic*** *if $\mathcal{A}^R$ is deterministic.*

Definition 5. *A state $q \in Q$ is called* ***accessible*** *if there exists a path from I to q, and* ***co-accessible*** *if there exists a path from q to F. An automaton where all states are both accessible and co-accessible is called* ***trim****.*

Transforming a nondeterministic automaton into an equivalent deterministic one is known as **determinization**. The most commonly implemented practical algorithm for determinization is the **subset construction** [1], a dynamic version of powerset construction which only keeps track of accessible states; hence, the states in the DFA returned by the subset construction are always a subset of the states in the DFA returned by the powerset construction. Algorithm 1 provides the pseudocode for an example implementation of subset construction. The algorithm roughly works as follows. Given an input NFA $\mathcal{A} = (\Sigma, Q, I, F, \delta)$, it explores all accessible subsets of states Q by following the labeled transitions in δ. Each new accessible state $\mathcal{Q} \subseteq Q$ will be placed on the stack, and for every subset of states Q on the stack, we iteratively search for all of its direct neighbors and place them on the stack until the stack is empty. Algebraically, this can be seen as multiplying the characteristic vector for the initial state $\mathcal{Q}_I$ with all possible sequences of transition matrices and terminating as soon as no new states can be produced. We will refer to the DFA $\mathcal{A}_{\text{DET}}$ obtained by applying subset construction on $\mathcal{A}$ as the **subset automaton** for $\mathcal{A}$.

Definition 6. *Given a finite-state automaton $\mathcal{A}$, we call the number of states in its* ***minimal*** *equivalent deterministic automaton its* ***state complexity****.*

Another way of characterizing FSA is by using the algebraic approach and studying the semigroups defined by the underlying transition matrices.

Definition 7. *Consider an FSA* $\mathcal{A} = (\Sigma, Q, I, F, \delta)$ *and, for each* $w \in \Sigma$*, define a binary relation* $T^{(w)}$ *over* Q *with* $(q, q') \in T^{(w)} \Leftrightarrow (q, w, q') \in \delta$ *for all* $q, q' \in Q$*. A* ***transition monoid*** $\mathbb{S}(\mathcal{A})$ *is a binary relation monoid over* Q *generated by* $\{T^{(w)} \mid w \in \Sigma\}$ *and closed under the relation composition operator* $\circ$ *with the identity relation* id.

It is often more convenient to think of $\mathbb{S}(\mathcal{A})$ as a monoid of $|Q| \times |Q|$ matrices over the Boolean semifield $\mathbb{B} := \langle \{0, 1\}, \vee, \wedge, 0, 1 \rangle$ closed under Boolean matrix multiplication with the identity element $\mathcal{I}$, such that:

$$T^{(w)}_{i,j} = 1 \Longleftrightarrow (q_i, q_j) \in T^{(w)}. \tag{1}$$

Notice that the monoid $\mathbb{S}(\mathcal{A})$ is, by construction, closely related to the regular language $\mathcal{L}(\mathcal{A})$. This duality has been extensively studied; for a more detailed overview, we refer to [18].

3 The Complexity of Determinization

As mentioned in Sect. 1, the problem of converting an NFA into an equivalent DFA is difficult because the state complexity of many NFAs can be exponentially large. Two classical examples demonstrating this phenomenon are the n-state Moore automaton [17] and the n-state Meyer–Fischer automaton [11], both of which exhibit a state complexity of 2^n; see Fig. 1.

Example 1. The blow-up occurring in a Meyer–Fischer automaton $\mathcal{A}_{\text{MF}}$ has a particularly intuitive explanation. Let $|\boldsymbol{w}|_a$ denote the number of times the symbol a appears in a word $\boldsymbol{w} \in \{a, b\}^*$. Then, the language accepted by an n-state $\mathcal{A}_{\text{MF}}$ can be described as

$$\mathcal{L}(\mathcal{A}_{\text{MF}}) = \{\boldsymbol{xy} \mid \boldsymbol{x} \in \{\varepsilon\} \cup (\{a, b\}^* b),\ \boldsymbol{y} \in \{a, b\}^* \text{ and } |\boldsymbol{y}|_a \equiv 0 \pmod{n}\}. \tag{2}$$

For every word $\boldsymbol{w} \in \mathcal{L}(\mathcal{A}_{\text{MF}})$, the nondeterministic Meyer–Fischer automaton guesses a prefix that is either empty or ends with b, such that the number of symbols a in the remaining suffix is a multiple of n. To accomplish that, any deterministic counterpart of $\mathcal{A}_{\text{MF}}$ needs to keep track of all parities modulo n for all occurrences of b in $\boldsymbol{w}$, i.e., exactly 2^n possible options.

We emphasize that not all NFAs will exhibit exponential blow-up. For example, as mentioned in Sect. 1, an NFA with no accepting states can be converted to an equivalent DFA with a single state accepting the empty language. Nevertheless, due to the possibility of an exponential blow-up, it immediately follows that there does not exist a polynomial-time (in the size of the NFA) algorithm that outputs the equivalent minimal DFA when given an NFA as input.

The next logical step would be to instead look for an efficient *parameterized* algorithm to find a minimal equivalent DFA, i.e., a polynomial-time algorithm parameterized by the state complexity of the NFA. Somewhat surprisingly, this

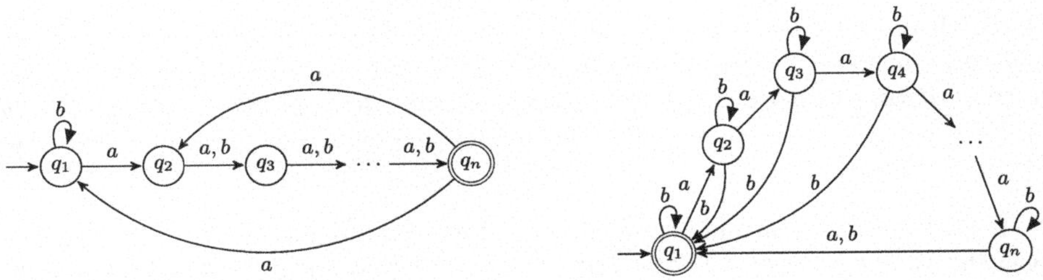

Fig. 1. An n-state Moore automaton $\mathcal{A}_{\text{MOORE}}$ (left) and an n-state Meyer–Fischer automaton $\mathcal{A}_{\text{MF}}$ (right). Both of them are nondeterministic with state complexity 2^n for every $n \geq 2$.

is likely impossible as well. To see this, consider the following one-state deterministic automaton

$$\mathcal{A}_{\text{UNIV}} := (\{a, b\}, \{q\}, \{q\}, \{q\}, \{(q, a, q), (q, b, q)\}), \tag{3}$$

which is minimal and accepts the **universal** language $\mathcal{L}(\mathcal{A}_{\text{UNIV}}) = \{a, b\}^*$, i.e., all words over a binary alphabet. The subsequent result demonstrates that the minimization becomes intractable even for this specific case.

Theorem 1 (NFA Universality [12]). *Given an n-state NFA $\mathcal{A}$, deciding whether $\mathcal{L}(\mathcal{A}) = \mathcal{L}(\mathcal{A}_{\text{UNIV}})$ is* PSPACE*-complete.*

Under the assumption that PSPACE $\neq$ P, we conclude that no parameterized polynomial algorithm for determinization exists—otherwise, we could decide universality by simply executing this algorithm and terminating it after some fixed polynomial number of steps. For the same reason, there is no efficient algorithm to find an almost minimal equivalent DFA because DFAs can be minimized efficiently. Furthermore, this result also implies that it is likely impossible to devise an algorithm that efficiently determines the state complexity of an NFA.

Corollary 1. *Determining the state complexity of a given NFA, i.e., the number of states in a minimal equivalent DFA, is* PSPACE*-hard.*

Proof. This follows immediately from Theorem 1. Note that the state complexity of Eq. (3) is 1. An NFA with state complexity of 1 must either be universal or accept the empty language. However, checking the emptiness of an NFA is a simple graph connectivity problem, which can be solved in linear time. Thus, given that we can efficiently determine whether an NFA accepts only the empty language, we have obtained a polynomial reduction from determining universality to determining state complexity. ■

We now relax the original question and ask whether it is possible to find some approximation to the state complexity of a given NFA in polynomial time. Perhaps even more surprisingly, this question remains equally hard as the previous one, even if we allow for arbitrary polynomial slackness in our approximation. Let us denote with $\mathfrak{A}$ the set of all FSA. To formalize the notion of approximation, we will require an additional definition.

Definition 8. *Let $\mathcal{A}$ be an arbitrary NFA and let $f\colon \mathbb{N} \to \mathbb{N}$ be some function satisfying $f(i) \geq i$ for all $i \in \mathbb{N}$. We say that metric $\mathcal{F}\colon \mathfrak{A} \to \mathbb{N}$ causes an* ***f-blow-up*** *for $\mathcal{A}$ if*

$$\mathcal{F}(\mathcal{A}) > f(|\mathcal{A}|). \tag{4}$$

Furthermore, we say that $\widehat{m}$ is an ***f-approximation*** *of $\mathcal{F}$ on $\mathcal{A}$ if*

$$\mathcal{F}(\mathcal{A}) \leq \widehat{m} \leq f(\mathcal{F}(\mathcal{A}) + |\mathcal{A}|), \tag{5}$$

i.e., $\widehat{m}$ is an upper bound with slackness specified by f.

For our purposes, only two particular choices for $\mathcal{F}$ are relevant: the state complexity of $\mathcal{A}$ and the size of automaton produced by the subset construction applied to $\mathcal{A}$.

Proposition 1. *For any polynomial p, it is* PSPACE*-hard both to compute a p-approximation to the state complexity and to decide whether a p-blow-up will occur.*

Proof. To show PSPACE-hardness, we construct a polynomial reduction from the NFA universality problem. Let $n = |\mathcal{A}|$ and m be the (unknown) state complexity of $\mathcal{A}$. Further, assume that there exists an algorithm that produces a p-approximation for m (the proof for p-blow-up is analogous). We show that we could use such an algorithm to decide whether $\mathcal{A}$ accepts the universal language, which is PSPACE-hard by Theorem 1.

Without loss of generality, we assume that $\Sigma = \{a, b\}$. Next, we construct an automaton $\mathcal{A}'$ over the alphabet $\Sigma' = \{a, b, \#\}$ with $2(n+1)$ states using a copy of $\mathcal{A}$, a copy of $\mathcal{A}_{\text{MOORE}}$ and two copies of $\mathcal{A}_{\text{UNIV}}$ as shown in Fig. 2. Specifically, $\mathcal{A}'$ is the union of the following two NFAs:

1. We construct the first automaton as follows. Let $\mathcal{A}_{\text{UNIV}}$ be the 1-state minimal DFA that accepts Σ^*, and let $\mathcal{A}_{\text{MOORE}}$ be the n-state Moore automaton. Then, concatenate $\mathcal{A}_{\text{UNIV}}$ to $\mathcal{A}_{\text{MOORE}}$ by adding a #-labeled transition from unique state in $\mathcal{A}_{\text{UNIV}}$ with the initial state of $\mathcal{A}_{\text{MOORE}}$. Then, the initial state of $\mathcal{A}_{\text{MOORE}}$ no longer serves as an initial state, and the single state in $\mathcal{A}_{\text{UNIV}}$ no longer serves as a final state.
2. We construct the second automaton as follows. Let $\mathcal{A}_{\text{UNIV}}$ be another copy of the 1-state minimal DFA that accepts Σ^*. Then, concatenate $\mathcal{A}$ to $\mathcal{A}_{\text{UNIV}}$ by adding a #-labeled transition from all final states in $\mathcal{A}$ to the initial state of $\mathcal{A}_{\text{UNIV}}$. The unique state in $\mathcal{A}_{\text{UNIV}}$ no longer serves as an initial state, and $\mathcal{A}$ no longer has any final states.

Clearly, the first automaton accepts the language $\Sigma^*\#\mathcal{L}(\mathcal{A}_{\text{MOORE}})$ while the second accepts the language $\mathcal{L}(\mathcal{A})\#\Sigma^*$. Thus, $\mathcal{A}'$ accepts $\Sigma^*\#\mathcal{L}(\mathcal{A}_{\text{MOORE}}) \cup \mathcal{L}(\mathcal{A})\#\Sigma^*$. On the one hand, if $\mathcal{A}$ is universal, then $\mathcal{L}(\mathcal{A}) = \Sigma^*$, and the union of these languages is precisely $\Sigma^*\#\Sigma^*$. Consequently, the state complexity of

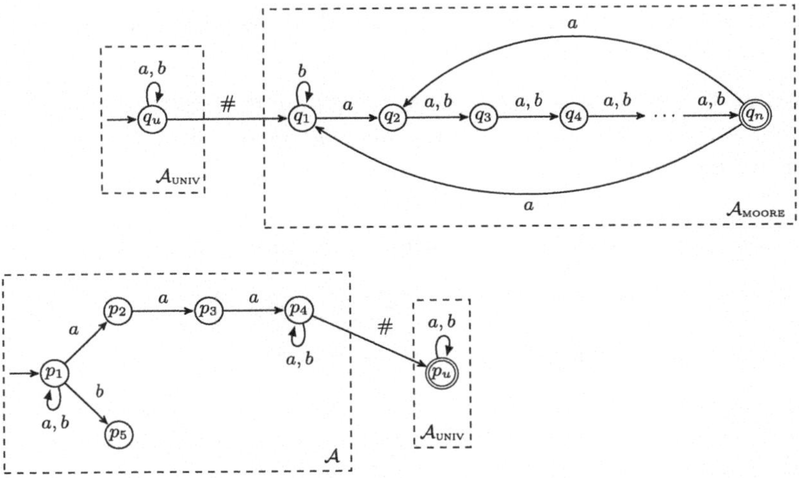

Fig. 2. Construction for automaton $\mathcal{A}'$ consisting of a union of two nondeterministic automata: the upper one is a connection of $\mathcal{A}_{\text{UNIV}}$ and $\mathcal{A}_{\text{MOORE}}$ using symbol #, and the lower one is the connection of $\mathcal{A}$ and $\mathcal{A}_{\text{UNIV}}$ using symbol #. In both cases the final states of the first automaton are connected to the initial states of the second one, with the corresponding initial/final labels dropped.

$\mathcal{A}$ is 3. On the other hand, if $\mathcal{L}(\mathcal{A})$ is not universal, then there exists a word $\boldsymbol{x} \in \{a, b\}^*$ such that $\boldsymbol{x} \notin \mathcal{L}(\mathcal{A})$, meaning that

$$\{\boldsymbol{x}\#\boldsymbol{y} \mid \boldsymbol{y} \in \mathcal{L}(\mathcal{A}_{\text{MOORE}})\} \subset \mathcal{L}(\mathcal{A}') \quad \text{and} \quad \{\boldsymbol{x}\#\boldsymbol{y} \mid \boldsymbol{y} \in \mathcal{L}(\mathcal{A}_{\text{MOORE}})^{\mathsf{c}}\} \cap \mathcal{L}(\mathcal{A}') = \emptyset.$$

Consider the minimal deterministic automaton for $\mathcal{A}'$, which we denote with $\mathcal{A}'_{\text{DET}}$. Let q be the state in $\mathcal{A}'_{\text{DET}}$ to which the path $\boldsymbol{\pi}$ with the yield $\boldsymbol{y}\#$ leads. Now, observe that the right language of q is $\mathcal{L}(\mathcal{A}_{\text{MOORE}})$. Because $\mathcal{L}(\mathcal{A}_{\text{MOORE}})$ has a state complexity 2^n, the state complexity of $\mathcal{A}'_{\text{DET}}$ is at least 2^n. Thus, depending on whether $\mathcal{A}$ is universal or not, the state complexity of $\mathcal{A}'$ will be either 3 or at least 2^n. Because 2^n is exponentially larger than 3, any algorithm producing a p-approximation for the state complexity of $\mathcal{A}'$ would necessarily decide the universality of $\mathcal{A}$. An analogous proof holds for deciding p-blow-up. ■

Proposition 1 shows that it is PSPACE-hard to give any polynomial-time approximation to the blow-up in an NFA's state complexity. Thus, instead, we relativize our results with respect to a specific determinization procedure which, given an NFA, produces an equivalent DFA, albeit one that is not necessarily minimal. In this article, we focus on the subset construction, discussed in Sect. 2. The question of optimality for subset construction was resolved in [5], who presented a characterization of all NFAs for which subset construction produces a minimal DFA. A well-known special case of this result is given below.

Theorem 2 (Brzozowski [6]). *If an NFA $\mathcal{A}$ is trim and co-deterministic, then the subset construction produces the minimal equivalent DFA.*

Even though the subset construction will not produce the minimal DFA for most NFAs, it does have one major advantage—it produces a DFA where all states are accessible. A more fine-grained analysis says that, if $\mathcal{A}$ is an NFA and $\mathcal{A}_{\mathrm{SS}}$ is the (possibly non-minimal) DFA produced by the subset construction, then the running time of Algorithm 1 is in $\mathcal{O}\left(|\Sigma||\mathcal{A}_{\mathrm{SS}}||\mathcal{A}|^2\right)$ if the algorithm is implemented with well-chosen data structures [8]. This reduces the question of whether it is possible to efficiently find an equivalent DFA to one of computing the size of the subset automaton. Clearly, we can decide whether $\mathcal{A}$ causes an f-blow-up by simulating $f(|\mathcal{A}|)$ steps of Algorithm 1 as each step produces a new state, or the algorithm halts. However, the running time of this algorithm is not polynomial, so it is not an efficient procedure. In other words, the question we care about is whether it is possible *a priori* to find an approximation to the size of subset automaton of $\mathcal{A}$ in polynomial time?

Proposition 2. *For any polynomial p, it is* PSPACE*-hard to both compute a p-approximation to the size of the subset automaton or to decide whether a p-blow-up will occur.*

Proof. To show PSPACE-hardness of computing a p-approximation, we again construct a polynomial reduction from the NFA universality problem; the p-blow-up case is analogous. Assume that we have access to an algorithm which, given any $\mathcal{A} = (\Sigma, Q, I, F, \delta)$, computes a p-approximation $\widehat{m}$ to the size of $\mathcal{A}$'s subset automaton. Let k be the degree of the polynomial p and without loss of generality assume that $\Sigma = \{a, b\}$. Consider an $n(k+1)$-state Meyer–Fischer automaton $\mathcal{A}_{\mathrm{MF}}$ over Σ. As with the $n(k+1)$-state Moore automaton, the $n(k+1)$-state Meyer–Fischer $\mathcal{A}_{\mathrm{MF}}$ has a state complexity of $2^{n(k+1)}$. However, the Meyer–Fischer automaton also has a unique initial state p_1 which is also the unique accepting state, as shown in the top part of Fig. 3.

Claim 1. Let $\mathcal{A}_{\mathrm{MF}}$ be an n-state Meyer–Fischer automaton. Consider the state $\mathcal{Q}_1 = \{p_1, \ldots, p_n\}$ created by applying the subset construction (Algorithm 1) to $\mathcal{A}_{\mathrm{MF}}$. Then, all transitions leaving $\mathcal{Q}_1$ are self-loops.

Because being in the state $\mathcal{Q}_1$ corresponds to simultaneously being in the states $\{p_1, \ldots, p_n\}$ in $\mathcal{A}_{\mathrm{MF}}$ (see Fig. 3), the claim follows by noting that every state in $\mathcal{A}_{\mathrm{MF}}$ has at least one incoming transition with label a and one with b. In other words, once you are in $\mathcal{Q}_1$, you will always transition back to all states in $\mathcal{Q}_1$. Without loss of generality, assume that $\mathcal{A}$ has an explicit dead state $q_\varnothing$, i.e., if some state $q \in Q$ is missing an explicit transition for some symbol $w \in \Sigma$, we augment $\mathcal{A}$ with transition $q \xrightarrow{w} q_\varnothing$. In other words, we assume that $\mathcal{A}$'s transition function is total.

Claim 2. An NFA $\mathcal{A}$ is universal if and only if every state $\mathcal{Q}$ in $\mathcal{A}_{\mathrm{SS}}$, the DFA produced by the subset construction (Algorithm 1), contains a final state from $\mathcal{A}$.

To show the left implication, observe that if all states generated by applying the subset construction contain a final state, then all states in $\mathcal{A}_{\mathrm{SS}}$ are accepting by the design of Algorithm 1; hence, $\mathcal{A}_{\mathrm{SS}}$'s language is universal. To show the

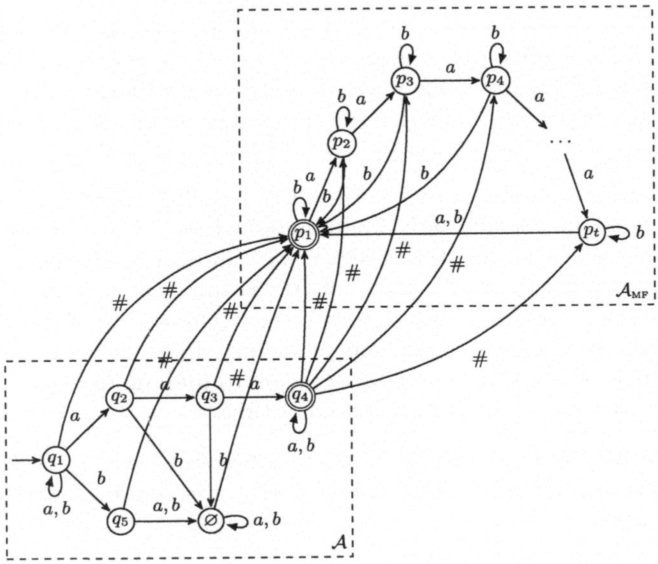

Fig. 3. The construction of the automaton $\mathcal{A}'$ from an arbitrary NFA $\mathcal{A}$ with an explicit dead state $\varnothing$ and the $n(k+1)$-state Meyer–Fischer automaton $\mathcal{A}_{\text{MF}}$. All non-final states of $\mathcal{A}$ are connected to the initial state p_1 of $\mathcal{A}_{\text{MF}}$ using symbol # and all final states are connected to all states of $\mathcal{A}_{\text{MF}}$ using the same symbol #. In the diagram, $t = n(k+1)$.

right implication, observe that, if there exists a state $\mathcal{Q}$ generated by Algorithm 1 that does *not* contain a final state, then, because all states in $\mathcal{A}_{\text{SS}}$ are accessible, there exists some path $\boldsymbol{\pi}$ with yield $\boldsymbol{y}$ from $\mathcal{Q}_I$ to $\mathcal{Q}$, meaning that $\boldsymbol{y} \notin \mathcal{L}(\mathcal{A}_{\text{SS}})$.

Next, we create an automaton $\mathcal{A}'$ over the alphabet $\Sigma' = \{a, b, \#\}$ by conjoining $\mathcal{A}$ and $\mathcal{A}_{\text{MF}}$ as follows (see Fig. 3).

1. We add #-labeled transitions from all nonfinal states of $\mathcal{A}$ to $\mathcal{A}_{\text{MF}}$'s initial state p_1. The state p_1 is no longer initial in $\mathcal{A}'$.
2. We add #-labeled transitions from all final states in $\mathcal{A}$ to all states of $\mathcal{A}_{\text{MF}}$.

Next, we analyze an application of the subset construction to $\mathcal{A}'$ by breaking its computation into two stages. In the first stage, we only traverse transitions with symbols a and b. This corresponds *exactly* to running the subset construction on $\mathcal{A}$. After the first stage is completed, i.e., after no new states can be generated, we allow the subset construction to consider other symbols from Σ'. Note that our decomposition into two stages is little more than an enforcement of a specific ordering of the computation performed by the subset construction when determinizing $\mathcal{A}'$—it does not change *what* computation performed. We denote the resulting subset automaton as $\mathcal{A}'_{\text{SS}}$.

Let us observe the (incomplete) subset automaton after the first stage. We first consider the case where $\mathcal{A}$ is universal. Due to Claim 2, all states in the (incomplete) subset automaton contain at least one final state. Hence, in the second stage of the subset construction, any #-labeled transition leads to the state $\mathcal{Q}_1$, where, due to Claim 1, we either remain forever or transition into the state corresponding to $\emptyset$. This means that exactly 2 additional states are produced in the second stage. We next consider the case where $\mathcal{A}$ is *not* universal. In this case, due to Claim 2, the subset construction will have produced some state $\mathcal{Q}$ such that $\mathcal{Q} \cap F = \emptyset$. Moreover, because we have an explicit dead state, we know that every $\mathcal{Q}$ will be non-empty. Thus, there exists some non-final $q \in \mathcal{Q}$, and, in the second stage, the subset construction will take the #-labeled transition from $\mathcal{Q}$, generating the state $\mathcal{Q}' = \{p_1\}$. Subsequently, the subset construction will begin to determinize the $n(k+1)$-state Meyer–Fischer automaton $\mathcal{A}_{\text{MF}}$, which produces $2^{n(k+1)}$ additional states.

In summary, if $\mathcal{A}$ is universal, then the subset automaton $\mathcal{A}'_{\text{SS}}$ will have exactly 2 more states than $\mathcal{A}_{\text{SS}}$, while if $\mathcal{A}$ is not universal, it will have at least $2^{n(k+1)}$ more states. Moreover, since $\mathcal{A}$ has only n states, the size of $\mathcal{A}_{\text{SS}}$ will be at most 2^n. Thus, if $\mathcal{A}$ is universal, we have $|\mathcal{A}'_{\text{SS}}| \leq 2^n + 2$. And, if $\mathcal{A}$ is not universal, we have $|\mathcal{A}'_{\text{SS}}| \geq 2^{n(k+1)}$. It follows that if $\mathcal{A}$ is not universal, any p-approximation $\widehat{m}$ (with p having degree k) for $\mathcal{A}'$ will satisfy

$$\widehat{m} \leq p(m + |\mathcal{A}'|) \in \mathcal{O}\left((m + n(k+2))^k\right) \leq \mathcal{O}\left((2^n + 2 + n(k+2))^k\right) < 2^{n(k+1)} \tag{6}$$

for sufficiently large values of n. And, if $\mathcal{A}$ is universal, $\widehat{m} \geq 2^{n(k+1)}$. By comparing $\widehat{m}$ and $2^{n(k+1)}$, we are able to decide the universality of $\mathcal{A}$. An analogous proof holds for p-blow-up. ■

While we believe the next result to be known, we were unable to find a formal presentation or reference for it in the literature, hence we state it as an observation and provide a proof sketch.

Observation 1 *Given an NFA $\mathcal{A}$, determining the state complexity and the size of the subset automaton can be computed in polynomial space. Hence, the corresponding decision problems are in* PSPACE.

Proof (sketch). Consider the following two decision problems. (i) For a given automaton $\mathcal{A}$ and $k \in \mathbb{N}$, is the size of the subset automaton larger than k? (ii) For a given automaton $\mathcal{A}$ and $k \in \mathbb{N}$, is the state complexity of $\mathcal{A}$ larger than k? We claim that both of these problems are in NPSPACE, and, hence, due to Savitch's theorem, also in PSPACE [21].

First, let $\mathcal{A} = (\Sigma, Q, I, F, \delta)$ be an NFA. Consider the set of characteristic vectors for the set of states Q in the NFA $\mathcal{A}$. Additionally, consider a $|Q|$-bit counter which stores the number of distinct accessible states in the corresponding subset automaton.

To demonstrate that (i) is in NPSPACE, we enumerate the $2^{|Q|}$ characteristic vectors in an arbitrary total ordering. For each vector in the enumeration, consider the corresponding subset of the states $\mathcal{Q} \subseteq Q$. Nondeterministically guess the path from $\mathcal{Q}_I$ (defined in Algorithm 1) to $\mathcal{Q}$ if one exists. The nondeterministic guessing procedure has at most $2^{|Q|}$ steps, where, in each step, we either nondeterministically choose a symbol $w \in \Sigma$ that leads us to the next state or halt. In the case that we successfully guessed a path to $\mathcal{Q}$, we increase the $|Q|$-bit counter by 1; otherwise, we keep it unchanged. After repeating this for all $2^{|Q|}$ characteristic vectors, we compare the counter value and k, i.e., accept or reject the input. Thus, (i) is in NPSPACE and, by Savitch's theorem, in PSPACE.

To demonstrate that (ii) is in NPSPACE, we borrow an idea suggested by Stefan Kiefer [14]. Because DFA minimization is in NL [9] and, hence, due to Savitch's theorem, in polyL, we are only required to keep track of polynomially many states from subset construction at once to compute the number of equivalence classes, i.e., determine the state complexity. ■

4 Bounding the State Complexity

Due to Proposition 1 and Proposition 2, no reasonable approximation to the state complexity or the size of the DFA produced by the subset construction is possible assuming PSPACE $\neq$ P. Thus, an alternative is to look for some easily computable lower and upper bounds and keep them as general as possible. We focus on bounding the size of the DFA produced by the subset construction (Algorithm 1), which directly tells us how hard it would be to determinize the chosen NFA in practice. Note, however, that, by the results in Sect. 3, we repeat that such bounds cannot be both (i) arbitrarily good, and (ii) easy to compute for all NFAs.

One way of achieving such a bound for the subset construction is to consider the transition monoid $\mathbb{S}(\mathcal{A})$. It is known that the size of the transition monoid directly translates into an upper bound on the subset automaton. In the case of unary, commutative, and dense automata, this fact can be used to produce useful bounds [2]. However, it remains unclear how to bound the size of the transition monoid for an arbitrary NFA.

Lemma 2 (Monoid bound [2]). *Given an NFA $\mathcal{A}$, the DFA produced by the subset construction $\mathcal{A}_{\text{ss}}$ satisfies $|\mathcal{A}_{\text{ss}}| \leq |\mathbb{S}(\mathcal{A})|$.*

Another natural way to bound the size of subset automaton is to consider the range $\mathcal{R}(T^{(w)})$ for all transition matrices in

$$\mathcal{T} := \{T^{(w)} \mid w \in \Sigma\}. \tag{7}$$

Because every state in the subset construction corresponds to a characteristic vector over Q, it has to be in the image of some transition matrix. Hence, the size of their combined images is an upper bound on the size of the subset automaton.

Lemma 3 (Range bound). *Let $\mathcal{A}$ be an NFA with a set of transition matrices $\mathcal{T}$. Then the DFA output by the subset construction $\mathcal{A}_{\text{ss}}$ satisfies*

$$|\mathcal{A}_{\text{ss}}| \leq 1 + \sum_{w \in \Sigma} \left|\mathcal{R}\left(T^{(w)}\right)\right|, \tag{8}$$

where $\mathcal{R}(T)$ is the range of the matrix T over the Boolean semifield $\mathbb{B}$.

Proof. Let $\mathcal{A}_{\text{ss}} = (\Sigma, Q_{\text{ss}}, I, F, \delta_{\text{ss}})$. Consider any $\mathcal{Q}_J \in Q_{\text{ss}}$ and let $w_1 \cdots w_N \in \Sigma^*$ be a word such that $\mathcal{Q}_J = \delta(\mathcal{Q}_I, w_1 \cdots w_N)$ Then, $\mathcal{Q}_J$'s characteristic vector is given by

$$J = I^\top T^{(w_1)} T^{(w_2)} \cdots T^{(w_N)}. \tag{9}$$

Moreover, because this holds for any J, we have

$$Q_{\text{ss}} \setminus \{\mathcal{Q}_I\} \subseteq \bigcup_{w \in \Sigma} \mathcal{R}\left(T^{(w)\top}\right) = \bigcup_{w \in \Sigma} \mathcal{R}\left(T^{(w)}\right). \tag{10}$$

Applying the union bound and adding 1 to account for the initial state $\mathcal{Q}_I$ concludes the proof. ■

Serendipitously, both the range and monoid bounds can be naturally combined, admitting a more fine-grained perspective on the nondeterministic blow-up, each compensating for the slackness of the other.

Definition 9. *Given an NFA $\mathcal{A} = (\Sigma, Q, I, F, \delta)$, we define the **subset complexity** $\|\mathcal{A}\|$ as*

$$\|\mathcal{A}\| = \min_{\mathcal{J} \subseteq \Sigma} \left(1 + \sum_{w \in \Sigma \setminus \mathcal{J}} \left|\mathcal{R}\left(T^{(w)}\right)\right|\right) |\mathbb{S}(\mathcal{J})|, \tag{11}$$

where $\mathbb{S}(\mathcal{J})$ denotes the submonoid generated by transitions $\{T^{(w)} \mid w \in \mathcal{J}\}$.

Essentially, subset complexity allows us to split $\mathcal{A}$ into subautomata according to whether the symbols on the transitions are in $\mathcal{J}$ or $\Sigma \setminus \mathcal{J}$, respectively. Then, we either apply the monoid or the range bound independently. The subset complexity is then the best possible split.

Theorem 3 (Subset complexity). *Let $\mathcal{A}$ be an NFA and let $\mathcal{A}_{\text{ss}}$ be the DFA output by the subset construction with $\mathcal{A}$ as input. Then, we have $|\mathcal{A}_{\text{ss}}| \leq \|\mathcal{A}\|$.*

Proof. Let $\mathcal{J} \subseteq \Sigma$ be arbitrary. We first show that

$$|\mathcal{A}_{\text{ss}}| \leq \left(1 + \sum_{a \in \Sigma \setminus \mathcal{J}} \left|\mathcal{R}\left(T^{(w)}\right)\right|\right) |\mathbb{S}(\mathcal{J})|. \tag{12}$$

For any word $\boldsymbol{x} \in \Sigma^*$, let $\boldsymbol{x} = \boldsymbol{y}\boldsymbol{z} = \boldsymbol{y} z_1 \cdots z_M$ be the unique decomposition where $z_m \in \mathcal{J}$ and M is maximal. Furthermore, let $\mathcal{Q}_J = \delta(\mathcal{Q}_I, \boldsymbol{x})$. Similar to the proof of Lemma 3, we consider a characteristic vector J for $\mathcal{Q}_J$. For clarity, we will denote transition matrices corresponding to symbols $w \in \mathcal{J}$ with $M^{(w)}$ and transition matrices which correspond to symbols $w \notin \mathcal{J}$ with $R^{(w)}$. Then, the characteristic vector J can be written as

$$J = J' M^{(z_1)} \cdots M^{(z_M)}, \tag{13}$$

for some $J' \in \cup_{w \in \Sigma} \mathcal{R}(R^{(w)})$.[2] Thus, there are at most $1 + \sum_{w \in \Sigma \setminus \mathcal{J}} |\mathcal{R}(T^{(w)})|$ choices for a vector J' and $|\mathbb{S}(\mathcal{J})|$ choices for the matrix $M^{(z_1)} \cdots M^{(z_M)}$. Thus, the total number of choices for J is bounded by the corresponding product. The minimum bound follows. ■

Our notion of subset complexity is a direct improvement over both monoid and range bounds, because it allows us to cherry-pick individual transition matrices according to their properties to achieve the tightest bound.

Example 2. Consider the n-state Moore automaton $\mathcal{A}_{\text{MOORE}}$ from Fig. 1 with state complexity of 2^n. We define a modified n-state Moore automaton $\mathcal{A}'_{\text{MOORE}}$ as follows. Take the n-state Moore automaton and replace the labels on the transitions $q_n \xrightarrow{c} q_1$ and $q_n \xrightarrow{c} q_2$ with a new symbol $c \notin \{a, b\}$. The new automaton $\mathcal{A}'_{\text{MOORE}}$ operates over the alphabet $\Sigma = \{a, b, c\}$; it is still nondeterministic.

Claim. For an n-state modified Moore automaton $\mathcal{A}'_{\text{MOORE}}$, the following inequality holds $\|\mathcal{A}'_{\text{MOORE}}\| \leq 3n^2 + 3n$.

Proof. Let $\mathcal{J} = \{a, b\}$ and observe that $T^{(a)}T^{(b)} = T^{(b}T^{(a)}$, which means that all matrices in the transition monoid $\mathbb{S}(\mathcal{J})$ can be obtained from a product sequence of the following form

$$T^{(b)}T^{(b)} \cdots T^{(b)}T^{(a)}T^{(a)} \cdots T^{(a)}.$$

Moreover, we have that $(T^{(a)})^n = 0$, i.e., the zero matrix and $(T^{(b)})^{n-1} = (T^{(b)})^n$, meaning that there are at most $n+1$ distinct powers of $T^{(w)}$ and n distinct powers of $T^{(b)}$ (counting the empty set). Hence, $|\mathbb{S}(\mathcal{J})| \leq n(n+1) = n^2 + n$. Moreover, we have that $\mathcal{R}(T^{(c)}) = 2$ because $T^{(c)}$ is a rank 1 matrix. Applying Theorem 3 concludes the proof. ■

5 A Simple Upper Bound

In this section, we discuss how to efficiently compute the estimates for the subset complexity from Definition 9. This requires computing the size of the range space as well as the size of the transition monoid. The size of the range space is known to be equivalent to counting maximal independent sets in bipartite graphs [22], which is a #P-complete problem [19]. The monoid size is generally hard to determine.[3] Despite these obstacles, we can still derive an efficiently computable upper bound for subset complexity. We start by considering the case where our NFA is unary: for some automaton $\mathcal{A}_1$ let A be its unique transition matrix. Then the bound on $|\mathbb{S}(\mathcal{A}_1)|$ relies solely on the **precedence graph** $\mathcal{G}(A)$, i.e., a directed graph with $|\mathcal{A}|$ vertices and edges defined by the transition matrix A.

[2] Note that J' will, in general, be the product of both M and R matrices.

[3] One notable exception is when all the matrices are permutations, in which case we use the Schreier–Sims algorithm to compute the size in almost quadratic time [15].

Definition 10. *Given a directed graph $\mathcal{G}$ the* **cyclicity** *of $\mathcal{G}$, denoted with $c(\mathcal{G})$, is the least common multiple of cyclities of all maximal strongly connected components of $\mathcal{G}$, where the cyclicity of a strongly connected component $\mathcal{C}$ is the greatest common divisor of all cycles in $\mathcal{C}$.*

Lemma 4 (Sect. 3 in [2]). *Let $\mathcal{A}_1 = (\{w\}, Q_1, \delta_1, I_1, F_1)$ be a n-state unary automaton with transition matrix A. Then*

$$c(\mathcal{G}(A)) \leq |\mathbb{S}(\mathcal{A}_1)| \leq c(\mathcal{G}(A)) + n^2 - 2n + 2. \tag{14}$$

Now we turn our attention to the range of a Boolean matrix and the methods that can be used to bound its size.

Lemma 5 (Lemma 1 in [7]). *Given an $n \times n$ Boolean matrix A, let* $\operatorname{rank}(A)$ *be the rank of A over the Galois field $\mathbb{F}_2$. Then the range of A satisfies*

$$\operatorname{rank}(A) \leq |\mathcal{R}(A)| \leq 2^{\operatorname{rank}(A)^2/4+\mathcal{O}(\operatorname{rank}(A))}.$$

Remark 1. Other possibilities for bounding the range exist. For example, one can consider the size of maximum matching or the notion of Boolean width; see [7] for in-depth discussion.

Using the simplified bounds for range on symbols $\Sigma \setminus \{a\}$ and monoid size on the remaining symbol a we get a simple upper bound on the subset complexity for any automaton $\mathcal{A}$.

Proposition 3 (All-but-one). *Given an n-state NFA $\mathcal{A} = (\Sigma, Q, I, F, \delta)$, an arbitrary target symbol $a \in \Sigma$ and any $\varepsilon > 0$, the following holds*

$$\|\mathcal{A}\| \in \mathcal{O}\left(|\Sigma|(c(\mathcal{G}(T^{(a)})) + n^2) \max_{b\in\Sigma\setminus\{a\}} 2^{\operatorname{rank}(T^{(b)})^2/(4-\varepsilon)}\right).$$

This bound has an intuitive interpretation—if all but one of the transition matrices is of low rank, then the subset complexity will be polynomially bounded; the cyclicity is large only in very exceptional cases. Note that cyclicity can be computed using a simple breadth-first search, while rank can be calculated using Gaussian elimination over $\mathbb{F}_2$.

6 Conclusion

Given an NFA, we have attempted to forecast the state complexity of the minimal equivalent DFA as well as the size of the subset automaton. In both cases, we show that such forecasting is PSPACE-hard; in fact, even the approximate forecasting is PSPACE-hard. As a potential workaround, we propose subset complexity—a tractable algebraic criterion, which gives us a sufficient condition for when determinization can be performed efficiently.

References

1. Allauzen, C., Riley, M., Schalkwyk, J., Skut, W., Mohri, M.: OpenFST: a general and efficient weighted finite-state transducer library: (extended abstract of an invited talk). In: Implementation and Application of Automata: 12th International Conference, pp. 11–23 (2007)
2. Baburin, I., Cotterell, R.: An analysis of on-the-fly determinization of finite-state automata (2023)
3. Bonchi, F., Pous, D.: Hacking nondeterminism with induction and coinduction. Commun. ACM **58**(2), 87–95 (2015)
4. Bordihn, H., Holzer, M., Kutrib, M.: Determination of finite automata accepting subregular languages. Theor. Comput. Sci. **410**(35), 3209–3222 (2009). descriptional Complexity of Formal Systems
5. Brzozowski, J., Tamm, H.: Theory of átomata. Theoret. Comput. Sci. **539**, 13–27 (2014)
6. Brzozowski, J.A.: Canonical regular expressions and minimal state graphs for definite events. In: Proceedings of the Symposium on Mathematical Theory of Automata, pp. 529–561 (1962)
7. Bui-Xuan, B.M., Telle, J.A., Vatshelle, M.: Boolean-width of graphs. Theoret. Comput. Sci. **412**(39), 5187–5204 (2011)
8. Champarnaud, J.M.: Subset construction complexity for homogeneous automata, position automata and ZPC-structures. Theoret. Comput. Sci. **267**(1–2), 17–34 (2001)
9. Cho, S., Huynh, D.T.: The parallel complexity of finite-state automata problems. Inf. Comput. **97**(1), 1–22 (1992)
10. De Wulf, M., Doyen, L., Henzinger, T.A., Raskin, J.F.: Antichains: a new algorithm for checking universality of finite automata. In: Computer Aided Verification, pp. 17–30 (2006)
11. Fischer, M.J., Meyer, A.R.: Economy of description by automata, grammars, and formal systems. In: 2013 IEEE 54th Annual Symposium on Foundations of Computer Science, pp. 188–191. IEEE Computer Society (1971)
12. Holzer, M., Kutrib, M.: Descriptional and computational complexity of finite automata–a survey. Inf. Comput. **209**(3), 456–470 (2011)
13. Hopcroft, J.E., Motwani, R., Ullman, J.D.: Introduction to Automata Theory, Languages, and Computation. Association for Computing Machinery (2001)
14. (https://cstheory.stackexchange.com/users/64968/stefan kiefer), S.K.: Complexity of NFA to DFA minimization with binary threshold. Theoretical Computer Science Stack Exchange. https://cstheory.stackexchange.com/q/50706
15. Knuth, D.E.: Efficient representation of perm groups. Combinatorica **11**(1), 33–43 (1991)
16. Leung, H.: Descriptional complexity of NFA of different ambiguity. Int. J. Found. Comput. Sci. **16**(05), 975–984 (2005)
17. Moore, F.R.: On the bounds for state-set size in the proofs of equivalence between deterministic, nondeterministic, and two-way finite automata. IEEE Trans. Comput. **100**(10), 1211–1214 (1971)
18. Pin, J.E.: Syntactic semigroups. Handbook of Formal Languages: Volume 1 Word, Language, Grammar, pp. 679–746 (1997)
19. Provan, J.S., Ball, M.O.: The complexity of counting cuts and of computing the probability that a graph is connected. SIAM J. Comput. **12**(4), 777–788 (1983)

20. Rabin, M.O., Scott, D.: Finite automata and their decision problems. IBM J. Res. Dev. **3**(2), 114–125 (1959)
21. Savitch, W.J.: Relationships between nondeterministic and deterministic tape complexities. J. Comput. Syst. Sci. **4**(2), 177–192 (1970)
22. Vatshelle, M.: New Width Parameters of Graphs. Ph.D. Thesis, University of Bergen (2012)

k-Local Graphs

Christian Beth(✉), Pamela Fleischmann(✉), Annika Huch, Daniyal Kazempour, Peer Kröger, Andrea Kulow, and Matthias Renz

Department of Computer Science, Kiel University, Kiel, Germany
{cbe,fpa,ahu,dka,pkr,mr}@informatik.uni-kiel.de,
stu229089@mail.uni-kiel.de

Abstract. In 2017 Day et al. introduced the notion of locality as a structural complexity-measure for patterns in the field of pattern matching established by Angluin in 1980. In 2019 Casel et al. showed that determining the locality of an arbitrary pattern is NP-complete. Inspired by hierarchical clustering, we extend the notion to coloured graphs, i.e., given a coloured graph determine an enumeration of the colours such that colouring the graph stepwise according to the enumeration leads to as few clusters as possible. Besides initial theoretical results on graph classes, we propose a priority search algorithm to compute the k-locality of a graph. This algorithm guarantees a correct result, while being faster by orders of magnitude than an exhaustive search over all permutations of colour enumerations. Finally, we perform a case study on a DBLP subgraph to demonstrate the potential of k-locality for knowledge discovery.

1 Introduction

The notion of locality was firstly introduced by Day et al. as a structural complexity-measure for patterns [6]. A pattern is a word that consists of constants from an alphabet of terminal symbols and variables. In their work, the authors investigated the *matching problem* where one decides whether, given a word w and a pattern α, the word may be obtained from substituting the variables in α. While this problem is NP-complete in general [2], they showed that the matching and also the membership problem can be solved efficiently for the class of k-local patterns for any fixed k. Extending the idea of the matching algorithm for *non-cross patterns* [18], for k-local patterns one has at every given point during the substitution at most k separate factors within the pattern, i.e., the algorithm in [6] tracks the possible extensions of such factors via dynamic programming. In [4] the research on k-locality is continued from a combinatorial perspective. The authors investigated the problem of computing the locality number of words and showed via a reduction from the decision problem cutwidth on graphs (asking to decide whether the cutwidth of a graph is upper bounded by a given number) that the computation of the locality number is NP-complete. The studies of k-local words from a word combinatorial perspective continued in [9]. A first connection between k-locality and graphs was introduced in [8], where the authors characterised the graphs which are represented by 1-local words.

Published by Springer Nature Switzerland AG 2025
A. Malcher and L. Prigioniero (Eds.): DCFS 2025, LNCS 15759, pp. 34–49, 2025.
https://doi.org/10.1007/978-3-031-97100-6_3

Hierarchical clustering is an archetype of clustering methods that allow for partitioning a given dataset. It operates on distances between objects (instances) and depending on the used linkage distance (e.g., single or complete link) and the clustering strategy like agglomerative (bottom-up) or divisive (top-down) a hierarchy of partitions among all objects is computed. Unlike other archetypes like, e.g., density-based or variance-minimising approaches, hierarchical clustering allows one to see and understand either single objects or clusters within their local context (e.g., a cluster A and B are most similar to each other within a cluster C). To combine hierarchical clustering [19] and the notion of locality on graphs, we investigate coloured graphs and enumerations of the used colours. In the first step, all vertices of the first colour in the enumeration form a singleton cluster each. In an arbitrary step, the vertices of the actual colour are either extending an existing cluster (if there is an edge from the vertex to a vertex in the cluster) or they form a new singleton cluster (otherwise). See Fig. 1 for an example.

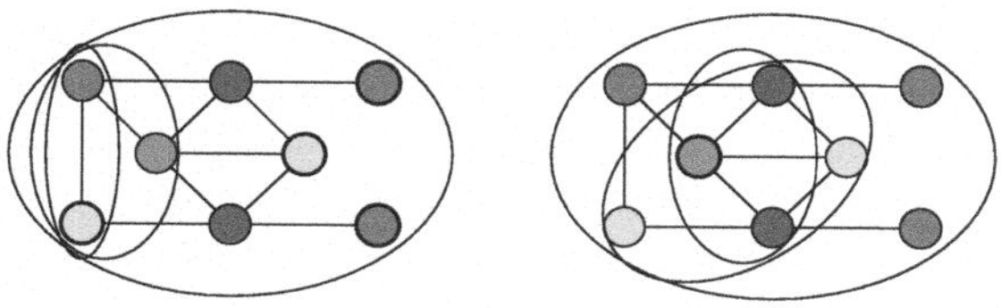

Fig. 1. A 4-coloured graph G marked with the marking sequences ($\texttt{yellow}, \texttt{red}, \texttt{cyan}, \texttt{blue}$) and ($\texttt{cyan}, \texttt{blue}, \texttt{yellow}, \texttt{red}$) (Color figure online)

Since all words (strings, subsequences) can be interpreted as linear graphs, determining the locality of a graph remains NP-complete (cf. [4]). But similar to the locality of sort-of palindromic structured words [6], some graph classes and some graphs with a specific colouring yield an efficiently determinable locality.

Besides theoretical interest, the locality of graphs bears a variety of potential relationships to the machine learning and data science community. In co-location pattern mining, a *co-located pattern* refers to instances (objects) of different types (subsets of features) frequently occurring together at the same (or at a close) location [12,14,16]. Applications for co-location pattern mining are co-occurrences of buildings/companies/institutions [13], social events, and biological and societal phenomena in temporal context. In this context, one is interested in the largest locality a colour enumeration may provide. Another related data mining task is motif discovery in gene or protein sequences. While the locality of words is researched as a structural complexity measure [9], this measure can contribute to finding motifs (frequently re-occurring patterns) and clustering of similar motifs. More explicitly, according to [23], determining the length of motifs is still an open challenge and the authors of [23] propose a deep learning based approach to determine the length. The locality of words can provide here the means to estimate that motif size $|M|_\mu$. Knowing the maximum number of blocks and the total sequence length $|S|$, the average motif length would be $|M|_\mu = \frac{|S|}{k}$. Being aware that this is not an exact value, it can serve as an orientation for domain experts *around* which value the motif length parameter can be chosen from. This orientation for parameter selection is common, e.g., the silhouette score as a cluster quality metric [15], which informs a meaningful choice of cluster numbers for k-means and other variance minimising clustering algorithms. However, not only the discovery of motifs alone requires the length of the motifs, but also their clustering [11] requires both their length and number. All these applications require a feasible solution to compute the k-locality. However, since an exhaustive search over all possible marking sequences would be infeasible, a more scalable solution is required.

Our Contribution. In this work, we extend the notion of k-locality to graphs. We consider (not necessarily valid or minimally) coloured, undirected graphs and enumerations of the colours. Similar as for the k-locality of words, we count the number of connected components (instead of blocks) within the graph after each marking step. We present first theoretical results regarding the complexity and special graph classes. Further, we propose a priority search algorithm that is optimal in the number of marking prefix expansions to compute the k-locality of graphs. We demonstrate its efficiency on scale-free graphs and conduct a case study on the DBLP publication graph to show some of its potential for knowledge discovery.

Structure of the Work. In Sect. 2 all required definitions and notions are introduced. Afterwards our theoretical results and practical applications follow in Sects. 3 and 4. In Sect. 5 we give a perspective of future work.

2 Preliminaries

Let $\mathbb{N} = \{1, 2, \ldots\}$ denote the natural numbers and set $\mathbb{N}_0 = \mathbb{N} \cup \{0\}$ as well as $[n] = \{1, \ldots, n\}$ and $[i, n] = \{i, i+1, \ldots, n\}$ for all $i, n \in \mathbb{N}_0$ with $i \leq n$. Set $\mathbb{N}_{\geq k} = \mathbb{N} \backslash [k-1]$ for a natural number $k \geq 2$. For q, n, r, z with $q \cdot n + r = z$, we denote the division without remainder by $q = z \operatorname{div} n$ and the rest by $r = z \bmod n$. Before we can introduce the new notion of k-local graphs, we need some basic definitions from combinatorics on words and from graph theory.

An *alphabet* Σ is a finite set of symbols, called *letters*. A *word* w is a finite sequence of letters from a given alphabet and its length $|w|$ is the number of w's letters. For $i \in [|w|]$ let $w[i]$ denote w's i^{th} letter. The set of all finite words (strings, sequences) over the alphabet Σ, is denoted by Σ^*. The empty word ε is the word of length 0. Let Σ^n denote all words in Σ^* exactly of length $n \in \mathbb{N}_0$. Set $\operatorname{alph}(w) = \{\mathtt{a} \in \Sigma \mid \exists i \in [|w|] : w[i] = \mathtt{a}\}$ as w's alphabet. For $u, w \in \Sigma^*$, u is called a *factor* of w, if $w = xuy$ for some words $x, y \in \Sigma^*$. For $1 \leq i \leq j \leq |w|$ define the factor from w's i^{th} letter to the jth letter by $w[i, j] = w[i] \cdots w[j]$. Further, given a pair of indices $i < j$, set $w[j, i] = \varepsilon$.

A *finite, undirected graph* G is a pair $G = (V, E)$ with finite sets V of vertices and edges $E \subseteq \{M \subseteq V \mid |M| = 2\}$ (the latter set is abbreviated by $\binom{V}{2}$). A *path* in G is a finite sequence of vertices $(v_1, \ldots, v_k)$ with $\{v_i, v_{i+1}\} \in E$ for all $i \in [k-1]$ and $k \in \mathbb{N}_{\geq 2}$. We say that this path has length $k-1$. Further, two vertices are *connected* if there exists a path between them. By convention set $n = |V|$ and $m = |E|$ and since we are only investigating finite, undirected graphs, we call them simply *graphs*. Moreover, given a graph G, let $V(G)$ and $E(G)$ denote its sets of vertices and edges resp. For $v \in V$, define the *connected component* of v by $C(v) = \{u \in V \mid \exists \text{ path from } u \text{ to } v\}$. Let $\gamma(G)$ denote the number of connected components in G. We say that G is *connected*, if $V = C(v)$ for all $v \in V$, i.e., $\gamma(G) = 1$. For $n \in \mathbb{N}$, the *complete graph* on $|V| = n$ vertices is defined by $K_n = (V, \binom{V}{2})$. A graph $H = (U, F)$ is called a *subgraph* of G ($H \leq G$) if we have $U \subseteq V$ and $F \subseteq E \cap \binom{U}{2}$. Moreover, we say that $H \leq G$ is *induced* by U if $F = E \cap \binom{U}{2}$; this is notated as $G|_U$. A fully connected subgraph of G is called a *clique*. For $\ell \in \mathbb{N}$, a *valid ℓ-colouring* of G is a function $c : V \to [\ell]$ such that $\{u, v\} \in E$ implies $c(u) \neq c(v)$ for all $u, v \in V$. If there exists a valid ℓ-colouring for G, we say that G is ℓ-colourable. Let $\mathcal{C}(G, c) = \{c(v) \mid v \in V\}$ denote the set of colours that occur in G w.r.t. the colouring c. For $x \in \mathcal{C}(G, c)$ and a valid ℓ-colouring c with $\ell \in \mathbb{N}$, denote the *set of all x-coloured vertices* by $V_x = \{v \in V \mid c(v) = x\}$. Further, let $G|_C = G|_{\bigcup_{x \in C} V_x}$ for $C \subseteq \mathcal{C}(G, c)$ be the *subgraph of G induced by the colours in C*.

Now, we define the k-locality on graphs generalising the definitions from words (cf. [6]). From now on let $G = (V, E)$ be an undirected graph.

Definition 1. *Let $\overline{V} = \{\overline{x} \mid x \in V\}$ be a copy of V that we refer to as the* set of marked vertices *and $c : V \to [\ell]$ with $\ell \in \mathbb{N}$ an ℓ-colouring of G. For G and c, we define a* marking sequence *e of the colours occurring in G as an enumeration $(x_1, x_2, \ldots, x_{|\mathcal{C}(G,c)|})$ of $\mathcal{C}(G, c)$ such that $x_i \leq_e x_j$, if x_i is enumerated before x_j in e for $i, j \in [|\mathcal{C}(G, c)|]$. A vertex v is marked in marking step $j \in \mathbb{N}$ if $c(v) = x_i$ for some $i \leq j$. Set $G_i = G|_{\{x_1, \ldots, x_i\}}$ for all $i \in [\ell]$, i.e., G_i is the graph induced by the first i colours.*

Definition 2. *Let $e = (x_1, \ldots, x_{|\mathcal{C}(G,c)|})$ be a marking sequence of $\mathcal{C}(G, c)$. Define* $\mathrm{loc}(G, c, e) = \max_{x_i \in e} |C(G_i)|$, *i.e., the* locality of G *w.r.t. e is given by the maximal number of connected components occurring during the marking process. Define the* locality of G *by* $\mathrm{loc}(G, c) = \min_e \mathrm{loc}(G, c, e)$.

Definition 3. *A graph G with an ℓ-colouring c is k-*local *for $k, \ell \in \mathbb{N}$, if there exists a marking sequence $(x_1, \ldots, x_{|\mathcal{C}(G,c)|})$ of $\mathcal{C}(G, c))$ such that for all $i \leq |\mathcal{C}(G, c)|$, G_i contains at most k connected components in marking step i.*

Definition 4. *A graph G is* strictly k-local *if G is k-local but not $(k-1)$-local.*

Notice that in general, we are not only interested in valid or minimal colourings. In the next section, we will show that a restriction to valid colourings is w.l.o.g. possible. We finish this section by revisiting the example from Fig. 1. Consider the marking sequence $e = (\texttt{yellow}, \texttt{red}, \texttt{cyan}, \texttt{blue})$. When marking all `yellow` vertices, we obtain 2 connected components. Then marking `red` we result in 4 connected components. Marking `cyan` we still have 4 components and then `blue` both result in one component. By Definition 2 we have $\mathrm{loc}(G, c, e) = 4$. One can verify that we have $\mathrm{loc}(G, c, e') = 1$ for the marking sequence $e' = (\texttt{cyan}, \texttt{blue}, \texttt{yellow}, \texttt{red})$. Thus, $\mathrm{loc}(G, c) = 1$.

The computational model we use is the standard unit-cost RAM with logarithmic word size (cf. e.g., [5]).

3 Theoretical Results: Complexity and Graph Classes

We start this section with a reduction from the NP-complete problem Loc_w [4] to the locality in the graph setting. First, we define the locality problem on graphs formally and obtain two immediate results from the locality on words.

Problem 5. Let Loc_G be the problem of deciding whether for a connected graph with a valid ℓ-colouring c, we have $\mathrm{loc}(G, c) \leq k$. The subproblem to decide whether we have $\mathrm{loc}(G, c) = 1$ is abbreviated by $\mathsf{Loc}_{G,1}$.

Proposition 6. *For an undirected graph G, the problem Loc_G is NP-complete.*

Theorem 7. *For every undirected graph G, we have $\mathsf{Loc}_{G,1} \in \mathsf{P}$.*

Proof. Let us firstly sketch a nondeterministic algorithm that decides this problem: Guess the first colour that occurs in the graph, and mark all vertices in the graph. Now as long as possible pick a colour for which every vertex is connected to a marked vertex. If there is no vertex left in the graph then stop and accept the input.

The algorithms finds only valid colour orderings. However, it remains to show that the algorithm always finds such an ordering if it exists. Assume there is a valid colour ordering, then the algorithm would non-deterministically guess the first colour correctly. Now assume that our algorithm would not accept. This can only happen when all remaining colours are connected to at least on not marked vertex. Consider all colours of the valid ordering, there is a first colour that has not been marked yet. The valid ordering guarantees that the number of connected components would not exceed 1. Indeed there are already more vertices marked, however since these are all connected to the first colour they would not increase the number of components.

Since we only have a constant number of guesses and a polynomial number of possible vertices, the algorithm runs deterministically in polynomial time. □

Note that we cannot restrict the investigations of k-locality w.l.o.g. to connected graphs since the locality of a graph does not depend (to our knowledge) just on the locality of the connected components. Consider the two graphs G and G' from Fig. 2. One can verify with the respective marking sequences that all the connected components of G and G' each are 1-local. But both possible marking sequences for G lead to 3-locality. Also in G' both connected components are 1-local; G' itself is 2-local witnessed by $(\texttt{red}, \texttt{yellow}, \texttt{blue})$.

Note that for any coloured graph G with colouring c, we have $\mathrm{loc}(G, c) \geq \gamma(G)$.

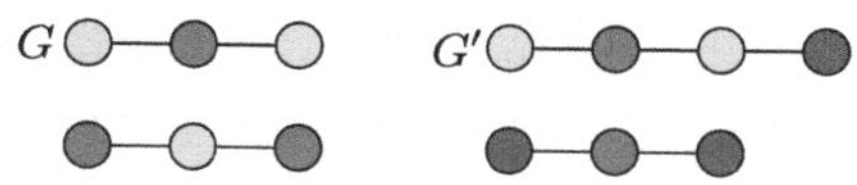

Fig. 2. A 2-coloured graph G and a 3-coloured graph G'

Proposition 8. *For every graph $G = (V, E)$ there is a (valid) colouring c such that* $\mathrm{loc}(G, c) = \gamma(G)$.

Proof. If c is restricted to be a valid colouring, then consider a colouring where every colour appears only for one vertex. We can find a permutation that certifies the claimed locality. Just iterate over all connected components, and each time pick an arbitrary vertex. Then, the induced graph has exactly $\gamma(G)$ components/single vertices. Then, greedily pick remaining vertices that are in the neighbourhood of the already chosen ones. □

Remark 9. Note that Proposition 8 implies that there always exists a (not necessarily minimal) valid colouring for any connected graph G such that G is 1-local for this colouring.

The more general version with non-connected graphs is at least as hard as the more restricted version because computing components can be done in polynomial time.

In this work, we only investigate connected graphs. The following proposition justifies why we mostly consider validly coloured graphs. The idea is to contract adjacent vertices coloured with the same colour.

Proposition 10. *For every graph G with colouring c there exists a validly coloured (by c) induced minor G' of G such that* $\mathrm{loc}(G, c) = \mathrm{loc}(G', c)$.

Proof. Consider an edge $\{v, w\} \in E$ with $c(v) = c(w)$. For every edge $\{w, u\} \in E$ where $u \neq v$ replace $\{w, u\}$ by $\{v, u\}$, and finally remove u and $\{v, w\}$ from G. Repeat this step, until no such an edge exists. Thus, build the minor induced by contracting adjacent vertices coloured with the same colour. This graph is moreover validly coloured. Since the colours occurring in the neighbourhood of a vertex remains the same, the locality does not change. □

A last result on arbitrary graphs narrows the locality a graph may have.

Theorem 11. *For all graphs G coloured by c, we have $\gamma(G) \leq \mathrm{loc}(G, c) \leq \alpha(G)$ where $\alpha(G)$ denotes the size of a maximal independent set.*

Proof. The lower bound follows immediately from the fact that for vertices of different connected components are not connected. For the upper bound consider a marking sequence $(x_1, \ldots, x_\ell)$ satisfying $\mathrm{loc}(G, c) = k$. Thus, there exists $t \leq \ell$ such that

$$\gamma(G|_{\bigcup_{j=1}^{t} V_{c_j}}) = \mathrm{loc}(G, c),$$

i.e., at marking stage t, k connected components are reached. Pick a set I of k many vertices that are pairwise not connected in G - one vertex of each component. Hence, I is an independent set of size $\operatorname{loc}(G, c)$, so the maximum independent set in G has size at least $\operatorname{loc}(G, c)$, which completes the proof. □

The remainder of this section dedicated to several graph classes and is meant a beginning of this line of research. We start with cycles, stars, complete, wheel, web and friendship graphs (cf. Table 1). Due to Remark 9 we focus on validly (not necessarily minimally) coloured graphs.

Remark 12. The triangle C_3 is 1-local for every colouring. For $n \geq 4$, the cycle graph C_n is 2-colourable if n is even and 3-colourable otherwise. Thus, minimal coloured cycle graphs are $\min\{|V_1|, |V_2|\}$-local for the sets of vertices V_1, V_2 containing at least two nodes.

Proposition 13. *Complete, star, wheel and friendship graphs are* 1*-local independent of the colouring.*

Proof. Let c be an arbitrary colouring of a complete graph $K_n = (V, E)$ on n vertices. Since $|V_c| = 1$ holds for all $c \in \bigcup_{v \in V} c(v)$ the claim follows.

In a star we can pick the colour of the vertex that has more than one neighbour first. Since, there is the only one such vertex, which is also connected to all other vertices, we have at most one component after this step. Now, we can pick the remaining colours in an arbitrary ordering. The number of components remains one, because every other vertex is connected with the first vertex.

By the same argument as for star graphs, we can start with the central vertex for wheel and friendship graphs, too. Now, every other vertex is connected to the marked one. Thus, the remaining colours can be picked again in an arbitrary order. □

Proposition 14. *If $\ell \in \mathbb{N}_{\geq 2}$ is even, web graphs are $\frac{\ell r}{2}$-local for every valid* 2*-colouring. If ℓ is odd, there exists a* 3*-colouring such that $W_{\ell,r}$ is $(\ell \operatorname{div} 3)r$-local.*

Proposition 15. *For a minimal valid colouring, sunflower graphs S_d and helm graphs H_d for $d \in \mathbb{N}$ are $\lfloor \frac{d-1}{2} \rfloor$-local.*

We now focus on the class of bipartite graphs for which we can determine the locality for a 2-colouring by inspecting the number of vertices coloured in each of the two colours.

Proposition 16. *Let $G = (V_1 \dot\cup V_2, E)$ be a bipartite, graph that is* 2*-coloured. Then G is strictly* $\min\{|V_1|, |V_2|\}$*-local.*

Proof. Let x_1, x_2 be two colours. A valid 2-colouring of the bipartite graph $G = (V_1 \dot\cup V_2, E)$ is given by $c : V_1 \dot\cup V_2 \to \{x_1, x_2\}$ with $c(v) = x_i$ for $v \in V_i$, $i \in [2]$. Let w.l.o.g. $|V_1| \leq |V_2|$ then the marking sequence $e = (x_1, x_2)$ shows the $|V_1|$-locality of G. □

Corollary 17. *For $d \in \mathbb{N}$, hypercubes Q_d are strictly 2^{d-1}-local, every knight's graph on $KG = (V_1 \dot\cup V_2, E)$ and gear graphs G_d are strictly $\min\{|V_1|, |V_2|\}$-local and d-crown graphs $(\{x_1, \cdots, x_d, y_1, \dots, y_d\}, \{(x_i, y_j) \mid i, j \in [d], i \neq j\})$ are strictly d-local for $d \in \mathbb{N}_{\geq 3}$.*

Corollary 18. *For a complete bipartite graph we have $\mathrm{loc}(G, c) = \min\{|V_1|, |V_2|\}$ for any valid colouring c.*

Corollary 19. *For $d \geq 2$, every complete d-partite graph $K_{i_1,\dots,i_d}$ for $i_1, \dots, i_d \in \mathbb{N}$ is $\min\{i_1, \dots, i_d\}$-local where i_j denotes the number of vertices in every disjoint vertex set, $j \in [d]$.*

We now inspect bipartite graphs that are coloured with more than 2 colours.

Proposition 20. *Let $G = (V_1 \dot\cup V_2, E)$ be a bipartite graph that is (> 2)-coloured by a colouring c. If there exists a colour $x \in \mathcal{C}(G, c)$ such that for all $v \in V_i$ we have $c(v) = x$ for exactly one $i \in [2]$ and $|V_i| \leq |V_j|$ for $j \in [2] \setminus \{i\}$ then G is strictly $|V_i|$-local. Otherwise G is strictly $|V_j|$-local.*

Proof. Let w.l.o.g. V_1 the set of nodes such that there exists a colour x with $c(v) = x$ for all $v \in V_1$ and $|V_1| \leq |V_2|$. Then for any marking sequence that starts with x the graph is $|V_1|$-local. Further, any marking sequence σ' that does not start with c but c' there exists a set of nodes $V_{c'}$ such that there are $|V_{c'}|$ connected components. Suppose that x is the last colour of the marking sequence σ'. Then the number of connected components after $|\sigma'| - 1$ marking steps is $|V_2|$, but $|V_2| \geq |V_1|$ which implies that the locality of G w.r.t. σ' is larger than the one w.r.t. σ, i.e., G is $|V_1|$-local. In the case of a marking sequence σ'' such that there exists $i \in [2, \sigma - 1]$ with $\sigma[i] = x$, i.e., we mark the x-coloured nodes somewhen in the middle, the number of connected components is given by $\max\{|V_1|, |S|\}$ where $S \subseteq V_2$ is given by $\bigcup_{j \in [i-1]} \{v \in V_2 \mid c(v) = x_j\}$. If $|V_1| \geq |S|$ then the locality of G is given by $|V_1|$. Otherwise, the marking sequence σ' is not an optimal one.

In the case that $|V_1| < |V_2|$ a marking sequence that firstly marks all nodes of V_2 results in a locality of $|V_2|$. □

The previous results raise the hope that for all bipartite graphs and all colourings, we can determine the locality efficiently. Theorem 22 shows that this is not the case.

Proposition 21. *Let $\tilde{\Sigma} = \{\tilde{\mathtt{a}}_i \mid \mathtt{a}_i \in \Sigma\}$. For all condensed $w \in \Sigma^*$ there exists $\tilde{w} \in (\Sigma \cup \tilde{\Sigma})^*$ such that for all $x \in \mathrm{alph}(w)$ we have either $\{i \mid w[i] = x\} \subset 2\mathbb{N}$ or $\{i \mid w[i] = x\} \subset 2\mathbb{N} + 1$. Further, w is strictly k-local iff $\tilde{w}$ is strictly k-local.*

Theorem 22. *Let G be a bipartite graph that is coloured by c with more than $\ell > 2$ colours. Then $(G, c, k) \in \mathsf{Loc}_G$ is NP-complete.*

Proof. First of all, the NP-membership follows directly from the NP-membership for arbitrary graphs. To show the problems NP-hardness, we reduce from the problem Loc_w that was used for Proposition 6 before. Let $w' \in \Sigma^*$ and $k \in \mathbb{N}$ such that $(w', k) \in \mathsf{Loc}_w$. By Proposition 21 and its proof we can conclude that for $w = \mathrm{cond}(w')$ and $\tilde{w} = f_{|w|}(w)$ with f from the proof of Proposition 21 we have

$$(w', k) \in \mathsf{Loc}_w \iff (w, k) \in \mathsf{Loc}_w \iff (\tilde{w}, k) \in \mathsf{Loc}_w.$$

Since all modifications are polynomial-time computable and $\tilde{w}$ a linear representation a bipartite graph coloured with $\mathrm{alph}(\tilde{w})$ colours the NP-completeness follows by Proposition 6. □

Now, we investigate snarks, i.e., connected bridgeless cubic graphs with a minimal number of colours for colouring edges of 4 (cf. Gardner [10]). In 1880, Tait showed that the famous four-colour theorem holds true iff every snark is non-planar [21]. One of the most famous snarks is the Peterson graph.

Remark 23. Note that the Peterson graph is 3-local since it is 3-colourable and there exists a colour x that occurs exactly 3 times for every 3-colouring.

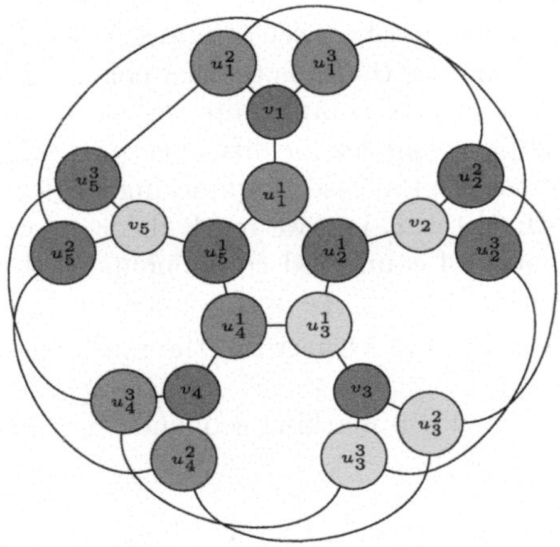

Fig. 3. Flower snark J_5 with a 3-colouring

Remark 24. Note that the chromatic number of flower snarks is 3. See Fig. 3 for en exemplary 3-colouring of J_5.

Proposition 25. *For every flower snark J_d, $d \in 2\mathbb{N}+1$ there exists a $\chi(J_d)$-colouring such that J_d is $(d - (d \bmod 3))$-local.*

Remark 26. Note that there also exists a colouring of J_n that uses the most infrequent colour (here b) only three times. This colouring is given by

$$c(v) = \begin{cases} b, & \text{if } v \in \{u_1^1, u_1^2, u_1^3\}, \\ r, & \text{if } v \in \{u_i^1, u_i^2, u_i^3 \mid i \in [n-1] \land i \text{ odd}\} \cup \{v_i \mid i \text{ even}\}, \\ b, & \text{if } v \in \{u_i^1, u_i^2, u_i^3 \mid i \in [n] \land i \text{ odd}\} \cup \{v_1\} \cup \{v_i \mid i \text{ even}\}. \end{cases}$$

Nevertheless, this colouring results in a higher locality since not all of the r- or g-coloured vertices are adjacent to the three b-coloured vertices.

Remark 27. The reader may verify that for the first and second Blanuša snark and the double-star snark there exist 3-colourings such that they are 5-, 6- and 9-local, resp.

Table 1. A summary of upper and lower bounds for the locality of graph classes

Class	Lower Bound	Upper Bound
Complete Graphs, Star Graphs Wheel Graphs, Friendship Graphs	1	1
Paths Cycles, Web graphs 1/2-regular Graphs	1	$\lfloor n/2 \rfloor$
Complete Bipartite Graphs K_{n_1,n_2} Crown Graphs, Hypercubes Bipartite Graphs with 2-colouring Knight's graph, Gear graph	1	$\min\{n_1, n_2\}$
Sunflower graphs S_d, Helm graphs H_d	1	$\lfloor \frac{d-1}{2} \rfloor$
Peterson Graph	1	3
Edgeless Graphs, 0-regular Graphs	n	n

4 Practical Application

In addition to theoretical properties, we are also interested in practical applications of k-locality in graphs. One application could be to optimize utility of a location of a shop type (groceries, pharmacy, restaurant, etc.) in a road network by determining the largest number of involved features (types of buildings) in a k block radius. This could make customer trips more convenient, since they could visit more points of interest in a shorter trip. Further, k-locality could be used as part of data exploration, by yielding valuable insights into the organising principles of the underlying graph.

In order to calculate the minimal k-locality of a given graph, the naïve approach would be to enumerate all valid colour permutations, and to compute the

k-locality w.r.t. every marking sequence. However, since this approach would not scale well for increasing numbers of colours or larger graphs, we propose a priority-based search (cf. Algorithm 1) to make the calculation feasible. First, we initialise the priority queue with an empty marking prefix ε and $\max_k = 0$ (line 3). The queue is maintained in ascending order of the k-locality of the respective marking prefixes. Since the first queue element marks the prefix with the least number of components, we pop it as the most promising candidate. For each remaining colour we expand the current sequence prefix by one colour, count the resulting components, and sort the expanded sequences back into the queue (lines 6–9). Once a sequence contains all colours, it is complete and the minimal k-locality may be updated (lines 11–15). Note that this algorithm finds *all* sequences that have minimal k-locality. If one is only interested in finding the minimal k-locality, it is sufficient to find only one of the sequences with minimal k-locality. This can be achieved by requiring the first queue element to have strictly fewer connected components than the current best ('<' instead of '≤' in line 4), and only keeping a single best sequence (removing lines 11 and 12). We demonstrate experimentally that this yields even further improvements in runtime.

Theorem 28. *Algorithm 1 is optimal in the number of successive expansions of a marking prefix beginning with an empty sequence and is guaranteed to find the correct solution.*

Algorithm 1: Priority Search

Input : Graph $G = (V, E)$, valid colouring $c : V \to [\ell]$
Output : minimum k-locality of G, all marking sequences of that k-locality

```
1  min_k ← ∞
2  minSequences ← ∅
3  queue ← [(0, ε)]                      // [(max_k, prefix), ...] sorted asc. by max_k
4  while queue ≠ ∅ ∧ queue[0][0] ≤ min_k do
5      (current_k, prefix) ← queue.pop()
6      if prefix incomplete then
7          forall the remaining colours c_j not in prefix do
8              count ← no. components in G marked with prefix + [c_j]
9              queue.insort((max(current_k, count), prefix + [c_j]))
10     else                                // current sequence is complete
11         if current_k = min_k then
12             minSequences ← minSequences ∪ {prefix}
13         if current_k < min_k then
14             min_k ← current_k
15             minSequences ← {prefix}
16 return min_k, minSequences
```

In the following we further empirically demonstrate the efficiency of the algorithm for various graphs. Many systems in nature and society, such as biological neural networks, bibliographical networks, or the internet, frequently exhibit a common organising principle (next to sheer size), which is referred to scale-free power-law distributed vertex connectivity [1,3]. Barabási and Albert identified two main reasons that result in this phenomenon: (1) new vertices enter the network, causing it to expand over time, and (2) new vertices tend to connect to already well-connected vertices (a.k.a. preferential attachment or rich-get-richer) [1,3]. Based on these principles they developed a random graph model, which creates scale-free power-law distributed graphs [1,3]. Since the Barabási-Albert random graph represents a large class of real-world graphs, we use it as a proxy to benchmark the efficiency and scalability of our approach on graphs with good control over the number of vertices and colours, while still retaining typical, real-world properties (such as degree distribution, diameter, and clustering coefficient). Due to space considerations, we neglect other random graph models, such as the Erdős-Rényi model [7] and the Watts-Strogatz model [22], since these generally feature less natural degree distributions, although they would lend themselves for considerations in future work for more extensive comparisons. We vary the network size from 10k to 100k vertices, where each vertex added connects to 10 existing vertices. The vertex colours are distributed uniformly at random. We investigate the impact of graph size and number of colours separately to avoid excessive parameter combinations that yield little additional insight. Therefore, when measuring the impact of the graph size alone, we keep the number of colours fixed at 5, and for impact of the number of colours fix the number of vertices at 5000. Different combinations of these parameters yield a similar result, which we omit for the sake of brevity. We report the average runtime with standard deviation over 5 runs of the naïve approach, the priority search (Algorithm 1), as well as a variant of Algorithm 1, named priority*, which does not yield *all* marking sequences with minimal k-locality, but terminates once it has found at least one that is guaranteed to have minimal k-locality. Figure 4a shows that the priority-based search outperforms the naïve approach substantially and scales better to larger graphs. Since counting the number of components takes longer for larger graphs, the priority-based searches benefit from requiring fewer counts. This is drastically emphasised in Fig. 4b , which shows that the naïve search does not scale well for increasing numbers of colours (note the log-scale). Depending on the application scenario it may be preferable to chose priority* over the full variant, since it can shave off even more computation time in case only the minimum k-locality is needed, and outperforms the naïve approach by up to 4 orders of magnitude. However, there may still be a benefit particularly for exploration purposes to have the ability to find all sequences with minimal k-locality.

One limitation of the previous experiments is the uniform distribution of colours in the graph. In real-world, *heterogeneous* graphs [17,20], where the colours could represent vertex types, the distribution would not be random, but rather organised by some underlying principle. As a familiar example, we look at a commonly studied subset of the DBLP publication graph, that covers the 4 areas of *databases*, *data mining*, *machine learning*, and *information retrieval*

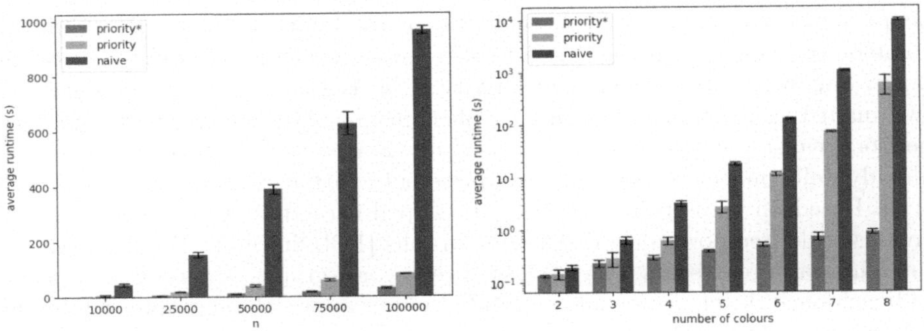

(a) Sensitivity to $|V|$

(b) Sensitivity to number of colours.

Fig. 4. Efficiency and scalability on Barabási-Albert random graphs

[17,20]. The graph contains about 5.9k author vertices (A), 5.2k papers (P), 18 venues V, and 4.4k topics (T), which are linked following the network schema in Fig. 5 (left). The average runtime of the search algorithms over 5 runs is shown in Fig. 5 (right), where the speed-up of the priority-based search again is substantial (almost 2 orders of magnitude), despite only considering 4 colours/types. Since only two marking sequences with minimal k-locality exist, the difference between priority and priority* is negligible.

In addition to the efficiency, the computed result itself is of great interest. The minimum k-locality of the DBLP subset is 18, with the two minimal sequences being (V, P, A, T) and (V, P, T, A). This suggests that the 18 venues, despite being few in numbers, play a pivotal role in the network and act as hubs, which span large areas of the network through the connecting papers. This matches the expectation one would have for such a graph, since the publishing activity revolves around the venues. The next smallest sequences have k-localities larger than 4.4k, starting with T. From this we can infer that no other vertex types act in a similarly central capacity as the venues, but instead are scattered across the graph. This hierarchy of centrality is not dissimilar to the underlying principles of hierarchical clustering. We believe that further study of the k-locality and the corresponding colour/type sequences can provide great insights for data exploration. A similar evaluation of other areas of computer science like theoretical computer science is ajar but not of less interest. The choice for our sample subset of the DBLP graph is based on the experience of some authors with the evaluation of this particular subgraph, and demonstrates the capability of k-locality to be a helpful tool in data exploration.

5 Conclusions

In this work, we extended the notion of k-local words introduced by Day et al. [6] to graphs. Not astonishingly the general problem of deciding whether a graph is k-local for some $k \in \mathbb{N}$ is NP-complete since words can be interpreted

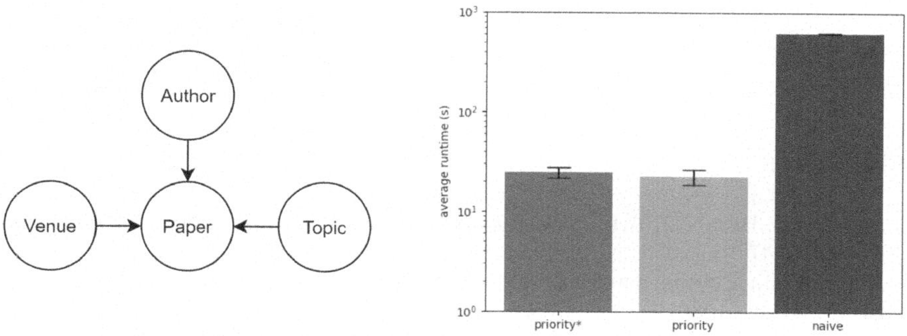

Fig. 5. Schema of the DBLP graph (left) and runtime comparison (right)

as linear graphs. Nevertheless, some graph classes yield a determinable locality based on a minimal colouring. In this field, it remains open to determine the exact colouring since not all minimal colourings lead to the same locality. As mentioned in Remark 9 every connected graph is 1-local colourable if the number of colours is not limited. Fixing ℓ and characterising the graphs for which an ℓ-local colouring exists, is a topic for further research. For several graph classes, we provided the minimal and maximal locality based on a minimal colouring of the graphs. The theoretical results so far follow the notion of k-locality on words, i.e., find an enumeration such that the k-locality is minimal. Regarding pattern mining, one could also alter the question in finding the maximum: Find a route, more explicitly a sequence of supermarkets and pharmacies to be visited, which contains as many co-located supermarkets and pharmacies together in a specific range, i.e., maximise k that denotes the number of co-occurring *blocks* of supermarkets and pharmacies. The benefit that comes with this task, is that users have multiple options if one co-location of supermarkets and pharmacies is too crowded (long queues, many items out of stock, etc.) the closest options are provided. Another application is that for a given k determine the largest number of involved features m (types of buildings) involved, i.e., get me for $k = 2$ blocks the largest number of different shop types (groceries, pharmacy, fast-food restaurant etc.). The purpose behind this application is to maximise the *utility* of a specific location by having as many different shop types d as the customer needs while at the same time having $k - 1$ further locations to visit where the d shop types co-occur. This allows for minimising travel time by having multiple shop types at the customers' disposal per location. In order to enable such tasks for the future, we have proposed a priority search algorithm, which is prefix expansion-optimal and able to calculate the minimum k-locality of a graph and its corresponding marking sequences several orders of magnitude faster than an exhaustive search on scale-free graphs. Since scale-free graphs are ubiquitous [1,3], we believe our solution bears great potential for future studies, not only in the theoretical field, but also in the practical.

Acknowledgements. We would like to thank Max Bannach, Malte Skambath and Philipp Sieweck for helpful discussions and some main ideas included in this work.

References

1. Albert, R., Barabási, A.L.: Statistical mechanics of complex networks. Rev. Mod. Phys. **74**, 47–97 (2002)
2. Angluin, D.: Finding patterns common to a set of strings. J. Comput. Syst. Sci. **21**(1), 46–62 (1980)
3. Barabási, A.L., Albert, R.: Emergence of scaling in random networks. Science **286**(5439), 509–512 (1999)
4. Casel, K., Day, J.D., Fleischmann, P., Kociumaka, T., Manea, F., Schmid, M.L.: Graph and string parameters: connections between pathwidth, cutwidth and the locality number. In: ICALP. LIPIcs, vol. 132, pp. 109:1–109:16 (2019)
5. Crochemore, M., Hancart, C., Lecroq, T.: Algorithms on strings. Cambridge University Press (2007)
6. Day, J.D., Fleischmann, P., Manea, F., Nowotka, D.: Local patterns. In: IARCS. LIPIcs, vol. 93, pp. 24:1–24:14 (2017)
7. Erdős, P., Rényi, A., et al.: On the evolution of random graphs. Publ. math. inst. hung. acad. sci **5**(1), 17–60 (1960)
8. Fleischmann, P., Haschke, L., Löck, T., Nowotka, D.: Word-representable graphs from a word's perspective. In: SOFSEM 2024. LNCS, vol. 14519, pp. 255–268. Springer (2024). (accepted at Acta Informatica)
9. Fleischmann, P., Haschke, L., Manea, F., Nowotka, D., Tsida, C.T., Wiedenbeck, J.: Blocksequences of k-local words. In: SOFSEM 2021. Springer International Publishing (2021)
10. Gardner, M.: Mathematical games. Sci. Am. **234**(4), 126–131 (1976)
11. Hamady, M., Widmann, J., Copley, S., Knight, R.: MotifCluster: an interactive online tool for clustering and visualizing sequences using shared motifs. Genome Biol. **9**, 1–13 (2008)
12. Mamoulis, N.: Co-location Patterns, Algorithms, pp. 103–107. Springer US, Boston, MA (2008)
13. Masrur, A., Thakur, G., Sparks, K., P., R., Peuquet, D.: Co-location pattern mining of geosocial data to characterize urban functional spaces. In: Big Data, pp. 4099–4102. IEEE (2019)
14. Morimoto, Y.: Mining frequent neighboring class sets in spatial databases. In: SIGKDD, pp. 353–358 (2001)
15. Rousseeuw, P.: Silhouettes: a graphical aid to the interpretation and validation of cluster analysis. J. Comput. Appl. Math. **20**, 53–65 (1987)
16. Shekhar, S., Huang, Y.: Discovering spatial co-location patterns: a summary of results. In: SSTD, pp. 236–256. Springer (2001)
17. Shi, C., Li, Y., Zhang, J., Sun, Y., Philip, S.Y.: A survey of heterogeneous information network analysis. IEEE Trans. Knowl. Data Eng. **29**(1), 17–37 (2016)
18. Shinohara, T.: Polynomial time inference of pattern languages and its applications. In: MFCS, pp. 191–209 (1982)
19. Sibson, R.: SLINK: an optimally efficient algorithm for the single-link cluster method. Comput. J. **16**(1), 30–34 (1973)

20. Sun, Y., Han, J., Yan, X., Yu, P.S., Wu, T.: PathSim: meta path-based top-k similarity search in heterogeneous information networks. Proc. VLDB Endowment **4**(11), 992–1003 (2011)
21. Tait, P.: Remarks on the colourings of maps. Proc. R. Soc. Edinburgh **10**, 729–729 (1880)
22. Watts, D.J., Strogatz, S.H.: Collective dynamics of 'small-world' networks. Nature **393**(6684), 440–442 (1998)
23. Yu, Q., Zhang, X., Hu, Y., Chen, S., Yang, L.: A method for predicting DNA motif length based on deep learning. EEE/ACM Trans. Comput. Biol. Bioinform. **20**(1), 61–73 (2022)

Word-Representable Graphs and Locality of Words

Philipp Böll, Pamela Fleischmann(✉), Annika Huch, Jana Kreiß, Tim Löck, Kajus Park, and Max Wiedenhöft

Kiel University, Kiel, Germany
{stu238462,stu201977,stu229765,stu222002}@mail.uni-kiel.de,
{fpa,ahu,maw}@informatik.uni-kiel.de

Abstract. In this work, we investigate the relationship between k-representable graphs and graphs representable by k-local words. In particular, we show that every graph representable by a k-local word is $(k+1)$-representable. A previous result about graphs represented by 1-local words is revisited with new insights. Moreover, we investigate both classes of graphs w.r.t. hereditary and in particular the speed as a measure. We prove that the latter ones belong to the factorial layer and that the graphs in this classes have bounded clique-width.

1 Introduction

The locality of a word is a complexity measure introduced by Day et al. in [13] for pattern matching. A pattern is a word consisting of letters (constants) and variables. It is matched to a word by replacing the variables with letters. The matching problem, which is about deciding if a pattern can be matched to a certain word, is NP-complete in general (cf. [3]), but can be solved in polynomial time for patterns with bounded locality. The idea of locality is to iteratively mark all letters in a word according to a given marking sequence, which is an enumeration of the word's letters. In each step, every occurrence of a letter is marked and consecutive marked letters form a block. A word is k-local if it can be marked with at most k blocks of marked letters in every step. For example, the word `reappear` is 2-local witnessed, for instance, by the marking sequence $(\mathtt{e}, \mathtt{a}, \mathtt{r}, \mathtt{p})$: marking the letters step by step leads to the marked words $\mathtt{r\overline{e}app\overline{e}ar}$, $\mathtt{r\overline{ea}pp\overline{ea}r}$, $\mathtt{\overline{rea}pp\overline{ear}}$, $\mathtt{\overline{reappear}}$ (where the marked letters are visualised by overlines). Some combinatorial properties of the locality have been investigated in [19], e.g., relating the different roles occurrences of letters in a word may play during the marking process. In [8], the connection between the locality, cutwidth, and pathwidth of graphs was established by reductions showing that determining the locality of a word is NP-complete. Very recently, in [6], locality was generalised to coloured graphs.

As started in [18], we are going to connect this measure on patterns and words with the field of word-representable graphs. A word *represents* a graph if the pairs of alternating letters exactly correspond to the edges in the graph.Two distinct

Published by Springer Nature Switzerland AG 2025
A. Malcher and L. Prigioniero (Eds.): DCFS 2025, LNCS 15759, pp. 50–63, 2025.
https://doi.org/10.1007/978-3-031-97100-6_4

letters are called *alternating* in a word if removing all other letters does not yield two consecutive occurrences of the same letter. Thus, the word's alphabet (the distinct letters occurring in it) determines the set of nodes and the projections onto two letters give the edge set. For instance, the word `analog` represents the graph in Fig. 1.

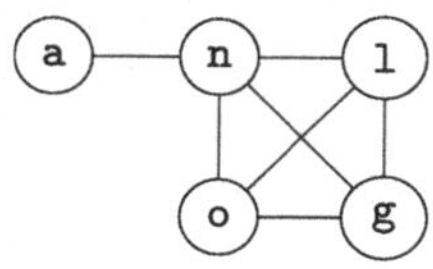

Fig. 1. Graph represented by the word `analog`.

The theory of word-representable graphs was introduced by Kitaev and Pyatkin in [26] as a tool for semigroup theory, and an introduction to this theory can be found in [25]. It has applications in periodic scheduling [23,25], topology [31], and the power domination problem from physics [9], but is also important from a theoretical perspective since word-representable graphs generalise several important classes of graphs such as circle graphs, 3-colourable graphs, and comparability graphs, see [25]. A fundamental result was presented in [22]. The authors characterised word-representable graphs using a special type of graph orientation. The study of word-representable graphs focuses on word-representability of certain graphs classes, operations that preserve word-representability, the concept of k-representability, and various generalisations of word-representability. For instance, in [17], word-representability is generalised from the perspective of language theory. The important notion of k-representability takes into account how many occurrences of a letter are necessary in order to represent the graph, i.e., a graph is k-representable for $k \in \mathbb{N}$ if it is represented by a word with at most k copies of each letter. Thus, each complete graph on $n \in \mathbb{N}$ nodes $V = \{v_1, \ldots, v_n\}$ is 1-representable witnessed by the word $v_1 \cdots v_n$. We denote the class of k-representable graphs by $\mathcal{R}^k$. In [18], the authors showed that k-representability is related to the locality of words. They proved that $\mathcal{R}^k$ is a subset of $\mathcal{L}^{2k}$ for every $k \in \mathbb{N}$, where $\mathcal{L}^k$ denotes the class of graphs represented by k-local words. There also $\mathcal{L}^1$ was characterised.

Our Contribution. We further investigate the relation between locality and word-representability. In particular, we prove that $\mathcal{L}^k$ is a strict subset of $\mathcal{R}^{k+1}$ for every $k \in \mathbb{N}$. We show that $\mathcal{L}^1$ is the class of threshold graphs, which means the classes $\mathcal{L}^k$ are a generalisation of them motivating further research. Moreover, we investigate the number of graphs in $\mathcal{R}^k$ and $\mathcal{L}^k$ and prove that $\mathcal{L}^k$ belongs to the factorial layer for $k > 1$. Finally, we show that the clique-width of graphs in $\mathcal{L}^k$ is bounded by $2^k + 1$.

Structure of the Work. After introducing the necessary definitions in Sect. 2, we prove that $\mathcal{L}^k$ is a subset of $\mathcal{R}^{k+1}$ in Sect. 3. In Sect. 4, we investigate the number of graphs in $\mathcal{R}^k$ and $\mathcal{L}^k$. We present our results regarding the clique-width in Sect. 5. At the end, there is a conclusion in Sect. 6.

2 Preliminaries

Let $\mathbb{N}$ denote the natural numbers starting with 1 and set $\mathbb{N}_0 = \mathbb{N} \cup \{0\}$ as well as $[n] = \{1, \dots, n\}$ and $[n]_0 = [n] \cup \{0\}$ for $n \in \mathbb{N}$. For a set M, define $\binom{M}{2} = \{N \subseteq M \mid |N| = 2\}$ as the set of all of M's subsets with two elements. Before we introduce our main definitions about word-representable graphs, we present some basic definitions from combinatorics on words and graph theory.

An *alphabet* Σ is a finite set whose elements are called *letters*. A *word* $w = \mathtt{a}_1 \cdots \mathtt{a}_n$ is a finite sequence of letters $\mathtt{a}_i \in \Sigma$ for $i \in [n]$, $n \in \mathbb{N}_0$ from a given alphabet Σ of length n, which is denoted by $|w|$. The ith letter of w, i.e., $\mathtt{a}_i$, is also denoted by $w[i]$ for all $i \in [|w|]$ if $|w| > 0$. The set of all finite words (strings, sequences) over the alphabet Σ is denoted by Σ^*. The empty word ε is the word of length 0. Let Σ^n denote all words in Σ^* exactly of length $n \in \mathbb{N}_0$. For all $\mathtt{a} \in \Sigma$, define $|w|_{\mathtt{a}} = |\{i \in [|w|] \mid w[i] = \mathtt{a}\}|$ as the number of occurrences of $\mathtt{a}$ in the word w. Set $\text{alph}(w) = \{\mathtt{a} \in \Sigma \mid \exists i \in [|w|] : w[i] = \mathtt{a}\}$ as w's alphabet. A word w is k-*uniform* for $k \in \mathbb{N}$ if $|w|_{\mathtt{a}} = k$ for every $\mathtt{a} \in \text{alph}(w)$. For $u, w \in \Sigma^*$, u is called a *factor* of w, if $w = xuy$ for some words $x, y \in \Sigma^*$. A mapping $f : \Sigma^* \to \Sigma^*$ is called a *morphism* if $f(uv) = f(u)f(v)$ holds for all $u, v \in \Sigma^*$. Thus, a morphic mapping is already completely defined, if the images for all letters in Σ are given. For $S \subseteq \Sigma$, we define the *projection* π_S *onto* S as the morphism given by $\pi_S(x) = x$ if $x \in S$ and $\pi_S(x) = \varepsilon$ otherwise for all $x \in \Sigma$. For further definitions on words, see [29]. This leads us to the main definition of the field of combinatorics on words for the word-representability.

Definition 1. *Two distinct letters* $\mathtt{a}, \mathtt{b} \in \Sigma$ alternate *in a word* $w \in \Sigma^*$ *if* $\pi_{\{\mathtt{a},\mathtt{b}\}}(w)$ *is* $(\mathtt{ab})^n$, $(\mathtt{ab})^n\mathtt{a}$, $(\mathtt{ba})^n$, *or* $(\mathtt{ba})^n\mathtt{b}$ *for some* $n \in \mathbb{N}$.

A *finite, undirected graph* G is a pair $G = (V, E)$ with finite sets V of *nodes* and *edges* $E \subseteq \binom{V}{2}$. By convention, set $n = |V|$ and $m = |E|$, and since we are only investigating finite, undirected graphs, we call them simply *graphs*. Moreover, given a graph G, let $V(G)$ and $E(G)$ denote its sets of nodes and edges resp. A *node labelled graph* is a graph (V, E, f) with a function $f : V \to M$ for a set of *labels* M. For $v, v' \in V$, a *path* from v to v' is a sequence $(v_1, \dots, v_k)$ for some $k \in \mathbb{N}$ with $v = v_1$, $v' = v_k$, and $\{v_i, v_{i+1}\} \in E$ for all $i \in [k-1]$. The *connected component of* $v \in V$ is defined as $C(v) = \{u \in V \mid \exists \text{ path from } u \text{ to } v\}$. A graph G is called *connected* if $V = C(v)$ for all $v \in V$. For $n \in \mathbb{N}$, the *complete graph* on $|V| = n$ nodes is defined by $K_n = (V, \binom{V}{2})$ and the empty graph as $E_n = (V, \emptyset)$. A graph $H = (U, F)$ is called a *subgraph* of G ($H \leq G$) if we have $U \subseteq V$ and $F \subseteq E \cap \binom{U}{2}$. Moreover, we say that $H \leq G$ is *induced* by U if $F = E \cap \binom{U}{2}$; this is notated as $G|_U$. A complete subgraph of G is called a *clique* and an empty subgraph *independent set.* A *component* is a maximal connected induced subgraph. For $n \in \mathbb{N}$, the *crown graph* $H_{n,n}$ is the graph $([2n], E)$ with $E = \{\{x, y + n\} \mid x, y \in [n] \text{ and } x \neq y\}$.

With these definitions at hand, we define the main notion of interest, the word-representable graphs.

Definition 2. *A graph* $G = (V, E)$ *is* represented *by a word* $w \in \Sigma^*$ *if* $\mathrm{alph}(w) = V$ *and for all* $\mathtt{a}, \mathtt{b} \in V$, $\mathtt{a}$ *and* $\mathtt{b}$ *alternate in* w *iff* $\{\mathtt{a}, \mathtt{b}\} \in E$. *A graph is* word-representable *if there is a word representing it. A graph is* k-representable *for some* $k \in \mathbb{N}$ *if there exists a* k*-uniform word representing it. The graph represented by a word* w *is denoted by* $\mathrm{G}(w)$.

For example, the graph $G = (\{\mathtt{a}, \mathtt{b}, \mathtt{l}, \mathtt{n}, \mathtt{o}\}, \{\{\mathtt{b}, \mathtt{a}\}, \{\mathtt{a}, \mathtt{n}\}, \{\mathtt{b}, \mathtt{n}\}\})$ is represented by the word $\mathtt{balloon}$.

Remark 3. As shown in [26], a graph is k-representable iff there is a word w representing it with $|w|_{\mathtt{a}} \leq k$ for all $\mathtt{a} \in \mathrm{alph}(w)$.

We finish this section with our second notion of interest, the k-local words. In the following, we give the main definitions on k-locality, following [13].

Definition 4. *Let* Σ *be an alphabet with* $|\Sigma| = n \in \mathbb{N}$. *Set* $\overline{\Sigma} = \{\overline{\mathtt{a}} \mid \mathtt{a} \in \Sigma\}$ *as the alphabet containing the* marked letters *and* $\overline{w} = \overline{w[1]} \cdots \overline{w[|w|]}$ *for* $w \in \Sigma^*$. *We assume w.l.o.g.* $\mathrm{alph}(w) = \Sigma$. *A* marking sequence σ *is an enumeration of* Σ, *i.e.,* $\sigma = (\mathtt{a}_1, \ldots, \mathtt{a}_n)$ *such that* $\mathtt{a}_i \neq \mathtt{a}_j$ *for all* $i, j \in [n]$ *with* $i \neq j$. *Let* $i \leq n$. *We call* w_i *the* marked version *of* w *at stage* i *w.r.t.* σ *if* $w_i[j] = \overline{w[j]}$ *for all* $j \in [|w|]$ *for which we have* $w[j] = \mathtt{a}_\ell$ *and* $\ell \leq i$ *with* $\ell \in [n]$, *and otherwise* $w_i[j] = w[j]$. *A* marked block *(or just* block*) is a maximal consecutive factor of marked letters.*

Definition 5. *A word* $w \in \Sigma^*$ *is called* k-local *for some* $k \in \mathbb{N}$ *if there is a marking sequence* σ *such that* w_i *contains at most* k *marked blocks at every stage* i. *It is called* strictly k-local *if it is* k*-local but not* $(k-1)$*-local.*

For example, consider the word $\mathtt{pepper}$ and the marking sequence $\sigma = (\mathtt{r}, \mathtt{p}, \mathtt{e})$. We have $\mathtt{peppe}\overline{\mathtt{r}}$ at the first stage, $\overline{\mathtt{p}}\mathtt{e}\overline{\mathtt{pp}}\mathtt{e}\overline{\mathtt{r}}$ at the second stage, and $\overline{\mathtt{pepper}}$ at the third stage. At every stage, there are at most three blocks, which means that this word is 3-local. One can verify that it is strictly 2-local witnessed by the marking sequence $\sigma' = (\mathtt{p}, \mathtt{e}, \mathtt{r})$.

Definition 6. *We denote the class of word-representable graphs by* $\mathcal{R}$. *For every* $k \in \mathbb{N}$, *we denote the class of* k*-representable graphs by* $\mathcal{R}^k$ *and the class of graphs representable by* k*-local words by* $\mathcal{L}^k$.

We present some section specific definitions within the following sections.

3 About k-Representability and Locality

In [18], it has been shown that every k-local word for $k \in \mathbb{N}$ represents a $2k$-representable graph. We improve this result by showing that every k-local word also represents a $(k+1)$-representable graph. To do so, we need the following two lemmata.

Lemma 7. *Let $w \in \Sigma^*$ be a k-local word for $k \in \mathbb{N}$. Every letter $\mathtt{a} \in \mathrm{alph}(w)$ with $|w|_{\mathtt{a}} > k+1$ does not alternate with any other letter.*

Proof. Let $\mathtt{a} \in \mathrm{alph}(w)$ with $|w|_{\mathtt{a}} > k+1$. Let $\mathtt{b} \in \mathrm{alph}(w) \setminus \{\mathtt{a}\}$. Let s be a marking sequence of w witnessing its k-locality. For every $p \in [|\mathrm{alph}(w)|]$, w_p w.r.t. s is of the form

$$u_1\overline{m_1}u_2\overline{m_2}\cdots u_k\overline{m_k}u_{k+1}$$

for some $u_1, m_1, \ldots, u_k, m_k, m_{k+1} \in \Sigma^*$.

First, assume $\mathtt{b}$ occurs before $\mathtt{a}$ in s at position p. This implies $|m_i|_{\mathtt{a}} = 0$ for every $i \in [k]$ and $|u_j|_{\mathtt{b}} = 0$ for every $j \in [k+1]$. Since $|w|_{\mathtt{a}} > k+1$, there is $j \in [k+1]$ with $|u_j|_{\mathtt{a}} > 1$.

Now, assume $\mathtt{a}$ occurs before $\mathtt{b}$ in s at position p. This implies $|m_i|_{\mathtt{b}} = 0$ for every $i \in [k]$ and $|u_j|_{\mathtt{a}} = 0$ for every $j \in [k+1]$. Since $|w|_{\mathtt{a}} > k+1$, there is $i \in [k]$ with $|m_i|_{\mathtt{a}} > 1$.

In both cases, there is a factor of w with two occurrences of $\mathtt{a}$ and no occurrence of $\mathtt{b}$. This means $\mathtt{a}$ does not alternate with $\mathtt{b}$ in w. □

Lemma 8. *Let $w \in \Sigma^*$ be k-local and $S \subseteq \mathrm{alph}(w)$. Then $\pi_S(w)$ is also k-local.*

Proof. Let s be a marking sequence witnessing the k-locality. Let $i \in [n]$. At every stage, the marked version of w w.r.t. s is of the form

$$u_1\overline{m_1}u_2\overline{m_2}\cdots u_k\overline{m_k}u_{k+1}$$

for some $u_1, m_1, \ldots, u_k, m_k, m_{k+1} \in \Sigma^*$, and the marked version of $\pi_S(w)$ w.r.t. s is

$$\pi_S(u_1)\overline{\pi_S(m_1)}\pi_S(u_2)\cdots\pi_S(u_k)\overline{\pi_S(m_k)}\pi_S(u_{k+1}).$$

Since there are at most k blocks, $\pi_S(w)$ is k-local. □

Using the previous two lemmata, for each k-local word w, we can provide a construction such that we obtain a k-local and $(k+1)$-uniform word w' that represents the same graph.

Lemma 9. *Let $k \in \mathbb{N}$. Let w be a k-local word. There is a k-local word w' with $|w'|_{\mathtt{a}} \leq k+1$ for every $\mathtt{a} \in \mathrm{alph}(w')$ such that $\mathrm{G}(w) = \mathrm{G}(w')$.*

Proof. Let $S = \{\mathtt{a}_1, \ldots \mathtt{a}_\ell\}$ be the set of letters that occur more than $k+1$ times in w. Define

$$w' = \pi_{\mathrm{alph}(w)\setminus S}(w)\mathtt{a}_1\mathtt{a}_1\cdots\mathtt{a}_\ell\mathtt{a}_\ell.$$

We have $|w'|_{\mathtt{a}} \leq k+1$ for every $\mathtt{a} \in \mathrm{alph}(w')$. By Lemma 7, w and w' represent the same graph. By Lemma 8, $\pi_{\mathrm{alph}(w)\setminus S}(w)$ is k-local. Since we can mark $\mathtt{a}_1, \ldots, \mathtt{a}_\ell$ at the end in this order, w' is also k-local. □

Remark 10. Notice that if w is k-local for some $k \in \mathbb{N}$ there exists a $k' \leq k$ such that w is strictly k'-local. Since w remains the same, we can alter Lemma 9 to the existence of a k'-local word w' with $|w'|_{\mathtt{a}} \leq k'+1$ for every $\mathtt{a} \in \mathrm{alph}(w')$ such that $\mathrm{G}(w) = \mathrm{G}(w')$.

Lemma 9, together with Remark 3, immediately implies the following result.

Theorem 11. *Every k-local word for $k \in \mathbb{N}$ represents a $(k+1)$-representable graph.*

We have proven $\mathcal{L}^k \subseteq \mathcal{R}^{k+1}$ for every $k \in \mathbb{N}$, but we do not know yet if the inclusion is strict. In Sect. 5, we will show, among other results, that this is the case.

4 Forbidden Subgraphs and Speed

In this section we first show that $\mathcal{R}, \mathcal{R}^k$, and $\mathcal{L}^k$ are hereditary. This leads to the first main result of this section, namely that $\mathcal{L}^1$ is exactly the class of threshold graphs. The second main result stems from the fact that hereditary graph classes have an asymptotic growth in their size w.r.t. their number of nodes. For this purpose, we use the notion of *speed* and give an upper and a lower bound for $\mathcal{R}^k$ and $\mathcal{L}^k$.

Definition 12. *A class of graphs is called* hereditary *if it is closed under induced subgraphs. By* $\mathrm{Free}(M)$*, we denote the class of graphs that do not contain a graph from the set of graphs M as an induced subgraph. The graphs from M are called the* forbidden induced subgraphs *of* $\mathrm{Free}(M)$*. A class of graphs X is called* finitely defined *if there is a finite set M such that $X = \mathrm{Free}(M)$.*

Remark 13. Note that for a finitely defined class, it can be checked in polynomial time in the size of a graph if it is contained in the class. A class of graphs X is hereditary iff $X = \mathrm{Free}(M)$ for some set of graphs M (cf. [25]).

Therefore, every hereditary class of graphs can be characterised in terms of forbidden induced subgraphs, and is a crucial task to find a characterisation with a minimal set of forbidden induced subgraphs. However, for many important graph classes such a characterisation has not yet been found. First, we prove that the classes $\mathcal{R}$, $\mathcal{R}^k$, $\mathcal{L}^k$ are hereditary.

Theorem 14. *The classes $\mathcal{R}$, $\mathcal{R}^k$, and $\mathcal{L}^k$ are hereditary for all $k \in \mathbb{N}$.*

Proof. If we have a word w and remove all occurrences of a letter $\mathtt{a}$, the resulting word represents the graph $\mathrm{G}(w)|_{\mathrm{alph}(w)\setminus\{\mathtt{a}\}}$. If w is k-uniform or k-local for some $k \in \mathbb{N}$, the resulting word is still k-uniform or k-local, respectively. Therefore, $\mathcal{R}$, $\mathcal{R}^k$, and $\mathcal{L}^k$ are hereditary for every $k \in \mathbb{N}$. □

We provide a forbidden induced subgraph characterisation for $\mathcal{L}^1$ using the following theorem. Notice that we hereby connect the notion of 1-local representable graphs with the one of threshold graphs [14].

Definition 15. *A graph G is a* threshold graph *if it can be constructed from the empty graph by repeatedly adding either an isolated node or a node that is connected to all other nodes.*

Theorem 16. *$\mathcal{L}^1$ is exactly the class of threshold graphs.*

Proof. In [18], the authors introduced the class of 1-local representable graphs and showed that it contains exactly the graphs represented by 1-local words, i.e., $\mathcal{L}^1$. The definition of threshold graphs and 1-local representable graphs is the same. □

It is well known that a graph is a threshold graph iff it does not contain one of the forbidden induced subgraphs shown in Fig. 2, cf. [30]. Note that the class of threshold graphs is equivalent to several other classes, which are listed in [14].

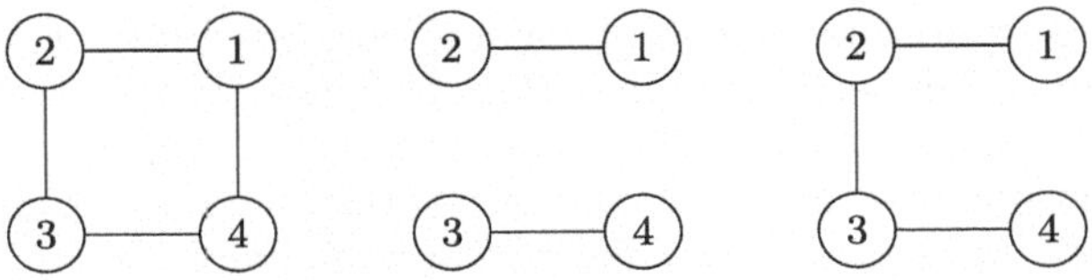

Fig. 2. Forbidden induced subgraphs of $\mathcal{L}^1$.

This means that the classes $\mathcal{L}^k$ for $k \in \mathbb{N}$ are a generalisation of the important threshold graphs, which further motivates to investigate them. However, we have not found a forbidden induced subgraph characterisation of $\mathcal{L}^k$ for $k > 1$, and it is unknown if these classes are finitely defined.

Another important aspect of hereditary graph classes is the asymptotic growth of their size w.r.t. the number of nodes. First, we define a way to count the size in our case (cf. [10]).

Definition 17. *For a class of graphs X and $n \in \mathbb{N}$ we define $X_n = \{G \in X \mid V(G) = [n]\}$, i.e. the graphs in X with nodes from 1 to n. We call $n \mapsto |X_n|$ the* speed *of X.*

For $X = \mathcal{R}$, the speed was analysed in [10]. The authors proved $|\mathcal{R}_n| = 2^{\frac{n^2}{3}+o(n^2)}$ and concluded that there are $2^{\frac{n^2}{3}+o(n^2)}$ non-isomorphic word-representable graphs with n nodes. We will investigate the speed of $\mathcal{L}^k$ and $\mathcal{R}^k$ with a similar approach based on the index (also called *colouring number*) of a hereditary class. See [7] for an introduction.

Definition 18. *Let $\mathscr{E}_{i,j}$ be the class of graphs whose nodes can be partitioned into i independent sets and j cliques as induced subgraphs. The* index $c(X)$ *of a hereditary class of graphs X is the largest $k \in \mathbb{N}$ such that $\mathscr{E}_{i,k-i} \subseteq X$ holds for some $i \in \mathbb{N}$.*

We want to determine the index of $\mathcal{R}^k$ and $\mathcal{L}^k$ for every $k \in \mathbb{N}$. First, we observe that there are graphs in $\mathscr{E}_{0,2}$ and $\mathscr{E}_{1,1}$ that are not word-representable. These graphs are depicted in Fig. 3 and Fig. 4.

Lemma 19. *We have $\mathscr{E}_{0,2} \nsubseteq \mathcal{R}$ and $\mathscr{E}_{1,1} \nsubseteq \mathcal{R}$.*

Proof. The graph depicted in Fig. 3 can be partitioned into two cliques as indicated by the colouring. Therefore, it belongs to $\mathscr{E}_{0,2}$. Since we know from [27] that this graph is not word-representable, $\mathscr{E}_{0,2}$ is not a subset of $\mathcal{R}$.

The graph depicted in Fig. 4 can be partitioned into a clique and an independent set as indicated by the colouring. Therefore, it belongs to $\mathscr{E}_{1,1}$. Since we know from [27] that this graph is not word-representable, $\mathscr{E}_{1,1}$ is not a subset of $\mathcal{R}$. □

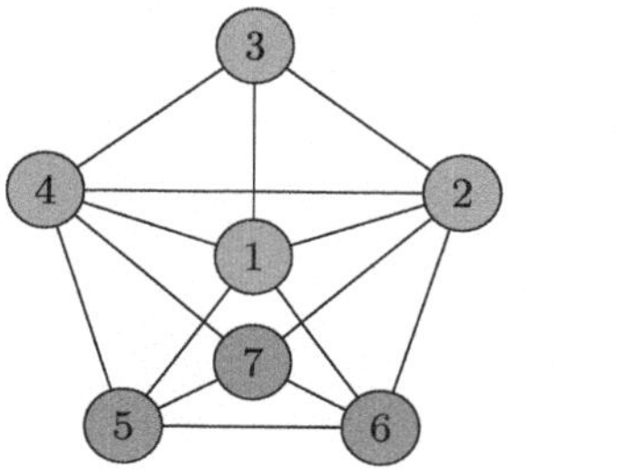

Fig. 3. A graph in $\mathscr{E}_{0,2}$ that is not in $\mathcal{R}$ (the colouring indicates a partition into two cliques).

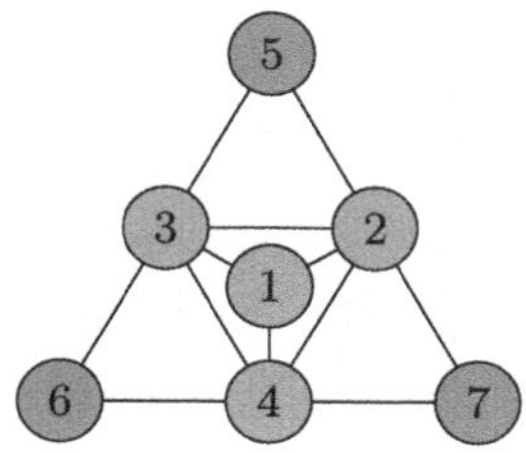

Fig. 4. A graph in $\mathscr{E}_{1,1}$ that is not in $\mathcal{R}$ (the colouring indicates a partition into a clique and an independent set).

With this we can show that the indices of $\mathcal{R}^{k+1}$ and $\mathcal{L}^k$ are both 1 for every $k \in \mathbb{N}$.

Theorem 20. *For every* $k \in \mathbb{N}$, $c(\mathcal{R}^{k+1}) = c(\mathcal{L}^k) = 1$ *holds.*

Proof. Let $k \in \mathbb{N}$. Note that $\mathscr{E}_{1,0}$ contains only the empty graphs, all of which are in $\mathcal{R}^{k+1}$ and $\mathcal{L}^k$. Due to Lemma 19, we only need to show that $\mathscr{E}_{2,0}$ is not contained in $\mathcal{R}^{k+1}$ and $\mathcal{L}^k$. We know from [20] that the crown graph $H_{2k+3,2k+3}$ has representation number $\lceil k + \frac{3}{2} \rceil > k + 1$. By Theorem 11, this implies that it is neither contained in $\mathcal{R}^{k+1}$ nor in $\mathcal{L}^k$. Since this graph is 2-colourable and thus in $\mathscr{E}_{2,0}$, it follows that $\mathscr{E}_{2,0}$ is not contained in $\mathcal{R}^{k+1}$ and $\mathcal{L}^k$. Hence, we have $c(\mathcal{R}^{k+1}) = c(\mathcal{L}^k) = 1$. □

The speed is closely related to the entropy, which can be considered as a coefficient of compressibility (cf. [25]).

Definition 21. *For a class of graphs* X, *its* entropy *is defined by*

$$e(X) = \lim_{n\to\infty} \frac{\log_2 |X_n|}{\binom{n}{2}}.$$

With the Alekseev–Bollobás–Thomason Theorem (cf. [1]) we immediately get the following result.

Corollary 22. *For* $X \in \{\mathcal{R}^{k+1}, \mathcal{L}^k\}$ *with* $k \in \mathbb{N}$, *the entropy is* $e(X) = 0$.

Unfortunately, this only gives us an upper bound for the speed of $\mathcal{R}^k$ and $\mathcal{L}^k$. We continue with a lower bound based on the Bell number.

Definition 23. *For every $n \in \mathbb{N}$, the nth* Bell number *B_n is defined as the number of partitions of a set with n elements.*

The hereditary properties are partitioned into properties below the Bell number with $|X_n| < B_n$ and properties above the Bell number with $|X_n| \geq B_n$ for sufficiently large $n \in \mathbb{N}$. The properties below the Bell number are of particular interest since they are finitely defined ([4]) and all contained graphs have bounded clique-width ([2]).

Lemma 24. *Let G be a graph with every component being a clique. Then, $G \in X$ for $X \in \{\mathcal{R}^k, \mathcal{L}^k\}$ for $k > 1$.*

Proof. Let $C_1, \ldots, C_n$ be the components of G. Let w_i be a word containing every node from C_i exactly once for every $i \in [n]$. Then, $w = w_1 w_1 w_2 w_2 \cdots w_n w_n$ represents G. Note that w is 2-uniform and 2-local, witnessed by the marking sequence

$$(w_1[1], \ldots, w_1[|w_1|], \ldots, w_n[1], \ldots, w_n[|w_n|]).$$

This implies $G \in \mathcal{R}^k$ and $G \in \mathcal{L}^k$. □

Theorem 25. *Let $X \in \{\mathcal{R}^k, \mathcal{L}^k\}$ for $k > 1$. We have $B_n \leq |X_n|$.*

Proof. Let $n \in \mathbb{N}$, and let P be a partition of $[n]$. Set $G = ([n], E)$ with

$$E = \bigcup_{C \in P} \{\{x, y\} \mid x, y \in C\}.$$

By Lemma 24, $G \in X_n$. Since we get a unique graph for every partition, it follows $B_n \leq |X_n|$. □

Thus, $\mathcal{L}^k$ and $\mathcal{R}^k$ are above the Bell number for $k > 1$. This means that we cannot draw any conclusion regarding forbidden induced subgraphs or the clique-width of these classes. Nevertheless, we are going to inspect the clique-width of $\mathcal{L}^k$ from a constructive perspective.

5 Clique-Width

In this last section, we prove that $\mathcal{L}^k$ is a proper subset of $\mathcal{R}^{k+1}$ for all $k \in \mathbb{N}$. Therefore, we first introduce the well-known graph parameter *clique-width* and show that $\mathcal{L}^k$ has bounded clique-width based on k. Afterwards, we show that $\mathcal{L}^k$ belongs to the factorial layer, a subclass of the hereditary graph classes depending on their speed.

We start with a folklore definition on constructing labelled graphs. Note that every labelled graph can be constructed using only these operations.

Definition 26. *We define the following operations on labelled graphs:*

- *$i(v)$, create a node v with label i,*
- *$G \oplus H$, disjoint union of G and H,*
- *$\eta_{i,j}$, connect every node with label i to every node with label j for $i \neq j$,*
- *$\rho_{i \to j}$, rename label i to j.*

A k-expression *with $k \in \mathbb{N}$ is an expression consisting of these operations with not more than k distinct labels. For a graph G, its* clique-width $\mathrm{cwd}(G)$ *is the minimum number such that there is k-expression for a labelled version of it. We define an* M-expression *for a set M as an expression with the above operations using only labels from M. For every $k \in \mathbb{N}$, we define $\Sigma_k = \{0,1\}^k \cup \{2\}$. For a marked word $m \in (\Sigma \cup \overline{\Sigma})^*$ and $k \in \mathbb{N}$, define the function* $\mathrm{label}_m^k : \Sigma \to \Sigma_k$ *that maps a letter* a *to a tuple such that the ith component is 1 if there is one occurrence of* a *in the ith block of m and it is 0 if there are less than i blocks or there is no occurrence of* a *in the ith block. If there is a block with two or more occurrences,* a *is mapped to 2 instead.*

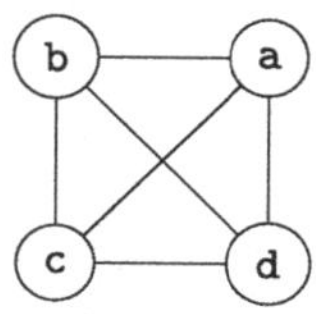

Fig. 5. Graph with clique-width 2.

The graph in Fig. 5 can be constructed using only the labels 1 and 2 with the expression

$$\eta_{1,2}(\rho_{2\to1}(\eta_{1,2}(1(\mathtt{a}) \oplus 2(\mathtt{b}))) \oplus \rho_{1\to2}(\eta_{1,2}(1(\mathtt{c}) \oplus 2(\mathtt{d})))).$$

Note that a graph with clique-width 1 cannot have any edges because we can only add edges between distinct labels. Therefore, this graph has a clique-width of 2.

Using these definitions, we can show that $\mathcal{L}^k$ has a bounded clique-width based on k. For the proof, we need the following lemma.

Lemma 27. *Let w be a k-local word witnessed by a marking sequence s. Let $i \in [|s|]$ and* $\mathtt{a} = s[i]$. *For every $j \in [|s|]_0$, let $u_j = \pi_{\mathrm{alph}(s[1]\cdots s[j])}(w)$ and let w_j be the marked version of w at stage j w.r.t. s. Let E be a Σ_k-expression for* $\mathrm{G}(u_{i-1})$ *such that every node v has label* $\mathrm{label}_{w_{i-1}}^k(v)$. *There is a Σ_k-expression for* $\mathrm{G}(u_i)$ *such that every node v has label* $\mathrm{label}_{w_i}^k(v)$.

Proof. Let N be the tuple with 0 in all k components. Let $l_1, \ldots, l_n$ for $n \in \mathbb{N}_0$ be the labels of the letters alternating with a in u_i. Note that for each letter alternating with a, every letter with the same label also alternates with a since they have the same number of occurrences in each block. Thus,

$$\eta_{l_1,N}(\ldots\eta_{l_n,N}(N(\mathtt{a})\oplus E)\ldots)$$

is a Σ_k-expression for $\mathrm{G}(u_i)$. Because no label is changed, every node v except a has label $\mathrm{label}^k_{w_{i-1}}(v)$.

Now, we need to adjust the labels because blocks can merge and new blocks can arise. If the jth and the $(j+1)^{\text{th}}$ block merge, we need to add the numbers of occurrences in both blocks and append a 0 at the end. This means every label $(x_1,\ldots,x_p)$ is renamed to $(x_1,\ldots,x_{j-1},x_j+x_{j+1},x_{j+2},\ldots,x_p,0)$ if $x_j+x_{j+1}<2$, else to 2, and 2 is not renamed. We define a function g that maps the labels of the letters from u_{i-1} to the corresponding labels after all merges. This function induces a directed graph with self-loops where every label has an edge to the new label after all merges. Note that there is no cycle except for self-loops in this graph. Hence, we find a topological ordering $l_1,\ldots,l_n$. Let w' be the word that we get from w_{i-1} by marking every occurrence of a that does not create a new block. It follows that

$$E' = \rho_{l_1\to g(l_1)}(\ldots\rho_{l_n\to g(l_n)}(E)\ldots)$$

is a Σ_k-expression for $\mathrm{G}(u_i)$ such that every node v has label $\mathrm{label}^k_{w'}(v)$.

If there arises a new block between the jth and the $(j+1)^{\text{th}}$ one, we need to insert a component with value 0 into the tuples. This means every label $(x_1,\ldots,x_p)$ is renamed to $(x_1,\ldots,x_j,0,x_{j+1},\ldots,x_{p-1})$ and 2 is not renamed. We define a function h that maps the labels of the letters from u_{i-1} to the corresponding labels after all new blocks are there. Again, this induces a directed graph with self-loops. Note that there is no cycle except for self-loops in this graph. Hence, we find a topological ordering $k_1,\ldots,k_n$. Also, a has to get the correct label. Let $y=\mathrm{label}^k_{w_i}(\mathtt{a})$. It follows that

$$\rho_{N\to y}(\rho_{k_1\to h(k_1)}(\ldots\rho_{k_n\to h(k_n)}(E')\ldots))$$

is a Σ_k-expression for $\mathrm{G}(u_i)$ such that every node v has label $\mathrm{label}^k_{w_i}(v)$. □

Now, we can prove the first main theorem of this section.

Theorem 28. *Let $G\in\mathcal{L}^k$ for $k\in\mathbb{N}$. We have* $\mathrm{cwd}(G)\le 2^k+1$.

Proof. We apply Lemma 27. Starting with the empty expression, we get a Σ_k-expression for G by induction. It follows $\mathrm{cwd}(G)\le|\Sigma_k|=2^k+1$. □

Consider the 2-local word banana and the marking sequence (n, a, b). We start with

$$E_1=\rho_{N\to(1,1)}(N(\mathtt{n})).$$

Next, we add a alternating with all nodes that have the label $(1,1)$ and get

$$E_2=\rho_{N\to 2}(\rho_{2\to 2}(\rho_{(1,1)\to 2}(\eta_{(1,1),N}(N(\mathtt{a})\oplus E_1)))).$$

Here, n needs to get the label 2 since the first and the second block merge such that there are two copies of n in the first block. Finally, we have

$$E_3 = \rho_{N \to (1,0)}(\rho_{2\to 2}(\rho_{2\to 2}(N(\mathtt{b}) \oplus E_2))),$$

which is a Σ_2-expression for G(banana).

Remark 29. The theorem implies that $\mathcal{L}^k$ has bounded clique-width for every $k \in \mathbb{N}$. This is interesting from an algorithmic point of view since many problems that cannot be solved in polynomial time in general can be solved in polynomial time on classes with bounded clique-width. These problems include the Hamiltonian path problem and the minimum maximal matching problem, see [15]. Courcelle et al. showed in [12] that all problems which can be formulated in a certain form of monadic second-order logic called MSO_1 can even be solved in linear time on graphs with clique-width bounded by some $k \in \mathbb{N}$ given a k-expression. An example for such a problem is 3-colourability, see [28]. Note that for a class with bounded clique-width, there is $k \in \mathbb{N}$ such that a k-expression for every graph in this class can be determined in polynomial time by [32]. In [16], it was shown that it is NP-complete to decide if the clique-width of a graph G is at most k. There are several other graph parameters related to clique-width. By [11], a graph with treewidth k has a clique-width not greater than $3 \cdot 2^{k-1}$. By [24], a graph with NLC-width k has a clique-width not smaller than k and not greater than $2k$. By [32], a graph with rank-width k has a clique-width not smaller than k and not greater than $2^{k+1} - 1$. A thorough investigations of these graph parameters for $\mathcal{L}^k$ remains for future work.

With the following theorem by Allen et al., we can apply our knowledge about the clique-width of $\mathcal{L}^k$ to learn more about its speed.

Theorem 30 ([2]). *If X is a class of graphs with bounded clique-width, there is C such that $|X_n| \leq n!C^n$.*

Corollary 31. *For every $k \in \mathbb{N}$, there is a constant C such that $|\mathcal{L}^k_n| \leq n!C^n$.*

Hereditary classes of graphs are divided into layers by their speed, first introduced in [33]. One of these layers is the factorial layer. A class with speed $f(n)$ belongs to the factorial layer if there are constants $C_1, C_2 > 0$ such that

$$n^{C_1 n} \leq f(n) \leq n^{C_2 n}.$$

Since the factorial layer is split into classes above and below the Bell number ([5]), $\mathcal{L}^k$ belongs to the factorial layer for every $k > 1$ by Theorem 25.

To finish off this section, we can use our knowledge about the clique-width of $\mathcal{L}^k$ to show that $\mathcal{L}^k$ is a proper subset of $\mathcal{R}^{k+1}$.

Theorem 32. *For every $k \in \mathbb{N}$, $\mathcal{L}^k \subsetneq \mathcal{R}^{k+1}$.*

Proof. By [21], the class of circle graphs has unbounded clique-width. The circle graphs are exactly the 2-representable graphs, as shown in [26]. Thus, $\mathcal{R}^{k+1}$ has unbounded clique-width for every $k \in \mathbb{N}$. By Theorem 28 and Theorem 11, we get $\mathcal{L}^k \subsetneq \mathcal{R}^{k+1}$. □

6 Conclusion

In this work, we investigated the connection between locality of words and word-representable graphs. We proved that $\mathcal{L}^k$ is a subset of $\mathcal{R}^{k+1}$ for every $k \in \mathbb{N}$, and we later proved that this inclusion is strict. We found out that $\mathcal{L}^1$ is the class of threshold graphs, which gave us a characterisation in terms of forbidden induced subgraphs. Moreover, we analysed the speed of $\mathcal{R}^k$ and $\mathcal{L}^k$. In particular, we showed that both classes are above the Bell number for $k > 1$ and $\mathcal{L}^k$ belongs to the factorial layer. Finally, we showed that the clique-width of graphs in $\mathcal{L}^k$ is bounded by $2^k + 1$, which connects the complexity of words with the complexity of the graphs represented by them.

It remains an open problem to characterise $\mathcal{L}^k$ for $k > 1$. In particular, it is unknown if $\mathcal{L}^k$ is finitely defined for $k > 1$. It is unclear if $\mathcal{R}^k$ also belongs to the factorial layer. Also, we do not know if 2^{k+1} is optimal as an upper bound of the clique-width of $\mathcal{L}^k$. Moreover, a thorough investigation of well-known graph-parameters for $\mathcal{L}^k$ remains future work.

References

1. Alekseev, V.E.: On the entropy values of hereditary classes of graphs. Discret. Math. Appl. **3**(2), 191–200 (1993)
2. Allen, P., Lozin, V.V., Rao, M.: Clique-width and the speed of hereditary properties. Electron. J. Comb. **16**(1) (2009)
3. Angluin, D.: Finding patterns common to a set of strings. J. Comput. Syst. Sci. **21**(1), 46–62 (1980)
4. Atminas, A.: Well-quasi-ordering of combinatorial structures. Unpublished doctoral dissertation (2015)
5. Atminas, A., Collins, A., Foniok, J., Lozin, V.V.: Deciding the Bell number for hereditary graph properties. SIAM J. Discret. Math. **30**(2), 1015–1031 (2016)
6. Beth, C., et al.: k-local graphs. (2025) accepted at DCFS
7. Bollobás, B.: Hereditary and monotone properties of combinatorial structures. Surv. Comb. **346**(1), 2007 (2007)
8. Casel, K., Day, J.D., Fleischmann, P., Kociumaka, T., Manea, F., Schmid, M.L.: Graph and string parameters: connections between pathwidth, cutwidth and the locality number. In: *ICALP 2019*, vol. 132 of LIPIcs, pp. 109:1–109:16. Schloss Dagstuhl - Leibniz-Zentrum für Informatik (2019)
9. Chandrasekaran, S., Sulthana, A.: k-Power domination of crown graph. IJAER **14**(13), 3066–3068 (2019)
10. Collins, A., Kitaev, S., Lozin, V.V.: New results on word-representable graphs. Discret. Appl. Math. **216**, 136–141 (2017)
11. Corneil, D.G., Rotics, U.: On the relationship between clique-width and treewidth. SIAM J. Comput. **34**(4), 825–847 (2005)
12. Courcelle, B., Makowsky, J.A., Rotics, U.: Linear time solvable optimization problems on graphs of bounded clique-width. Theory Comput. Syst. **33**(2), 125–150 (2000)
13. Day, J.D., Fleischmann, P., Manea, F., Nowotka, D.: Local patterns. In: 37th IARCS, FSTTCS 2017, vol. 93 of LIPIcs, pp. 24:1–24:14. Schloss Dagstuhl - Leibniz-Zentrum für Informatik (2017)

14. de Ridder, H.N., et al.: Information system on graph classes and their inclusions (ISGCI). https://www.graphclasses.org/classes/gc_328.html
15. Espelage, W., Gurski, F., Wanke, E.: How to solve NP-hard graph problems on clique-width bounded graphs in polynomial time. In: *Graph-Theoretic Concepts in Computer Science*, vol. 2204 of LNCS, pp. 117–128. Springer (2001)
16. Fellows, M.R., Rosamond, F.A., Rotics, U., Szeider, S.: Clique-width is NP-complete. SIAM J. Discret. Math. **23**(2), 909–939 (2009)
17. Feng, Z., Fernau, H., Fleischmann, P., Mann, K., Sacher, S.C.: Generalized word-representable graphs. *CoRR*, abs/2411.03274 (2024). https://doi.org/10.48550/arXiv.2411.03274
18. Fleischmann, P., Haschke, L., Löck, T., Nowotka, D.: Word-representable graphs from a word's perspective. Acta Informatica **61**(4), 383–400 (2024)
19. Fleischmann, P., Haschke, L., Manea, F., Nowotka, D., Tsida, C.T., Wiedenbeck, J.: Blocksequences of k-local Words. In: Bureš, T., et al. (eds.) SOFSEM 2021. LNCS, vol. 12607, pp. 119–134. Springer, Cham (2021). https://doi.org/10.1007/978-3-030-67731-2_9
20. Glen, M., Kitaev, S., Pyatkin, A.V.: On the representation number of a crown graph. Discret. Appl. Math. **244**, 89–93 (2018)
21. Golumbic, M.C., Rotics, U.: On the clique-width of some perfect graph classes. Int. J. Found. Comput. Sci. **11**(3), 423–443 (2000)
22. Halldórsson, M.M., Kitaev, S., Pyatkin, A.V.: Semi-transitive orientations and word-representable graphs. Discret. Appl. Math. **201**, 164–171 (2016)
23. Halldórsson, M.M., Kitaev, S., Pyatkin, A.: Graphs capturing alternations in words. In: Gao, Y., Lu, H., Seki, S., Yu, S. (eds.) DLT 2010. LNCS, vol. 6224, pp. 436–437. Springer, Heidelberg (2010). https://doi.org/10.1007/978-3-642-14455-4_41
24. Johansson, O.: Clique-decomposition, NLC-decomposition, and modular decomposition-relationships and results for random graphs. *Congressus Numerantium*, pp. 39–60 (1998)
25. Kitaev, S., Lozin, V.V.: *Words and Graphs.* Monographs in Theoretical Computer Science. An EATCS Series. Springer (2015)
26. Kitaev, S., Pyatkin, A.V.: On representable graphs. J. Autom. Lang. Comb. **13**(1), 45–54 (2008)
27. Kitaev, S., Sun, H.: Human-verifiable proofs in the theory of word-representable graphs. RAIRO Theor. Informatics Appl. **58**, 9 (2024)
28. Knop, D., Koutecký, M., Masaník, T., Toufar, T.: Simplified algorithmic metatheorems beyond MSO: treewidth and neighborhood diversity. *Log. Methods Comput. Sci.***15**(4) (2019)
29. Lothaire, M.: Combinatorics on Words. Cambridge University Press, Cambridge Mathematical Library (1997)
30. Mahadev, N.V.R., Peled, U.N.: *Threshold graphs and related topics*, vol. 56 of *Annals of Discrete Mathematics.* Elsevier (1995)
31. Oliveros, D., Torres, A.J.: From word-representable graphs to altered tverberg-type theorems. *Discrete & Computational Geometry*, pp. 1–17 (2025)
32. Oum, S., Seymour, P.D.: Approximating clique-width and branch-width. J. Comb. Theory B **96**(4), 514–528 (2006)
33. Scheinerman, E.R., Zito, J.S.: On the size of hereditary classes of graphs. J. Comb. Theory B **61**(1), 16–39 (1994)

Automata for Synchronised Shuffle on Backbones

Sabine Broda, António Machiavelo, Nelma Moreira(✉), and Rogério Reis

CMUP and DM-DCC, Faculdade de Ciências da Universidade do Porto, Rua do Campo Alegre, 4169-007 Porto, Portugal
{sabine.broda,antonio.machiavelo,nelma.moreira,rogerio.reis}@fc.up.pt

Abstract. Considering regular expressions extended with synchronised shuffle on backbones, we present two equivalent automata: the location based position automaton and the partial derivative automaton. We show that the latter is a quotient of the former. Using the framework of analytic combinatorics, we study the average complexity of the partial derivative automaton. Surprisingly, for binary and ternary alphabets the average number of partial derivatives by a symbol is exponential on the size of the expression, while it is constant for larger alphabets which is what happens with the results for all other regular operators studied so far. Furthermore, we prove that the average number of states of the partial derivative automaton is bounded from above by $(1.57708 + o(1))^m$, while in the worst-case that value is $O(3^m)$, where m is the alphabetic size of the expression.

1 Introduction

Synchronised shuffle operators allow to specify symbols on which the synchronisation can be strict or not, instead of pure interleave. Simulations of regular expressions extended with those operators by automata where studied by several authors [6–8,14,15]. The synchronised shuffle on backbones was introduced by Manea et al. [12] as an operation where the synchronisation can be done along a predefined set of words, the backbones. This operation may model some phenomena of gene linkage, in molecular biology, and also ensure compositionality of team automata, a framework for modelling the collaboration between components of computational systems. In this paper, we introduce regular expressions with synchronised shuffle on backbones, and define a location based position automaton and a partial derivative automaton for expressions with this operator. We show that the latter is a quotient of the former, which extends the corresponding result for standard regular expressions and other synchronised shuffle operators. Moreover, using the framework of analytic combinatorics, we

This work was partially supported by project Avatar (2023.12169.PEX) and project CMUP (UIDB/00144/2020), member of LASI (UIDP/00144/2020) which are financed by funds through FCT.

Published by Springer Nature Switzerland AG 2025
A. Malcher and L. Prigioniero (Eds.): DCFS 2025, LNCS 15759, pp. 64–78, 2025.
https://doi.org/10.1007/978-3-031-97100-6_5

give asymptotic estimates of the average complexity of several measures for partial derivative automata. Asymptotically, and on average, the number of partial derivatives by a symbol depends on the size of the alphabet, k. While for $k > 3$ the number of partial derivatives of an expression tends to a constant, for $k = 2$ and $k = 3$ that value is exponential on the size of the expression. This result contrasts with the ones for standard and other (syn chronised) shuffle operators, where this value always tends to some constant. Furthermore, we prove that the average number of partial derivatives (number of states of the partial derivative automaton) is bounded from above by $(1.57708 + o(1))^m$, while in the worst-case that value is $O(3^m)$, where m is the alphabetic size of the expression.

2 Preliminares

Given an alphabet Σ and a word $w \in \Sigma^\star$, let $|w|$ and Σ_w denote respectively the length of w and the set of symbols that occur in w. The empty word is ε. We denote by RE the set of *regular expressions*, α, over Σ and by $\mathcal{L}(\alpha)$ the *language* associated to an expression α. The *size* $|\alpha|$ of $\alpha \in$ RE is the number of symbols in α (disregarding parentheses). The *alphabetic size* $|\alpha|_\Sigma$ is its number of letters. We define $\varepsilon(\alpha)$ by $\varepsilon(\alpha) = \varepsilon$ if $\varepsilon \in \mathcal{L}(\alpha)$, and $\varepsilon(\alpha) = \emptyset$, otherwise. We say that two expressions α and β are equivalent, and write $\alpha \doteq \beta$, if and only if $\mathcal{L}(\alpha) = \mathcal{L}(\beta)$. We also consider $\varepsilon S = S\varepsilon = S$ and $\emptyset S = S\emptyset = \emptyset$, for any set S of expressions. For a singleton $S = \{\alpha\}$, we usually write $\varepsilon\alpha$ instead of $\varepsilon\{\alpha\}$, etc. A *nondeterministic finite automaton* (NFA) is a five-tuple $A = \langle Q, \Sigma, \delta, I, F\rangle$ where Q is a finite set of states, Σ is a finite alphabet, $I \subseteq Q$ is the set of initial states, $F \subseteq Q$ is the set of final states, and $\delta : Q \times \Sigma \to 2^Q$ is the transition function. When $I = \{q_0\}$, we use $I = q_0$. The *size* $|A|$ of an NFA A is $|Q|$. The *language accepted* by A is represented by $\mathcal{L}(A)$. Two automata are *equivalent* if they accept the same language. Two automata $A_1 = \langle Q_1, \Sigma, \delta_1, I_1, F_1\rangle$ and $A_2 = \langle Q_2, \Sigma, \delta_2, I_2, F_2\rangle$ are *isomorphic*, $A_1 \simeq A_2$, if there is a bijection $\varphi : Q_1 \longrightarrow Q_2$ such that $\varphi(I_1) = I_2$, $\varphi(F_1) = F_2$, and $\varphi(\delta_1(q_1, \sigma)) = \delta_2(\varphi(q_1), \sigma)$, for all $q_1 \in Q_1, \sigma \in \Sigma$. An equivalence relation $\equiv$ on Q is *right invariant* w.r.t. an NFA A (or a *bisimulation*) if and only if (i) $\equiv \subseteq (Q - F)^2 \cup F^2$ (ii) $\forall p, q \in Q, \sigma \in \Sigma$, if $p \equiv q$, then $\forall p' \in \delta(p, \sigma)\ \exists q' \in \delta(q, \sigma)$ such that $p' \equiv q'$. If $\equiv$ is right-invariant w.r.t. A, the *quotient automaton* $A/\equiv$ is given by $A/\equiv\ = \langle Q/\equiv, \Sigma, \delta/\equiv, I/\equiv, F/\equiv\rangle$, where $\delta/\equiv([p], \sigma) = \{[q] \mid q \in \delta(p, \sigma)\} = \delta(p, \sigma)/\equiv$. We have $\mathcal{L}(A/\equiv) = \mathcal{L}(A)$.

2.1 Synchronised Shuffle on Backbones

The shuffle of two words $u, v \in \Sigma^\star$ is the set of words $u \sqcup\!\sqcup v$ obtained by arbitrarily interleaving the letters in u and v. Formally, we have $u \sqcup\!\sqcup \varepsilon = \varepsilon \sqcup\!\sqcup u = \{u\}$ and $\sigma u \sqcup\!\sqcup \tau v = \{\sigma w \mid w \in u \sqcup\!\sqcup \tau v\} \cup \{\tau w \mid w \in \sigma u \sqcup\!\sqcup v\}$. In the remaining of this section we briefly review several synchronised shuffle operators, that were studied by Beek et al. [15] and by Manea et al. [12].

Given $\Gamma \subseteq \Sigma$ and $u, v \in \Sigma^\star$, the strongly synchronised shuffle $u\ {}^{\mathsf{s}}\|_\Gamma\ v$ imposes synchronisation on all letters of Γ, while the arbitrary synchronised shuffle $u \,{}^{\mathsf{a}}\|_{\Gamma}\, v$ permits symbols in Γ to synchronise, but does not force their synchronisation. Formally, $u \,{}^{\mathsf{s}}\|_{\Gamma}\, v$, is the finite set of words defined as follows [15]:

$$\begin{aligned} u \,{}^{\mathsf{s}}\|_{\Gamma}\, v = \{x \mid \sigma_i \in \Gamma \wedge u_i, v_i \in (\Sigma \setminus \Gamma)^{\star} \ \wedge \ u = u_1\sigma_1 \cdots \sigma_{n-1}u_n \ \wedge \\ v = v_1\sigma_1 \cdots \sigma_{n-1}v_n \ \wedge x \in (u_1 \sqcup\!\sqcup v_1)\sigma_1 \cdots \sigma_{n-1}(u_n \sqcup\!\sqcup v_n)\}, \end{aligned}$$

and

$$\begin{aligned} u \,{}^{\mathsf{a}}\|_{\Gamma}\, v = \{x \mid \ \sigma_i \in \Gamma \wedge u_i, v_i \in \Sigma^{\star} \ \wedge \ u = u_1\sigma_1 \cdots \sigma_{n-1}u_n \wedge \\ v = v_1\sigma_1 \cdots \sigma_{n-1}v_n \ \wedge x \in (u_1 \sqcup\!\sqcup v_1)\sigma_1 \cdots \sigma_{n-1}(u_n \sqcup\!\sqcup v_n)\}. \end{aligned}$$

Example 1. In $abca \,{}^{\mathsf{s}}\|_{\{a\}}\, ada$ it is mandatory to synchronise the first occurrences of a in $abca$ and in ada, as well as the last occurrences. In between, there may be any word obtained by shuffling bc with d. Thus, $abca \,{}^{\mathsf{s}}\|_{\{a\}}\, ada = \{abcda, abdca, adbca\}$ or $ab \,{}^{\mathsf{s}}\|_{\{a\}}\, da = \{dab\}$. While, for the of arbitrary synchronised we have $ab \,{}^{\mathsf{a}}\|_{\{a\}}\, da = \{abda, adba, adab, dab, daab, daba\}$.

Manea et al. [12] introduced a different kind of shuflle operator where two words synchronise on a predefined set of words, called the backbones. Informally, for $u, v, t \in \Sigma^{\star}$ the synchronised shuffle of u and v on the backbone t requires that t is a subword of both u and v, and they have to synchronise on the positions forming t in both words. Formally, $u \,|||_t\, v$ the synchronised shuffle of u and v on the backbone t is defined as,

$$\begin{aligned} u \,|||_t\, v = \{x \mid \ t = \sigma_1 \cdots \sigma_{n-1} \wedge \ u_i, v_i \in \Sigma^{\star} \ \wedge u = u_1\sigma_1 \cdots \sigma_{n-1}u_n \ \wedge \\ v = v_1\sigma_1 \cdots \sigma_{n-1}v_n \ \wedge x \in (u_1 \sqcup\!\sqcup v_1)\sigma_1 \cdots \sigma_{n-1}(u_n \sqcup\!\sqcup v_n)\}. \end{aligned} \tag{1}$$

Moreover, given a language $L \subseteq \Sigma^{\star}$, we define

$$x \,|||_L\, y = \bigcup_{t \in L} x \,|||_t\, y. \tag{2}$$

Example 2. We have $acab \,|||_{ab}\, bab = \{acbab, abcab, bacab\}$.

Note that the operator $|||$ is commutative, but not associative. Given languages $L_1, L_2, L \subseteq \Sigma^{\star}$, $\Gamma \subseteq \Sigma$, and $\circ \in \{{}^{\mathsf{s}}\|_{\Gamma}, {}^{\mathsf{a}}\|_{\Gamma}, |||_L\}$ one has, as usual,

$$L_1 \circ L_2 = \bigcup_{u \in L_1, v \in L_2} u \circ v.$$

If L_1, L_2, and L are regular, then $L_1 \circ L_2$ is regular.

2.2 Regular Expressions with Synchronised Shuffle on Backbones

Let RE($|||$) denote the set of regular expressions RE extended with the ternary operator $|||$, i.e., the set of expressions containing $\emptyset$ and all terms generated by the following grammar

$$\alpha \rightarrow \varepsilon \mid \sigma \mid (\alpha + \alpha) \mid (\alpha \cdot \alpha) \mid (\alpha^{\star}) \mid (\alpha \,|||_{\alpha}\, \alpha), \tag{3}$$

where for expressions of the form $\alpha \mid\mid\mid_\gamma \beta$, we have $\mathcal{L}(\alpha \mid\mid\mid_\gamma \beta) = \mathcal{L}(\alpha) \mid\mid\mid_{\mathcal{L}(\gamma)} \mathcal{L}(\beta)$. Then, it follows by (1) that $\varepsilon(\alpha \mid\mid\mid_\gamma \beta) = \varepsilon(\alpha)\varepsilon(\gamma)\varepsilon(\beta)$. The following properties of $\mid\mid\mid$ are straightforward.

Lemma 1. *For all* $\alpha, \alpha', \beta, \gamma, \gamma' \in \mathrm{RE}(\mid\mid\mid)$, *we have*

1. $\alpha \mid\mid\mid_\gamma \beta \doteq \beta \mid\mid\mid_\gamma \alpha$;
2. $(\alpha + \alpha') \mid\mid\mid_\gamma \beta \doteq \alpha \mid\mid\mid_\gamma \beta + \alpha' \mid\mid\mid_\gamma \beta$;
3. $\alpha \mid\mid\mid_{\gamma+\gamma'} \beta \doteq \alpha \mid\mid\mid_\gamma \beta + \alpha \mid\mid\mid_{\gamma'} \beta$;
4. $\alpha \mid\mid\mid_\gamma \varepsilon \doteq \begin{cases} \alpha, & \text{if } \varepsilon(\gamma) = \varepsilon; \\ \emptyset, & \text{otherwise;} \end{cases}$
5. $\alpha \mid\mid\mid_\gamma \beta \doteq \emptyset$, *if* α, γ, *or* β *is* $\emptyset$.

3 Automata for Synchronised Shuffle on Backbones

In this section, we define a position (location) automaton $\mathcal{A}_{\mathrm{POS}}(\alpha)$ and a partial derivative automaton, $\mathcal{A}_{\mathrm{PD}}(\alpha)$, for $\alpha \in \mathrm{RE}(\mid\mid\mid)$. For standard regular expressions and several other extended expressions, the second is a quotient of the first. We show that this also holds for $\alpha \in \mathrm{RE}(\mid\mid\mid)$.

3.1 Location Based Position Automaton

Location automata are an extension of the classic position automata for regular expressions with shuffle operators [7,8]. Given a standard regular expression $\alpha \in$ RE, one can mark each occurrence of an alphabet symbol σ with its position i in α, reading it from left to right, i.e., representing this occurrence by σ^i. The resulting regular expression is a *marked* regular expression $\overline{\alpha}$ with all alphabet symbols occurring only once (linear) and belonging to $\Sigma_{\overline{\alpha}}$. The *Position* or *Glushkov automaton*, $\mathcal{A}_{\mathrm{POS}}(\alpha)$, is an NFA equivalent to α that is computed from sets of positions, specifying which occurrences of letters can appear at the beginning (First), which can follow each other (Follow), or appear as the last letter in a word generated by α (Last). In this section, we define a Glushkov automaton for expressions in $\mathrm{RE}(\mid\mid\mid)$, where locations are used instead of positions. Locations allow to specify how far a word has advanced in each of the components of an expression with nested shuffles [7,8]. Given $\alpha \in \mathrm{RE}(\mid\mid\mid)$, each location $p \in \mathsf{Loc}(\overline{\alpha})$ is a ternary tree, whose leaves are labelled either with 0, or with a position i. Additionally, instead of defining the set Last explicitly, we annotate each location p with a Boolean b. Whenever, $p \in \mathsf{Last}(\overline{\alpha})$, then the annotation of p is true, i.e., $\langle p : \mathsf{true}\rangle \in \mathsf{Loc}(\overline{\alpha})$. Furthermore, we define $\mathsf{Last}_0(\overline{\alpha}) = \mathsf{Last}(\overline{\alpha}) \cup \{0\}$ if $\varepsilon(\alpha) = \varepsilon$, and $\mathsf{Last}_0(\overline{\alpha}) = \mathsf{Last}(\overline{\alpha})$ otherwise. The set of *annotated locations* $\mathsf{Loc}(\overline{\alpha})$ is inductively defined as follows:

$$
\begin{aligned}
\mathsf{Loc}(\sigma^i) &= \{\langle i : \mathsf{true}\rangle\}, \quad \mathsf{Loc}(\varepsilon) = \emptyset, \\
\mathsf{Loc}(\overline{\alpha} + \overline{\beta}) &= \mathsf{Loc}(\overline{\alpha}) \cup \mathsf{Loc}(\overline{\beta}), \quad \mathsf{Loc}(\overline{\alpha}^\star) = \mathsf{Loc}(\overline{\alpha}), \\
\mathsf{Loc}(\overline{\alpha}\overline{\beta}) &= \begin{cases} \mathsf{Loc}(\overline{\alpha}) \cup \mathsf{Loc}(\overline{\beta}), \text{if } \varepsilon(\beta) = \varepsilon, \\ \{\langle p : \mathsf{false}\rangle \mid \langle p : \mathsf{b}\rangle \in \mathsf{Loc}(\overline{\alpha})\} \cup \mathsf{Loc}(\overline{\beta}), \text{otherwise}, \end{cases} \\
\mathsf{Loc}(\overline{\alpha} \mathbin{|||_{\overline{\gamma}}} \overline{\beta}) &= \{\langle (p,0,0) : \mathsf{b} \wedge (\varepsilon(\beta) = \varepsilon) \wedge (\varepsilon(\gamma) = \varepsilon)\rangle \mid \langle p : \mathsf{b}\rangle \in \mathsf{Loc}(\overline{\alpha})\} \\
&\cup \{\langle (0,0,r) : \mathsf{b} \wedge (\varepsilon(\alpha) = \varepsilon) \wedge (\varepsilon(\gamma) = \varepsilon)\rangle \mid \langle r : \mathsf{b}\rangle \in \mathsf{Loc}(\overline{\beta})\} \\
&\cup \{\langle (p,0,r) : \mathsf{b}_1 \wedge \mathsf{b}_2 \wedge (\varepsilon(\gamma) = \varepsilon)\rangle \mid \\
&\qquad\qquad \langle p : \mathsf{b}_1\rangle \in \mathsf{Loc}(\overline{\alpha}), \langle r : \mathsf{b}_2\rangle \in \mathsf{Loc}(\overline{\beta})\} \\
&\cup \{\langle (p,q,r) : \mathsf{b}_1 \wedge \mathsf{b}_2 \wedge \mathsf{b}_3\rangle \mid \\
&\qquad\qquad \langle p : \mathsf{b}_1\rangle \in \mathsf{Loc}(\overline{\alpha}), \langle r : \mathsf{b}_2\rangle \in \mathsf{Loc}(\overline{\beta}), \langle q : \mathsf{b}_3\rangle \in \mathsf{Loc}(\overline{\gamma})\}.
\end{aligned}
$$

Furthermore, let $\mathsf{Loc}_0(\overline{\alpha}) = \mathsf{Loc}(\overline{\alpha}) \cup \{\langle 0 : (\varepsilon(\alpha) = \varepsilon)\rangle\}$. It follows from the definition, that $\langle p : \mathsf{b}\rangle$, $\langle p : \mathsf{b}'\rangle \in \mathsf{Loc}(\overline{\alpha})$ implies $\mathsf{b} = \mathsf{b}'$. As such, we will omit the Boolean of an annotated location whenever convenient.

Example 3. Let $\theta = \alpha \mathbin{|||_\gamma} \beta$, where $\alpha = (ab^\star)^\star$, $\beta = (ba^\star)^\star$, and $\gamma = (ab)^\star$. Then $\overline{\theta} = (a^1(b^2)^\star)^\star \mathbin{|||_{(a^3b^4)^\star}} (b^5(a^6)^\star)^\star$, and $|\mathsf{Loc}_0(\overline{\theta})| = 17$, where

$$
\begin{aligned}
\mathsf{Loc}(\overline{\theta}) &= \{\langle (1,0,0) : \mathsf{true}\rangle, \langle (2,0,0) : \mathsf{true}\rangle\} \\
&\cup \{\langle (p,0,r) : \mathsf{true}\rangle \mid p \in \{0,1,2\}, r \in \{5,6\}\} \\
&\cup \{\langle (p,4,r) : \mathsf{true}\rangle \mid p \in \{1,2\}, r \in \{5,6\}\} \\
&\cup \{\langle (p,3,r) : \mathsf{false}\rangle \mid p \in \{1,2\}, r \in \{5,6\}\}.
\end{aligned}
$$

Due to the resemblance of $|||$ to the operator ${}^{\mathsf{a}}\|_\Gamma$, the definition of the sets First, Follow, and Last for expressions in RE($|||$) are extensions of the ones for ${}^{\mathsf{a}}\|_\Gamma$. For this reason, the proofs of Lemma 2, Lemma 3, and Lemma 4 show similarities to those for ${}^{\mathsf{a}}\|_\Gamma$, in [7]. The set Last can be restricted to the set of locations that occur in First and Follow. First, we define the set $\mathsf{First}(\overline{\alpha}) \subseteq \Sigma \times \mathsf{Loc}(\overline{\alpha})$. For the standard operators, the set First is defined inductively as usual, but explicitly associating a letter with each location.

$$
\mathsf{First}(\varepsilon) = \emptyset, \quad \mathsf{First}(\sigma^i) = \{(\sigma, i)\}, \quad \mathsf{First}(\overline{\alpha} + \overline{\beta}) = \mathsf{First}(\overline{\alpha}) \cup \mathsf{First}(\overline{\beta}),
$$

$$
\mathsf{First}(\overline{\alpha}^\star) = \mathsf{First}(\overline{\alpha}), \quad \mathsf{First}(\overline{\alpha}\overline{\beta}) = \begin{cases} \mathsf{First}(\overline{\alpha}) \cup \mathsf{First}(\overline{\beta}), & \text{if } \varepsilon(\alpha) = \varepsilon, \\ \mathsf{First}(\overline{\alpha}), & \text{otherwise}, \end{cases}
$$

$$
\begin{aligned}
\mathsf{First}(\overline{\alpha} \mathbin{|||_{\overline{\gamma}}} \overline{\beta}) &= \{(\sigma, (p,q,r)) \mid (\sigma, p) \in \mathsf{First}(\overline{\alpha}), (\sigma, q) \in \mathsf{First}(\overline{\gamma}), (\sigma, r) \in \mathsf{First}(\overline{\beta})\} \\
&\cup \{(\sigma, (p,0,0)) \mid (\sigma, p) \in \mathsf{First}(\overline{\alpha})\} \cup \{(\sigma, (0,0,r)) \mid (\sigma, r) \in \mathsf{First}(\overline{\beta})\}.
\end{aligned}
$$

Example 4. For θ from Example 3, we have

$$
\mathsf{First}(\overline{\theta}) = \{(a, \langle (1,0,0) : \mathsf{true}\rangle), (b, \langle (0,0,5) : \mathsf{true}\rangle)\}.
$$

Lemma 2. *Given $\alpha \in$ RE($|||$), if there is some $\sigma w \in \mathcal{L}(\alpha)$, then there is a location p such that $(\sigma, p) \in \mathsf{First}(\overline{\alpha})$.*

Now, we define the set $\mathsf{Follow}(\overline{\alpha}) \subseteq \mathsf{Loc}(\overline{\alpha}) \times \Sigma \times \mathsf{Loc}(\overline{\alpha})$. Again, for the standard operators the set First is defined inductively as usual, but considering explicitly the letter associated with each location. For the location $0 \in \mathsf{Loc}_0(\overline{\alpha})$ we define $\mathsf{Follow}(\overline{\alpha}, 0) = \mathsf{First}(\overline{\alpha})$.

$$\mathsf{Follow}(\varepsilon, p) = \mathsf{Follow}(\sigma^i, p) = \emptyset,$$

$$\mathsf{Follow}(\overline{\alpha} + \overline{\beta}, p) = \begin{cases} \mathsf{Follow}(\overline{\alpha}, p), & \text{if } p \in \mathsf{Loc}(\overline{\alpha}), \\ \mathsf{Follow}(\overline{\beta}, p), & \text{if } p \in \mathsf{Loc}(\overline{\beta}), \end{cases}$$

$$\mathsf{Follow}(\overline{\alpha}\overline{\beta}, p) = \begin{cases} \mathsf{Follow}(\overline{\alpha}, p), & \text{if } \langle p : \mathsf{false} \rangle \in \mathsf{Loc}(\overline{\alpha}), \\ \mathsf{Follow}(\overline{\alpha}, p) \cup \mathsf{First}(\overline{\beta}), & \text{if } \langle p : \mathsf{true} \rangle \in \mathsf{Loc}(\overline{\alpha}), \\ \mathsf{Follow}(\overline{\beta}, p), & \text{if } p \in \mathsf{Loc}(\overline{\beta}), \end{cases}$$

$$\mathsf{Follow}(\overline{\alpha}^\star, p) = \begin{cases} \mathsf{Follow}(\overline{\alpha}, p), & \text{if } \langle p : \mathsf{false} \rangle \in \mathsf{Loc}(\overline{\alpha}), \\ \mathsf{Follow}(\overline{\alpha}, p) \cup \mathsf{First}(\overline{\alpha}), & \text{if } \langle p : \mathsf{true} \rangle \in \mathsf{Loc}(\overline{\alpha}), \end{cases}$$

$$\begin{aligned} \mathsf{Follow}(\overline{\alpha} \mathbin{|||_{\overline{\gamma}}} \overline{\beta}, (p, q, r)) = {} & \{(\sigma, (p', q, r)) \mid (\sigma, p') \in \mathsf{Follow}(\overline{\alpha}, p)\} \\ \cup {} & \{(\sigma, (p, q, r')) \mid (\sigma, r') \in \mathsf{Follow}(\overline{\beta}, r)\} \\ \cup {} & \{(\sigma, (p', q', r')) \mid (\sigma, p') \in \mathsf{Follow}(\overline{\alpha}, p) \wedge \\ & \quad (\sigma, q') \in \mathsf{Follow}(\overline{\gamma}, q) \wedge (\sigma, r') \in \mathsf{Follow}(\overline{\beta}, r)\}. \end{aligned}$$

Example 5. For θ from Example 3, we have for instance,

$$\mathsf{Follow}(\overline{\theta}, (1,0,0)) = \{(a, (1,0,0)), (b, (2,0,0)), (b, (1,0,5))\},$$
$$\mathsf{Follow}(\overline{\theta}, (0,0,5)) = \{(a, (1,3,6)), (a, (0,0,6)), (a, (1,0,5)), (b, (0,0,5))\}.$$

Lemma 3. *Given $\alpha \in \mathrm{RE}(|||)$, if $x = \sigma_1 \cdots \sigma_n \in \mathcal{L}(\alpha)$ $(n \geq 0)$, then there is a sequence $p_0, p_1, \ldots, p_n \in \mathsf{Loc}_0(\overline{\alpha})$, such that $p_0 = 0$ and $(\sigma_i, p_i) \in \mathsf{Follow}(\overline{\alpha}, p_{i-1})$, $1 \leq i \leq n$ and $p_n \in \mathsf{Last}_0(\overline{\alpha})$.*

Lemma 4. *Given $\alpha \in \mathrm{RE}(|||)$, if there are $s_0 = 0, s_1, \ldots, s_n \in \mathsf{Loc}_0(\overline{\alpha})$ and $\sigma_1, \ldots, \sigma_n \in \Sigma$ $(n \geq 0)$ such that, (1) $(\sigma_i, s_i) \in \mathsf{Follow}(\overline{\alpha}, s_{i-1})$, $1 \leq i \leq n$, and (2) $s_n \in \mathsf{Last}_0(\overline{\alpha})$, then $\sigma_1 \cdots \sigma_n \in \mathcal{L}(\alpha)$.*

The *position automaton* for and expression $\alpha \in \mathrm{RE}(|||)$ is defined as follows.

$$\mathcal{A}_{\mathrm{POS}}(\alpha) = \langle \mathsf{Loc}_0(\overline{\alpha}), \Sigma, \delta_{\mathrm{POS}}, 0, \mathsf{Last}_0(\overline{\alpha}) \rangle,$$

where $\delta_{\mathrm{POS}}(p, \sigma) = \{q \mid (\sigma, q) \in \mathsf{Follow}(\overline{\alpha}, p)\}$ for $p \in \mathsf{Loc}_0(\overline{\alpha})$, $\sigma \in \Sigma$. The following proposition, states the correctness of this construction and is a consequence Lemma 2, Lemma 3, and Lemma 4.

Proposition 1. $\mathcal{L}(\mathcal{A}_{\mathrm{POS}}(\alpha)) = \mathcal{L}(\alpha)$.

Example 6. Consider again $\theta = \alpha \mathbin{|||}_\gamma \beta$, where $\alpha = (ab^\star)^\star$, $\beta = (ba^\star)^\star$, and $\gamma = (ab)^\star$. Let $\overline{\theta} = \overline{\alpha} \mathbin{|||}_{\overline{\gamma}} \overline{\beta} = (a^1(b^2)^\star)^\star \mathbin{|||}_{(a^3b^4)^\star} (b^5(a^6)^\star)^\star$. The sets needed to obtain the Glushkov automaton are $\mathsf{First}(\alpha \mathbin{|||}_\gamma \beta)$, that was computed in Example 4, and $\mathsf{Follow}(\alpha \mathbin{|||}_\gamma \beta)$, for which some elements were given in Example 5. The remaining elements of the Follow set can be obtained from the diagram of $\mathcal{A}_{\text{POS}}(\alpha \mathbin{|||}_\gamma \beta)$, which is depicted below. In the diagram each location $(p, q, r) \in \mathsf{Loc}_0(\overline{\alpha} \mathbin{|||}_{\overline{\gamma}} \overline{\beta})$ is represented by the sequence pqr. Transitions corresponding to synchronisations by letter a are drawn in red and the letter is omitted. The same applies to synchronisations by b, where the transitions are drawn in blue.

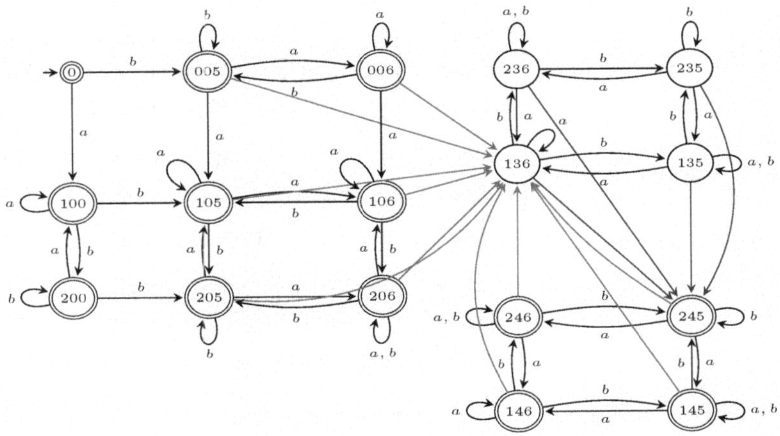

3.2 Partial Derivative Automaton

Partial derivatives [1] have been defined for the synchronised operators such as ${}^{\mathsf{s}}\|_\Gamma$ and ${}^{\mathsf{a}}\|_\Gamma$ by Sulzmann and Thiemann [14]. In the following, we define partial derivatives for the synchronised shuffle on backbones. Given $\alpha \in \text{RE}(|||)$, the set of partial derivatives of α by a symbol σ, $\partial_\sigma(\alpha)$, is defined as follows:

$$
\begin{aligned}
&\partial_\sigma(\emptyset) = \partial_\sigma(\varepsilon) = \emptyset,\ \partial_\sigma(\sigma') = \begin{cases} \{\varepsilon\} \text{ if } \sigma = \sigma', \\ \emptyset \text{ otherwise,} \end{cases} \quad \partial_\sigma(\alpha^\star) = \partial_\sigma(\alpha)\alpha^\star, \\
&\partial_\sigma(\alpha + \beta) = \partial_\sigma(\alpha) \cup \partial_\sigma(\beta), \quad \partial_\sigma(\alpha\beta) = \partial_\sigma(\alpha)\beta \cup \varepsilon(\alpha)\partial_\sigma(\beta), \\
&\partial_\sigma(\alpha \mathbin{|||}_\gamma \beta) = \partial_\sigma(\alpha) \mathbin{|||}_{\partial_\sigma(\gamma)} \partial_\sigma(\beta) \ \cup\ \partial_\sigma(\alpha) \mathbin{|||}_\gamma \{\beta\} \ \cup\ \{\alpha\} \mathbin{|||}_\gamma \partial_\sigma(\beta),
\end{aligned} \tag{4}
$$

where, for any $S, T, R \subseteq \text{RE}(|||) \setminus \{\emptyset\}$ we define $S \mathbin{|||}_\gamma T = \{\alpha \mathbin{|||}_\gamma \beta \mid \alpha \in S \wedge \beta \in T\}$, $S \mathbin{|||}_R T = \{\alpha \mathbin{|||}_\gamma \beta \mid \alpha \in S, \beta \in T, \gamma \in R\}$, and for $\alpha' \neq \varepsilon$, $S\alpha' = \{\alpha\alpha' \mid \alpha \in S \wedge \alpha \neq \varepsilon\} \cup (\varepsilon \in S)\{\alpha'\}$.

Proposition 2. *For* $\alpha, \beta, \gamma \in \text{RE}(|||)$, $\sigma \in \Sigma$, $\mathcal{L}(\partial_\sigma(\alpha \mathbin{|||}_\gamma \beta)) = \sigma^{-1}(\mathcal{L}(\alpha \mathbin{|||}_\gamma \beta))$.

Remark 1. Given $S, T, R \subseteq \text{RE}(|||)$, and $\sigma \in \Sigma$, one has that

$$\partial_\sigma(S \mathbin{|||}_T R) = \partial_\sigma(S) \mathbin{|||}_{\partial_\sigma(T)} \partial_\sigma(R) \ \cup\ \partial_\sigma(S) \mathbin{|||}_T R \ \cup\ S \mathbin{|||}_T \partial_\sigma(R).$$

As usual, the set of partial derivatives of $\alpha \in \mathrm{RE}(|||)$ w.r.t. a word $w \in \Sigma^\star$ is inductively defined by $\partial_\varepsilon(\alpha) = \{\alpha\}$ and $\partial_{\sigma w}(\alpha) = \partial_w(\partial_\sigma(\alpha))$. Moreover, $\mathcal{L}(\partial_w(\alpha)) = \{w_1 \mid ww_1 \in \mathcal{L}(\alpha)\}$. Let $\partial(\alpha) = \bigcup_{w \in \Sigma^\star} \partial_w(\alpha)$, and $\partial^+(\alpha) = \bigcup_{w \in \Sigma^+} \partial_w(\alpha)$. The partial derivative automaton of $\alpha \in \mathrm{RE}(|||)$ is

$$\mathcal{A}_{\mathrm{PD}}(\alpha) = \langle \partial(\alpha), \Sigma, \{\alpha\}, \delta_{\mathrm{PD}}, F_{\mathrm{PD}} \rangle,$$

with $F_{\mathrm{PD}} = \{\beta \in \partial(\alpha) \mid \varepsilon(\beta) = \varepsilon\}$ and $\delta_{\mathrm{PD}}(\beta, \sigma) = \partial_\sigma(\beta)$, for $\beta \in \partial(\alpha)$, $\sigma \in \Sigma$.

Example 7. For $\theta = \alpha \,|||_\gamma\, \beta$ from Example 3, where $\alpha = (ab^\star)^\star$, $\beta = (ba^\star)^\star$, and $\gamma = (ab)^\star$, the partial derivative automaton $\mathcal{A}_{\mathrm{PD}}(\theta)$ is depicted below. In the diagram the transitions corresponding to synchronisation are coloured in red and blue.

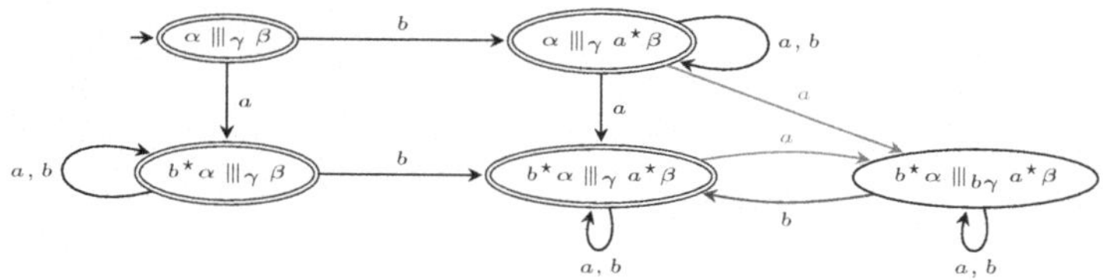

The following result is a consequence of Proposition 2.

Proposition 3. *For* $\alpha \in \mathrm{RE}(|||)$, *one has* $\mathcal{L}(\mathcal{A}_{\mathrm{PD}}(\alpha)) = \mathcal{L}(\alpha)$.

Support. For standard regular expressions, the set of partial derivatives has also been defined as the solution of a set of equations [9,13]. Formally, given an expression α over $\Sigma = \{\sigma_1, \ldots, \sigma_k\}$, a *support* for $\alpha = \alpha_0$ is a set of expressions $\{\alpha_1, \ldots, \alpha_n\}$ that satisfies a system of equations

$$\alpha_i \doteq \sigma_1\alpha_{i,1} + \cdots + \sigma_k\alpha_{i,k} + \varepsilon(\alpha_i), \quad 0 \le i \le n \tag{5}$$

where each of $\alpha_{i,1}, \ldots, \alpha_{i,k}$ is a (possibly empty) sum of elements in $\{\alpha_1, \ldots, \alpha_n\}$. Mirkin [13] showed that for a standard regular expression $\alpha \in \mathrm{RE}$, a support $\pi(\alpha)$ can be computed as follows:

$$\begin{array}{lll} \pi(\emptyset) = \pi(\varepsilon) = \emptyset, & \pi(\alpha + \beta) = \pi(\alpha) \cup \pi(\beta), & \pi(\alpha^\star) = \pi(\alpha)\alpha^\star, \\ \pi(\sigma) = \{\varepsilon\} \quad (\sigma \in \Sigma), & \pi(\alpha\beta) = \pi(\alpha)\beta \cup \pi(\beta), & \end{array} \tag{6}$$

Champarnaud et al., [9] showed that for $\alpha \in \mathrm{RE}$, $\pi(\alpha) = \partial^+(\alpha)$. The inductive definition of the support allows us to obtain average estimations of the size of $\partial(\alpha)$. Here, we extend the notion of support to $\alpha \in \mathrm{RE}(|||)$ by:

$$\pi(\alpha \,|||_\gamma\, \beta) = \pi(\alpha) \,|||_{\pi(\gamma)}\, \pi(\beta) \cup \pi(\alpha) \,|||_\gamma\, \pi(\beta) \cup \pi(\alpha) \,|||_\gamma\, \{\beta\} \cup \{\alpha\} \,|||_\gamma\, \pi(\beta). \tag{7}$$

Proposition 4. *Given* $\alpha \in \mathrm{RE}(|||)$, $\pi(\alpha) = \{\alpha_1, \ldots, \alpha_n\}$ *is a support for* $\alpha = \alpha_0$, *satisfying a system of equations of the form* (5).

Proposition 5. *Given $\alpha \in \mathrm{RE}(|||)$, one has $|\pi(\alpha)| \leq 3^{|\alpha|_\Sigma} - 1$.*

We now relate the set of partial derivatives of an expression α with the support $\pi(\alpha)$. For that, we first obtain an expression for the set of partial derivatives of α by a word w. Given a word $w \in \Sigma^\star$, let

$$\mathsf{Part}(w) = \{(w_1, w_2, w_3) \mid w \in w_1 \,|||_{w_3}\, w_2\}.$$

Proposition 6. *For $w \in \Sigma^\star$ we have,*

$$\frac{(|w|+1)(|w|+2)}{2} \;\leq\; |\mathsf{Part}(w)| \;\leq\; 3^{|w|}.$$

Proposition 7. *For $\alpha, \beta, \gamma \in \mathrm{RE}(|||)$ and $w \in \Sigma^\star$ the following holds:*

$$\partial_w(\alpha \,|||_\gamma\, \beta) = \bigcup_{(w_1,w_2,w_3)\in\mathsf{Part}(w)} \partial_{w_1}(\alpha) \,|||_{\partial_{w_3}(\gamma)}\, \partial_{w_2}(\beta).$$

Finally, we have the following result.

Proposition 8. *Given $\alpha \in \mathrm{RE}(|||)$, we have $\partial^+(\alpha) \subseteq \pi(\alpha)$.*

Example 8. For $\alpha \in \mathrm{RE}(|||)$ the inclusion $\pi(\alpha) \subseteq \partial^+(\alpha)$ does not hold in general. Let $\alpha = ab \,|||_{ab}\, b$. One has $b \,|||_b\, \varepsilon \in \pi(\alpha)$, but $b \,|||_b\, \varepsilon \notin \partial^+(\alpha)$.

3.3 $\mathcal{A}_{\mathrm{PD}}(\alpha)$ as a Quotient of $\mathcal{A}_{\mathrm{POS}}(\alpha)$

We show that $\mathcal{A}_{\mathrm{PD}}(\alpha)$ is a quotient of $\mathcal{A}_{\mathrm{POS}}(\alpha)$, for $\alpha \in \mathrm{RE}(|||)$. Again, the proof follows the lines of the one for regular expressions with the operator ${}^{\mathsf{a}}\|_\Gamma$, [7]. We associate to each location $p \in \mathsf{Loc}_0(\overline{\alpha})$, that is reachable in $\mathcal{A}_{\mathrm{POS}}$, a unique partial derivative of α, which will be denoted by $\mathsf{d}(\overline{\alpha}, p)$. For $\alpha \in \mathrm{RE}$ and a position $i \in \mathsf{Pos}(\overline{\alpha})$, $\mathsf{d}(\overline{\alpha}, i)$ corresponds to the unmarked c-continuation $\overline{\mathsf{c}(\overline{\alpha}, i)}$ [10]. Given a marked expression $\overline{\alpha}$, and a location $p \in \mathsf{Loc}_0(\overline{\alpha})$, we define $\mathsf{d}(\overline{\alpha}, p)$ as follows:

$$\mathsf{d}(\overline{\alpha}, 0) = \alpha, \quad \mathsf{d}(\sigma^i, i) = \varepsilon, \quad \mathsf{d}(\overline{\alpha}^\star, p) = \mathsf{d}(\overline{\alpha}, p)\alpha^\star,$$

$$\mathsf{d}(\overline{\alpha_1} + \overline{\alpha_2}, p) = \begin{cases} \mathsf{d}(\overline{\alpha_1}, p), & \text{if } p \in \mathsf{Loc}(\overline{\alpha_1}), \\ \mathsf{d}(\overline{\alpha_2}, p), & \text{if } p \in \mathsf{Loc}(\overline{\alpha_2}), \end{cases}$$

$$\mathsf{d}(\overline{\alpha_1}\overline{\alpha_2}, p) = \begin{cases} \mathsf{d}(\overline{\alpha_1}, p)\alpha_2, & \text{if } p \in \mathsf{Loc}(\overline{\alpha_1}), \\ \mathsf{d}(\overline{\alpha_2}, p), & \text{if } p \in \mathsf{Loc}(\overline{\alpha_2}), \end{cases}$$

$$\mathsf{d}(\overline{\alpha_1} \,|||_{\overline{\alpha_2}}\, \overline{\alpha_3}, (p_1, p_2, p_3)) = \mathsf{d}(\overline{\alpha_1}, p_1) \,|||_{\mathsf{d}(\overline{\alpha_2}, p_2)}\, \mathsf{d}(\overline{\alpha_3}, p_3).$$

Example 9. For $\alpha \,|||_\gamma\, \beta$ from Example 6, where $\alpha = (ab^\star)^\star$, $\beta = (ba^\star)^\star$, and $\gamma = (ab)^\star$ we have,

$$\begin{aligned} \mathsf{d}((a^1b^{2^\star})^\star \,|||_{(a^3b^4)^\star}\, (b^5a^{6^\star})^\star, (1,0,0)) &= \mathsf{d}((a^1b^{2^\star})^\star, 1) \,|||_{\mathsf{d}((a^3b^4)^\star, 0)}\, \mathsf{d}((b^5a^{6^\star})^\star, 0) \\ &= \mathsf{d}(a^1b^{2^\star}, 1)(ab^\star)^\star \,|||_{(ab)^\star}\, (ba^\star)^\star \\ &= \mathsf{d}(a^1, 1)b^\star(ab^\star)^\star \,|||_{(ab)^\star}\, (ba^\star)^\star \\ &= b^\star(ab^\star)^\star \,|||_{(ab)^\star}\, (ba^\star)^\star = b^\star\alpha \,|||_\gamma\, \beta. \end{aligned}$$

Equally, we have $\mathsf{d}((a^1b^{2^\star})^\star \,|||_{(a^3b^4)^\star}\, (b^5a^{6^\star})^\star, (2,0,0)) = b^\star\alpha \,|||_\gamma\, \beta$.

Lemma 5. *For* $\alpha \in \mathrm{RE}(|||)$, $\partial^+(\alpha) \subseteq \{\mathsf{d}(\overline{\alpha}, p) \mid p \in \mathsf{Loc}(\overline{\alpha})\}$.

Lemma 6. *For* $\alpha \in \mathrm{RE}(|||)$ *and* $p \in \mathsf{Loc}(\overline{\alpha})$, $\varepsilon(\mathsf{d}(\overline{\alpha}, p)) = \varepsilon \iff p \in \mathsf{Last}(\overline{\alpha})$.

The following proposition relates derivatives of $\mathsf{d}(\overline{\alpha}, p)$ with $\mathsf{Follow}(\overline{\alpha}, p)$.

Proposition 9. *For* $\alpha \in \mathrm{RE}(|||)$, $p \in \mathsf{Loc}_0(\overline{\alpha})$, *and* $\sigma \in \Sigma_\alpha$, *one has*

$$\partial_\sigma(\mathsf{d}(\overline{\alpha}, p)) = \{\mathsf{d}(\overline{\alpha}, q) \mid (\sigma, q) \in \mathsf{Follow}(\overline{\alpha}, p)\}.$$

Consider the equivalence relation $\equiv_c \subseteq \mathsf{Loc}_0(\overline{\alpha}) \times \mathsf{Loc}_0(\overline{\alpha})$ defined by $p \equiv_c q$ iff $\mathsf{d}(\overline{\alpha}, p) = \mathsf{d}(\overline{\alpha}, q)$.

Lemma 7. *The relation* $\equiv_c$ *is right-invariant w.r.t.* $\mathcal{A}_{\mathrm{POS}}(\alpha)$.

Finally, considering the isomorphism $\varphi_c : \mathsf{Loc}_0(\overline{\alpha})/\!\equiv_c \longrightarrow \partial^+(\alpha)$, defined by $\varphi_c([p]) = \mathsf{d}(\overline{\alpha}, p)$, we have for $\alpha \in \mathrm{RE}(|||)$

Proposition 10. $\mathcal{A}_{\mathrm{POS}}(\alpha)/\!\equiv_c \simeq \mathcal{A}_{\mathrm{PD}}(\alpha)$.

Example 10. Consider the expression $\theta = \alpha \,|||_\gamma\, \beta$, where $\alpha = (ab^\star)^\star$, $\beta = (ba^\star)^\star$ and $\gamma = (ab)^\star$, from Example 6. $\mathcal{A}_{\mathrm{PD}}(\theta)$ can be obtained by merging states in $\mathcal{A}_{\mathrm{POS}}(\theta)$, which belong to the same equivalence class under $\equiv_c$. For this, one can compute $\mathsf{d}(\overline{\theta}, p)$, where p is a state in $\mathcal{A}_{\mathrm{POS}}(\theta)$ as defined in Example 6. We have,

$$\begin{aligned}
\mathsf{d}(\overline{\alpha} \,|||_{\overline{\gamma}}\, \overline{\beta}, 0) &= \alpha \,|||_\gamma\, \beta, \\
\mathsf{d}(\overline{\alpha} \,|||_{\overline{\gamma}}\, \overline{\beta}, p) &= \alpha \,|||_\gamma\, a^\star\beta, && \text{for } p \in \{005, 006\}, \\
\mathsf{d}(\overline{\alpha} \,|||_{\overline{\gamma}}\, \overline{\beta}, p) &= b^\star\alpha \,|||_\gamma\, \beta, && \text{for } p \in \{100, 200\}, \\
\mathsf{d}(\overline{\alpha} \,|||_{\overline{\gamma}}\, \overline{\beta}, p) &= b^\star\alpha \,|||_\gamma\, a^\star\beta, && \text{for } p \in \{105, 106, 205, 206, 145, 146, 245, 246\}, \\
\mathsf{d}(\overline{\alpha} \,|||_{\overline{\gamma}}\, \overline{\beta}, p) &= b^\star\alpha \,|||_{b\gamma}\, a^\star\beta, && \text{for } p \in \{135, 136, 235, 236\}.
\end{aligned}$$

Therefore, the partial derivative automaton $\mathcal{A}_{\mathrm{PD}}(\alpha \,|||_\gamma\, \beta)$ is the one depicted in Example 7.

4 Average Case Complexity of Partial Derivatives

To better gauge the size of the automaton, and not only in its worst case, we turn to the techniques of Analytic Combinatorics. Recall that, given a measure of the objects of a combinatorial class, $\mathcal{A}$, for each $n \in \mathbb{N}_0$, let a_n be the sum of the values of this measure for all objects of size n. Set $A(z) = \sum_n a_n z^n$, the corresponding generating function (*cf.* [11]). We will use the notation $[z^n]A(z)$ for a_n. The generating function $A(z)$ can be seen as a complex analytic function, and when this function has a unique dominant singularity ρ, the study of the behaviour of $A(z)$ around it gives us access to the asymptotic form of its coefficients. In particular, if $A(z)$ is analytic in some indented disc neighbourhood of ρ, then one has the following [11, Corol. VI.1, p. 392]:

Theorem 1. *The coefficients of the series expansion of the complex function*

$$f(z) \underset{z \to \rho}{\sim} \lambda \left(1 - \frac{z}{\rho}\right)^{\nu},$$

where $\nu \in \mathbb{C} \setminus \mathbb{N}_0$, $\lambda \in \mathbb{C}$, *have the asymptotic approximation*

$$[z^n]f(z) = \frac{\lambda}{\Gamma(-\nu)} n^{-\nu-1}\rho^{-n} + o\left(n^{-\nu-1}\rho^{-n}\right).$$

Here Γ *is, as usual, the Euler's gamma function and the notation* $f(z) \underset{z \to z_0}{\sim} g(z)$ *means that* $\lim_{z \to z_0} \frac{f(z)}{g(z)} = 1$.

We consider the set of expressions RE(|||) defined in (3). Let $R_k(z)$ be the generating function, whose coefficient $[z^n]R_k(z)$ is the cumulative number of regular expressions in RE(|||) of size n. Then

$$R_k(z) = (k+1)z + 2zR_k(z)^2 + zR_k(z) + zR_k(z)^3.$$

Regular expressions that have ε in their language, denoted by α_ε, are unambiguously generated by the following grammar

$$\alpha_\varepsilon \to \varepsilon \mid (\alpha_\varepsilon + \alpha) \mid (\alpha_{\overline{\varepsilon}} + \alpha_\varepsilon) \mid (\alpha_\varepsilon \alpha_\varepsilon) \mid (\alpha^\star) \mid (\alpha_\varepsilon \mathbin{|||}_{\alpha_\varepsilon} \alpha_\varepsilon), \tag{8}$$

where $\alpha_{\overline{\varepsilon}}$ represents regular expressions that do not have ε in their language. Using $R_{\overline{\varepsilon},k}(z) = R_k(z) - R_{\varepsilon,k}(z)$, the generating function for α_ε satisfies

$$R_{\varepsilon,k}(z) = z + 2zR_k(z)R_{\varepsilon,k}(z) + zR_k(z) + zR_{\varepsilon,k}(z)^3.$$

Using the techniques expounded in [5], we got:

$$[z^n]R_k(z) \underset{n \to \infty}{\sim} \frac{r_k}{2\sqrt{\pi}} \rho_k^{-n} n^{-\frac{3}{2}}, \tag{9}$$

where ρ_k is the only real zero of the polynomial $(27k^2 + 50k + 23)z^3 + 4(9k + 16)z^2 + 8z - 4$, since its discriminant is $-16(k+1)(27k+19)^3$, which is negative, and r_k has the following asymptotic behaviour

$$r_k \underset{k \to \infty}{\sim} \sqrt[3]{\frac{k}{2}}, \qquad \text{while} \qquad \rho_k \underset{k \to \infty}{\sim} \frac{1}{3}\left(\frac{2}{k}\right)^{\frac{2}{3}}. \tag{10}$$

4.1 Average Case of the Alphabetic Size

Let $\ell(\alpha)$ be the cost function for an upper bound of the alphabetic size of $\alpha \in$ RE(|||). By the grammar (3), we have:

$$\ell(\varepsilon) = 0, \quad \ell(\sigma) = 1, \quad \ell(\alpha^\star) = \ell(\alpha),$$
$$\ell(\alpha + \beta) = \ell(\alpha\beta) = \ell(\alpha) + \ell(\beta), \quad \ell(\alpha \mathbin{|||}_\gamma \beta) = \ell(\alpha) + \ell(\beta) + \ell(\gamma).$$

The corresponding generating function L_k satisfies the following equality:

$$L_k(z) = kz + zL_k(z) + 4zL_k(z)R_k(z) + 3zL_k(z)R_k(z)^2,$$

and its dominant singularity is the same, ρ_k, as above. One has:

$$[z^n]L_k(z) \underset{n\to\infty}{\sim} \frac{1}{c_k\sqrt{\pi}}\rho_k^{-n}n^{-\frac{1}{2}}, \quad \text{where} \quad c_k \underset{k\to\infty}{\sim} 3\sqrt[3]{\frac{2}{k}}.$$

From this one concludes:

Proposition 11. *The average of an upper bound of the alphabetic size of an* $\alpha \in RE(|||)$ *of size* n *is*

$$\frac{[z^n]L_k(z)}{[z^n]R_k(z)} \underset{n,\,k\to\infty}{\sim} \frac{2}{3}n. \tag{11}$$

We note that this result only depends on the number of different operators and their cardinalities occuring in the expressions generated by (3), and it is in line with the ones obtained for other sets of regular expressions [2–4].

4.2 Average Case of the Partial Derivatives by a Symbol

Let $\mathsf{t}(\alpha)$ be the cost function for an upper bound of the size of $\partial_\sigma(\alpha)$ for a given symbol $\sigma \in \Sigma$. Using (4), we have $\mathsf{t}(\varepsilon) = 0$ and

$$\begin{aligned}
&\mathsf{t}(\alpha+\beta) = \mathsf{t}(\alpha)+\mathsf{t}(\beta),\ \mathsf{t}(\alpha^\star) = \mathsf{t}(\alpha), && \mathsf{t}(\sigma) = 1, \qquad \mathsf{t}(\sigma') = 0, \quad \text{for } \sigma' \neq \sigma,\\
&\mathsf{t}(\alpha_\varepsilon\beta) = \mathsf{t}(\alpha_\varepsilon)+\mathsf{t}(\beta),\ \mathsf{t}(\alpha_{\overline{\varepsilon}}\beta) = \mathsf{t}(\alpha_{\overline{\varepsilon}}), && \mathsf{t}(\alpha \,|||_\gamma\, \beta) = \mathsf{t}(\alpha)\,\mathsf{t}(\beta)\,\mathsf{t}(\gamma)+\mathsf{t}(\alpha)+\mathsf{t}(\beta).
\end{aligned}$$

The corresponding generating function T_k satisfies the following equality:

$$T_k(z) = z + zT_k(z) + 3zT_k(z)R_k(z) + 2zT_k(z)R_k(z)^2 + zT_k(z)R_{\varepsilon,k}(z) + zT_k(z)^3.$$

Once more, using the techniques detailed in [5], we found that the asymptotic behaviour of the average number of transitions per state in the partial derivative automaton is dramatically different depending on whether $k \in \{2,3\}$ or not.

In all cases, one has

$$[z^n]T_k(z) \underset{n\to\infty}{\sim} \frac{s_k}{2\sqrt{\pi}}\rho_k^{-n}n^{-\frac{3}{2}}, \tag{12}$$

where, for $k \geq 4$, ρ_k is, as above, the only real zero of the polynomial $(27k^2 + 50k+23)z^3+4(9k+8)z^2+8z-4$, and s_k has the following asymptotic behaviour

$$s_k \underset{k\to\infty}{\sim} 4\left(\frac{2}{k}\right)^{\frac{2}{3}} \qquad (\text{for } k \geq 4). \tag{13}$$

Hence, from (12), (13), and (9) we have

Proposition 12. *For alphabets of size $k \geq 4$, the average of the upper bound (here considered) of the size of the set $\bigcup_{\sigma \in \Sigma} \partial_\sigma(\alpha)$ for $\alpha \in \mathrm{RE}(|||)$ of size n is*

$$\frac{k[z^n]T_k(z)}{[z^n]R_k(z)} \underset{n,\,k \to \infty}{\sim} 8 \qquad (\text{for } k \geq 4).$$

When $k = 2$ and $k = 3$, the singularity ρ_k is the largest real root of a 27th degree irreducible polynomial with integer coefficients, the largest of which has 23 digits, when $k = 2$, and 25 digits when $k = 3$. For these two cases, we have obtained

$$s_2 \simeq 4.31592, \qquad \rho_2 \simeq 0.1432765,$$
$$s_3 \simeq 7.87998, \qquad \rho_3 \simeq 0.1249227.$$

This, yields

Proposition 13. *For alphabets of size $k = 2$ and $k = 3$, the average of the upper bound (here considered) of the size of the set $\bigcup_{\sigma \in \Sigma} \partial_\sigma(\alpha)$ for $\alpha \in \mathrm{RE}(|||)$ of size n is*

$$\frac{2[z^n]T_2(z)}{[z^n]R_2(z)} \simeq 7.50281 \times (1.00528)^n,$$

and

$$\frac{3[z^n]T_3(z)}{[z^n]R_3(z)} \simeq 18.689 \times (1.00062)^n,$$

respectively.

This is a rather curious result, quite different from all we have seen so far: the average number of transitions per state in the partial derivative automaton grows exponentially with n, for alphabets of sizes 2 and 3, but for larger alphabets tends to 8, independently of the size of the alphabet! This last behaviour, of tending to a constant, is what we observed for the standard operator, as well as for several other shuffle operators [6].

Comparison with Experimental Results. Using the AsymptoticSolve function of Mathematica^{TM}, we explicitly calculated the coefficients of the series $R_k(z)$ and $T_k(z)$, for $n = 25, 50, 100$, and $k = 10, 20, 30$, and compare the coefficient $\frac{k[z^n]T_k(z)}{[z^n]R_k(z)}$ with experimental results obtained by uniformally randomly generate 10000 expressions for each n and k. The following table gives the respective results where for each k the first row is the estimates obtained as mentioned above and the second the average number $|\partial_\Sigma(\alpha)|$ obtained experimentally.

$k\backslash n$	25	50	100
10	4.04351	5.16564	6.19391
	3.88440	4.70930	5.40850
20	4.12441	5.16752	6.06656
	4.05950	4.86430	5.59510
30	4.17232	5.19746	6.06641
	4.10030	4.98480	5.72140

4.3 Average Case of the Support

Let $\mathsf{p}(\alpha)$ be the cost function for an upper bound of the size of $\pi(\alpha)$. Using (6) and (7), we have:

$$\begin{aligned}&\mathsf{p}(\varepsilon) = 0,\ \mathsf{p}(\sigma) = 1,\ \mathsf{p}(\alpha^\star) = \mathsf{p}(\alpha),\ \mathsf{p}(\alpha+\beta) = \mathsf{p}(\alpha\beta)\,\mathsf{p}(\alpha) + \mathsf{p}(\beta),\\ &\mathsf{p}(\alpha \,|||_\gamma\, \beta) = \mathsf{p}(\alpha)\,\mathsf{p}(\beta)\,\mathsf{p}(\gamma) + \mathsf{p}(\alpha)\,\mathsf{p}(\beta) + \mathsf{p}(\alpha) + \mathsf{p}(\beta).\end{aligned} \tag{14}$$

The generating function for $\mathsf{p}(\alpha)$, $P_k(z)$, satisfies the following equality:

$$P_k(z) = kz + 4zP_k(z)R_k(z) + 2zP_k(z)R_k(z)^2 + zP_k(z)^2R_k(z) + zP_k(z) + zP_k(z)^3.$$

Using again the techniques described in [5], we got:

$$[z^n]P_k(z) \underset{n\to\infty}{\sim} \frac{p_k}{2\sqrt{\pi}}\,\xi_k^{-n} n^{-\frac{3}{2}}, \tag{15}$$

where ξ_k is the dominant singularity of $P_k(z)$, which, using Puiseux expansions, can be seen to be the only real root of a polynomial of degree 9, and

$$p_k \underset{k\to\infty}{\sim} \frac{(1+\sqrt{17})^{\frac{1}{9}}}{2^{\frac{11}{9}}3^{\frac{5}{6}}} k^{\frac{1}{3}}. \tag{16}$$

Using Newton's polygon technique, one can see that

$$\xi_k \underset{k\to\infty}{\sim} \zeta\, k^{-\frac{2}{3}},$$

where ζ is the only real root of the polynomial $658\,503\,x^3 - 73\,600\,x^2 + 2\,652\,x - 36$. From (15), (16), and (9) it follows that

$$\frac{[z^n]P_k(z)}{[z^n]R_k(z)} \underset{n\to\infty}{\sim} \frac{(1+\sqrt{17})^{\frac{1}{9}}}{2^{\frac{8}{9}}\,3^{\frac{5}{6}}} \left(\frac{\rho_k}{\xi_k}\right)^n. \tag{17}$$

It turns out that

$$\frac{\rho_k}{\xi_k} \underset{k\to\infty}{\sim} 1.35488,$$

the only real root of the polynomial $6561x^9 - 71604x^6 + 294400x^3 - 390244$. The value of $(1+\sqrt{17})^{\frac{1}{9}}/2^{\frac{8}{9}}\,3^{\frac{5}{6}}$ is approximately 0.25921, which gives

$$\frac{[z^n]P_k(z)}{[z^n]R_k(z)} \underset{n\to\infty,\,k\to\infty}{\sim} 0.25921 \times (1.35488 + o(1))^n. \tag{18}$$

Taking into account Proposition 5, one gets the following significant improvement, when compared with the worst case, for the average case upper bound.

Proposition 14. *An upper bound for the average size of* $\mathcal{A}_{\mathrm{PD}}$ *for expressions in* RE(|||) *is* $0.25921 \times (1.57708 + o(1))^{|\alpha|_\Sigma}$, *for large sizes of the alphabet and regular expressions.*

References

1. Antimirov, V.M.: Partial derivatives of regular expressions and finite automaton constructions. Theoret. Comput. Sci. **155**(2), 291–319 (1996)
2. Bastos, R., Broda, S., Machiavelo, A., Moreira, N., Reis, R.: On the average complexity of partial derivative automata for semi-extended expressions. J. Autom. Lang. Comb. **22**(1–3), 5–28 (2017)
3. Broda, S., Machiavelo, A., Moreira, N., Reis, R.: On the average size of Glushkov and partial derivative automata. Int. J. Found. Comput. Sci. **23**(5), 969–984 (2012)
4. Broda, S., Machiavelo, A., Moreira, N., Reis, R.: Automata for regular expressions with shuffle. Inf. Comput. **259**(2), 162–173 (2018)
5. Broda, S., Machiavelo, A., Moreira, N., Reis, R.: Analytic combinatorics and descriptional complexity of regular languages on average. ACM SIGACT News **51**(1), 38–56 (2020)
6. Broda, S., Machiavelo, A., Moreira, N., Reis, R.: Average complexity of partial derivatives for synchronised shuffle expressions. In: Nagy, B., (ed.), *27th CIAA*, volume 14151 of *LNCS*, pp. 103–115. Springer (2023)
7. Broda, S., Machiavelo, A., Moreira, N., Reis, R.: Location automata for synchronised shuffle expressions. *J. Log. Algebr. Program.***133** (2023)
8. Broda, S., Machiavelo, A., Moreira, N., Reis, R.: Location based automata for expressions with shuffle and intersection. Inf. Comput. **295**, 104917 (2023)
9. Champarnaud, J.M., Ziadi, D.: From Mirkin's prebases to Antimirov's word partial derivatives. Fundam. Inform. **45**(3), 195–205 (2001)
10. Champarnaud, J.M., Ziadi, D.: Canonical derivatives, partial derivatives and finite automaton constructions. Theoret. Comput. Sci. **289**, 137–163 (2002)
11. Flajolet, P., Sedgewick, R.: *Analytic Combinatorics*. CUP (2008)
12. Manea, F., Mitrana, V., Voinescu, D.-C.: Synchronized shuffle on backbones. Fundam. Inform **73**(1–2), 191–202 (2006)
13. Mirkin, B.G.: An algorithm for constructing a base in a language of regular expressions. Eng. Cybern. **5**, 51–57 (1966)
14. Sulzmann, M., Thiemann, P.: Derivatives and partial derivatives for regular shuffle expressions. J. Comput. Syst. Sci. **104**, 323–341 (2019)
15. ter Beek, M.H., Martín-Vide, C., Mitrana, V.: Synchronized shuffles. Theoret. Comput. Sci. **341**, 263–275 (2005)

Two-Word Shuffle: Some Results

Guilherme Duarte, Nelma Moreira(✉), and Rogério Reis

CMUP and DCC, Faculdade de Ciências da Universidade do Porto,
Rua do Campo Alegre, 4169-007 Porto, Portugal
{guilherme.duarte,nelma.moreira,rogerio.reis}@fc.up.pt

Abstract. In this paper, we study the shuffle operator on two words. First, we give a combinatorial analysis of the number of distinct languages generated by such shuffle operations, relying on known results that ensure their uniqueness. We establish a bijection between two-word shuffles and initial segments of natural numbers, enabling the enumeration and a natural uniform random generation of shuffle languages. As the shuffle of two words corresponds to a language where all the words have the same length, a block language, we show how to inductively construct its bitmap representation. We then turn our attention to both deterministic and nondeterministic state complexity of the shuffle square of a word, i.e., the shuffle of a word with itself. Finally, we examine the average state complexity of the partial derivative automata for the two-word shuffle.

1 Introduction

The shuffle of two words u and v (denoted by $u \sqcup\!\sqcup v$) is the set of words corresponding to the interleaving of u and v, while maintaining the internal order of the symbols in each word. It is naturally extended to languages, by shuffling words from each language in all possible combinations.

This operation has been extensively studied in the context of formal languages. It is known that determining whether a word w belongs to the shuffle of two words u and v lies in P [15]. However, deciding if w is in the shuffle of n words becomes NP-COMPLETE [16]. Berstel and Boasson [1] established that a finite set of words S can be decomposed into a multiset P such that S is the shuffle of the words in P, and P is unique up to normalisation. This result was extended by Biegler et al. [2], showing that if the shuffle of two words u and v is equal to the shuffle of two languages L_1 and L_2, then L_1 and L_2 must each be singletons containing the words u and v. Biegler et al. [4] provides an algorithm that given a deterministic finite automaton (DFA) $\mathcal{A}$ outputs in polynomial time two words u and v such that if the language of the automaton is a shuffle language $u \sqcup\!\sqcup v = \mathcal{L}(\mathcal{A})$, otherwise the answer is meaningless. To decide if the shuffle of two words is contained in the language recognised by a DFA is

Rogério Reis: This work was partially supported by CMUP through the FCT projects UIDB/00144/2020 and UIDP/00144/2020, by AVATAR through the FCT project 2023.12169.PEX, and by the FCT grant 2024.01528.BD.

Published by Springer Nature Switzerland AG 2025
A. Malcher and L. Prigioniero (Eds.): DCFS 2025, LNCS 15759, pp. 79–93, 2025.
https://doi.org/10.1007/978-3-031-97100-6_6

in P [4]. However, given a nondeterministic finite automaton (NFA) $\mathcal{A}$ and two words u and v, the problems of deciding if $u \sqcup\!\sqcup v \not\subseteq \mathcal{L}(\mathcal{A})$ or $\mathcal{L}(\mathcal{A}) \not\subseteq u \sqcup\!\sqcup v$ are both NP-COMPLETE [11].

Regular languages are closed under the shuffle operation. Brzozowski et al. [7] showed that a (complete) DFA with $2^{mn-1} + 2^{(m-1)(n-1)}(2^{m-1} - 1)(2^{n-1} - 1)$ states is sufficient to accept the shuffle of two regular languages accepted by DFAs with m and n states, respectively. The tightness is only known if $2 \leq m \leq 5$ and $n \geq 2$, and also if $m = n = 6$. For incomplete DFAs, Câmpeanu et al. [8] shown that $2^{mn} - 1$ is a tight bound for the shuffle of two regular languages. For the shuffle of two words u and v, $O(2^{m+1}n)$ states are sufficient for a DFA to recognise their shuffle, where m and n are the lengths of u and v, respectively, with $m \leq n$ [3]. But this upper bound seems not possible to attain. For both the shuffle of two languages and the shuffle of two words, an NFA recognising the shuffle of the operands requires at most mn states and it is tight [3,7].

Despite all these advances, several questions remain open. For example, it is not known whether a language L can be expressed as the result of the shuffle of two other languages; what is the complexity of deciding whether $\mathcal{L}(\mathcal{A}) \neq u \sqcup\!\sqcup v$, given a DFA $\mathcal{A}$ and words u and v; and if the bounds for the size of the DFAs are tight.

In this paper we study the shuffle operator on two words. First, we give a combinatorial analysis of the number of distinct languages generated by such shuffle operations. Then, we establish a bijective correspondence between two-word shuffles and initial segments of natural numbers, enabling the enumeration and a natural uniform random generation of shuffle languages. As the shuffle of two words corresponds to a language where all the words have the same length, we show how to inductively obtain its bitmap representation. We then explore both the deterministic and nondeterministic state complexity associated with the operation of shuffling a word with itself. Finally, we examine the average state complexity of the partial derivative automata for the two-word shuffle.

2 Preliminaries

In this section, we establish the notation used. Given two integers i, j with $i < j$, let $[i, j]$ denote the range from i to j, including both i and j, namely $\{i, \ldots, j\}$. Moreover, we shall omit the left bound if it is equal to 0, thus $[j] = \{0, \ldots, j\}$.

Given an *alphabet* $\Sigma = \{a_1, \ldots, a_k\}$, a *word* w is a sequence of symbols, and a *language* $L \subseteq \Sigma^\star$ is a set of words over Σ. We represent a singleton language by its element. Let $|w|$ denote the length of a word w and the empty word be denoted by ε. The number of occurrences of an alphabetic symbol $a \in \Sigma$ in a word w is denoted by $|w|_a$. We consider the alphabet Σ ordered. Given two words $u, v \in \Sigma^\star$ we say that u is *lexicographically* less than v, denoted as $u < v$ if either $|u| < |v|$, or $|u| = |v|$ and the words can be written as $u = xay_1$, $v = xby_2$ with $a < b$, for $a, b \in \Sigma$ and $x, y_1, y_2 \in \Sigma^\star$.

The *(left) quotient* of a language $L \subseteq \Sigma^\star$ w.r.t. a symbol $a \in \Sigma$ is $a^{-1}L = \{x \mid ax \in L\}$. The left quotient of L w.r.t. a word $w \in \Sigma^\star$ is then inductively defined by $\varepsilon^{-1}L = L$ and $(xa)^{-1}L = a^{-1}(x^{-1}L)$.

A *nondeterministic finite automaton* (NFA) is a five-tuple $\mathcal{A} = \langle Q, \Sigma, \delta, I, F\rangle$ where Q is the set of states, Σ is the alphabet, $\delta : Q \times \Sigma \to 2^Q$ is the transition function, $I \subseteq Q$ is the set of initial states, and $F \subseteq Q$ is the set of final states. When $I = \{q_0\}$, we use $I = q_0$. The *size* of an NFA $\mathcal{A}$ is $|Q|$. The *right language* of $q \in Q$ is $\mathcal{L}_q(\mathcal{A}) = \{ w \in \Sigma^\star \mid \delta(q, w) \cap F \neq \emptyset \}$. The *language accepted* by $\mathcal{A}$ is $\mathcal{L}(\mathcal{A}) = \bigcup_{q\in I} \mathcal{L}_q(\mathcal{A})$. An NFA $\mathcal{A}$ is *minimal* if there is no smaller NFA with the same language. An NFA is *deterministic* (DFA) if $|I| = 1$ and $|\delta(q, a)| \leq 1$, for all $(q, a) \in Q \times \Sigma$. We can convert an NFA into an equivalent DFA by using the well-known subset construction. Two states $q_1, q_2 \in Q$, are *equivalent* (or *indistinguishable*) if $\mathcal{L}_{q_1}(\mathcal{A}) = \mathcal{L}_{q_2}(\mathcal{A})$. A DFA is *minimal* if it has no equivalent states, in which case it is unique up to renaming of states. The *state complexity* of a language L, $sc(L)$, is the size of the minimal DFA accepting L. The *nondeterministic state complexity* of a language L, $nsc(L)$, is defined analogously.

A NFA $\mathcal{A} = \langle Q, \Sigma, \delta, q_0, F\rangle$ for a non-empty finite language, whose longest word is $\ell \geq 0$, is *acyclic* and *ranked*, i.e., the set of states Q can be partitioned into $\ell + 1$ sets $Q_0, Q_1, \ldots Q_\ell$ such that for every state $q \in Q_i$, $\mathcal{A}$ reaches a final state by words of length at most i, and all transitions from states in Q_i lead only to states in Q_j, with $j < i$. We define the i-th *layer* of an automaton as the set of states that are reachable from the initial state by words of length i, and the i-th *rank* as the set of states whose longest word that reaches a final state has length i. A DFA for a finite language is also ranked but it may have a *dead state*, which is the only cyclic state with no rank nor layer.

3 Shuffle of Two Words

Given u, $v \in \Sigma^\star$, the *shuffle* of u and v is the set $u \sqcup\!\sqcup\, v$ defined as follows

$$u \sqcup\!\sqcup\, v = \{ u_1v_1 \cdots u_mv_n \mid u = u_1 \cdots u_m, v = v_1 \cdots v_n,\\ u_i \in \Sigma^\star, v_j \in \Sigma^\star, i \in [1, m], j \in [1, n] \}.$$

Alternatively, the shuffle operation can be inductively defined as follows, where $a, b \in \Sigma$:

$$\begin{aligned} \varepsilon \sqcup\!\sqcup\, u &= u \sqcup\!\sqcup\, \varepsilon = u \\ au \sqcup\!\sqcup\, bv &= \{ aw \mid w \in u \sqcup\!\sqcup\, bv \} \cup \{ bw \mid w \in au \sqcup\!\sqcup\, v \}, \end{aligned}$$

It is clear that the shuffle operation is commutative. We say that $L \subseteq \Sigma^\star$ is *(two-word) shuffle decomposable* (or, alternatively, a *shuffle language*) if there exists words $u, v \in \Sigma^\star$ such that $L = u \sqcup\!\sqcup\, v$. Note that if L is shuffle decomposable, then every word in L is of the same length, i.e., L is a *block language*.

Lemma 1 (Berstel and Boasson [1]). *If $L \subseteq \Sigma^\star$ is two-word shuffle decomposable, then there is a unique decomposition into words u and v such that $u \sqcup\!\sqcup v = L$, provided that u and v contain at least two distinct symbols within.*

Let $|\Sigma| = k$ and $k > 1$. If we consider pairs of words lexicographically ordered, each pair represents uniquely a shuffle language. Formally, let $\mathcal{S}_k$ be the set

$$\mathcal{S}_k = \{ (u, v) \in \Sigma^\star \times \Sigma^\star \mid \sum_{a\in\Sigma} |uv|_a > 1,\ |u| < |v| \text{ or } |u| = |v| \wedge u \leq v \}.$$

We define the *block length* of a pair $(u, v) \in \mathcal{S}_k$ as $\ell = |u| + |v|$. Moreover, we denote the restriction of $\mathcal{S}_k$ to a specific block length $\ell > 1$ as $\mathcal{S}_k^\ell$. Then, we have

Theorem 1. *Let $\ell, k > 1$, then*

$$|\mathcal{S}_k^\ell| = \begin{cases} (k^\ell - k)(\frac{\ell-1}{2} + 1), & \textit{if } \ell \textit{ is odd;} \\ (k^\ell - k)\frac{\ell}{2} + \frac{k^{\ell/2}(k^{\ell/2}-1)}{2}, & \textit{otherwise.} \end{cases}$$

Proof. The factor $k^\ell - k$ represents the number of words of length ℓ that contain at least two distinct symbols, for an alphabet of size k. For the odd case (resp. even case), the factor $\frac{\ell-1}{2} + 1$ (resp. $\frac{\ell}{2}$) is the number of ways to split a word of length ℓ such that the length of the first half is strictly smaller than the length of the second. Finally, for the even case, the pairs (u, v), with $|u| = |v| = k^{\frac{\ell}{2}}$, are included. □

3.1 Bijection Between Shuffle Pairs and Natural Numbers

Let $\mathsf{ind}_k(w)$ be the index of $w \in \Sigma$ in the lexicographical ordered list of all words in $\Sigma^{|w|}$, with $|\Sigma| = k$. First, let us define a relation $\leq$ on the set $\mathcal{S}_k$. Given $(u_1, v_1), (u_2, v_2) \in \mathcal{S}_k$ we say that $(u_1, v_1) \leq (u_2, v_2)$ if either $u_1v_1 < u_2v_2$, or $u_1v_1 = u_2v_2$ and $|u_1| \leq |u_2|$.

Lemma 2. *The binary relation $\leq$ on the set $\mathcal{S}_k$ is a total order.*

Proof. We shall prove that this relation is antisymmetric and comparable, and omit the proofs for reflexivity and transitivity. Let $(u_1, v_1), (u_2, v_2) \in \mathcal{S}_k$, then the relation $\leq$ is:

- *antisymmetric*: suppose that $(u_1, v_1) \leq (u_2, v_2)$ and $(u_2, v_2) \leq (u_1, v_1)$. This implies $u_1v_1 = u_2v_2$, which leads to $|u_1| \leq |u_2|$ and $|u_2| \leq |u_1|$. Consequently, $u_1 = u_2$ and $(u_1, v_1) = (u_2, v_2)$;
- *comparable*: suppose that $(u_1, v_1) \not\leq (u_2, v_2)$. Then, we have $u_1v_1 \geq u_2v_2$ and either $u_1v_1 \neq u_2v_2$ or $|u_1| > |u_2|$. If $u_1v_1 \neq u_2v_2$, it follows that $u_1v_1 > u_2v_2$, and so $(u_2, v_2) \leq (u_1, v_1)$. On the other hand, if $|u_1| > |u_2|$ and $u_1v_1 = u_2v_2$, by definition, $(u_2, v_2) \leq (u_1, v_1)$.

□

For a word $w \in \Sigma^\star$, we use $\mathsf{indShuffle}_k(w)$ as the index of the first occurrence of a pair (u, v) satisfying $uv = w$ in the ordered set of $\mathcal{S}_k^\ell$, where $\ell = |w|$ and $u, v \in \Sigma^\star$. In fact, such pair has the format (ε, w), according to the relation $\leq$ on the set $\mathcal{S}_k$. The value of $\mathsf{indShuffle}_k(w)$ can be computed in a similar way to the calculation of $|\mathcal{S}_k^\ell|$ in Theorem 1, as follows:

Lemma 3. *Given $w = a_1 \cdots a_\ell \in \Sigma^\ell$, with $|\Sigma| = k > 1$ and $\ell > 1$, let $i = \mathsf{ind}_k(w)$. Then,*

$$\mathsf{indShuffle}_k(w) = \begin{cases} (i-d)(\frac{\ell-1}{2}+1), & \text{if } \ell \text{ is odd;} \\ (i-d)\frac{\ell}{2} + j_1(k^{\ell/2} - \frac{j_1-1}{2}) + \max(j_2 - j_1, 0) - d, & \text{otherwise,} \end{cases}$$

where $d = \mathsf{ind}_k(a_0) + 1$ is the number of words of the form a^ℓ, with $a \in \Sigma$, that have an index smaller than that of w, and j_1 (resp. j_2) equals $\mathsf{ind}_k(a_1 \cdots a_{\frac{\ell}{2}})$ (resp. $\mathsf{ind}_k(a_{\frac{\ell}{2}+1} \cdots a_\ell)$) when ℓ is even.

Proof. Let us consider the case where ℓ is even. The proof for when ℓ is odd follows similarly. First, observe that, by definition of $\mathsf{ind}_k(w)$, there are i words in Σ^ℓ lexicographically smaller than w. Moreover, note that no pair $(u, v) \in \mathcal{S}_k^\ell$ satisfies $uv = a^\ell$, for any $a \in \Sigma$, due to the definition of $\mathcal{S}_k^\ell$, and that there are exactly $\mathsf{ind}_k(a_0)+1$ of those pairs. Thus, the expression includes the factor $i-d$. Then, the factor $\frac{\ell}{2}+1$ accounts for all possible ways to split a word into two such that the second part is no longer than the first. Now, let w_1 (resp. w_2) be the first (resp. second) half of w with index j_1 (resp. j_2). The term $j_1 k^{\frac{\ell}{2}}$ accounts for all pairs (u, v) such that $u < w_1$. However, we must exclude the cases where $v > u$ or $u = v = a^\ell$, for some $a \in \Sigma$, which total exactly $\frac{j_1(j_1-1)}{2} - d$. Finally, we add the number of pairs where $u = w_1$ and $\mathsf{ind}_k(v) < j_2$, which is $j_2 - j_1$ when this value is positive. □

Now, let $f : \mathcal{S}_k \to \mathbb{N}$ and let g be the inverse of f, namely f^{-1}. Considering the results in Theorem 1 and Lemma 3, the following holds.

Lemma 4. *Given $(u, v) \in \mathcal{S}_k$, for some $k > 1$, the function f defined as*

$$f((u, v)) = \sum_{\ell=2}^{|u|+|v|-1} |\mathcal{S}_k^\ell| + \mathsf{indShuffle}_k(uv) + |u|$$

is bijective. Moreover, given $n \in \mathbb{N}$, the function $g = f^{-1}$ is defined as

$$g(n) = (u, v),$$

where $\ell = \max\{\ell' \in \mathbb{N} \mid \sum_{i=2}^{\ell'-1} |\mathcal{S}_k^i| \leq n\}$ is the block length of $g(n)$, $m = n - \sum_{i=2}^{\ell-1} |\mathcal{S}_k^i|$ is the index of $g(n)$ in $\mathcal{S}_k^\ell$, $w = a_1 \cdots a_\ell = \max\{w' \in \Sigma^\ell \mid \mathsf{indShuffle}_k(w') \leq m\}$ is the word obtained by concatenating the first element of $g(n)$ with the second, $t = m - \mathsf{indShuffle}_k(w)$ is the length of u, and $u = a_1 \cdots a_t$, $v = a_{t+1} \cdots a_\ell$.

Note that for $k, \ell > 1$, $|\mathcal{S}_k^\ell| \geq k^\ell$. Thus, in the definition of g in Lemma 4, the block length ℓ can be computed in $O(\log_k n)$ time. Moreover, the word w can also be found in $O(\log_2 \ell)$ time. This bijection allows a straightforward uniform random generator for shuffle languages: given an alphabet size $k > 1$, a natural number n is sampled uniformly at random from the initial segment of $\mathbb{N}$ of some length N, i.e., $n \in \{0, \ldots, N-1\}$, and the corresponding shuffle language is then determined from the pair encoded by $g(n)$.

4 Bitmap for the Shuffle of Two Words

A *bitmap* of a block language $L \subseteq \Sigma^\ell$, denoted as $\mathsf{B}(L)$, over a k-symbol alphabet Σ and for $\ell > 1$, is a binary word of length k^ℓ that characterises L, and it was studied by Duarte et al. [9,10]. In particular, given an alphabet size k and a block length ℓ, the i-th bit on the bitmap indicates whether the i-th word, according to the lexicographical order, belongs, or not, to the language. Bitwise operations on bitmaps correspond to set operations on block languages. For example, the bitmap representing the union (resp. intersection) of two block languages with the same block length can be obtained by the bitwise or (resp. and) of their respective bitmaps.

Example 1. Let $L = \{aaa, aba, abb, bab, bbb\}$, with $k = 2$ and $\ell = 3$. Then, the bitmap of L is $\mathsf{B}(L) = 10110101$.

The authors showed how to construct minimal automata, both deterministic and nondeterministic, from a bitmap representation of a block language. As previously mentioned, if $L = u \sqcup\!\sqcup\, v$, for $u, v \in \Sigma^\star$, then $L \subseteq \Sigma^{|u|+|v|}$ is a block language, thus the previous constructions can be used. Let $L_1 \subseteq \Sigma^{\ell_1}$ and $L_2 \subseteq \Sigma^{\ell_2}$ be two block languages over an alphabet Σ of size $k > 1$, with $\ell_1, \ell_2 > 1$, and let $\mathsf{B}(L_1)$ and $\mathsf{B}(L_2)$ denote their bitmap representation with lengths k^{ℓ_1} and k^{ℓ_2}, respectively. Now, consider the operation that, for each 1 in $\mathsf{B}(L_1)$, replaces it with $\mathsf{B}(L_2)$, and for each 0, replaces it with $0^{k^{\ell_2}}$. We denote this operation by $\mathsf{B}(L_1) \circ \mathsf{B}(L_2)$ and define it as

$$\mathsf{B}(L_1) \circ \mathsf{B}(L_2) = c_0 \cdots c_{k^{\ell_1}-1}, \text{ where } c_i = \begin{cases} \mathsf{B}(L_2), & \text{if } b_i = 1 \\ 0^{k^{\ell_2}}, & \text{otherwise,} \end{cases}$$

for $i \in [k^{\ell_1} - 1]$, where $\mathsf{B}(L_1) = b_0 \cdots b_{k^{\ell_1}-1}$. Then, the resulting word corresponds to the bitmap representation of the concatenation of L_1 and L_2, $\mathsf{B}(L_1 L_2)$. From this observation, it is possible to construct the bitmap of the shuffle of two words u and v directly.

Lemma 5. *The bitmap representation of* $u \sqcup\!\sqcup\, v$, *with* $u, v \in \Sigma^\star$, *namely* $\mathsf{B}(u \sqcup\!\sqcup\, v)$, *is inductively defined by*

$$\begin{aligned} \mathsf{B}(\varepsilon \sqcup\!\sqcup\, \varepsilon) &= 1 \\ \mathsf{B}(\varepsilon \sqcup\!\sqcup\, u) = \mathsf{B}(u \sqcup\!\sqcup\, \varepsilon) &= \mathsf{B}(\{u\}) \\ \mathsf{B}(au \sqcup\!\sqcup\, bv) &= \mathsf{B}(\{a\}) \circ \mathsf{B}(u \sqcup\!\sqcup\, bv) + \mathsf{B}(\{b\}) \circ \mathsf{B}(au \sqcup\!\sqcup\, v), \end{aligned}$$

where the + corresponds to the bitwise or operation between bitmaps.

5 State Complexity of the Shuffle Square of a Word

The deterministic and nondeterministic state complexity of the shuffle operation of two words was studied by Biegler et al. [3]. Firstly, in their work, it is introduced the definition of *naive* NFA for the shuffle of two words. Let $u = u_1 \cdots u_m$, $v = v_1 \cdots v_n$ be two words over an alphabet Σ, with $m \leq n$. The NFA $\mathcal{A} = \langle Q, \Sigma, \delta, q_0, F \rangle$ where $Q = [m] \times [n]$, $q_0 = (m, n)$, $F = \{(0,0)\}$, and δ:

$$\begin{aligned} (p-1, q) &\in \delta((p,q), u_{m-p+1}), \quad \text{for } p \in [1, m], q \in [n]; \\ (p, q-1) &\in \delta((p,q), v_{n-q+1}), \quad \text{for } p \in [m], q \in [1, n], \end{aligned}$$

satisfies $\mathcal{L}(\mathcal{A}) = u \sqcup\!\sqcup\, v$ and is referred to as the *naive shuffle* NFA for u and v. The correctness of the construction follows from the fact that the right language of each state $(p, q) \in Q$ is $u_{m-p+1} \cdots u_m \sqcup\!\sqcup\, v_{n-q+1} \cdots v_n$. The next result follows directly from this construction:

Lemma 6 (Biegler et al. [3]**).** *Let u and v be two words of length m and n, respectively, over an alphabet $|\Sigma| \geq 2$. Then, $\mathsf{nsc}(u \sqcup\!\sqcup\, v) \leq (m+1)(n+1)$, and the bound is tight.*

The upper bound derived for the deterministic state complexity of the shuffle of two words is based on the observation that during the subset construction applied to naive shuffle NFAs, only states from the same layer appear within the same state of the DFA.

Lemma 7 (Biegler et al. [3]**).** *Let u and v be two words of length m and n, with $m < n$. Then, $\mathsf{sc}(u \sqcup\!\sqcup\, v) \in O(2^{m+1} n)$.*

The *shuffle square* of a word $w \in \Sigma^\star$ is $w \sqcup\!\sqcup\, w$. Naturally, the naive shuffle NFA recognises the square shuffle of a word. Let $\mathcal{A}$ be a naive shuffle NFA for $w \sqcup\!\sqcup\, w$, with $w = a_1 \cdots a_n$, and let (p, q) be a state from $\mathcal{A}$. It is easy to see that the right languages of the states (p, q) and (q, p) are the same, namely, $a_{n-p+1} \cdots w_n \sqcup\!\sqcup\, a_{n-q+1} \cdots w_n$. Thus, an NFA with half as many states compared to the naive suffices, as suggested by the following construction.

Let $w = a_1 \cdots a_n$ be a word over an alphabet Σ. The NFA $\mathcal{A} = \langle Q, \Sigma, \delta, q_0, F \rangle$, where $Q = \{\, (p, q) \in [n] \times [n] \mid p \leq q \,\}$, $q_0 = (n, n)$, $F = \{(0,0)\}$, and δ:

$$\begin{aligned} (p-1, q) &\in \delta((p,q), a_{n-p+1}), \quad \text{for } p \in [1, q], q \in [n]; \\ (p, q-1) &\in \delta((p,q), a_{n-q+1}), \quad \text{for } p \in [q], q \in [1, n]. \end{aligned}$$

Directly from the correctness of the naive shuffle NFA for two words, we also have the following:

Lemma 8. *Given a word $w \in \Sigma^\star$, the construction above described results in an NFA $\mathcal{A}$ such that $\mathcal{L}(\mathcal{A}) = w \sqcup\!\sqcup\, w$. We refer to this NFA as the* naive shuffle square NFA *for w.*

Example 2. Let $w = abba$. The naive shuffle square NFA for w is depicted in Fig. 1.

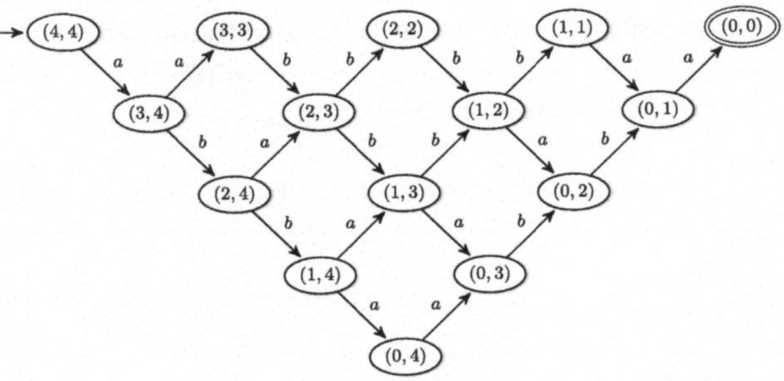

Fig. 1. Naive shuffle square NFA for $w = abba$

The naive shuffle square of a word w of length n consists of exactly $2n+1$ layers. This NFA has two phases: the *growing phase* and the *shrinking phase*. The growing phase consists of the first $n+1$ layers, from layer 0 to n. During this phase, in every layer up to the n-th, each state has two outgoing transitions, indicating what symbols are being read from both copies of w. The shrinking phase corresponds to the last n layers, from $n+1$ to $2n$, or, alternatively, to the first n ranks, from 0 to $n-1$. For each rank $i \in [1, n-1]$ of this phase, the state $(0, i)$ has a single outgoing transition, while all other states have two. In these states, every symbol from the first copy of w has been read. Given a layer (resp. rank) $i \in [n]$ of the naive shuffle square NFA, the number of states in the i-th layer (resp. rank) is $\lceil \frac{i+1}{2} \rceil$.

The size of the automaton resulting from the construction above serves as an upper bound on the nondeterministic state complexity of the operation.

Lemma 9. *Let w be a word of length n over an alphabet Σ. Then, $\frac{(n+1)(n+2)}{2}$ states are sufficient for an NFA to recognise $w \sqcup\!\sqcup\, w$. We next examine whether or not we can reach the upper bound of Lemma 9.*

Lemma 10. *The upper bound $\frac{(n+1)(n+2)}{2}$ for the nondeterministic state complexity of the shuffle square cannot be reached with an alphabet of size 2.*

Proof. Let $\mathcal{A}$ be the naive shuffle square NFA for a word $w = a_1 \cdots a_n$ over the alphabet $\{a, b\}$, where $n \geq 1$. Suppose that w contains two consecutive a symbols, that is, $w = uaav$, for some $u, v \in \Sigma^\star$. Then, $\mathcal{A}$ is nondeterministic on the state $(|v|+1, |v|+2)$, with outgoing transitions to $(|v|+1, |v|+1)$ and $(|v|, |v|+$

2) by a. These two states have right languages $av \sqcup\!\sqcup av$ and $v \sqcup\!\sqcup aav$, respectively. It is easy to see that $av \sqcup\!\sqcup av \subseteq v \sqcup\!\sqcup aav$, hence the state $(|v|+1, |v|+1)$ can be eliminated, as it is only accessible through the state $(|v|+1, |v|+2)$. Consequently, $\mathcal{A}$ is not minimal. Now, suppose that w does not contain the subwords aa or bb. In this case, let $w = (ab)^m$, with $m = \frac{n}{2}$, assuming that w has an even length. In particular, $\mathcal{A}$ is nondeterministic on the state $(n-2, n)$, as it has two outgoing transitions on a to the states $(n-3, n)$ and $(n-2, n-1)$. Now, these two states have the right languages $b(ab)^{m-2} \sqcup\!\sqcup (ab)^m$ and $(ab)^{m-1} \sqcup\!\sqcup b(ab)^{m-1}$, respectively. Again, the first language is a proper subset of the second, and since $(n-3, n)$ is only accessible through $(n-2, n)$, it can be eliminated. Thus $\mathcal{A}$, is not minimal. The other cases for the binary alphabet follow similarly.

Now, consider the word $w_n = c(ab)^m$ of size $n = 2m+1$ over the alphabet $\Sigma = \{a, b, c\}$, for $m > 0$. We claim that $\frac{(n+1)(n+2)}{2}$ states are necessary to recognise $w_n \sqcup\!\sqcup w_n$.

Lemma 11. *For $m > 0$, any NFA recognising the shuffle square of w_n requires at least $\frac{(n+1)(n+2)}{2}$ states.*

Proof. Let $\mathcal{A}$ be the naive shuffle square NFA for w with set of states Q. Note that $\mathcal{A}$ is nondeterministic on every state $(p, q) \in Q$, where $p, q \in [1, n-1]$ and p and q have the same parity, with two outgoing transitions: one to $(p-1, q)$ and another to $(p, q-1)$. These transitions occur on a if both p and q are even, or on b if both are odd. We now show that $\mathcal{A}$ is minimal.

Let $i \in [n]$ be a layer of $\mathcal{A}$ and Q_i the set of states at that layer. Suppose that i is even; the proof follows similarly when i is odd. Then, up to the i-th layer, the NFA has read i symbols in total within the two copies of w. Therefore, the right language of a state (p, q) in Q_i, for the case where $p, q \in [1, n-1]$, is either $(ab)^{m_1} \sqcup\!\sqcup (ab)^{m_2}$, for some $m_1 \leq m_2 \leq m$ such that $m_1 + m_2 = \frac{n-i}{2}$, or $b(ab)^{m_1} \sqcup\!\sqcup b(ab)^{m_2}$, for some $m_1 \leq m_2 \leq m$ such that $m_1 + m_2 = \frac{n-i}{2} - 1$. To determine whether the NFA can be minimised, we must examine states whose right languages share the same format, as the right languages of different cases have disjoint intersections. For the first case, one can observe that $(ab)^{m_1} \sqcup\!\sqcup (ab)^{m_2} \subseteq (ab)^{m_1'} \sqcup\!\sqcup (ab)^{m_2'}$, if $m_1 + m_2 = m_1' + m_2'$ and $m_1 \leq m_1'$, thus a hierarchy of subsets can be observed among the right languages of states within the same case. However, the language $(ab)^{m_1} \sqcup\!\sqcup (ab)^{m_2}$, for some $m_1 \leq m_2 \leq m$, cannot be reconstructed by the union of its proper subsets, since that no other subset produces the word $(aabb)^{m_1}(ab)^{m_2-m_1}$. A similar argument can be made for the case where the right language of the state has a different format. Thus, $|Q_i|$ states are required at the i-th rank of $\mathcal{A}$. □

From Lemmas 9 to 11, we establish the following result.

Theorem 2. *Let w be a word of length n over an alphabet Σ. Then,*

$$\mathsf{nsc}(w \sqcup\!\sqcup w) \leq \frac{(n+1)(n+2)}{2},$$

and the bound is tight for $|\Sigma| \geq 3$.

Analogously to the general case of the two-word shuffle, applying the subset construction to naive shuffle square NFAs results only on subsets of states where all elements belong to the same layer of the NFA.

Lemma 12. *Let w be a word of length n over Σ. Then,*

$$\mathsf{sc}(w \sqcup\!\sqcup w) \leq \begin{cases} 5\sqrt{2^{n+1}} + n - 7, & \text{if } n \text{ is odd} \\ 7\sqrt{2^{n}} + n - 5, & \text{otherwise.} \end{cases}$$

Proof. Let us prove the obtained result for the case when n is odd; the other case follows analogously. Let $\mathcal{A}$ be the naive shuffle square NFA for w, and $\mathcal{B}$ the resulting DFA from the subset construction.

As we previously saw, the growing phase of the naive shuffle square NFA has $n+1$ layers, with the i-th layer containing $\lceil \frac{i+1}{2} \rceil$ states, $i \in [n]$. As n is odd, there is an even number of layers in this phase, and this implies that there are two layers with exactly m states, for each $m \in [1, \frac{n+1}{2}]$. Moreover, notice that the state $(n-i, n)$, for $i \in [n]$, has a single path from the initial state to itself. In other words, there exists a single word $x \in \Sigma^i$ such that $\delta((n, n), x) = \{(n-i, n)\}$. This result must be preserved on the determinised DFA, thus this state appears in exactly one subset of states at the i-th rank of $\mathcal{B}$. Using this insight, and considering the remaining subsets of states except the empty set (it is sufficient to add the empty set once), we obtain for the first phase an upper bound of

$$2 \sum_{i=1}^{n+1/2} 2^{i-1} = 2^{n+2/2} - 2.$$

The shrinking phase follows similarly; however, we now must consider every subset of each layer, as the observation on the number of paths from the starting state no longer holds. □

We now introduce a family of words that cause an exponential blow-up in the size of the minimal DFA recognising its shuffle square.

Theorem 3. *There exists a word w over an alphabet Σ, such that the size of the minimal DFA accepting $w \sqcup\!\sqcup w$ is $\Omega(\sqrt[8]{2}^{|w|})$.*

Proof. For $n > 1$, let $w_n = (aabb)^n aabababb(aabb)^n$ and

$$X_n = a(aabb)^n aaabbbabaaa(bbbbaaaa + bbbabaaa)^n bbbb(aabb)^n.$$

Let $\mathcal{A}_n = \langle Q, \Sigma, q_0, F, \delta \rangle$ be the naive shuffle NFA for w_n. By restricting the input words to X_n, one can follow the proof of Theorem 13 in [3] to show that the determinisation of $\mathcal{A}$ results in an automaton with at least $\sqrt[8]{2}^{|w|}$ distinguishable states. □

Considering $w = (aabb)^{2n+2}$, with $n > 1$, it is not hard to see that the minimal DFA recognising the shuffle square of w has $O(n^2)$ states. Theorem 3 is especially interesting because the word there used, $(aabb)^n aabababb(aabb)^n$, differs from w only by switching two letters, and yet this subtle change is sufficient to cause an exponential blow-up in size.

6 Partial Derivative Automata for the Two-Word Shuffle

Regular expressions (REs) with the shuffle operator are, in general, exponentially more succinct than equivalent standard REs [12–14]. Broda et al. [6] extended the partial derivative automaton to handle REs with the shuffle operator.

We consider the set of REs with shuffle where the $\sqcup\!\sqcup$ operator only occurs in expressions of the form $u \sqcup\!\sqcup v$, with $u, v \in \Sigma^\star$. We denote this set by $\mathcal{W}_{\sqcup\!\sqcup}$ and it is described by the expressions τ generated by the following grammar:

$$\tau \rightarrow \alpha \sqcup\!\sqcup \alpha \tag{1}$$

$$\alpha \rightarrow \beta \mid \varepsilon \tag{2}$$

$$\beta \rightarrow a \mid (a \cdot \beta) \quad (a \in \Sigma). \tag{3}$$

where the $\cdot$ is often omitted. It is easy to see that the expressions α and β generate, respectively, $\Sigma^\star$ and Σ^+. We denote by $\mathcal{L}(\tau)$ the language represented by an expression $\tau \in \mathcal{W}_{\sqcup\!\sqcup}$. We have that $\mathcal{L}(u \sqcup\!\sqcup v) = u \sqcup\!\sqcup v$, for $u, v \in \Sigma^\star$. For the *size* of a regular expression $\tau \in \mathcal{W}_{\sqcup\!\sqcup}$, denoted by $\|w\|$, we will consider the number of symbols in τ.

The *set of partial derivatives* of an expression $\tau \in \mathcal{W}_{\sqcup\!\sqcup}$ w.r.t. a letter $a \in \Sigma$, denoted by $\partial_a(\tau)$, where $\tau = u \sqcup\!\sqcup v$ with $u, v \in \Sigma^\star$, is defined by

$$\partial_a(u \sqcup\!\sqcup v) = \partial_a(u) \sqcup\!\sqcup v \cup u \sqcup\!\sqcup \partial_a(v), \tag{4}$$

where $\partial_a(\varepsilon) = \partial_a(\emptyset) = \emptyset$, $\partial_a(b) = \varepsilon$, if $a = b$, or equals $\emptyset$, otherwise, and $\partial_a(b \cdot \beta) = \beta$, if $a = b$, or $\emptyset$, otherwise. Moreover, let $\emptyset \sqcup\!\sqcup u = u \sqcup\!\sqcup \emptyset = \emptyset$.

Note that for $u, v \in \Sigma^\star$ and $a \in \Sigma$, the shuffle operation satisfies $a^{-1}(u \sqcup\!\sqcup v) = (a^{-1}u) \sqcup\!\sqcup v \cup u \sqcup\!\sqcup (a^{-1}v)$. Thus, we have that $\mathcal{L}(\partial_a(u \sqcup\!\sqcup v)) = a^{-1}(u \sqcup\!\sqcup v)$. The set of partial derivatives of a regular expression $\tau \in \mathcal{W}_{\sqcup\!\sqcup}$ w.r.t. a word $w \in \Sigma^\star$, denoted by $\partial_w(\tau)$, is inductively defined by $\partial_\varepsilon(\tau) = \{\tau\}$, and $\partial_{xa}(\tau) = \partial_a(\partial_x(\tau))$, where for a set $S \subseteq \mathcal{W}_{\sqcup\!\sqcup}$, we define $\partial_a(S) = \bigcup_{\tau \in S} \partial_a(\tau)$. Moreover, $\mathcal{L}(S) = \bigcup_{\tau \in S} \mathcal{L}(\tau)$.

Lemma 13. *The set $\partial_w(u \sqcup\!\sqcup v)$, for $u \sqcup\!\sqcup v \in \mathcal{W}_{\sqcup\!\sqcup}$ and $w \in \Sigma^\star$, satisfies*

$$\partial_w(u \sqcup\!\sqcup v) = \bigcup_{w \in u' \sqcup\!\sqcup v'} \partial_{u'}(u) \sqcup\!\sqcup \partial_{v'}(v).$$

Proof. The proof proceeds by induction on the word w. For $w = \varepsilon$, it is clear that $\partial_\varepsilon(u \sqcup\!\sqcup v) = \partial_\varepsilon(u) \sqcup\!\sqcup \partial_\varepsilon(v) = u \sqcup\!\sqcup v$. For the inductive step, w can be decomposed as $w = xa$, for $x \in \Sigma^\star$ and $a \in \Sigma$. We have:

$$\begin{aligned}
\partial_{xa}(u \sqcup\!\sqcup v) &= \partial_a(\partial_x(u \sqcup\!\sqcup v)) \\
&\overset{i.h.}{=} \partial_a\Big(\bigcup_{x \in u_1 \sqcup\!\sqcup v_1} \partial_{u_1}(u) \sqcup\!\sqcup \partial_{v_1}(v)\Big) \\
&= \bigcup_{x \in u_1 \sqcup\!\sqcup v_1} \partial_a(\partial_{u_1}(u) \sqcup\!\sqcup \partial_{v_1}(v)) \\
&= \bigcup_{x \in u_1 \sqcup\!\sqcup v_1} \partial_a(\partial_{u_1}(u)) \sqcup\!\sqcup \partial_{v_1}(v) \cup \partial_{u_1}(u) \sqcup\!\sqcup \partial_a(\partial_{v_1}(v)) \\
&= \bigcup_{x \in u_1 \sqcup\!\sqcup v_1} (\partial_{u_1 a}(u) \sqcup\!\sqcup \partial_{v_1}(v) \cup \partial_{u_1}(u) \sqcup\!\sqcup \partial_{v_1 a}(v)) \\
&= \bigcup_{xa \in u_1 a \sqcup\!\sqcup v_1} \partial_{u_1 a}(u) \sqcup\!\sqcup \partial_{v_1}(v) \;\cup \bigcup_{xa \in u_1 \sqcup\!\sqcup v_1 a} \partial_{u_1}(u) \sqcup\!\sqcup \partial_{v_1 a}(v) \\
&= \bigcup_{xa \in u' \sqcup\!\sqcup v'} \partial_{u'}(u) \sqcup\!\sqcup \partial_{v'}(v).
\end{aligned}$$

□

Let $\partial(\tau)$ denote the set of all partial derivatives of an expression $\tau \in \mathcal{W}_{\sqcup\!\sqcup}$, i.e., $\partial(\tau) = \bigcup_{w \in \Sigma^\star} \partial_w(\tau)$. It is well known that the set of partial derivatives of a regular expression gives rise to an equivalent NFA, and this remains valid for the expressions considered in this study.

The partial derivative automaton, denoted as $\mathcal{A}_{pd}$, for a regular expression $\tau \in \mathcal{W}_{\sqcup\!\sqcup}$ is defined as

$$\mathcal{A}_{pd} = \langle \partial(\tau), \Sigma, \tau, \delta_\tau, F_\tau \rangle,$$

where $\delta_\tau(\tau', a) = \partial_a(\tau')$ and $F_\tau = \{\, \tau' \in \partial(\tau) \mid \varepsilon \in \mathcal{L}(\tau') \,\}$, and $\mathcal{L}(\mathcal{A}_{pd}) = \mathcal{L}(\tau)$.

6.1 Average State Complexity

We now estimate the asymptotic average number of states in the partial derivative automata. In [6], the authors analyse the average state complexity of $\mathcal{A}_{pd}$ for regular expressions extended with the shuffle operator. Similarly, we study regular expressions of the form $\tau \in \mathcal{W}_{\sqcup\!\sqcup}$.

Let $A(z) = \sum_{n \geq 0} a_n z^n$ be a *generating function* associated with some combinatorial class. Given some measure defined on the objects of the class, the coefficient a_n denotes the sum of this measure over all objects of size n. We use the notation $[z^n]A(z)$ for a_n. Generating functions are also complex analytic functions, and their coefficients can be estimated by analysing their behaviour around their singularities. For an introduction to this approach applied to formal languages, we refer to [5].

Considering the grammar (3), the generating function for the number of words in Σ^+, namely $R_k(z)$, satisfies $R_k(z) = kz + kzR_k(z)$, thus,

$$R_k(z) = \frac{kz}{1 - kz} = \sum_{n \geq 1} (kz)^n,$$

where $1/k$ is the single point of singularity of $R_k(z)$. Now, let $W_k(z)$ be the extension of $R_k(z)$ to also count the word ε. Of course, $W_k(z) = z + R_k(z)$.

Now, notice that the set of partial derivatives of a word $w \in \Sigma^\star$ has exactly $|w| + 1$ elements. Let $\ell(w) = |w| + 1$. Then, the generating function for the number of partial derivatives of Σ^+, namely $P_k(z) = \sum_{w \in \Sigma^+} \ell(w) z^{\|w\|}$, satisfies

$$P_k(z) = \sum_{a} \ell(a) z^{\|a\|} + \sum_{a,\beta} \ell(a \cdot \beta) z^{\|a \cdot \beta\|} = 2kz + kzR_k(z) + kzP_k(z),$$

and, therefore,

$$P_k(z) = \frac{kz(2 + R_k(z))}{1 - kz} = 2R_k(z) + R_k(z)^2.$$

Now, let $S_k(z)$ be the generating function for the number of $\mathcal{W}_{\sqcup\!\sqcup}$-expressions. From specification (1) it follows that $S_k(z) = zW_k(z)^2$. Hence,

$$S_k(z) = zR_k(z)^2 + 2z^2 R_k(z) + z^3 = z^3 + \sum_{n \geq 3} \left[2k^{n-2} + (n-2)k^{n-1}\right] z^n,$$

thus, for $n \geq 3$,

$$[z^n]S_k(z) = 2k^{n-2} + (n-2)k^{n-1}. \tag{5}$$

Given $\tau = u \sqcup\!\sqcup v \in \mathcal{W}_{\sqcup\!\sqcup}$, an upper bound, denoted as $p(\tau)$, for the number of elements in the set $\partial(\tau)$ satisfies:

$$p(u \sqcup\!\sqcup v) = \ell(u)\ell(v) + \ell(u) + \ell(v).$$

This upper bound corresponds to the case where all unions in (4) are disjoint. Then, the generating function for the size of $\partial(\tau)$, namely $D_k(z)$, satisfies

$$D_k(z) = \sum_{\alpha,\beta} p(\alpha \sqcup\!\sqcup \beta) z^{\|\alpha \sqcup\!\sqcup \beta\|} = 2zC_k(z)W_k(z) + zC_k(z)^2.$$

In fact, we have

$$D_k(z) = (3 + 10k + 8k^2)z^3 + 7(2k^2 + 11k^3)z^4 + \sum_{n \geq 5} \left(2(2n-1)k^{n-2} + \left[8(n-2) + 6\binom{n-2}{2} + \binom{n-2}{3} \right] k^{n-1} \right) z^n,$$

hence, for $n \geq 5$,

$$[z^n]D_k(z) = \frac{1}{6}\left((24n - 12)k^{n-2} + (n-2)(n^2 + 11n + 6)k^{n-1}\right). \tag{6}$$

Consequently, using the results obtained in (5) and (6), the average number of partial derivatives in $\partial(\tau)$, which we denote by avD, for an expression $\tau \in \mathcal{W}_{\sqcup\!\sqcup}$ of size at least 5 is

$$avD = \frac{[z^n]D_k(z)}{[z^n]S_k(z)} \sim \frac{n^2}{6}.$$

Theorem 4. *An upper bound for the average number of states of $\mathcal{A}_{pd}$ for regular expressions $\tau \in \mathcal{W}_{\sqcup\sqcup}$ is $O(n^2)$.*

This result shows that, even in terms of average state complexity, the shuffle operation requires a quadratic number of states relative to the size of the block of the shuffle language.

References

1. Berstel, J., Boasson, L.: Shuffle factorization is unique. Theor. Comput. Sci. **273**(1–2), 47–67 (2002). https://doi.org/10.1016/S0304-3975(00)00433-3
2. Biegler, F., Daley, M., Holzer, M., McQuillan, I.: On the uniqueness of shuffle on words and finite languages. Theor. Comput. Sci. **410**(38–40), 3711–3724 (2009). https://doi.org/10.1016/J.TCS.2009.04.016
3. Biegler, F., Daley, M., McQuillan, I.: On the shuffle automaton size for words. J. Autom. Lang. Comb. **15**(1/2), 53–70 (2010). https://doi.org/10.25596/JALC-2010-053
4. Biegler, F., Daley, M., McQuillan, I.: Algorithmic decomposition of shuffle on words. Theor. Comput. Sci. **454**, 38–50 (2012). https://doi.org/10.1016/J.TCS.2012.04.001
5. Broda, S., Machiavelo, A., Moreira, N., Reis, R.: A hitchhiker's guide to descriptional complexity through analytic combinatorics. Theor. Comput. Sci. **528**, 85–100 (2014). https://doi.org/10.1016/J.TCS.2014.02.013
6. Broda, S., Machiavelo, A., Moreira, N., Reis, R.: Automata for regular expressions with shuffle. Inf. Comput. **259**(2), 162–173 (2018). https://doi.org/10.1016/J.IC.2017.08.013
7. Brzozowski, J.A., Jirásková, G., Liu, B., Rajasekaran, A., Szykula, M.: On the state complexity of the shuffle of regular languages. In: Câmpeanu, C., Manea, F., Shallit, J.O. (eds.) 18th DCFS, 2016. LNCS, vol. 9777, pp. 73–86. Springer (2016). https://doi.org/10.1007/978-3-319-41114-9_6
8. Câmpeanu, C., Salomaa, K., Yu, S.: Tight lower bound for the state complexity of shuffle of regular languages. J. Autom. Lang. Comb. **7**(3), 303–310 (2002)
9. Duarte, G., Moreira, N., Prigioniero, L., Reis, R.: Block languages and their bitmap representations. In: Fazekas, S.Z. (ed.) 28th CIAA 2024. LNCS, vol. 15015, pp. 124–137. Springer (2024). https://doi.org/10.1007/978-3-031-71112-1_9
10. Duarte, G., Moreira, N., Prigioniero, L., Reis, R.: Operational state complexity of block languages. In: Manea, F., Pighizzini, G. (eds.) 14th NCMA, 2024. EPTCS, vol. 407, pp. 59–76 (2024). https://doi.org/10.4204/EPTCS.407.5
11. Eremondi, J., Ibarra, O.H., McQuillan, I.: On the complexity and decidability of some problems involving shuffle. Inf. Comput. **259**(2), 214–224 (2018). https://doi.org/10.1016/J.IC.2017.09.002
12. Gelade, W.: Succinctness of regular expressions with interleaving, intersection and counting. Theor. Comput. Sci. **411**(31–33), 2987–2998 (2010). https://doi.org/10.1016/J.TCS.2010.04.036
13. Gruber, H.: On the descriptional and algorithmic complexity of regular languages. Ph.D. thesis, Justus Liebig University Giessen (2010)
14. Gruber, H., Holzer, M.: Finite automata, digraph connectivity, and regular expression size. In: Aceto, L., Damgård, I., Goldberg, L.A., Halldórsson, M.M., Ingólfsdóttir, A., Walukiewicz, I. (eds.) 35th ICALP, 2008. LNCS, vol. 5126, pp. 39–50. Springer (2008). https://doi.org/10.1007/978-3-540-70583-3_4

15. Mansfield, A.: An algorithm for a merge recognition problem. Discret. Appl. Math. **4**(3), 193–197 (1982). https://doi.org/10.1016/0166-218X(82)90039-7
16. Warmuth, M.K., Haussler, D.: On the complexity of iterated shuffle. J. Comput. Syst. Sci. **28**(3), 345–358 (1984). https://doi.org/10.1016/0022-0000(84)90018-7

Matrix Forbidding Grammars

Henning Fernau[1], Lakshmanan Kuppusamy[2], Indhumathi Raman[3], and György Vaszil[4(✉)]

[1] Fachbereich 4 – Abteilung Informatikwissenschaften, Universität Trier, 54286 Trier, Germany
fernau@uni-trier.de

[2] School of Computer Science and Engineering, VIT University, Vellore 632 014, India
klakshma@vit.ac.in

[3] Department of Computing Technologies, SRM Institute of Science and Technology, Kattankulathur, Chennai 603203, India
indhumar2@srmist.edu.in

[4] Faculty of Informatics, Department of Computer Science, University of Debrecen, Debrecen 4028, Hungary
vaszil.gyorgy@inf.unideb.hu

Abstract. Matrix grammars are one of the first approaches ever proposed in regulated rewriting, prescribing that rules have to be applied in a certain order. Semi-conditional grammars introduced the notion of permitting and forbidding contexts in context-free rules. In this paper, we introduce a new form of matrix grammars, called matrix forbidding grammars, where matrices of context-free rules are considered and each context-free rule is associated with a context so that a rule (in a matrix) can be applied only if this context is not a subword of the current sentential form. For matrix forbidding grammars, we study a range of descriptional complexity parameters, such as degree (length of forbidden contexts), number of nonterminals, number of conditional rules, number of matrices containing conditional rules, and matrix length, in order to explore the Pareto frontier (set of solutions that represents the best trade-off between all the parameters) of computational completeness.

Keywords: Matrix grammars · (Generalized) Forbidding Grammars · Generalized Forbidding Matrix · Computational Completeness · Descriptional Complexity

1 Introduction

Matrix grammars are presumably the oldest type of regulated rewriting mechanism, introduced by S. Ábrahám [1,2]. It has been observed that context conditions in the form of appearance checks are necessary to obtain computational complete classes of matrix grammars with context-free core rules; see [3,4,6,13,17,18]. However, not all variations of adding such appearance checks

Published by Springer Nature Switzerland AG 2025
A. Malcher and L. Prigioniero (Eds.): DCFS 2025, LNCS 15759, pp. 94–107, 2025.
https://doi.org/10.1007/978-3-031-97100-6_7

are known to be computationally complete, see [7,11]. Due to these subtleties, every variation of context conditions has to be studied carefully. This has been undertaken, e.g., in [10] for the concept of generalized forbidding grammars, studied in [14,15]: forbidding conditions are attached to matrices in the form of sets of forbidden strings. Aspects of descriptional complexity, with a certain focus on nonterminal complexity, also have quite some tradition with matrix languages and their variations; see [5,8,16].

In this paper, we propose a novel way to blend generalized forbidding and matrix grammars, where forbidding conditions are attached to individual rules in the matrices as forbidden strings. We first introduce our new grammatical mechanism formally in Sect. 2. Then, we provide basic properties of two variations of Geffert normal forms that are central for obtaining our results (characterizing the family RE of recursively enumerable languages) that we present thereafter, grouped to reflect the two different simulation variations. Due to space restrictions, some proofs can be found in the long version only. We present our main results of the paper in Sect. 3 and conclude with Sect. 4.

2 Preliminaries

A *matrix forbidding grammar* $G = (N, T, M, S)$ is specified by a set N of nonterminals, a set T of terminals, a finite set M of matrices and the start symbol S. Matrices of length ℓ in G are of the form $m = [(A_1 \to x_1, f_1), \ldots, (A_\ell \to x_\ell, f_\ell)]$ with (for $1 \le j \le \ell$) $A_j \in N$, $x_j \in (N \cup T)^*$, where $f_j \in (N \cup T)^+ \cup \{\emptyset\}$ is called a *forbidden string* or *forbidden context*. A rule $(A_j \to x_j, f_j)$ in a matrix with $f_j \neq \emptyset$ is called a *conditional rule*. When all forbidden contexts are $\emptyset$ in a matrix m, then m is *unconditional* and is the same as a (context-free) matrix (without appearance checking). Otherwise, such a matrix is called a *conditional matrix*. Abusing notation, instead of $(A \to x, \emptyset)$, we also write $A \to x$.

As with generalized forbidding grammars, we can apply a rule $(A_j \to x_j, f_j)$ to a string w if f_j is no substring of w and if A_j occurs in w. If the rule is applicable, we get a string w' from w by replacing exactly one occurrence of A_j in w by x_j; we also write $w \rightsquigarrow w'$ then. Matrix m is applicable on string w_0 if (for $j = 1, \ldots, \ell$) $w_{j-1} \rightsquigarrow w_j$; finally, w_ℓ is the result of applying m to w, and we can denote this as $w \Rightarrow_m w_\ell$. With $\Rightarrow = \bigcup_{m \in M} \Rightarrow_m$, we can define $L(G) = \{w \in T^* \mid S \Rightarrow^* w\}$, where $\Rightarrow^* = \bigcup_{r \ge 0} \Rightarrow^r$ is the reflexive-transitive closure of $\Rightarrow$.

$\mathrm{MF}(d; n, r, m, \ell)$ is the language family that can be described by matrix forbidding grammars of degree (i.e., longest length of a forbidden context) of at most d, with at most n nonterminals, using at most r conditional rules that are spread over at most m conditional matrices, so that no matrix length is beyond ℓ. When a complexity measure cannot be bounded, this is denoted by *. A survey of computational completeness results is collected in Table 1.

According to [12], a type-0 grammar is said to be in (4, 1)-Geffert normal form (GNF) if it has exactly four nonterminals S, A, B, C that uses context-free rules with S as its left-hand side and a single non-context-free erasing rule of

Table 1. RE characterizations of this paper and the literature, sorted by increasing degree and increasing number of nonterminals and finally number of conditional rules.

Degree	# Non-terminals	# Conditional rules	# Conditional matrices	Max. Matrix Length	Reference
1	*	*	*	2	Theorem 2 in [10]
2	7	31	8	4	Theorem 7 in [9]
2	8	12	6	3	Theorem 12 in [10]
1	3	*	*	*	Theorem 13
2	4	8	1	8	Theorem 9
2	5	5	1	6	Theorem 7
2	5	14	4	5	Theorem 10
2	6	7	2	4	Theorem 5
2	7	6	2	3	Theorem 8
2	8	6	3	2	Theorem 6
3	5	8	2	4	Theorem 11
3	6	10	4	3	Theorem 12

the form $ABC \to \lambda$. The derivation occurs in two phases. In Phase 1, only the context-free rules are applied and this phase ends by applying the rule $S \to \lambda$. In Phase 2, the only non-context-free rule $ABC \to \lambda$ is applied repeatedly. The following properties hold for $(4,1)$-GNF grammars and are used in proofs later:

1. If $S \Rightarrow^* w$, then $w \in \{A, AB\}^*\{S, ABC, \lambda\}(\{C, BC\} \cup T)^*$.
2. No sentential form derivable in the grammar contains substrings BBB or CA (in fact, after any C no A can occur).
3. If $S \Rightarrow^* w$, with $w = w't$, where $w' \in \{A, B, C\}^+$ and $t \in (T\{C, BC\}^*)^*$, then w' contains exactly one occurrence from $\{ABC, AC, ABBC\}$ as a substring. We refer to this substring as the *central part* of w, while we call t the *terminal suffix*.
   (a) Only with ABC as central part, possibly $w' \Rightarrow^* \lambda$ as intended in a derivation that yields a terminal string.
   (b) Also only with $t \in T^*$, a terminal string could be produced.
   (c) If w contains a substring from $\{A, B\}T$, the derivation is blocked.
4. Again, the derivation proceeds in two phases, the first one split into two stages. Only in phase two, a central part will appear. Until then, S separates the central part. To the right of S, some string from $(T \cup \{C, BC\})^*$ is situated, ending with a terminal suffix $t \in (T\{C, BC\}^*)^*$.

In particular when simulating derivations of this kind of normal form with grammars that rely on forbidding strings, the problem is that we cannot really test if the terminal suffix consists of terminal symbols only. The easiest way to resolve this problem is to explicitly split the first two stages by using a new additional start symbol S' as discussed in the following theorem. As we somewhat artificially introduce another nonterminal, we call this variation $(4+1,1)$-GNF.

Proposition 1. *A type-0 grammar* $G = (N, T, P, S')$ *where* $N = \{S', S, A, B, C\}$ *is said to be in* $(4+1,1)$*-GNF if its rules can be classified* *to belong in one of the following groups: (a)* context-free terminal-generating*:* $S' \to uS'a$*, with* $u \in \{A, AB\}^+$ *and* $a \in T$*; (b)* context-free no-terminal-generating*:* $\{S' \to uSv, S \to uSv\}$*, with* $u \in \{A, AB\}^+$ *and* $v \in \{C, BC\}^*$*; (c)* context-free transient*:* $S \to \lambda$*; and (d)* non-context-free deleting*:* $ABC \to \lambda$*.*

There are some slight differences to the construction given by Geffert in [12]. Namely, first Geffert did not differentiate between S' and S; he only mentioned one symbol, say, S, instead; then, he had to use rules from $\{S \to uSv, S \to uv\}$ in the second stage of Phase 1 also to transition into Phase 2. He could prove that a possible mixture of context-free terminal-generating and context-free no-terminal-generating rules does no harm, as such unintended derivations will not terminate. However, in our simulations, we cannot control this, so that we will always have both S' and S in the grammar that we are going to simulate. This explains why we introduced the notation '$(4+1,1)$-GNF grammar' (in [10]) as opposed to $(4,1)$-GNF (which should mean the variation where 4 nonterminals S, A, B, C are used and one non-context-free deletion rule $ABC \to \lambda$ in order to describe any recursively enumerable language): We seemingly artificially have to add one more nonterminal. However, this is essential to ensure the correctness of our simulations. Notice one more technical detail: The rules $S \to uSa$, $S \to uSv$, $S \to uv$ proposed by Geffert guarantee that after removing the symbol S, as u is non-empty, the sentential form starts with some non-empty string over $\{A, B\}$. The same property is guaranteed by our proposalDue to these (informal) arguments, the following statement is true.

Theorem 2. *For each* $L \in \mathrm{RE}$*, there is a* $(4+1,1)$*-GNF grammar generating* L*.*

To prove our main results, we need another enhanced variant of a normal form as derived by Geffert in [12]. We are now describing a variant of a normal form that was originally introduced to prove that 3 nonterminals are sufficient to generate any recursively enumerable language by a type-0 grammar. It can be proved very similarly to Proposition 1.

Proposition 3. *A type-0 grammar* $G = (N, T, P, S')$ *where* $N = \{S', S, A, B\}$ *is said to be in* $(3+1,1)$*-GNF if its rules can be classified to belong in one of the following groups: (a)* context-free terminal-generating*:* $S' \to uS'a$*, with* $u \in \{AB, ABB\}^+$ *and* $a \in T$*; (b)* context-free no-terminal-generating*:* $\{S' \to uSv, S \to uSv\}$*, with* $u \in \{AB, ABB\}^+$ *and* $v \in \{BA, BBA\}^*$*; (c)* context-free transient*:* $S \to \lambda$*; and (d)* non-context-free deleting*:* $ABBBA \to \lambda$*.*

This normal form uses less nonterminals than $(4+1,1)$-GNF, but it also offers less structure (e.g., a characterization result of Phase 2 as in Proposition 1 is not possible) and some tests are more complicated here. Nonetheless, for each derivable sentential form v that does not contain S', S, we have $v = v't$ for some $v' \in \{AB, ABB\}^*\{BA, BBA\}^*$ and $t \in T^*$. Again, we can have the notion of a *center*, this time referring to strings of the form $ABBA$, $ABBBA$ and $ABBBBA$. Notice that only the second form is the intended 'good' one and it can be formed in two ways: $AB \cdot BBA$ and $ABB \cdot BA$. Also, the first possibility of $ABBA$ is particularly awkward, because once this type of 'center' has been produced, the position of the center has become undetectable, as this substring can occur multiple times in the sentential form, while the other two centers are unique if they exist. In similar lines of Theorem 2, we have the following:

Theorem 4. *For each* $L \in \mathrm{RE}$, *there is a* $(3{+}1, 1)$*-GNF grammar generating* L.

3 Main Results

We consider a type-0 grammar in $(4+1, 1)$-GNF for the proofs of Theorems 5, 6, 7, 8 and in $(3+1, 1)$-GNF for the proofs of Theorems 9, 10, 11, 12.

Theorem 5. $\mathrm{RE} = \mathrm{MF}(2; 6, 7, 2, 4)$.

Proof. We simulate a type-0 grammar G in $(4{+}1, 1)$-GNF by a matrix forbidding grammar G'. The idea is to 're-cycle' the nonterminal symbol S of G within G'.

$$\begin{aligned} m1 &= [(A \to A, \$), (B \to \$, BB), (C \to S, S'), (S \to \lambda, \$C)], \\ m2 &= [(A \to S, \$A), (S \to \lambda, A\$), (\$ \to \lambda, C\$)] . \end{aligned}$$

The intended derivation is: $\alpha ABC\beta t \Rightarrow_{m1} \alpha A\$\beta t \Rightarrow_{m2} \alpha\beta t$. We analyze a sentential form w that is derivable both in G and in G', i.e., $w = \alpha\gamma\beta t$ by Proposition 1 (note that S' must be absent and C present when applying $m1$ and that \$ is absent so that $m2$ is inapplicable), where $\gamma \in \{ABC, AC, ABBC\}$ is the center. First, the possibly bad center $ABBC$ is caught by the substring check BB in $m1$, hence we do not consider this anymore.

It could be that we try to delete any C that is not in the center of w (or it might be in the bad center AC). Then, assuming that we have turned (as intended) the B occurring in the center into \$, then the substring $\$C$ must occur before applying the last rule of $m1$, which stops this erroneous derivation, unless we made these replacements or deletions at the very right end of β. Hence, in order to pass $m1$, when some unintended C was deleted upon applying $m1$, we must have replaced some occurrence of B from α, or we have arrived at $\alpha\gamma\overline{\beta}t$, where $\overline{\beta}$ was obtained from β by deleting its last symbol C and replacing the last occurrence of symbol B by \$. Notice that this description also covers a situation like $\beta = BCBCC$ and $\overline{\beta} = BC\$C$.

What happens if we turn the 'wrong' B (i.e., any B from α) and not the B in the center into \$? This could also happen (similarly) if we had the center AC, not ABC. Let us hence call ζC as the center, with $\zeta = A$ or $\zeta = AB$ and α' as the string obtained from α by replacing any B within α by a \$, and similarly assume that β' is obtained from $C\beta$ by deleting any occurrence of C. In other words, we find when starting with the sentential form $w = \alpha\zeta C\beta t$: $w \Rightarrow_{m1} w' = \alpha'\zeta\beta' t$. As \$ is present, we cannot reapply $m1$ and in fact we must apply $m2$ to make any progress and possibly get rid of \$ again. Now, observe that in such a scenario, by the basic properties of $(4+1, 1)$-GNF, some A must occur to the right of \$, which is checked in the first rule of $m2$. Hence, after this check, we know that only the B occurring in the center (and therefore also, the center was ABC as intended) could have been replaced by \$ (as intended).

When applying the first rule of $m2$, that is again re-cycling the nonterminal S (but notice that $m2$ expects \$ to be present, so this matrix cannot be applied in the first simulation phase), we might replace some 'wrong' A by S, i.e., an A that is not in the center. In that case, the second context check (concerning $A\$$) will catch this mistake. There is only one way that we did not follow up here, namely, when $w \Rightarrow_{m1} w' = \alpha\gamma\overline{\beta}t$ as described above. Then, the checks concerning A and \$ will not help, but now, when trying to apply the last rule of $m2$ that is deleting \$, the context $\$C$ is checked and will also catch this erroneous derivation.

By induction, we can conclude that G' will (only) generate $L(G)$.

Theorem 6. $\mathrm{RE} = \mathrm{MF}(2; 8, 6, 3, 2)$.

Proof. Again, we simulate a type-0 grammar $G = (N, T, P, S')$ in $(4+1, 1)$-GNF. We now describe a matrix forbidding grammar $G' = (N', T, M, S')$, where $N' = N \cup \{\#_1, \#_2, \$\}$ and the set of matrices M contains singleton matrices for each context-free rules of G. The following matrices simulate $ABC \to \lambda$:

$$\begin{aligned} m1 &= [(C \to \#_1, \#_2), (A \to \#_2, S)] \\ m2 &= [(B \to \$\$, BB), (\#_1 \to \#_2, \$C)] \\ m3 &= [(\#_2 \to \lambda, A\$), (\$ \to \lambda, \$A)] \end{aligned}$$

The intended simulation of $ABC \to \lambda$ is $\alpha ABC\beta t \Rightarrow_{m1} \alpha\#_2 B\#_1\beta t \Rightarrow_{m2} \alpha\#_2\$\$\#_2\beta t \Rightarrow_{m3} \alpha\#_2\$\beta t \Rightarrow_{m3} \alpha\beta t$, proving that $L(G) \subseteq L(G')$.

Let us now consider a string w that is derivable both in G and in G'. As $m2, m3$ check for the presence of some nonterminal from $N' \setminus N$ and as $m1$ checks the presence of C as well as the absence of S, by Proposition 1 we can apply matrices only to strings w that can occur during Phase 2 of G. Also, we can assume that $w \notin T^*$ (then, no further derivations are possible in either of the grammars) and that both A and C are present in w (otherwise, no matrix would be applicable, as in particular applying $m1$ requires the presence of both nonterminals). Hence, we consider a string of the form $w = xyzt$ with $x \in \{A, AB\}^*$, $y \in \{ABC, ABBC, AC\}$, $z \in \{BC, C\}^*$ and $t \in T^*$. We now prove that we can only derive a string of the same form again again if the center y equals ABC and then, this would correspond to applying $ABC \to \lambda$.

As $m2, m3$ require some nonterminal from $N' \setminus N$, $w \Rightarrow_{m1} w'$ is enforced. We can think of w' being identical to w but one occurrence of C that has been turned into $\#_1$ and one occurrence of A that has been turned into $\#_2$. Also notice that $m1$ checks for the absence of $\#_2$ so that it cannot be reapplied. Neither can we apply matrix $m3$, as it requires the presence of \$ and of $\#_2$. Hence, we must continue with $w' \Rightarrow_{m2} w''$. Compared to w, this string w'' can be seen as being obtained by turning one occurrence of C and one occurrence of A into $\#_2$ and one occurrence of B into \$. Moreover, as the forbidden context BB is checked before applying the first rule $B \to \$\$$, we also know that $y = ABBBC$ is ruled out. The forbidden context $\$C$ associated to the second rule ensures that w'' will contain either the substring $\$A$ or the substring $\$\#_2$, as terminal symbols cannot be to the right of \$ that was originally replacing a B.

Notice that the presence of $\#_2$ in w'' blocks $m1$ and the absence of $\#_1$ blocks $m2$. Hence, we must now see $w'' \Rightarrow_{m3} w'''$. On applying the two deletion rules, we check the absence of substrings $A\$$ and $\$A$, so that in fact the string $\#_2\$\$\#_2$ was forming the center of w''. In fact, this reasoning also rules out the possible (bad) center $y = AC$, because then, any B that was turned into $\$\$$ would see C to its right or A to its left, and these cases are checked in the matrices $m2$ and $m3$. The arguments saying which matrix to apply remain the same for w''' as for w'', i.e., we have to apply $m3$ again to obtain $\alpha\beta_t$ as intended. Observe that it is important that we first check for the absence of $A\$$, as after removing the last occurrence of $\#_2$, we will see the substring $A\$$ also in some intended derivations. This argument finishes the induction step of our proof of the inclusion $L(G') \subseteq L(G)$, as finally $\alpha = \beta = \lambda$.

Theorem 7. $\mathrm{RE} = \mathrm{MF}(2; 5, 5, 1, 6)$.

Proof. Assume that S' is the start symbols of the type-0 grammar G in $(4+1, 1)$-GNF that we are going to simulate. Note that $(S \to \lambda)$ is an unconditional rule and is interpreted as a single-rule unconditional matrix (as any other context-free rule of G). We propose the following matrix m to simulate $ABC \to \lambda$:

$$[(B \to \lambda, AC), (A \to S', S), (C \to S, S'A), (S \to S, S'B), (S' \to \lambda, S'C), (S \to \lambda)]\,.$$

The intended simulation is $\alpha ABC\beta t \rightsquigarrow \alpha AC\beta t \rightsquigarrow \alpha S'C\beta t \rightsquigarrow \alpha S'S\beta t \rightsquigarrow \alpha S'S\beta t \rightsquigarrow \alpha S\beta t \rightsquigarrow \alpha\beta t$. By induction, $L(G) \subseteq L(G')$ follows.

First, observe that applying m is only possible on a string w that is derived in Phase 2 of G according to Proposition 1 as we test for the presence of C and for the absence of S. Also, because we actually test for the presence of A, B, C, we can assume that $w = \alpha\beta t$ for $\alpha \in \{A, AB\}^+$, $\beta \in \{BC, C\}^+$ and $t \in T^*$. Hence, $w = \alpha'\zeta\beta' t$, where α' is a prefix of α, β' is a suffix of β and $\zeta \in \{ABC, ABBC, AC\}$ is the center. Upon applying m, the forbidden context of the first rule excludes the possibility $\zeta = AC$. Consider $w \rightsquigarrow w'$. Then, w' originates from w by deleting an arbitrary occurrence of B within w. By the structure of the encoding, this could be in α', ζ, or β'. Next, with $w' \rightsquigarrow w''$, we substitute any occurrence of A in w' with S'. This can happen only in α' or in ζ. If it would have happened in α', then to the right of it, we would see either an A or a B, and this would be still true for w''' obtained from w'' by replacing any C by S. Therefore, the forbidden contexts of the third and fourth rules of m catch this situation, i.e., $w'' = \alpha'\zeta'\beta' t$ is enforced. Moreover, the same argument rules out the case $\zeta' = S'BC$, i.e., $w'' = \alpha' S'C\beta' t$. By looking at the forbidden context of the penultimate rule of m, we understand that only $w''' = \alpha' S'S\beta' t$ is possible, and deleting S' and S using the last two rules of m necessarily converts w''' into $w^4 = \alpha'\beta' t$ and we can finally observe that w^4 can be obtained (within G) by applying $ABC \to \lambda$ to w. This enables us to prove $L(G') \subseteq L(G)$ by induction.

Theorem 8. $\mathrm{RE} = \mathrm{MF}(2; 7, 6, 2, 3)$.

Proof. We assume that S' is the start symbols of the type-0 grammar G in $(4+1, 1)$-GNF that we are going to simulate. The simulation of $ABC \to \lambda$ is given below.

$$\begin{aligned} m1 &= [(B \to \lambda, AC), (A \to \$, \$), (C \to \#, S)] \\ m2 &= [(\# \to \#\#, \$A), (\# \to \#\#, \$B), (\$ \to \lambda, \$C)] \\ m3 &= [(\# \to \lambda), (\# \to \lambda), (\# \to \lambda)] \end{aligned}$$

Note that $m3$ is an unconditional matrix rule. After $m1$ is applied, $m3$ cannot be applied as there will be only one # present in the string after $m1$. As $m1$ also cannot be reapplied, $m2$ is the only possible application. After $m2$ is applied, the string will have three # and no \$, so $m2$ cannot be reapplied as the presence of \$ is required in the string.

In the following, we will obtain some computational completeness results using type-0 grammars in $(3+1, 1)$-GNF.

Theorem 9. $\mathrm{RE} = \mathrm{MF}(2; 4, 8, 1, 8)$.

Proof. We start with a type-0 grammar $G = (N, T, P, S')$ in $(3+1, 1)$-GNF. The rule $ABBBA \to \lambda$ is supposed to be simulated by the following matrix m:

$$\begin{aligned} m = [&(B \to S', S), (B \to S', S'A), (B \to S, AS'), (A \to \lambda, S'B) \\ &(A \to \lambda, BS), (S' \to \lambda, BS'), (S \to \lambda, AS), (S' \to \lambda, S'A)]\,. \end{aligned}$$

The intended simulation is as follows.

$$\begin{aligned} \alpha ABBBA\beta t &\leadsto \alpha ABS'BA\beta t \leadsto \alpha ABS'S'A\beta t \leadsto \alpha ASS'S'A\beta t \\ &\leadsto \alpha ASS'S'\beta t \leadsto \alpha SS'S'\beta t \leadsto \alpha SS'\beta t \leadsto \alpha S'\beta t \leadsto \alpha\beta t \end{aligned}$$

In order to analyze sentential forms that should not terminate, we first consider the case when the matrix m is applied to a sentential form that contains the symbol S' (the absence of the symbol S is checked by the first rule). In this case, the sentential form is $w = \beta S' t$ for some $\beta \in \{AB, ABB\}^*$, $t \in T^*$. Since the first three rules of m do not change any A into w, both of the first two rules have to rewrite occurrences of B that do not see A as their neighbors. This is not possible, as there is at most one B without a neighboring A (if the sentential form happens to be $w = \beta_1 ABBS't$).

Consider now the case when there is no S', S in the sentential form, but there is no substring BBB either, thus, when it is of the form $w = \alpha ABBA\beta t$ for some $\alpha \in \{AB, ABB\}^*$, $\beta \in \{BA, BBA\}^*$, $t \in T^*$. Since there are no B-occurrences without neighboring A, and as mentioned above, the first three rules of m do not change any A, the application of the first two rules must produce both AS' and $S'A$, so the third rule of m can never be applied.

Consider next the one remaining case when the derivation should not terminate successfully, the case when the sentential form is $w = \alpha ABBBBA\beta t$ for some $\alpha \in \{AB, ABB\}^*$, $\beta \in \{BA, BBA\}^*$, $t \in T^*$. Again, because AS' and $S'A$ are in the forbidding contexts of rules 2 and 3, the first two rules of the matrix must rewrite w as $\alpha ABS'S'BA\beta$, and now one more B should be replaced with S by the third rule. As the forbidding contexts of the fourth and the sixth rules, $S'B$ and BS', are present in the sentential form, the derivation is stuck.

Let us consider now the case when the derivation should terminate, that is, when the sentential form is $w = \alpha ABBBA\beta t$ for some $\alpha \in \{AB, ABB\}^*$, $\beta \in \{BA, BBA\}^*$, $t \in T^*$. The first two rules must rewrite two B occurrences to S, and because of the forbidding contexts of rules 2 and 3, there are three cases possible: (i) $w \Rightarrow^2 \alpha_1 ABS'\alpha_2 ABS'BA\beta t$, (ii) $w \Rightarrow^2 \alpha ABS'BA\beta_1 BS'A\beta_2 t$, (iii) $w \Rightarrow^2 \alpha ABS'S'A\beta t$, where $\alpha_1, \alpha_2 \in \{AB, ABB\}^*$, $\beta_1, \beta_2 \in \{BA, BBA\}^*$.

The first two cases can be treated analogously, as there are two occurrences of the substring BS' in both of them, and rule 3 can only eliminate one of these before rule 6 should be applied. Since the forbidding context of rule 6 is exactly BS', the derivation cannot be successful. In the last case, consider the possible applications of rule 3. We either obtain $w' = \alpha ASS'S'A\beta t$, or we rewrite another B somewhere in the sentential form and BS' remains a substring. As BS' would forbid the application of rule 6, we must apply rule 3 in a way which produces $\alpha ASS'S'A\beta t$ in order to be able to finish the derivation. For the application of rule 4, we again have three possibilities (i) $w' \Rightarrow \alpha' ASS'S'A\beta'$ (ii) $w' \Rightarrow \alpha SS'S'A\beta t$ (iii) $w' \Rightarrow \alpha ASS'S'\beta$ where $\alpha'\beta'$ is the result of erasing one A from $\alpha\beta$. In case 1, notice that after erasing one more A with rule 5, either AS or $S'S'A$ remains as a substring in the sentential form, and AS blocks the application of rule 7. If rule 5 is applied in such a way that we have $S'S'A$ in the sentential form, then the application of rule 8 is blocked, as rule 6 may only remove one occurrence of S', thus $S'A$, the forbidding context of rule 8 remains in the string. In case 2, notice that $\alpha \in \{AB, ABB\}$, so it ends with a symbol B making the forbidding context BS blocks the application of rule 4. In case 3, as mentioned above at case 1, the presence of AS will block the application of rule 7, so we must obtain $\alpha SS'S'\beta t$ by the application of rule 5, and then by rules 6, 7, and 8 we have $\alpha\beta t$, thus, we have successfully simulated with matrix m the application of the erasing rule $ABBBA \to \lambda$.

Theorem 10. RE $=$ MF$(2; 5, 14, 4, 5)$.

Proof. We start with a grammar $G = (N, T, P, S')$ in (3+1, 1)-GNF. The deletion rule $ABBBA \to \lambda$ should be simulated by the following four matrices.

$$\begin{aligned}
m1 &= [(B \to X, X), (B \to X, XA), (B \to S', XX), (A \to A, AS'), (S' \to \lambda, S'A)] \\
m2 &= [(X \to X, XB), (X \to \lambda, BX), (A \to XX, S'), (A \to X, S)] \\
m3 &= [(X \to X, AX), (X \to \lambda, XA), (X \to \lambda, S'), (X \to \lambda, S)] \\
m4 &= [(S \to \lambda, X)]
\end{aligned}$$

Notice that we are re-cycling the non-terminal S' in $m1$ but we do not check if S' was already present. We have to check that no unintended derivation can happen this way. However, upon applying $m1$, we also introduce the symbol X.

We have to delete X by applying either $m2$ or $m3$, but both test for the absence of S' and of S. But we also cannot finish Phase 1 simulations, trying to get rid of the symbol S finally, as this case is finally caught by $m4$, a matrix that is to be used before the simulation of Phase 2.

The intended simulation of $ABBBA \to \lambda$ works as follows, starting on a string $w = \alpha ABBBA\beta t$ with $\alpha \in \{AB, ABB\}^*$, $\beta \in \{BA, BBA\}^*$, $t \in T^*$. $w = \alpha ABBBA\beta t \Rightarrow_{m1} \alpha AXXA\beta t \Rightarrow_{m2} \alpha X^4\beta t \Rightarrow_{m3} \alpha\beta t$.

Next, we analyze how unintended derivations using $m1$ might work. If we look at a substring BA and replace this B by X using the first rule of $m1$, the context condition of the second rule of $m1$ will stop this derivation. To 'survive' this test, we have to replace the leftmost B within the substring BB (this also happened in the intended derivation), as if we replace the B within the substring BS' or BS, we are wrongly applying this matrix to a string that is meant to simulate Phase 1, and this case was already discussed above. Notice that by the encoding used in $(3+1,1)$-GNF, no terminal symbol can ever occur immediately to the right of a B-occurrence.

How could the situation look like after applying the second rule of $m1$? As the third rule will check for XX as a forbidden substring, the only somewhat local situation would look as follows: $xXBXy$ (as it also happens in the intended derivation). This means that we started with a sentential form containing the substring BBB and this is only possible when simulating Phase 2; even more, we must have seen the center $ABBBA$ or $ABBBBA$ in this case. If we do not have such a local replacement situation, it actually means that we are looking at an unintended situation, so we have to carefully analyze the different scenarios.

We might have seen $xBByBAz \rightsquigarrow xXByBAz \rightsquigarrow xXByXAz$. To avoid the 'local scenario' discussed above, we can assume that $y \neq \lambda$. The third rule will turn another B-occurrence into S'; then, the last two rules check if substrings AS' or $S'A$ appears. This is quite a strong check, as it enforces that we actually have another substring BB and then, next to this substring, a symbol different from A. This could be either realized by a substring BBB, leading to the substring $BS'B$ and then BB, or S' or S are already to the left or right of BB.

Let us consider the unintended derivation possibilities in Phase 2 further, assuming that the two X are not showing up in the center. As we have replaced one B-occurrence by X that does not see A to its right, this X-occurrence must now see B to its right, which blocks applying $m2$. Also, whatever way we replace a B by X outside the center, either subword AX or XA will be created, blocking matrix $m3$. This proves that all replacements of B by X must happen in the center. Also, our reasoning ruled out the possible center $ABBA$. If we face the center $ABBBBA$, then necessarily the last three rules of $m1$ will delete one of the central B's. This means that after finishing $m1$, we look at three possible centers: $ABXXA$, $AXBXA$, or $AXXBA$. In either case, any attempt to apply $m2$ or $m3$ is blocked. Hence, only the 'good center' $ABBBA$ remains as a possibility. Following similar arguments as above, now $ABBBA \Rightarrow_{m1} AXXA$ is enforced.

Let us therefore now consider a string of the form $w' = \alpha AXXA\beta t$, assuming that $w = \alpha ABBBA\beta t$ was a sentential form derivable both in G and in G'. As

$m1$ and $m3$ are blocked, we must apply $m2$ now. Apart from the checks that we already discussed, this will first delete one occurrence of X and then one occurrence of A is turned into X and another one into XX. This describes any possible w'' satisfying $w' \Rightarrow_{m2} w''$. Due to the presence of the substring XX, we cannot apply $m1$. Due to the structure of the encoding of $(3+1,1)$-GNF, the XB- and BX-checks suffice to avoid re-applying $m2$. If we apply $m3$ (as intended), then the absence of AX and XA is checked. All three occurrences of X will be deleted and we arrive at $w'' \Rightarrow_{m3} w''' = \alpha\beta t$ as we desired.

Theorem 11. $\mathrm{RE} = \mathrm{MF}(3; 5, 8, 2, 4)$.

Proof. We start with a type-0 grammar in $(3+1,1)$-GNF with the alphabet $N = \{S', S, A, B\}$. The context-free rules of G are translated into unconditional short matrices (of length 1) in the simulating GFM grammar G', with $N' = N \cup \{\#\}$. The matrices (two conditional and one unconditional) of G' for simulating $ABBBA \to \lambda$ are given below:

$$\begin{aligned} m1 &= [(B \to \#, \#), (B \to \#, S'), (B \to \#, S), (\# \to \#, A\#A)] \\ m2 &= [(\# \to \#, \#B), (A \to \#, B\#), (A \to \#, \#A), (\# \to \lambda, A\#)] \\ m3 &= [(\# \to \lambda), (\# \to \lambda), (\# \to \lambda), (\# \to \lambda)] \end{aligned}$$

For $\alpha \in \{AB, ABB\}^*$, $\beta \in \{BA, BBA\}^*$ and $t \in T^*$, the intended simulation is $\alpha ABBBA\beta t \Rightarrow_{m1} \alpha A\#^3A\beta t \Rightarrow_{m2} \alpha\#^4\beta t \Rightarrow_{m3} \alpha\beta t$ proving $L(G) \subseteq L(G')$.

To prove the converse, let us first consider any sentential form $v = \alpha'\beta' t$ where $\alpha' \in \{AB, ABB\}^*$, $\beta' \in \{BA, BBA\}^*$, $t \in T^*$.

<u>Case A</u>: $\alpha' \neq \lambda, \beta' = \lambda$ in v. In this case, between two As, there is either one or two occurrences of B, but there is no substring BBB. Since there are no B-occurrences without neighboring As, one of the first three rules of $m1$ surely changes such a B (with a neighboring A) into $\#$ which leads to either a substring $A\#$ or $\#A$. The forbidden context $A\#A$ in the last rule of $m1$ takes care that no B with A on either sides is turned into $\#$. So we assume that at the end of applying $m1$, every Bs that was turned into $\#$ has one neighbor A and another neighbor B. This leads to $B\#$ or $\#B$ as a substring at the end of applying $m1$ on v. Let $v \Rightarrow_{m1} v'$. The presence of $\#, B\#$ or $\#B$, three occurrences of $\#$ forbids us from applying any of the rules on v' and hence the derivation is stuck.

<u>Case B</u>: $\alpha' = \lambda, \beta' \neq \lambda$ in v: This case is similar to the previous case A.

<u>Case C</u>: $\alpha' \neq \lambda, \beta' \neq \lambda$ in v. Let $v = \alpha'\beta' t$ with $\alpha' \in \{AB, ABB\}^+$, $\beta' \in \{BA, BBA\}^+$, $t \in T^*$ be considered as $w = \alpha AB, ABBBBA, BA\beta t$ with $\alpha \in \{AB, ABB\}^*$, $\beta \in \{BA, BBA\}^*$, $t \in T^*$. We notice that the center here could be one of $ABBA, ABBBA, ABBBBA$.

<u>Case C.1</u>: when the center is $ABBA$. In this case, $w = \alpha ABBA\beta t$ for some $\alpha \in \{AB, ABB\}^*, \beta \in \{BA, BBA\}^*, t \in T^*$. On applying $m1$ to w, at least one non-central B is turned into $\#$ since there are only two centrals Bs but $m1$ turns three Bs into $\#$. Let us look at this non-central B that is turned

into # by $m1$. Since there are no B occurrences without neighboring A, as in Case A, the presence of $\#A$ or $A\#$ forbids us to apply $m2$. However, on close observation, one might notice that $m3$ can be applied only when there are at least four occurrences of #. However, application of $m1$ and not $m2$ produces only three occurrences of # and hence $m3$ also cannot be applied and hence the derivation is stuck.

Case C.2: when the center is $ABBBBA$. In this case, $w = \alpha ABBBBA\beta t$ for some $\alpha \in \{AB, ABB\}^*$, $\beta \in \{BA, BBA\}^*$, $t \in T^*$. Applying $m1$ on w will change three Bs into # which will again have one of $A\#, B\#, \#B, \#A$ as a substring. Similar to the above case, the derivation is stuck.

Case C.3: when the center is $ABBBA$. In this case, $w = \alpha ABBBA\beta T$ for some $\alpha \in \{AB, ABB\}^*$, $\beta \in \{BA, BBA\}^*$, $t \in T^*$. The matrix $m1$ changes three Bs into #. We intend to turn all the three central Bs into #. If this is not so, then at least one central B is not turned into # which leads to having either $\#B$ or $B\#$ as a substring in the center. This blocks the application of $m2$ and hence the derivation is stuck as discussed above. Hence, we safely assume that on applying $m1$, $w = \alpha ABBBA\beta t$ turns into $w = \alpha A\#\#\#A\beta t$. One cannot reapply $m1$ on w' since the first rule of $m1$ forbids #. Matrix $m3$ demands four occurrences of # and hence cannot be applied. On deterministically applying $m2$, the first rule just checks the absence of $\#B$ which w' passes the check and the second rule turns an occurrence of A into #. We intend to the change the rightmost A within the central $A\#\#\#A$ into #. If this was not done, then $\#A$ would be substring and this blocks the application of the third rule of $m2$ and hence the derivation is stuck. Hence, we can now safely assume that the rightmost A is deterministically turned into # to fruitfully continue our derivation. Let us call this string with the rightmost A turned into # in w' as w'_1. On applying the third rule of $m2$ on w'_1, yet another A-occurrence is changed into #. Here, we intend to the change the leftmost A within the central $A\#\#\#\#$ into #. If this was not done, then $A\#$ would be a substring and this blocks the application of the last rule of $m2$ and hence the derivation is stuck. Thus, we again safely assume that the leftmost A is changed into #; call this string $w'_2 = \alpha\#^5\beta$. The last rule of $m2$ erases one #, thus yielding $w'' = \alpha\#^4\beta$. We notice that $w' \Rightarrow_{m2} w'' = \alpha\#\#\#\#\beta t$. Matrix $m1$ cannot be applied on w'' due to the presence of #. Matrix $m2$ also cannot be applied on w'' due to the presence of $\#B$; recalling that the first symbol β is B if $\beta \neq \lambda$. Suppose that $\beta = \lambda$, then the last symbol of $\alpha \neq \lambda$ is always B, so that the presence of $B\#$ will block the application of second rule in $m2$, thereby blocking the whole derivation. However if $\alpha = \beta = \lambda$, this means that $w'' = \#^4$, on which the second rule of $m2$ cannot be applied due to the absence of any A. These arguments prove that $m1, m2$ can never be (re)applied on $w'' = \alpha\#^4\beta$. On applying $m3$, four occurrences of # are deleted, thus yielding $w''' = \alpha\beta t$.

By induction, this case analysis shows that $L(G') \subseteq L(G)$ and this concludes the proof of the theorem.

At the expense of one nonterminal, we can reduce the matrix length to three. Instead of a proof, we only mention our construction of the simulation of the deletion rule $ABBBA \to \lambda$ now.

$$\begin{aligned} m1 &= [(B \to \#, \#), (B \to \#, S'), (B \to \#, S)] \\ m2 &= [(\# \to \#, A\#A), (A \to \$, \$), (A \to \$, B\#)] \\ m3 &= [(\# \to \lambda, \#B), (\# \to \lambda, \#A), (\$ \to \lambda, A\#)] \\ m4 &= [(\# \to \lambda), (\$ \to \lambda, \#)] \end{aligned}$$

This idea yields:

Theorem 12. RE = MF(3; 6, 10, 4, 3). □

4 Conclusions

In this paper, we started to explore the Pareto frontier of computability for matrix forbidding grammars, a new formalism that we introduced here as well. We showed that matrix forbidding grammars of various sizes are computationally complete. The most interesting question is of course if this Pareto frontier is delineated correctly. More specifically, tools should be developed that allow to prove that certain language families are not characterizing RE. There are clearly links between this newly introduced regulated rewriting mechanism and other variants of regulated rewriting, like generalized forbidding (matrix) grammars and graph-controlled grammars. It is sometimes possible to carry over descriptional complexity results or constructions from these mechanisms to matrix forbidding grammars. One example is a generalized forbidding grammar of size (d, i, n, c) (studied in [9,14,15]) that can be interpreted as a matrix forbidding grammar of the same degree d, the same number n of nonterminals, with matrix length bounded by i and with at most c conditional matrices, so that we have at most $i \cdot c$ many conditional rules. Another example is a generalized forbidding matrix grammar of size (d, i, n, m, l) (see [10] for further formalities) that can be viewed as a matrix forbidding grammar of the same degree d, the same number n of nonterminals, with matrix length at most $i + m - 1$ and with at most m conditional matrices, so that we have at most $i \cdot m$ many conditional rules. Unfortunately, the results that can be derived from [9] are not very strong for matrix forbidding grammars, while from [10], further supplements to Table 1 could be derived, as detailed in the long version of this paper.

As a non-trivial result from graph-controlled grammars, we mention a result obtained similarly to Corollary 6 from [8]:

Theorem 13. *Each recursively enumerable language can be generated by a matrix forbidding grammar with at most three nonterminals and with degree one.*

Acknowledgement. The first and the second authors thank DST-DAAD project (DST/IND/DAAD P-01-2024) and the work was carried out under the scope of the project. The work was initiated when the second author visited the Institute of the fourth author during June 2024 and the visit was supported by the University of Debrecen Scientific Research Bridging Fund (DETKA).

References

1. Ábrahám, S.: Some questions of language theory. In: First International Conference on Computational Linguistics, COLING, pp. 1–11 (1965)
2. Ábrahám, S.: Some questions of phrase-structure grammars. I. Comput. Linguistics **4**, 61–70 (1965)
3. Cremers, A., Mayer, O.: On matrix languages. Inf. Control (Now Inf. Comput.) **23**, 86–96 (1973)
4. Dassow, J., Fernau, H., Păun, Gh.: On the leftmost derivation in matrix grammars. Int. J. Found. Comput. Sci. **10**(1), 61–80 (1999)
5. Dassow, J., Păun, G.: Regulated rewriting in formal language theory. In: EATCS Monographs in Theoretical Computer Science, vol. 18. Springer, Cham (1989)
6. Ferment, D.: Principality results about some matrix languages families. In: Paredaens, J. (ed.) ICALP 1984. LNCS, vol. 172, pp. 151–161. Springer, Heidelberg (1984). https://doi.org/10.1007/3-540-13345-3_14
7. Fernau, H.: Unconditional transfer in regulated rewriting. Acta Informatica **34**, 837–857 (1997)
8. Fernau, H., Freund, R., Oswald, M., Reinhardt, K.: Refining the nonterminal complexity of graph-controlled, programmed, and matrix grammars. J. Autom. Lang. Comb. **12**(1/2), 117–138 (2007)
9. Fernau, H., Kuppusamy, L., Oladele, R.O., Raman, I.: Improved descriptional complexity results on generalized forbidding grammars. Discret. Appl. Math. **319**, 2–18 (2022)
10. Fernau, H., Kuppusamy, L., Raman, I.: On the computational completeness of generalized forbidding matrix grammars. Theoret. Comput. Sci. **999**, 114539 (2024)
11. Fernau, H., Stephan, F.: Characterizations of recursively enumerable languages by programmed grammars with unconditional transfer. J. Autom. Lang. Comb. **4**(2), 117–142 (1999)
12. Geffert, V.: Normal forms for phrase-structure grammars. RAIRO Informatique théorique et Applications/Theoretical Informatics and Applications **25**, 473–498 (1991)
13. Hauschildt, D., Jantzen, M.: Petri net algorithms in the theory of matrix grammars. Acta Informatica **31**, 719–728 (1994)
14. Meduna, A., Svec, M.: Descriptional complexity of generalized forbidding grammars. Int. J. Comput. Math. **80**(1), 11–17 (2003)
15. Meduna, A., Svec, M.: Grammars with Context Conditions and Their Applications. Wiley-Interscience (2005)
16. Păun, G.: Six nonterminals are enough for generating each r.e. language by a matrix grammar. Int. J. Comput. Math. 15(1-4), 23–37 (1984)
17. Salomaa, A.K.: Periodically time-variant context-free grammars. Inf. Control (now Inf. Comput.) **17**, 294–311 (1970)
18. Salomaa, A.K.: Matrix grammars with a leftmost restriction. Inf. Control (now Inf. Comput.) **20**, 143–149 (1972)

On the Decidability and Expressive Power of Several Theories Based on String Constraints

Justus Greve-Kramer, Tore Koß, Florin Manea, and Timo Specht(✉)

Institute of Computer Science, University of Göttingen, Göttingen, Germany
{tore.koss,timo.specht}@uni-goettingen.de,
florin.manea@informatik.uni-goettingen.de

Abstract. In this paper we show a series of results related to the decidability and expressive power of quantifier-free first order logical formulas containing language membership predicates (for the classes of regular and visibly push-down languages), string concatenation, letter-count and string-length functions, as well as linear integer arithmetic.

1 Introduction

String solving is a popular and intensely studied field within the more general setting of constraint solving and satisfiability modulo theories. The typical problem is checking the satisfiability of given quantifier-free first order logical formulas involving strings over some finite alphabet Σ of constants, string-variables (to be substituted by strings from Σ^*), the concatenation operation of strings or variables, from various finite or infinite domains (e.g., integer variables), and common string-related constraints such as string-equality, linear arithmetics over string-lengths (where the length of some string w is denoted by $|w|$), or membership predicates to various formal languages. Such a formula is satisfiable if there exists an assignment for the variables, from their respective domains, such that the formula evaluates to True. For example, if $a, b, c \in \Sigma$ are the constant letters, and x, y, z are variables, the formula $\phi = xyz \in a^*b^*c^* \wedge x \in a^* \wedge y \in ab^*c \wedge z \in c^* \wedge |x| = |y| \wedge |z| = |x| + 5$ is satisfied when x is substituted by a word a^n, for some $n \geq 2$, y is substituted by the word $ab^{n-2}c$, and z by the word c^{n+5}.

String solving has received, over the last years, significant interest in the formal methods community, as many concrete problems, which appear in tasks related to the formal analysis of string-heavy programs (e.g., symbolic execution and path analysis [10,30], or sanitisation and input-validation [33]), can be modelled as satisfiability problems for logical formulas over string constraints. To address these problems arising from practice, multiple solvers have been devel-

Published by Springer Nature Switzerland AG 2025
A. Malcher and L. Prigioniero (Eds.): DCFS 2025, LNCS 15759, pp. 108–122, 2025.
https://doi.org/10.1007/978-3-031-97100-6_8

oped, based on different approaches (see, e.g., [1,6,23,25,26,28]), but also significant work was done in theory (see the surveys [5,13,17,21] and the references therein).

While the most prominent and relevant class of string constraints is that of word equations (see the surveys [5,17,21]), in this paper, we continue the work of [7–9,13,18], and address the decidability and expressive power of logical formulas involving language-membership predicates, linear-arithmetic over length, as well as additional letter-count functions, but no word equations.

In [7–9] a series of results of (un)decidability related to the satisfiability of formulas involving language membership predicates for the class of regular languages, alongside other types of predicates and functions extracted from real-world string solving benchmarks (e.g., concatenation of strings, linear arithmetic over string-lengths, string-to-integer conversion), were shown, and solvers for the resulting first-order logics were developed. In particular, it was shown that the theory allowing regular-language-membership predicates, concatenation and linear arithmetics over string-length, as well as string-to-integer conversion is undecidable, while its subtheory where the conversion function is not allowed stays decidable. These results were further extended in [18], where it was shown that the theory allowing regular-language-membership predicates, linear arithmetics over string-length, and string-to-integer conversion (but no concatentaion) is decidable. The case of the theory allowing regular-language-membership predicates, concatenation, linear integer arithmetics, and string-to-integer conversion (without a string-length function) remains open, but formulas from this particular theory also do not appear in any real-world benchmark. Further, an additional point of view, more focused on understanding the solution sets of formulas over string constraints, was considered in [13,14,17]. In the respective works, a series of results were shown regarding the classes of formal languages which can be expressed using language-membership predicates for the classes of regular languages, visibly push-down languages, and deterministic context-free languages, as well as concatenation and linear arithmetic over string-lengths. Interestingly, these results were used to derive a series of (un)decidability results for the respective classes of languages. For instance, it was shown that the theory allowing visibly push-down-language-membership predicates (all acting on the same visibly push-down alphabet) and string concatenation can express all recursively enumerable languages, so that theory is undecidable.

Coming back to our work, as mentioned above, we consider logical theories based on language-membership predicates (for regular and visibly push-down languages) and linear-arithmetic over length, extended with additional letter-count functions (i.e., functions that return, for a string term and a letter, the number of occurrences of that letter in the string term). This is a theoretically-motivated extension of the practically-relevant theories containing language-membership predicates considered in the literature. More precisely, the usage of letter-count functions is rooted in the fundamental work of [11], where undecidability was shown for the first order theory of word equations, over binary alphabets, extended with two predicates checking, for two string terms and each letter of the alphabet, respectively, whether the string terms have the same number of occurrences of that letter. Other undecidability results, for related theories involving word equations, were shown in [16]. In this paper, we extend the existing work as follows: we consider strings over arbitrary alphabets, language membership predicates (for regular and visibly push down languages), do not use word equations, and, instead of the two aforementioned predicates, we use letter-count functions, as well as string-length and integer arithmetic. In this setting, we show first a series of positive results. If we allow membership to regular languages or visibly push-down languages, over a fixed visibly push-down alphabet, the considered theories are all decidable, and in the case of regular languages this result holds even if we allow concatenation; clearly, this more general setting covers also the case when we have predicates that only allow us to compare whether two words have exactly the same number of occurrences of some letter. We also show that as soon as we allow predicates testing the membership to visibly push-down languages, over distinct visibly push down alphabets, the resulting theory becomes undecidable. Further, following [13,14,17], we also consider the expressive power of such theories, and show both upper-bounds (from the Chomsky hierarchy) for the classes of expressed languages, as well as inexpressibility results.

2 Preliminaries

Let $\mathbb{N} = \{0, 1, 2, \ldots\}$ denote the natural numbers as well as $[n] = \{1, \ldots, n\}$ and $[i, n] = \{i, i+1, \ldots, n\}$, for all $i, n \in \mathbb{N}$ with $i \leq n$. An *alphabet* $\Sigma = \{\sigma_1, \sigma_2, \ldots, \sigma_K\}$ is a finite set of symbols, called *letters*. A *string* w is a finite concatenation of letters from a given alphabet and the amount of these letters is its *length* $|w|$. The string with no letters is the *empty string* ε, of length 0. The set of all finite strings over the alphabet Σ, denoted by Σ^*, is the free monoid generated by Σ with concatenation. A subset $L \subseteq \Sigma^*$ is called a *language*. By Σ^n we denote the set of all strings in Σ^* of length $n \in \mathbb{N}$.

For $1 \leq i \leq j \leq |w|$ we denote the ith letter of w by $w[i]$ and the *factor* of w starting at position i and ending at position j by $w[i:j] = w[i] \cdots w[j]$. If $i = 1$ the factor is also called a prefix, while if $j = |w|$ it is called a suffix of w. For each $a \in \Sigma$ set $|w|_a = |\{i \in [|w|] \mid w[i] = a\}|$. The *reverse* of $w = w[1]w[2] \cdots w[n]$, denoted w^R, is the word $w[n]w[n-1] \cdots w[1]$, i.e. it is the word one obtains by reading the letters of w from right to left.

We refer to [22,32] for basic definitions and results on regular languages (where REGLang^{Σ} denotes the regular languages over an alphabet Σ), context free languages (where CFLang^{Σ} denote the context-free languages over an alphabet Σ), context-sensitive language (where CSLang^{Σ} denote the context-sensitive languages over an alphabet Σ), and finite and push-down automata. We will also use the notions of visibly push-down automata (VPA) and visibly push-down languages (where VPLang^{Σ} denotes the visibly-push-down languages over a fixed visibly push-down alphabet Σ), see [2–4]; these are also overviewed in the appendix. The class VPLang^{Σ} is closed under union, intersection and complement, and the emptiness problem is decidable for VPLang^Σ, for inputs given as VPAs.

We now turn our focus to logical theories defined over string constraints, along the lines of [13]. By a *logical theory* (theory, for short), we mean a set $\mathfrak{T} = \{f_1, f_2, \ldots\}$ of formulas adhering to a given syntax, over variables of different sorts, and to which we associate some particular semantics. Here we focus on quantifier-free formulas. One typical question that we will consider with respect to a given theory is the *Satisfiability* problem: given a formula $F \in \mathfrak{T}$, does there exist an assignment of the variables in F such that F becomes true under the associated semantics? Another question that we consider here concerns the *Expressibility* of languages by formulas of some theory, whose formulas have string variables: given a formula $F \in \mathfrak{T}$ and a *string* variable x occurring in F, we are interested in (language theoretic properties of) the set of all values w for which there is an assignment mapping x to w which makes the formula true (in other words, the language expressed by x in F). Clearly, the emptiness problem for the language expressed by x in F is equivalent to the satisfiability problem for F. For more details see [13,24]

We now define the logical formulas foundation on which the theories considered here are built. Again, we follow [13]. Let $\mathcal{X} = \{x_1, x_2, \ldots\}$ be an infinite set of string variables. Let Σ be a finite alphabet. Let $\mathcal{T}_{str}^{\Sigma} = \mathcal{X} \cup \Sigma^*$ be the set of *basic string terms*. Let $\mathcal{T}_{str,con}^{\Sigma} = (\mathcal{X} \cup \Sigma)^*$ be the set of *extended string terms*, or *patterns*. Note that $\mathcal{T}_{str,con}^{\Sigma}$ is the closure of $\mathcal{T}_{str}^{\Sigma}$ under concatenation. A substitution $h : \mathcal{T}_{str,con}^{\Sigma} \to \Sigma^*$ is a morphism such that $h(\sigma) = \sigma$, for all $\sigma \in \Sigma$. Let $H_\Sigma = \{h \mid h : \mathcal{T}_{str,con}^{\Sigma} \to \Sigma^* \text{ is a morphism}, \forall \sigma \in \Sigma : h(\sigma) = \sigma\}$ denote the set of all substitutions.

Let $\mathcal{Z} = \{z_1, z_2, \ldots\}$ be an infinite set of integer variables, with $\mathcal{Z} \cap \mathcal{T}_{str}^{\Sigma} = \emptyset$. Let

$$\mathcal{T}_{\text{count}}^{\Sigma} = \Big\{ k_0 + \sum_{i=1}^{m} t_i z_i + \sum_{i=1}^{n} (k_i |x_i| + \sum_{\sigma \in \Sigma} k_{i,\sigma} |x_i|_\sigma) \\ \mid n \in \mathbb{N}, m \in \mathbb{N}, t_i, k_i, k_{i,\sigma} \in \mathbb{N}, x_i \in \mathcal{X} \Big\}$$

be the set of *linear letter-count terms over* Σ, $\mathcal{X}$, $\mathcal{Z}$.

Note that the above definition is purely syntactic, based on the notations $|x|$ and $|x|_\sigma$, for a variable $x \in \mathcal{X}$. We interpret $|x|$ as the length of the string variable x and $|x|_\sigma$ as the number of occurrences of σ in the string variable x, so $\mathcal{T}_{\text{count}}^{\Sigma}$ is the set of linear combinations of integer variables and lengths and letter-counts of string terms. Note that since we can express the length of a concatenation of string terms as a linear combination of lengths of basic string terms, it is no restriction that we only consider string-variables and not string terms in our linear letter-count terms. We have two types of atomic terms (atoms) as follows:

(A1) Language membership constraints: $s \in L$, where $s \in \mathcal{T}_{str,con}^{\Sigma}$ and $L \subseteq \Sigma^*$ is a formal language,

(A2) Letter-count constraints: $\ell_1 \sim \ell_2$, with $\ell_1, \ell_2 \in \mathcal{T}^{\Sigma}_{\text{count}}$, $\sim \in \{=, \leq, \geq, <, >, \neq\}$.

Formulas in our theories are constructed in general as follows:

(C1) Any atom is a well-formed formula,
(C2) If F_1, F_2 are well-formed formulas then $\neg F_1$ is a well-formed formula and $F_1 \oplus F_2$ is a well-formed formula for each $\oplus \in \{\wedge, \vee, \implies, \iff\}$.

All formulas considered here are quantifier-free. The semantics associated with them is defined as follows. Consider a pair of functions $H = (h, f)$, where $h \in H_\Sigma$ is a substitution and $f : \mathcal{Z} \to \mathbb{Z}$ is a function mapping the variables of $\mathcal{Z}$ to integers. A term $s \in \mathcal{T}^{\Sigma}_{str,con}$ is evaluated to $h(s)$ under H. A term

$$\ell = k_0 + \sum_{i=1}^{m} t_i z_i + \sum_{i=1}^{n} (k_i |x_i| + \sum_{\sigma \in \Sigma} k_{i,\sigma} |x_i|_\sigma)$$

is evaluated to

$$H(\ell) = k_0 + \sum_{i=1}^{m} t_i f(z_i) + \sum_{i=1}^{n} (k_i |h(x_i)| + \sum_{\sigma \in \Sigma} k_{i,\sigma} |h(x_i)|_\sigma)$$

.

Atoms of type A1 evaluate to true if the string term s evaluates to a word in the language L and false otherwise. Atoms $\ell_1 \sim \ell_2$ of type A2 evaluate to true if $H(\ell_1) \sim H(\ell_2)$ and false otherwise. Boolean combinations of the form C2 are evaluated canonically.

The most general logical theory we consider here consists of all well-formed formulas according to C1 and C2 using all atoms of type A1 and A2, where the language membership constraints are of the form $s \in L$ and L is a visibly push-down language; in this most general case, we only ask that all languages are over the same alphabet, but we do not ask that the partition of this alphabet (in call, return and internal symbols) is the same for all atoms. However, as this theory turns out to be undecidable, we will also consider various sub-theories in order to compare their expressive power and computability-related properties. As in [13], we will consider restrictions based on the types of terms/atoms we allow, as well as restrictions based on the classes of languages we allow in the language membership constraints (atoms of type A1). For the latter, we focus on two main classes: regular languages and visibly push-down languages (where both the alphabet and its partition are fixed). For technical completeness, we can assume that all language constraints are given as automata (DFA or VPA, respectively). We consider all combinations of atom-types A1 and A2. In particular, A1 atoms are always allowed: the case that only letter-count constraints (atoms of type A2) are allowed reduces to the existential fragment of Presburger arithmetic, which is already well understood (see [20] and the references therein). However, we will also consider a further restriction in which only basic string terms from $\mathcal{T}^{\Sigma}_{str}$ are allowed in A1 atoms (i.e. language membership constraints have the form $s \in L$ where s is a variable or concrete word from Σ^*).

It is convenient to introduce a naming convention for the considered theories. Each theory-name consists of abbreviations signifying the allowed atom-types, separated where necessary by +. If atoms of type A1 are allowed, we add either REG^{Σ} or VPL^{Σ} to the name of the theory-family depending on the class of languages permitted: $\mathrm{REGLang}^{\Sigma}$ and VPLang^{Σ}, respectively. If the A1-atoms are unrestricted in the sense that they may have the form $s \in L$ where s is an extended string term (arbitrary pattern), we also add the abbreviation CON (for concatenation). If we consider only restricted A1-atoms $s \in L$ where s may only be a basic string term, then we omit CON from the name. It is important to note that VPL^{Σ} is the theory which contains formulas consisting in boolean combinations of language membership constraints for visibly-push-down languages over Σ, with the additional important restriction that all languages occurring in these formulas are over the same, fixed, partition of the alphabet Σ in call, return, and internal alphabets. When we allow languages over different partitions of the same alphabet Σ, the resulting theory is called $\mathrm{VPLmixed}^{\Sigma}$. If atoms of type A2 are allowed, we add the abbreviation LETCOUNT.

Next, we state definitions related to expressibility of languages by formulas.

Definition 1 (Language expressed by a formula). *Let F be a formula and x_0 a string variable occurring in F. Then the* language expressed by the string variable x_0 in the formula F *is* $L(F, x_0) := \{h(x_0) \mid h \text{ is a solution for } F\}$.

Let $\mathfrak{T}_1, \mathfrak{T}_2$ be theories. We say that $\mathfrak{T}_1$ is *less expressive* than $\mathfrak{T}_2$, or $\mathfrak{T}_1 \preceq \mathfrak{T}_2$, if for every formula $F \in \mathfrak{T}_1$ and string-variable x occurring in F, there exists a formula $F' \in \mathfrak{T}_2$ and a string-variable x' occurring in F', such that $L(F, x) = L(F', x')$. We write $\mathfrak{T}_1 \sim \mathfrak{T}_2$ if $\mathfrak{T}_1 \preceq \mathfrak{T}_2$ and $\mathfrak{T}_2 \preceq \mathfrak{T}_1$.

It is immediate to see that the theories REG^{Σ} and VPL^{Σ} express exactly the classes of languages $\mathrm{REGLang}^{\Sigma}$ and VPLang^{Σ}, respectively. However, the theory $\mathrm{VPLmixed}^{\Sigma}$ can also express non-context-free languages. As every formula in REG^{Σ} can be seen as a formula in VPL^{Σ}, and every formula in VPL^{Σ} can be seen as a formula in $\mathrm{VPLmixed}^{\Sigma}$, we also have $\mathrm{REG}^{\Sigma} + \mathrm{LETCOUNT} \preceq \mathrm{VPL}^{\Sigma} + \mathrm{LETCOUNT} \preceq \mathrm{VPLmixed}^{\Sigma} + \mathrm{LETCOUNT}$.

We assume familiarity with semi-linear sets and their closure properties, for more details see [19]. Here, we just recall that a subset $M \subseteq \mathbb{N}^K$ is called linear if it is of the form $M = \{u_0 + t_1 u_1 + \ldots + t_m u_m \mid t_1, \ldots, t_m \in \mathbb{N}\}$ for some vectors $u_0, \ldots, u_m \in \mathbb{N}^K$; the set M is represented by $u_0, \ldots, u_m$. A subset $M' \subseteq \mathbb{N}^K$ is said to be semi-linear if it is a union of finitely many linear subsets, and its representation consists in the list of representations of the respective linear subsets. We also recall the definitions of the Parikh mapping and Parikh image of languages.

Definition 2. *Let $\Sigma = \{\sigma_1, \sigma_2, \ldots, \sigma_K\}$ be an alphabet and $w \in \Sigma^*$ be a word. The* Parikh-vector *of w is $\Psi(w) = (|w|_{\sigma_1}, |w|_{\sigma_2}, \ldots, |w|_{\sigma_K})$; the function $\Psi : \Sigma^* \to \mathbb{N}^K$, mapping a word to its Parikh-vector, is called the Parikh-mapping. The Parikh-image of a language $L \subseteq \Sigma^*$ is $\Psi(L) = \{\Psi(w) \mid w \in L\} \subseteq \mathbb{N}^K$.*

Note that the definition of the Parikh-mapping Ψ depends on the alphabet Σ; we prefer to not write this dependency explicitly, to keep the notation lighter.

An important result is that the Parikh-image of every context-free language is semi-linear, and there exists a regular language with the same Parikh image [29].

Theorem 1. *Let Σ be an alphabet and $K = |\Sigma|$. Let $L \subseteq \Sigma^*$ be a context-free language. Then $\Psi(L) \subseteq \mathbb{N}^K$, the Parikh-image of L, is a semi-linear set and the representation of $\Psi(L)$ can be computed. Moreover, If S is a semi-linear set, then there exists a regular language L' whose Parikh-image is S; a finite automaton for L' can be computed, given the representation of S.*

In particular, $\Psi(L)$ is semi-linear if L is in REGLang^{Σ} and VPLang^{Σ} since regular languages and visibly push-down languages are context-free.

The following result from [31] gives a sufficient criterion in which case the language described by a given Parikh-image is context-free.

Theorem 2. *Let $\Sigma = \{a, b\}$ be a binary alphabet. For a semi-linear set $M \subseteq \mathbb{N}^2$, the language $\Psi^{-1}(M) \subseteq \Sigma^*$ is in* CFLang^{Σ}.

Let $u, v \in \Sigma^*$. We say that u and v are *permutation equivalent* if v is a permutation of u, or, in other words, if $|u|_\sigma = |v|_\sigma$ holds for all $\sigma \in \Sigma$. For a language $L \subseteq \Sigma^*$, we define the *permutation closure of* L as $\{v \in \Sigma^* \mid \exists u \in L$ which is permutation equivalent to $v\}$. Note that $\Psi^{-1}(\Psi(L))$ is the permutation closure of L. We say that L is *permutation closed* if $L = \Psi^{-1}(\Psi(L))$.

Also, note that a language $L \subseteq \{a, b\}^*$ satisfies the assumptions of Theorem 2 (that is, $L = \Psi^{-1}(M)$ for a semi-linear set $M \subseteq \mathbb{N}^2$) if and only if L is permutation closed and has semi-linear Parikh-image.

Lemma 1. *Let $S \subseteq \mathbb{N}^K$ be a semi-linear set, and $L = \Psi^{-1}(S)$. Then L is in CSLang.*

Finally, we recall (see [19]) the alternative characterization of semi-linear sets as Presburger-sets. More precisely, a set $M \subset \mathbb{N}^n$ is a Presburger-set if there exists a Presburger formula $P(z_1, z_2, \dots, z_n)$ in n free variables $z_1, \dots, z_n$ and $M = \{(a_1, \dots, a_n) \mid P(a_1, \dots, a_n) \text{ is true}\}$. We also recall (see [19] and the reference therein) the following fundamental result about Presburger arithmetics.

Theorem 3. *Let $P(z_1, z_2, \dots, z_n)$ be a Presburger formula in n free variables. Then, it is decidable whether P is satisfiable, i.e. whether there exists an assignment h for the variables such that $P(h(z_1), h(z_2), \dots, h(z_n))$ is a true statement.*

3 Decidability

We start by giving an overview of the decidability of the considered results. Therefore, let us first note that in the case of membership atoms involving visibly push-down languages we do not consider concatenation, since $\text{VPL}^{\Sigma} + \text{CON}$ is already undecidable, see [15]. Hence, for VPL and VPLmixed, we only consider the theories with basic string terms and, additionally, LETCOUNT-terms. We prove the decidability of the theory $\text{VPL}^{\Sigma} + \text{LETCOUNT}$ and the undecidability of $\text{VPLmixed}^{\Sigma} + \text{LETCOUNT}$; the latter result holds already for VPLmixed, and follows from the fact that we are allowed to use different partitions of the underlying alphabet. However, we start by showing the decidability of REG^{Σ} + CON + LETCOUNT.

In this work, we always assume that our input formula F is given in its disjunctive normal form. That is, we assume that $F = C_1 \vee \cdots \vee C_n$, where C_i is a conjunction of atoms or negations of atoms, for $i \in [1, n]$. If this is not the case, we can bring F in disjunctive normal form, using standard techniques (see, e.g., [22], or [8], and the references therein, in a context closer to our work).

Before we prove that formulas over REG^{Σ} + CON + LETCOUNT are decidable, we show that the addition of concatenation to the theory REG^{Σ} + LETCOUNT does not change its computability properties and expressive power. That is, for every formula F_1 from REG^{Σ} + CON + LETCOUNT one can construct an *equivalent formula* F_2 over REG^{Σ} + LETCOUNT. More precisely, F_2 is satisfiable if and only if F_1 is satisfiable, and, moreover, the language $L(F_1, x)$ expressed by some variable x in F_1 equals $L(F_2, x')$ for some variable x' of F_2. This result uses the technique of automata splitting (see, e.g., [1]), which takes a given DFA and splits it up into multiple automata, keeping the original states and transition function, but potentially changing the initial state and having a single final state (which is not necessarily one of the final states of the initial DFA). This allows to obtain automata which accept exactly those words labelling the walks connecting, in the original automata, the new initial state with the new final state. The proof of our result is then rather straightforward. We first take each atom $s \in L$, where L is accepted by a DFA A and s is an extended string term such that $s = s_1 s_2 \cdots s_k$ with s_i being basic string terms. Then, we consider each choice of the split automata $A_1, \ldots, A_k$, such that the initial state of A_1 is the initial state of A, the final state of A_k is one of the final states of A, and the initial state of A_i is the final state of A_{i-1}, for $i \in [2 : k]$; we replace $s \in L$ by the disjunction of all formulas $s_1 \in L(A_1) \wedge \ldots \wedge s_k \in L(A_k)$, for each choice of the split automata $A_1, \ldots, A_k$. The resulting formula is in REG^{Σ} + LETCOUNT, as the letter-count atoms are not affected.

Lemma 2. *Every formula from* REG^{Σ} + CON + LETCOUNT *has an equivalent formula from* REG^{Σ} + LETCOUNT.

The next result now follows immediately. The idea of its proof is that the satisfiability of a formula from REG^{Σ} + CON + LETCOUNT is equivalent to the satisfiability of a REG^{Σ} + LETCOUNT formula, by Lemma 2, and further, using the closure properties of REGLang and the fact that the Parikh image of a regular language is semi-linear, it is equivalent to the satisfiability of a Presburger formula.

Theorem 4. *The theory* REG^{Σ} + CON + LETCOUNT *is decidable.*

Now, we shift our focus to theories over visibly push-down languages. As mentioned before we do not consider concatenation in this case, as VPL^{Σ} + CON was already shown to be undecidable, see [15]. Thus, we want to show the decidability of VPL^{Σ} + LETCOUNT. Note that in this theory all membership predicates are over the same partition of the alphabet, and act on basic string terms only, so we can apply the approach from Theorem 4: on the one hand, VPLang are also closed under intersection, union and complement, just as regular languages; on the other hand, as they are a subclass of CFLang, they have a semi-linear Parikh image as well. As we do not have concatenation, the approach from Theorem4 works unchanged, to obtain the following result.

Theorem 5. *The theory* $\mathrm{VPL}^{\Sigma}+\mathrm{LETCOUNT}$ *is decidable.*

Finally, we consider the theory $\mathrm{VPLmixed}^{\Sigma}+\mathrm{LETCOUNT}$, where we allow different partitions of the alphabet Σ into call, return, and internal symbols. Thus, now we do not have anymore closure under, e.g., intersection. It is therefore, maybe, not so surprising that the good properties of $\mathrm{VPL}^{\Sigma}+\mathrm{LETCOUNT}$ are not preserved. In fact, in this case, we obtain an undecidable theory already for the case of $\mathrm{VPLmixed}^{\Sigma}$ (that is, without letter-count atoms). This follows from a reduction from the halting problem of two-counter machines, which is known to be undecidable [27], and it can be shown by an adaptation a proof from [12], where a similar model was considered. Basically, given a two-counter machine M, one constructs two VPAs A_0 and A_1, over two different partitions in call, return, and internal symbols of the set of the instructions of M (seen as letters in an alphabet), such that $L(A_0)\cap L(A_1)$ (which is the language expressed by x in the formula $\phi = x \in L(A_1) \wedge x \in L(A_2))$ is exactly the set of halting sequences of instructions of M. Thus, ϕ is satisfiable (i.e., $L(A_0) \cap L(A_1) \neq \emptyset$) if and only if M halts.

Theorem 6. *The theory* $\mathrm{VPLmixed}^{\Sigma}$ *is undecidable.*

As VPLmixed is undecidable, the same holds for $\mathrm{VPLmixed}^{\Sigma}+\mathrm{LETCOUNT}$.

4 Expressibility

In terms of expressibility, we will show a series of positive and negative results. On the one hand, we prove results showing the containment of the languages expressible in our theories in classes of languages from the Chomsky hierarchy. On the other hand, we show several examples of languages that are not expressible in these theories. As $\mathrm{VPLmixed}^{\Sigma}+\mathrm{LETCOUNT}$ was shown to be undecidable, we first focus on the most general theory, from those considered in this paper, which is still decidable, namely $\mathrm{VPL}^{\Sigma}+\mathrm{LETCOUNT}$, and prove that only context-sensitive languages are expressible in it.

Before proving this, we first introduce some notation to ease the structure of the proof. Let $F = C_1 \vee \cdots \vee C_n$ be a $\mathrm{VPL}^{\Sigma}+\mathrm{LETCOUNT}$ formula. In the following, we always look at the language expressed by some variable x_0 (we can always rename the variables to achieve this). So, we denote by $L(F, x_0)$ the language expressed by x_0 in F. Since $L(F, x_0) = L(C_1, x_0) \cup \cdots \cup L(C_n, x_0)$, and the class of context-sensitive language is closed under union, we can also concentrate on $L(C_1, x_0)$ and prove that this is indeed context-sensitive. Hence, let us take a closer look at the structure of C_1. As before, as the class VPLang is closed under intersection (when the alphabet partition is fixed), we can assume that for every variable in C_1, there is only a single language membership atom in the respective conjunction. Thus, let $x_0, x_1, \ldots, x_r$ be the string-variables occurring in C_1. For each variable x_i, with $i \in [0, r]$, C_1 contains a single atom $c_i : x_i \in L_i$. Besides the language membership atoms C_1 contains also letter-count atoms; the conjunction of those is denoted by Λ. Putting these together, we structure C_1 in the following way $C_1 = c_0 \wedge \cdots \wedge c_r \wedge \Lambda$; further, let $C = c_1 \wedge \cdots \wedge c_r \wedge \Lambda$. Hence, $L(C_1, x_0) = L(c_0, x_0) \cap L(C, x_0)$. Firstly, we prove that $L(C, x_0)$ is context-sensitive. This follows by noting that the constraints of C do not restrict in any way the order of the letters occurring in the image of x_0, in a satisfying assignment for C, but just restrict the counts for each of these letters; so, if w is some assignment of x_0, part of a satisfying assignment for C, then every permutation of w has the same property. So, on the one hand, $L(C, x_0)$ is permutation closed. On the other hand, this also shows that it is enough to find the Parikh image of $L(C, x_0)$, and, since C contains only VPLang-membership constraints and linear letter-count constraints, it is not hard to show that this Parikh image is a semilinear set. Thus, $L(C, x_0)$ is a context-sensitive language, due to Lemma 1 (and context-free, in the case of binary alphabets). We therefore have the following result.

Lemma 3. *The language $L(C, x_0)$ is a permutation closed, context-sensitive language. If $|\Sigma| = 2$, then $L(C, x_0)$ is context-free.*

Recall that $L(C_1, x_0) = L(c_0, x_0) \cap L(C, x_0)$. Thus, since $L(C, x_0)$ is context-sensitive, it is enough to show that $L(c_0, x_0)$ is also context-sensitive. But, $L(c_0, x_0) = L_0$, and L_0 is in VPLang, so also context-sensitive. Because CSLang is closed under intersection, we then conclude that $L(C_1, x_0)$ is context-sensitive.

Theorem 7. *The class of languages expressible in* $\mathrm{VPL}^{\Sigma} + \mathrm{LETCOUNT}$ *is contained in the class CSLang.*

As an immediate consequence, in the case of $\mathrm{REG}^{\Sigma} + \mathrm{CON} + \mathrm{LETCOUNT}$, based on the second part of Lemma 3 and the fact that $L(c_0, x_0) = L_0$ is regular, we obtain the following result.

Corollary 1. *The languages expressible in* $\mathrm{REG}^{\Sigma} + \mathrm{CON} + \mathrm{LETCOUNT}$ *are context-sensitive. For Σ binary alphabet, the languages expressible in* $\mathrm{REG}^{\Sigma} + \mathrm{CON} + \mathrm{LETCOUNT}$ *are context-free.*

The result of Corollary 1 does not carry over to $\mathrm{VPL}^{\Sigma} + \mathrm{LETCOUNT}$: there are binary context-sensitive languages, expressible in this theory. In particular, for $F = x \in \{a^n b^n a^m \mid n, m \in \mathbb{N}\} \wedge y \in (aab)^* \wedge |x|_b = |y|_b \wedge |x|_a = |y|_a$, over the visibly push-down alphabet $\tilde{\Sigma} = (\Sigma_c, \Sigma_r, \Sigma_i)$, with $\Sigma_c = \{a\}$, $\Sigma_r = \{b\}$, and $\Sigma_i = \emptyset$, we have $L(F, x) = \{a^n b^n a^n \mid n \in \mathbb{N}\}$.

Lemma 4. *The language $\{a^n b^n a^n \mid n \in \mathbb{N}\}$ is expressible in the theory* $\mathrm{VPL}^{\Sigma} + \mathrm{LETCOUNT}$. *Hence, for $|\Sigma| = 2$,* $\mathrm{VPL}^{\Sigma} + \mathrm{LETCOUNT}$ *can express non-context-free languages.*

Proof. In the case of $\text{VPL}^\Sigma + \text{LETCOUNT}$ and a binary alphabet consider the following formula $F = x \in \{a^n b^n a^m \mid n, m \in \mathbb{N}\} \wedge y \in (aab)^* \wedge |x|_b = |y|_b \wedge |x|_a = |y|_a$. Clearly, $\{a^n b^n a^m \mid n, m \in \mathbb{N}\}$ and $(aab)^*$ are both visibly push-down over the same visibly push-down alphabet. Further, $|x|_b = |y|_b$ ensures that the images of x and y in a satisfying assignment of F have the same amount of b-letters. This means that the image of x in a satisfying assignment is in $\{a^n b^n a^m \mid m \in \mathbb{N}\}$ and that of y is $(aab)^n$, for some $n \in \mathbb{N}$. Moreover, since $|x|_a = |y|_a$, we get that $n + m = 2n$, so $n = m$ and the image of x must be $a^n b^n a^n$. □

While the binary languages expressed in $\text{REG}^\Sigma + \text{CON} + \text{LETCOUNT}$ are all context-free, we can show that this is not true for alphabets with more letters.

Proposition 1. *Let Σ be an alphabet with $\{a, b, c\} \subseteq \Sigma$. Then $L = \{a^n b^n c^n \mid n \in \mathbb{N}\}$ is expressible in* $\text{REG}^\Sigma + \text{CON} + \text{LETCOUNT}$.

Proof. Let $F = x \in a^* b^* c^* \wedge y \in (abc)^* \wedge |x|_a = |y|_a \wedge |x|_b = |y|_b \wedge |x|_b = |y|_b$. Clearly, the language $L = \{a^n b^n c^n\}$ is expressed by the variable x in F; further, F is a $\text{REG}^\Sigma + \text{LETCOUNT}$-formula. Thus, the statement holds. □

We move on to inexpressibility results. We first show that the language of even-length palindromes is not expressible in the most general theory considered here, namely $\text{VPLmixed}^\Sigma + \text{LETCOUNT}$. We first state a technical lemma.

Lemma 5. *Let $\tilde{\Sigma} = (\Sigma_c, \Sigma_r, \Sigma_i)$ be a visibly push-down alphabet where $\Sigma := \Sigma_c \cup \Sigma_r \cup \Sigma_i = \{a, b\}$. Let Γ be a finite stack alphabet containing the bottom-of-stack symbol $\perp$. Let A be a visibly push-down automaton over $\tilde{\Sigma}$ and Γ. Also, let $N \in \mathbb{N}$ and denote $W = W(N) = \{ab, ba\}^N$. Let $v, w \in W$ be such that*

- *The state of A after processing v is the same as its state after processing w.*
- *The upmost stack symbol of A after processing v is the same as the upmost stack symbol of A after processing w.*

Let $u \in \{a, b\}^*$ be any word. Then the state of A after processing vu is the same as the state of A after processing wu.

We make use of the previous result to show that the language of even-length palindromes are not expressible in $\text{VPLmixed}^\Sigma + \text{LETCOUNT}$. More precisely, we first argue that restricting ourselves to the scenario of Lemma 5 does not make a difference for our results. Therefore, we first show how to transform a given formula over $\text{VPLmixed}^\Sigma + \text{LETCOUNT}$ in order to obtain a setup allowing us to use Lemma 5. Recall, that we made the assumption that our input formula F is in disjunctive normal form, i.e. $F = C_1 \vee \cdots \vee C_n$.

Theorem 8. *Let Σ be an alphabet with $\{a, b\} \subseteq \Sigma$. Then the context-free language $L = \{ww^R \mid w \in \{a, b\}^*\}$ of even-length palindromes over $\{a, b\}^*$ is not expressible in* $\text{VPLmixed}^\Sigma + \text{LETCOUNT}$.

Proof. Let $F \in \text{VPLmixed}^{\Sigma} + \text{LETCOUNT}$ contain a variable x; assume for the sake of a contradiction that $L = L(F, x)$. Each conjunction C_i of F consists of m_i atomic formulas $\varphi_{i,j}$. Suppose, for every i, that the conjunction C_i starts with the language membership constraints on x, followed by language membership constraints on the other variables and the linear constraints. We may assume w.l.o.g. that all terms C_i contain the same number ℓ of VPL constraints on x.

To apply Lemma 5 we first alter the constraints affecting x. Let $(x \in L_0)$ be one such constraint occurring in F, where $L_0 \in \text{VPLang}$. Notice that $L_0 \cap \{a, b\}^* \in \text{VPLang}$ holds as well, and replace $(x \in L_0)$ by $(x \in L_0 \cap \{a, b\}^*)$.

We proceed like this for every VPL membership constraint on x in F. Call the new formula F'. Next, we show that $L(F', x) = L(F, x)$.

Showing $L(F', x) \subseteq L(F, x)$ is immediate: a solution for F' is automatically a solution for F, because the constraints in F' are more restrictive.

For $L(F', x) \supseteq L(F, x)$, let $h : \text{vars}(F) \to \Sigma^*$ be a solution for F. Since $L(F, x) = L \subseteq \{a, b\}^*$ by assumption, this means that $h(x) \in \{a, b\}^*$. So, h satisfies the more restrictive constraints on x in F' (i.e. that $x \in \{a, b\}^*$), and is therefore a solution for F'. Thus, we obtain that x only expresses languages over $\{a, b\}^*$. Hence, we are now in a setting allowing us to use Lemma 5 to get our result. Next, we will explain how this is done.

For $i \in [1, n]$ and $j \in [1, \ell]$, let $A_{i,j}$ be a VPA accepting $L_{i,j}$. Without loss of generality, all these automata have the same amount r of states. For given $i \in [1, n], j \in [1, \ell]$, denote the states of $A_{i,j}$ by $q_{i,j,k}$ (for $1 \leq k \leq r$). Furthermore, we may assume that all these VPA operate over the same stack alphabet Γ containing c elements, one of which is the bottom-of-stack symbol $\perp$. The underlying alphabet is $\Sigma = \{a, b\}$. The partition of Σ into a call, return, and internal alphabet can be, however, different for different automata.

After these preliminaries, we shall set up the pigeonhole principle argument. Choose a number $N \in \mathbb{N}$ such that $2^N > n \cdot (rc)^{\ell}$. Let $W = W(N) = \{ab, ba\}^N$ and consider a word $w \in W$. Since ww^R is a palindrome, there exists an $i \in [1, n]$ with $ww^R \in L(C_i, x)$. If there is more than one such i, choose the smallest. For all $j \in [1, \ell]$, let $k_j \in [1, r]$ be the unique index such that $A_{i,j}$ is in its state q_{i,j,k_j} after processing the word w. Let γ_j be the upmost stack symbol of $A_{i,j}$ after processing w; this way, we have constructed a map

$$W \to \{1, \dots, n\} \times (\{1, \dots, r\} \times \Gamma)^{\ell}, \text{ where } w \mapsto (i, k_1, \gamma_1, k_2, \gamma_2, \dots, k_{\ell}, \gamma_{\ell})$$

which maps a word $w \in W$ to the tuple of indices we constructed above.

Since the domain W contains 2^N-many words, whereas the co-domain contains only $n \cdot (rc)^{\ell}$-many elements, we have that there exist two distinct words v, w which are mapped to the same tuple $(i, k_1, \gamma_1, k_2, \gamma_2, \dots, k_{\ell}, \gamma_{\ell})$.

We have $vv^R \in L(C_i, x)$ and also $ww^R \in L(C_i, x)$; in particular, for all $j \in [1, \ell]$, the automaton $A_{i,j}$ accepts both of the words vv^R and ww^R.

For every $j \in [1, \dots, \ell]$, the automaton $A_{i,j}$ is in the same state after processing w as after processing v, and has the same upmost stack symbol; namely, $A_{i,j}$ reaches state q_{i,j,k_j}, and its upmost stack symbol is γ_j in both cases. According to Lemma 5, this means that $A_{i,j}$ reaches the same state after reading vw^R as after reading ww^R. Since ww^R is accepted by $A_{i,j}$; vw^R is accepted by $A_{i,j}$ as well.

Until now, we have that vw^R is accepted by each of the automata $A_{i,j}$ (for $j \in [1, \ell]$). We note that vw^R has $2N$-many symbols a and $2N$-many symbols b, just like ww^R. So, we modify an assignment h with $h(x) = ww^R$, which satisfies C_i, into an assignment h' with $h'(x) = vw^R$, which still satisfies C_i.

Finally, we show that $vw^R \in L(C_i, x)$. Let h be a satisfying assignment for C_i which maps x to ww^R and every other variable y to $h(y) \in \Sigma^*$; such an assignment for the variables exists because $ww^R \in L(C_i, x)$. Let h' be another satisfying assignment with $h'(x) = vw^R$, and $h'(y) = h(y)$. The subformula $\varphi_{i,j} = (x \in L_{i,j})$ is satisfied for $j \in [1, \ell]$, since $vw^R \in L_{i,j}$. For $j \geq \ell$, $\varphi_{i,j}$ is guaranteed to not be a VPL constraint on x. If the variable x does not occur in $\varphi_{i,j}$, then $\varphi_{i,j}$ is satisfied under h', since h' operates just like h on the occurring variables. If x does occur in $\varphi_{i,j}$, then $\varphi_{i,j}$ is a linear letter-count constraint. In this case, the formula is still satisfied, because for every variable y in F, we have $|h'(y)|_\sigma = |h(y)|_\sigma$ for $\sigma \in \Sigma$. For the variables $y \neq x$, this is direct from $h'(y) = h(y)$. For the variable x, we have $|h'(x)|_a = |v|_a + |w^R|_a = N + |w^R|_a = |w|_a + |w^R|_a = |h(x)|_a$; likewise for the letter b. This concludes the proof. □

Clearly, Theorem 8 also says that the context-free language of binary, even-length palindromes is not expressible in any of the theories considered in this paper, as all are at most as expressive as VPLmixed$^\Sigma$ + LETCOUNT.

We now shift our focus to REG$^\Sigma$ + LETCOUNT. Note first that that all languages from VPLang are expressible in VPL and all its extensions. However, for large enough alphabets, REG$^\Sigma$ + LETCOUNT is incomparable to VPLang. Indeed, we have that for $|\Sigma| \geq 3$, this theory already expresses $\{a^n b^n c^n \mid n \in \mathbb{N}\}$ which is not visibly push-down. For the other direction, we take the language of even-length palindromes and modify it such that it is accepted by a VPA. We consider the alphabet $\tilde{\Sigma} = (\Sigma_c, \Sigma_r, \Sigma_i)$ with $\Sigma_c = \{a, b\}$, $\Sigma_r = \{\bar{a}, \bar{b}\}$, and $\Sigma_i = \emptyset$, and $L = \{w\bar{w}^R \mid w \in \{a, b\}^*, \bar{w}^R \in \{\bar{a}, \bar{b}\}^*\}$. It is not hard to show that this language is visibly push-down, but, in a similar way to Theorem 8, we can show that it is not expressible in REG$^\Sigma$ + LETCOUNT (so neither in REG$^\Sigma$ + CON + LETCOUNT, which has the same expressive power, by Lemma 2).

Theorem 9. *Let Σ be an alphabet with $|\Sigma| > 3$. The languages expressed by formulas of* REG$^\Sigma$ + LETCOUNT *over Σ are incomparable to* VPL *over Σ.*

According to our last result, for an alphabet Σ with $|\Sigma| > 3$, we have that REG$^\Sigma$ + CON + LETCOUNT $\prec$ VPL$^\Sigma$ + LETCOUNT. Recall that, in Sect. 2, we have stated that REG$^\Sigma$ + LETCOUNT $\preceq$ VPL$^\Sigma$ + LETCOUNT $\preceq$ VPLmixed$^\Sigma$ + LETCOUNT, as an example when introducing the expressive power of a theory. So the first relation from the above is strict for large enough alphabets. Our results do not show that the inclusion VPL$^\Sigma$ + LETCOUNT $\preceq$ VPLmixed$^\Sigma$ + LETCOUNT is also strict, but Theorems 5 and 6 show that, in fact, given a VPLmixed$^\Sigma$ + LETCOUNT, we cannot algorithmically construct a VPL$^\Sigma$ + LETCOUNT expressing the same language. We leave open the problem of showing that there are languages expressible in VPLmixed$^\Sigma$ + LETCOUNT but not in VPL$^{\Sigma'}$ + LETCOUNT, even for some alphabet Σ' larger than Σ.

References

1. Abdulla, P.A., et al.: Norn: an SMT solver for string constraints. In: Proceedings of CAV. vol. 9206, pp. 462–469. Springer (2015)
2. Alur, R., Kumar, V., Parthasarathy, M., Viswanathan, M.: Congruences for visibly pushdown languages. vol. 3580 (2005). https://doi.org/10.1007/11523468_89
3. Alur, R., Madhusudan, P.: Visibly pushdown languages. In: Proceedings of STOC (2004). https://api.semanticscholar.org/CorpusID:7473479
4. Alur, R., Madhusudan, P.: Adding nesting structure to words. J. ACM **56**(3) (2009). https://doi.org/10.1145/1516512.1516518
5. Amadini, R.: A survey on string constraint solving. ACM Comput. Surv. **55**(1) (2021). https://doi.org/10.1145/3484198
6. Barbosa, H., et al.: cvc5: a versatile and industrial-strength SMT solver. In: Proc. TACAS 2022, Part of ETAPS 2022, Lecture Notes in Computer Science, vol. 13243, pp. 415–442. Springer (2022). https://doi.org/10.1007/978-3-030-99524-9_24
7. Berzish, M., et al.: String theories involving regular membership predicates: from practice to theory and back. In: Proceedings of WORDS 2021. Lecture Notes in Computer Science, vol. 12847, pp. 50–64. Springer (2021). https://doi.org/10.1007/978-3-030-85088-3_5
8. Berzish, M., et al.: Towards more efficient methods for solving regular-expression heavy string constraints. Theor. Comput. Sci. **943**, 50–72 (2023). https://doi.org/10.1016/J.TCS.2022.12.009
9. Berzish, M., et al.: An SMT solver for regular expressions and linear arithmetic over string length. In: Proceedings of CAV 2021. Lecture Notes in Computer Science, vol. 12760, pp. 289–312. Springer (2021). https://doi.org/10.1007/978-3-030-81688-9_14
10. Bjørner, N., Tillmann, N., Voronkov, A.: Path feasibility analysis for string-manipulating programs. In: International Conference on Tools and Algorithms for the Construction and Analysis of Systems, pp. 307–321. Springer (2009)
11. Büchi, J.R., Senger, S.: Definability in the Existential Theory of Concatenation and Undecidable Extensions of this Theory, pp. 671–683. Springer New York, New York, NY (1990). https://doi.org/10.1007/978-1-4613-8928-6_37
12. Carotenuto, D., Murano, A., Peron, A.: Ordered multi-stack visibly pushdown automata. Theoret. Comput. Sci. **656**, 1–26 (2016). https://doi.org/10.1016/j.tcs.2016.08.012
13. Day, J., Ganesh, V., Grewal, N., Manea, F.: On the expressive power of string constraints. In: Proceedings of the ACM on Programming Languages, POPL 2023, vol. 7, pp. 278–308 (2023). https://doi.org/10.1145/3571203
14. Day, J.D., Ganesh, V., Grewal, N., Konefal, M., Manea, F.: A closer look at the expressive power of logics based on word equations. Theory Comput. Syst. **68**(3), 322–379 (2024). https://doi.org/10.1007/S00224-023-10154-8
15. Day, J.D., Ganesh, V., Grewal, N., Manea, F.: Formal languages via theories over strings (2022). https://arxiv.org/abs/2205.00475
16. Day, J.D., Ganesh, V., He, P., Manea, F., Nowotka, D.: The satisfiability of word equations: decidable and undecidable theories. In: Proceedings of RP 2018. Lecture Notes in Computer Science, vol. 11123, pp. 15–29. Springer (2018). https://doi.org/10.1007/978-3-030-00250-3_2
17. Day, J.D., Ganesh, V., Manea, F.: Formal languages via theories over strings: an overview of some recent results. Bull. EATCS **140** (2023). http://eatcs.org/beatcs/index.php/beatcs/article/view/765

18. Draghici, A., Haase, C., Manea, F.: Semënov arithmetic, affine VASS, and string constraints. In: Proceedings of STACS 2024. LIPIcs, vol. 289, pp. 29:1–29:19. Schloss Dagstuhl - Leibniz-Zentrum für Informatik (2024). https://doi.org/10.4230/LIPICS.STACS.2024.29
19. Ginsburg, S., Spanier, E.H.: Bounded algol-like languages. Trans. Am. Math. Soc. **113**(2), 333–368 (1964)
20. Haase, C.: A survival guide to presburger arithmetic. ACM SIGLOG News **5**(3), 67–82 (2018). https://doi.org/10.1145/3242953.3242964
21. Hague, M.: Strings at MOSCA. ACM SIGLOG News **6**(4), 4–22 (2019)
22. Hopcroft, J.E., Motwani, R., Ullman, J.D.: Introduction to Automata Theory, Languages, and Computation, 3rd edn. Addison-Wesley Longman Publishing Co., Inc, USA (2006)
23. Kan, S., Lin, A.W., Rümmer, P., Schrader, M.: CertiStr: a certified string solver. In: Proceedings of CPP 2022. CPP '22, ACM (2022). https://doi.org/10.1145/3497775.3503691
24. Karhumäki, J., Mignosi, F., Plandowski, W.: The expressibility of languages and relations by word equations. J. ACM **47**(3), 483–505 (2000). https://doi.org/10.1145/337244.337255
25. Kiezun, A., Ganesh, V., Artzi, S., Guo, P.J., Hooimeijer, P., Ernst, M.D.: HAMPI: a solver for word equations over strings, regular expressions, and context-free grammars. ACM Trans. Softw. Eng. Methodol. **21**(4) (2013). https://doi.org/10.1145/2377656.2377662
26. Lu, Z., Siemer, S., Jha, P., Day, J.D., Manea, F., Ganesh, V.: Layered and staged monte carlo tree search for SMT strategy synthesis. In: Proc. IJCAI 2024, pp. 1907–1915. ijcai.org (2024). https://www.ijcai.org/proceedings/2024/211
27. Minsky, M.L.: Computation: finite and infinite machines. Prentice-Hall Inc, USA (1967)
28. Mora, F., Berzish, M., Kulczynski, M., Nowotka, D., Ganesh, V.: Z3str4: a multi-armed string solver. In: Proceedings of FM 2021, pp. 389–406. Springer-Verlag, Berlin, Heidelberg (2021). https://doi.org/10.1007/978-3-030-90870-6_21
29. Parikh, R.J.: On context-free languages. J. ACM **13**(4), 570–581 (1966).https://doi.org/10.1145/321356.321364
30. Redelinghuys, G., Visser, W., Geldenhuys, J.: Symbolic execution of programs with strings. In: Proceedings of SAICSIT 2012, pp. 139–148. SAICSIT '12 (2012)
31. Rigo, M.: The commutative closure of a binary slip-language is context-free: a new proof. Discret. Appl. Math. **131**(3), 665–672 (2003). https://doi.org/10.1016/S0166-218X(03)00335-4
32. Rozenberg, G., Salomaa, A. (eds.): Handbook of Formal Languages. Lecture Notes in Computer Science, Springer, Heidelberg (1997). https://doi.org/10.1007/978-3-642-59126-6
33. Saxena, P., Akhawe, D., Hanna, S., Mao, F., McCamant, S., Song, D.: A symbolic execution framework for JavaScript. In: 2010 IEEE Symposium on Security and Privacy, pp. 513–528. IEEE (2010)

Scattered Context Grammars with One Non-Context-Free Production and Six Nonterminals Are Computationally Complete

Martin Havel, Alexander Meduna, and Zbyněk Křivka(✉)

Brno University of Technology, Faculty of Information Technology, Božetěchova 1/2, 612 00 Brno, Czech Republic
{ihavelm,meduna,krivka}@fit.vut.cz

Abstract. The present paper explains how to reduce the size of scattered context grammars with respect to the number of both non-context-free productions and nonterminals. It proves that every recursively enumerable language is generated by a six-nonterminal scattered context grammar with a single non-context-free production. Open problems are proposed.

Keywords: Scattered context grammars · Size reduction · The number of non-context-free productions · The number of nonterminal symbols · Computational completeness · Descriptional complexity

1 Introduction

Over its history, formal language theory has always struggled to reduce its grammars with respect to various numbers of components (see Sects. 1.2 and 1.3 in Chap. 4 in [13]). Perhaps most intensively, it has studied how to reduce the number of nonterminals and productions without affecting the generative power of the grammars in question. The present paper continues with this study in terms of scattered context grammars (see [11]).

Recall that restricting the amount of nonterminals was always of great interest without disrupting its computational power or how computational power is changed. Restricting the number of nonterminals was already researched for phase-structured grammar (see [3]), automata, (see [4], context-free grammars (see [2,7]), EOL (see [8,14]) and countless others. For scattered context grammars, it was already demonstrated that scattered context grammars with a single non-context-free production are as powerful as their unlimited versions because they characterize the family of recursively enumerable languages (see [6]). This paper improves this result by reducing the number of non-context-free productions and, simultaneously, the number of nonterminals. Specifically, it demonstrates that six-nonterminal scattered context grammars with one non-context-free production characterize this family.

Published by Springer Nature Switzerland AG 2025
A. Malcher and L. Prigioniero (Eds.): DCFS 2025, LNCS 15759, pp. 123–136, 2025.
https://doi.org/10.1007/978-3-031-97100-6_9

Of course, concerning the number of non-context-free productions, this statement represents the best possible result because scattered context grammars without any non-context-free productions are as powerful as context-free grammars, so they are less powerful than their unlimited versions. With respect to the number of nonterminals, however, an improvement of this statement represents a challenging open problem. Indeed, as one-nonterminal scattered context grammars are weaker than their unlimited versions (see Theorem 6.1 in [11]), we ask whether there exists i in {2, 3, 4, 5, 6, ...} such that i-nonterminal scattered context grammars with one non-context-free production characterize the family of recursively enumerable languages.

2 Definitions

This paper assumes that the reader is familiar with the language theory (see [9]), including scattered context grammars (see [11,12]).

For a set, Q, card(Q) denotes the cardinality of Q. For an alphabet, V, V^* represents the free monoid generated by V under the operation of concatenation. The unit of V^* is denoted by ε. Set $V^+ = V^* - \{\varepsilon\}$; algebraically, V^+ is thus the free semigroup generated by V under the operation of concatenation. For $w \in V^*$, $|w|$ and rev(w) denote the length of w and the reversal of w, respectively. Furthermore, suffix(w) denotes the set of all suffixes of w, and prefix(w) denotes the set of all prefixes of w. For $w \in V^*$ and $T \subseteq V$, occur(w, T) denotes the number of occurrences of symbols from T in w, and erase(w, T) denotes the string obtained by removing all occurrences of symbols from T in w. For instance, occur($abdabc$, $\{a, d\}$) = 3 and erase($abdabc$, $\{a, d\}$) = bbc. If $T = \{a\}$, where $a \in V$, we simplify occur(w, $\{a\}$) and erase(w, $\{a\}$) to occur(w, a) and erase(w, a), respectively.

A *scattered context grammar* is a quadruple, $G = (N, T, P, S)$, where N and T are alphabets such that $N \cap T = \emptyset$. Symbols in N are referred to as nonterminals while symbols in T are terminals. N contains S—the start symbol of G. P is a finite non-empty set of productions or rules such that every $p \in P$ has the form

$$(A_1, A_2, \ldots, A_n) \rightarrow (x_1, x_2, \ldots, x_n),$$

where $n \geq 1$, and for all $i = 1, 2, \ldots, n$, $A_i \in N$ and $x_i \in (N \cup T)^*$. If each x_i satisfies $|x_i| \leq 1$, $i = 1, 2, \ldots, n$, then $(A_1, A_2, \ldots, A_n) \rightarrow (x_1, x_2, \ldots, x_n)$ is said to be simple. If $n = 1$, then $(A_1) \rightarrow (x_1)$ is referred to as a context-free production; for brevity, we hereafter write $A_1 \rightarrow x_1$ instead of $(A_1) \rightarrow (x_1)$. If for some $n \geq 1$, $(A_1, A_2, \ldots, A_n) \rightarrow (x_1, x_2, \ldots, x_n) \in P, v = u_1 A_1 u_2 A_2 \ldots u_n A_n u_{n+1}$, and $w = u_1 x_1 u_2 x_2 \ldots u_n x_n u_{n+1}$ with $u_i \in (N \cup T)^*$ for all $i = 1, 2, \ldots, n$, then v directly derives w in G, symbolically written as $v \Rightarrow w$ $[(A_1, A_2, \ldots, A_n) \rightarrow (x_1, x_2, \ldots, x_n)]$ or, simply, $v \Rightarrow w$ in G. In the standard manner, extend $\Rightarrow$ to $\Rightarrow^n$, where $n \geq 0$; then, based on $\Rightarrow^n$, define $\Rightarrow^+$ and $\Rightarrow^*$. The language of G, $L(G)$, is defined as $L(G) = \{w \in T^* : S \Rightarrow^* w\}$. A derivation of the form $S \Rightarrow^* w$ with $w \in T^*$ is called a successful derivation.

A *queue grammar* (see [5]) is a sextuple, $Q = (V, T, W, F, s, R)$, where V and W are alphabets satisfying $V \cap W = \emptyset$, $T \subseteq V$, $F \subseteq W$, $s \in (V - T)(W - F)$, and $R \subseteq (V \times (W - F)) \times (V^* \times W)$ is a finite relation such that for every $a \in V$, there exists an element $(a, b, z, c) \in R$. If $u, v \in V^*W$ such that $u = arb$; $v = rzc$; $a \in V$; $r, z \in V^*$; $b, c \in W$; and $(a, b, z, c) \in R$, then $u \Rightarrow v$ $[(a, b, z, c)]$ in Q or, simply, $u \Rightarrow v$. In the standard manner, extend $\Rightarrow$ to $\Rightarrow^n$, where $n \geq 0$; then, based on $\Rightarrow^n$, define $\Rightarrow^+$ and $\Rightarrow^*$. The language of Q, $L(Q)$, is defined as $L(Q) = \{w \in T^* : s \Rightarrow^* wf,\ f \in F\}$.

As a slight modification of the notion of a queue grammar, there is the notion of a left-extended queue grammar such that it is a queue grammar that during every derivation step shifts the rewritten symbol in front of the beginning of its sentential form (see # below); in this way, it records the derivation history, which plays a crucial role in the proof of correctness of Algorithm 1 in the next section. Formally, a *left-extended queue grammar* is a sextuple, $Q = (V, T, W, F, s, P)$, where V, T, W, F, and s are defined as in a queue grammar. $P \subseteq (V \times (W - F)) \times (V^* \times W)$ is a finite relation (as opposed to an ordinary queue grammar, this definition does not require that for every $a \in V$, there exists an element $(a, b, z, c) \in R$). Furthermore, assume that $\# \notin V \cup W$. If $u, v \in V^*\{\#\}V^*W$ so that $u = w\#arb; v = wa\#rzc; a \in V; r, z, w \in V^*; b, c \in W$; and $(a, b, z, c) \in R$, then $u \Rightarrow v$ $[(a, b, z, c)]$ in Q or, simply, $u \Rightarrow v$. In the standard manner, extend $\Rightarrow$ to $\Rightarrow^n$, where $n \geq 0$; then, based on $\Rightarrow^n$, define $\Rightarrow^+$ and $\Rightarrow^*$. The language of $Q, L(Q)$, is defined as $L(Q) = \{v \in T^* : \#s \Rightarrow^* w\#vf$ for some $w \in V^*$ and $f \in F\}$.

Next, we recall two already known properties of left-extended queue grammars (introduced in [6,10]), subsequently used in the proof of Algorithm 1.

Lemma 1. *For every recursively enumerable language, L, there exists a left-extended queue grammar, Q, satisfying $L(Q) = L$.*

Definition 1. *Let $Q = (V, T, W, F, s, R)$ be a left-extended queue grammar. Q is said to be in* normal form 2 *if every $(a, b, x, c) \in R$ satisfies $a \in V - T, b \in W - F$, and $x \in ((V - T)^* \cup T^*)$ and in addition, for every $q \in W - F$, there is no more than one $a \in V - T$ such that $(a, q, x, p) \in R$, where $x \in (V - T)^* \cup T^*$ and $p \in W$.*

Lemma 2. *For every left-extended queue grammar H, there exists an equivalent left-extended queue grammar Q in normal form 2.*

In general, two grammars are *equivalent* if both generate the same language.

3 Results

This section demonstrates that every recursively enumerable language, L, is generated by a scattered context grammar, $G = (N, T, P, S)$, such that $L = L(G)$, (i) P contains a single non-context-free production of the form $(1, 2, 0, 3, 0, 2, 1) \rightarrow (2, \varepsilon, \varepsilon, \varepsilon, \varepsilon, \varepsilon, 2)$, and (ii) N consists of six nonterminals. This demonstration is based on left-extended queue grammars, which are computationally complete.

First, we define certain *codes* and their counterparts, referred to as *anti-codes*. We establish several general results about these codes and anti-codes, which are used later in this section. Then, we give the major algorithm that turns any left-extended queue grammar to an equivalent scattered context grammar having firstly a single non-context-free production and secondly seven nonterminals. We establish several results about this algorithm, based on which, we verify that the algorithm is correct. Finally, we improve the result sketched about so we demonstrate that every recursively enumerable language L is generated by a scattered context grammar having no more than (i) one non-context-free production and (ii) six nonterminals.

Next, we explain how to turn any left-extended queue grammar Q in second normal form to an equivalent scattered context grammar G with a single non-context-free production and only seven nonterminals. The basic idea consists of the simulation of a derivation in Q by context-free productions in an utterly arbitrary way, after which the only scattered context production is repeatedly used to verify that the derivation is correct. More precisely, G generates every $x \in L(G)$ by performing (I) and (II).

First, we introduce a coding generated by context-free productions of G that handles any context dependency. It derives uxv from its start symbol, where u and v are codes over $\{0, 1, 2, 3\}$, where 0 through 3 are special encoding nonterminals. The first phase ends when precisely two 2 s are generated in the current sentential form. Then, in (II), by using its only non-context-free production π of the form

$$(1, 2, 0, 3, 0, 2, 1) \to (2, \varepsilon, \varepsilon, \varepsilon, \varepsilon, \varepsilon, 2),$$

it removes u and v. G completes its removal successfully and, thereby, generates x iff x belongs to $L(Q)$. Thus, $L(G) = L(Q)$.

Definition 2. *For $k \geq 1$, let $X_k, Y_k \subseteq \{0, 1, 3\}^*$ such that*

$$X_k = \{103\}^+\{1\}\{10\}^+ \cap \{x\colon x \in \{0, 1, 3\}^*, \mathrm{occur}(x, 1) = k\}$$

and

$$Y_k = \{301\}^+\{0301\}\{01\}^+ \cap \{x\colon x \in \{0, 1, 3\}^*, \mathrm{occur}(x, 1) = k\}$$

Let A, B be a finite (non-empty) sets. Let us define an injection $\iota\colon A \times B \to X_n$ where n is a positive integer great enough to allow us to introduce ι as injection (a proof that such a constant necessarily exists is simple and left to the reader). Extend the domain of ι to $(A \times B)^*$ in the standard way.

Let $\beta\colon \{0, 1\}^* \to \{0, 1, 3\}^*$ be a homomorphism such that $\beta(0) = 30$ and $\beta(1) = 1$.

Let $\kappa\colon A \times B \to Y_n$ be an injection with $\kappa(a, b) = z10301w$ where $z = \beta(\mathrm{rev}(v))$ and $w = \mathrm{rev}(\mathrm{erase}(u, \{3\}))$ where $u11v = \iota(a, b)$. Extend the domain of κ to $(A \times B)^*$ in the standard way too.

We refer to $x, y \in \{0, 1, 3\}^*$ as a code string *and its* anticode string *iff $x = \iota(a, b)$ and $y = \kappa(a, b)$ for some $a \in A$ and $b \in B$.*

Example 1. For instance, for $A = \{C, D\}$ and $B = \{s\}$ ($|A| = 2$, $|B| = 1$) and $n = 4$, we can define ι as $\iota(C, s) = 10311010$ and $\iota(D, s) = 103103110$. Then, $\kappa(C, s) = 301301030101$ and $\kappa(D, s) = 30103010101$.

The following lemma demonstrates that in scattered context grammar with two special productions, we can safely annihilate some code string and its corresponding anticode string.

Definition 3. *We say that a code string and its corresponding anticode string are* annihilated *if $xuwvz \Rightarrow^* \omega(x)w\omega'(z)$ where $u = \iota(a, b)$ and $v = \kappa(a, b)$, for some $a \in A$ and $b \in B$, $w \in (N \cup T)^*$, and ω and ω' replaces the last 1 by 2 and the first 1 by 2, respectively.*

Lemma 3. *Let $G = (N, T, P, S)$ be a scattered context grammar with $N = N' \cup D$, $D = \{0, 1, 2, 3\}$, and the only two productions in P that rewrite nonterminals from D are*

$$(1, 2, 0, 3, 0, 2, 1) \to (2, \varepsilon, \varepsilon, \varepsilon, \varepsilon, \varepsilon, 2)$$

$$2 \to \varepsilon$$

For any sentential form $xuwvz$ with $u = \iota(a, b)$ and $v = \kappa(a, b)$ for some $a \in A$ and $b \in B$ (will be specified later), where $x, u, v, z \in D^*$, u and v can be annihilated.

Claim. Any substrings from V^* in the sentential form do not matter for the annihilation (i.e. cannot block the annihilation of some code and its anticode).

More formally, if $u \in D^*$ can be annihilated by productions from P in G, then u scattered with x, where $x \in (V - D)^*$, can be rewritten to x in G as the rest of u.

Definition 4. *Based on $\iota \colon A \times B \to X_k$, define the substitution ν from A to 2^{X_k} by*

$$\nu(a) = \{\iota(a, b) \colon b \in B\}$$

for every $a \in A$; then, extend its domain to A^* in the standard way.

Next, using $\kappa \colon A \times B \to Y_k$, define the substitution μ from B to 2^{Y_n} by

$$\mu(b) = \{\kappa(a, b) \colon a \in A\}$$

for every $b \in B$; then, extend its domain to B^* in the standard way too.

Example 2. Notice that every $x \in \nu(a)$ is a string of the form

$$103103 \cdots 10311010 \cdots 10$$

in which there are n occurrences of 1 and precisely one occurrence of substring 11. Notice that every $y \in \mu(q)$ is a string of the form

$$301301 \cdots 30103010101 \cdots 01$$

in which there are n occurrences of 1 and precisely one occurrence of 030.

Before giving a proof of the correctness, we describe Algorithm 1 informally. Recall that the input Q is left-extended, so it records the prefix of all symbols rewritten at the beginning of the queue during the generation of $x \in L(Q)$.

In addition, apart from recording this prefix, Q also records all the states through which Q passes through. That is, it always records two identical states to the left. Furthermore, based on Q generate code two times denoted as δ defined later in this section and generates mirroring anticode later in the derivation to ensure that all terminals are generated.

When simulating this generation, G takes an advantage of this recorded rewriting history to verify that the entire simulation has been performed properly. To give a more precise insight into this simulation and subsequent verification, assume that Q generates $x \in L(Q)$ by using a sequence of productions $r_1, r_2, \ldots, r_m$. G simulates this generation as follows.

(I) During the first phase, G makes $S \Rightarrow^* q_0 u_1 q_1 q_1 u_2 q_2 q_2 \cdots u_{m-1} q_{m-1} q_{m-1} u_m q_m q_m x q_m q_m v_m q_{m-1} q_{m-1} v_{m-1} \cdots q_2 q_2 v_2 q_1 q_1 v_1 q_0$ where each u_j and v_j encodes a production applied during the jth derivation step in Q, and all of them have the same number of 1 s. More specifically, each $u_i = {}_p u_i \, {}_s u_i$ where ${}_p u_i$ is a prefix of u_i over $\{0, 1, 3\}$ and ${}_s u_i$ is a suffix of u_i over $\{0, 1\}$. Let us call the beginning of ${}_s u_i$ as u_i-*break*. Similarly, each $v_i = {}_p v_i \, {}_s v_i$ where ${}_p v_i$ is a prefix of v_i over $\{0, 1\}$ and ${}_s v_i$ is a suffix of v_i over $\{0, 1, 3\}$. Let us call the end of ${}_p v_i$ as v_i-*break*. The position of u_i-break and v_i-break encodes a production in Q so this encoding satisfies the following property:

if (a, q, x, p) and (b, o, y, r) are two productions
encoded by the same break position, then $p = r$ and $x = y$.

The states are encoded analogously.

(II) During the second phase, G has to make sure that the simulation of the generation of x in Q is performed correctly. To do so, G has to verify that for $j = m, \ldots, 2, 1$, both u_j and v_j encode the same production r_j in Q. G makes this verification solely by using π so it eliminates all u_m through u_1 and, simultaneously, v_m through v_1 in the insight-out way.
To explain the elimination process more precisely, consider this portion

$$u_1 u_2 \cdots {}_p u_i \cdot {}_s u_i \;\; x \;\; {}_p v_i \cdot {}_s v_i \cdots v_2 v_1$$

where $\cdot$ points out the position of u_i-break and v_i-break, respectively. G can eliminate the codes u_i and v_i if and only if u_i-break and v_i-break are simultaneously rewritten by π; thereby, it guaranties that ${}_s u_i$ and ${}_p v_i$ have the same number of 1 s and 0 s, therefore, u_i and v_i encode the same production r_i. Analogously, G verifies that during any two consecutive derivation steps, in the first step, Q enters the same state from which it performs the other step.

Definition 5. *Define function δ over $\{y \colon y \in \nu(a), a \in A\}^*$ as follows*

1. $\delta(\varepsilon) = \varepsilon$

2. *let* $z = x_1x_2x_3 \cdots x_n$ *for some* $n \geq 1$, $x_i \in \nu(a_i)$ *for some* $a_i \in A$; *then,* $\delta(z) = x_1^2x_2^2x_3^2 \cdots x_n^2$.

Let $D = \{0, 1, 2, 3\}$.

Algorithm 1. *Input: A left-extended queue grammar* $Q = (V, T, W, F, s, R)$ *in normal form 2.*
Output: A scattered context grammar $G = (N, T, P, S)$ *such that* $L(G) = L(Q)$.
Method:

1. *Set* $N = \{S, 4, 5\} \cup D$.
2. *Consider the definition of* ι *(see Definition 2) with* $A = V - T$ *and* $B = W - F$. *Based on* A, B, *and* ι, *consider specific definitions of* κ, μ, ν, *and* δ *(see Definitions 2, 4, and 5).*
3. *Initialize* M *with* $\emptyset$. *Perform (3i) through (3v), given next, to construct* M.
   (i) *if* $s = a_0q_0$, *where* $a_0 \in V - T$ *and* $q_0 \in W - F$, *then add* $S \to 1\delta(u)4w1$ *to* M, *for all* $u \in \nu(a_0)$ *and* $w \in \mu(q_0)$;
   (ii) *if* $(a, q, y, p) \in R$, *where* $a \in V - T$, $p, q \in W - F$, *and* $y \in (V - T)^*$, *then add* $4 \to \delta(u)4w$ *to* M, *for all* $u \in \nu(y)$ *and* $w \in \mu(p)\mu(q)$;
   (iii) *add* $4 \to 205$ *to* M;
   (iv) *if* $(a, q, y, p) \in R$, *where* $a \in V - T$, $p, q \in W - F$, $y \in T^*$, *then add* $5 \to y5w$ *to* M, *for all* $w \in \mu(p)\mu(q)$;
   (v) *if* $(a, q, y, p) \in R$, *where* $a \in V - T$, $q \in W - F$, $y \in T^*$, *and* $p \in F$, *then add* $5 \to y302w$ *to* M, *for all* $w \in \mu(q)$.
4. *Set* $O = \{(1, 2, 0, 3, 0, 2, 1) \to (2, \varepsilon, \varepsilon, \varepsilon, \varepsilon, \varepsilon, 2),\ 2 \to \varepsilon\}$.
5. *Set* $P = M \cup O$.

Hereafter, for brevity, we refer to $(1, 2, 0, 3, 0, 2, 1) \to (2, \varepsilon, \varepsilon, \varepsilon, \varepsilon, \varepsilon, 2)$ as π.

Basic Idea. Algorithm 1 extends the Algorithm proposed in [6], but for clarity, we explained it completely. Next, we sketch the reason why $L(G) = L(Q)$.

What we need to demonstrate is that for any $y \in T^*$,

$$S \Rightarrow^* y \text{ in } G \text{ if and only if } \#s \Rightarrow^* w\#yf \text{ in } Q$$

with $s = a_0q_0$, $w \in (V - T)^*$, and $f \in F$.

To rephrase this equivalence more precisely, we need to show that $S \Rightarrow^* y$ in G if and only if for some $m \geq 1$, Q makes $\#a_0q_0 \Rightarrow^* a_0 \cdots a_m\#yf$ according to (a_0, q_0, z_0, q_1) through (a_m, q_m, z_m, q_{m+1}), where $q_{m+1} = f$. To see why this equivalence holds true, take any $S \Rightarrow^* y$ with $y \in L(G)$. Examine the construction of P to see that $S \Rightarrow^* y$ in G has, in a greater detail, the form

$$S \Rightarrow^* 1\nu_1 20y302\nu_2 1 \Rightarrow^* y$$

with $\nu_1, \nu_2 \in D^*$, $\nu_1 \in \nu(a_0 \cdots a_\ell), \nu_2 \in \mu(q_k \ldots q_0)$, where $\ell, k \geq 1$. Consequently, we see that proving the equivalence requires a demonstration that in the derivation of the above form in G,

(I) $m = \ell = k$;
(II) $\nu_1 \in \nu(a_0 \cdots a_\ell)$ with $a_0, \ldots, a_\ell \in V - T$;
(III) $\nu_2 \in \mu(q_k \ldots q_0)$ with $q_0, \ldots, q_k \in W - F$.

Consider (II) above. Observe that ν_1 encodes the prefix of all the front queue symbols (including the erased symbols) rewritten during the generation of y. This is the reason why we assume that Q is a left-extended queue grammar, which records this prefix as opposed to any ordinary queue grammar, which throws it away.

During the sketch of this basic idea, we refer to all symbols that occur somewhere to the left of y as *left nonterminals*, and we refer to all symbols that occur somewhere to the right of y as *right nonterminals*. From the definition of ν, it follows that

$$\begin{aligned} 1\nu_1 20 = & 1103103 \cdots 103\underline{11}0 \cdots 1010 \cdots 103103 \cdots 103\underline{11}0 \cdots 101010 \cdots \\ & \cdots 103103 \cdots 103\underline{11}0 \cdots 1020 \end{aligned}$$

Counting from the right to the left, we refer to the ith underlined occurrence of 11 as the ith *left turn*, $1 \leq i \leq n$. From the definition of μ, it follows that

$$\begin{aligned} 302\nu_2 1 = & 302301 \cdots 301\underline{030}101 \cdots 0101 \cdots 301301301 \cdots 301\underline{030}101 \cdots \\ & \cdots 0101 \cdots 301301 \cdots 301\underline{030}101 \cdots 01011 \end{aligned}$$

Counting from the left to the right, we refer to the ith underlined occurrence of 030 as the ith *right turn*.

Let us examine $1\nu_1 20y302\nu_2 1 \Rightarrow^* y$ in a greater detail. The first 1 and the last 1 are produced by a production from step (3i) in the construction. Furthermore, in front of y, 20 is made by a production from (3iii), and behind y, 302 is produced by a production from (3v). Observe that all the left and right nonterminals can be removed only by π and $2 \rightarrow \varepsilon$. In $1\nu_1 20y302\nu_2 1$, there exist two occurrences of 2. Production π is applicable as soon as two occurrences of 2 appear in the rewritten string, and its application does not change the number of these occurrences. Consequently, during $1\nu_1 20y302\nu_2 1 \Rightarrow^* y$, $2 \rightarrow \varepsilon$ is applied only during the last two steps while all the preceding steps are made by using π. The first 2 is always a left nonterminal and the other occurs always as a right nonterminal. Considering these observations and π, we see that if a string contains 1 somewhere in between the left 2 and the right 2, then G cannot derive a terminal string from it. Consequently, during $1\nu_1 20y302\nu_2 1 \Rightarrow^* y$, G eliminates 1s in an inside-out way so that it always rewrites the rightmost occurrence within the left 1 s and, simultaneously, the leftmost occurrence among the right 1 s. Unless a string contains 0, 3, 0 in this order scattered somewhere in between the left 2 and the right 2, then G cannot apply π and derive a terminal string. More specifically, every successful derivation in G is of the form

$$S \Rightarrow^* 1\nu_1 20y302\nu_2 1 \Rightarrow^* 1203y021 \Rightarrow 2y2 \Rightarrow^2 y$$

Let $1v_3yv_41 \Rightarrow 1v_3'yv_4'1$ be a direct derivation step in $1\nu_120y302\nu_21 \Rightarrow^* 1203y021$. Then, in a greater detail, this step has one of these five forms

a) $1v_5\underline{1}0\underline{20}y\underline{302}30\underline{1}v_61 \Rightarrow 1v_520y302v_61$ with $v_51020 = v_3$ and $302301v_6 = v_4$;
b) $1v_5\underline{120}y\underline{302}030\underline{1}v_61 \Rightarrow 1v_52y0302v_61$ with $v_5120 = v_3$ and $3020301v_6 = v_4$;
c) $1v_5\underline{1}03\underline{2}y\underline{0302}0\underline{1}v_61 \Rightarrow 1v_5203y02v_61$ with $v_51032 = v_3$ and $030201v_6 = v_4$;
d) $1v_5\underline{1}03\underline{203}y\underline{02}0\underline{1}v_61 \Rightarrow 1v_5203y02v_61$ with $v_5103203 = v_3$ and $0201v_6 = v_4$;
e) $1v_5\underline{1}0\underline{203}y\underline{02}30\underline{1}v_61 \Rightarrow 1v_520y302v_61$ with $v_510203 = v_3$ and $02301v_6 = v_4$.

Hereafter, to point out that a derivation step $u \Rightarrow v$ $[\pi]$ satisfies one specific form of the five previous forms ($X \in \{a, b, c, d, e\}$), we write $u \Rightarrow_{X)} v$.

Suppose that the leftmost right turn occurs closer to y than the rightmost left turn does. For instance,

$$1103103\cdots 103103110101010101020y3020301010101\cdots 01011$$

From this string, G performs these steps

$$1103103\cdots 1031031101010101\underline{1}0\underline{20}\ y\ \underline{302}030\underline{1}010101\cdots 01011$$
$$\Rightarrow\quad 1103103\cdots 10310311010101\underline{1}0\underline{2}0\ y\ \underline{0302}0\underline{1}0101\cdots 01011$$
$$\Rightarrow\quad 1103103\cdots 1031031101010200\ y\ 020101\cdots 01011$$

Observe that in between the two 2s, no 3 occurs, so G cannot derive a terminal string from it.

Suppose that the leftmost right turn occurs farther from y than the rightmost left turn does. For instance,

$$1103103\cdots 10310311020y3023013013013010301010101\cdots 01011$$

From this string, G performs these steps

$$1103103\cdots 1031031\underline{1}0\underline{20}\ y\ \underline{302}30\underline{1}3013013010301010101\cdots 01011$$
$$\Rightarrow\quad 1103103\cdots 103103\underline{120}\ y\ \underline{302}30\underline{1}3013010301010101\cdots 01011$$
$$\Rightarrow\quad 1103103\cdots 1031032\ y\ 30230130103010101\cdots 01011$$

Observe that in between the two 2s, only one 0 occurs, so G cannot derive a terminal string from it.

Next, we give an example for some $a \in V - T$ and $q \in W - F$, where the right and left turns match.

$$1103103\cdots 103110101010\cdots 101020y302301301\cdots 30103010101\cdots 01011$$

where

$$\iota(aq) = 103103\cdots 103110101010\cdots 1010 \in \nu(a)$$

and

$$301301\cdots 30103010101\cdots 0101 \in \mu(q)$$

Consequently, G always simultaneously eliminates the ith left turn and the ith right turn in the way sketched next

$$
\begin{array}{lr}
 & 1103103\cdots 103110101010\cdots 10\underline{1}0\underline{20}\ y\ \underline{302}30\underline{1}301\cdots 30103010101\cdots 01011\\
\Rightarrow_{a)} & 1103103\cdots 103110101010\cdots \underline{1}0\underline{20}\ y\ \underline{302}30\underline{1}\cdots 30103010101\cdots 01011\\
\Rightarrow_{a)} & 1103103\cdots 103110101010\cdots 20\ y\ 302\cdots 30103010101\cdots 01011\\
\Rightarrow & \\
\Rightarrow & 1103103\cdots 1031031\underline{1}0\underline{20}\ y\ \underline{302}30\underline{1}0301010101\cdots 01011\\
\Rightarrow_{a)} & 1103103\cdots 103103\underline{120}\ y\ \underline{302}030\underline{1}010101\cdots 01011\\
\Rightarrow_{b)} & 1103103\cdots 103\underline{1}03\underline{2}\ y\ \underline{0302}0\underline{1}0101\cdots 01011\\
\Rightarrow_{c)} & 1103103\cdots 103203\ y\ 020101\cdots 01011
\end{array}
$$

In this way, G simulates the successful derivation of y performed by Q so

$$S \Rightarrow^* 1\nu_1 20y302\nu_2 1 \Rightarrow^* y$$

with $\nu_1, \nu_2 \in D^*$, $\nu_1 \in \nu(a_0 \cdots a_m)$ with $a_0, \ldots, a_m \in V - T$, and $\nu_2 \in \mu(q_m \ldots q_0)$ with $q_0, \ldots, q_m \in W - F$. Thus, $L(Q) = L(G)$.

Next, we illustrate the construction of a simulating scattered context grammar for a very simple left-extended queue grammar.

Example 3. To make this example as readable as possible, we introduce some notation. First, $\lceil \underline{a}, q \rceil$ denotes the code of $\iota(a, q)$ from $\nu(a)$ for any $a \in V - T$. Then, $\lfloor a, \underline{q} \rfloor$ denotes an element (code) based on $\iota(a, q)$ from $\mu(q)$ for any $q \in W - F$.

Consider a left-extended queue grammar $Q = (V, T, W, \{f\}, Ss, R)$ in normal form 2 with $V = \{S, X, a, b\}, T = \{a, b\}, W = \{s, p, q, f\}$. Let R consist of (S, s, XS, p), (X, p, aa, q) and (S, q, bb, f).

Considering the construction from Algorithm 1, we present the introduction of some productions in the resulting scattered context grammar, $G = (N, T, P, S)$, in the corresponding steps with rules not deriving words replaced with '...' for brevity:

(i): Add $\ldots$, $S \to 1\lceil \underline{S}, s\rceil \lceil \underline{S}, s\rceil 4\lfloor S, \underline{s}\rfloor 1$, $\ldots$ into P;
(ii): For $(S, s, XS, p) \in R$, add $\ldots$, $4 \to \lceil \underline{X}, p\rceil \lceil \underline{X}, p\rceil \lceil \underline{S}, q\rceil \lceil \underline{S}, q\rceil 4\lfloor X, \underline{p}\rfloor \lfloor S, \underline{s}\rfloor$, $\ldots$ into P;
(iii): Add $4 \to 205$ into P;
(iv): For $(X, p, aa, q) \in R$, add $\ldots$, $5 \to aa5\lfloor S, \underline{q}\rfloor \lfloor X, \underline{p}\rfloor$, $\ldots$ into P;
(v): For $(S, q, bb, f) \in R$, add $\ldots$, $5 \to bb302\lfloor S, \underline{q}\rfloor$, $\ldots$ into P.

Now, we explore how a derivation

$$\#Ss \Rightarrow S\#XSp \Rightarrow SX\#Saaq \Rightarrow SXS\#aabbf$$

in Q is simulated in G.

We explore the first phase of a derivation of $aabb$ in G:

$$
\begin{aligned}
& S \\
\Rightarrow\ & 1\lceil \underline{S}, s\rceil \lceil \underline{S}, s\rceil 4 \lfloor S, \underline{s}\rfloor 1 \\
\Rightarrow\ & 1\delta(\lceil \underline{S}, s\rceil)\lceil \underline{X}, p\rceil \lceil \underline{X}, p\rceil \lceil \underline{S}, q\rceil \lceil \underline{S}, q\rceil 4 \lfloor X, \underline{p}\rfloor \lfloor S, \underline{s}\rfloor \lfloor S, \underline{s}\rfloor 1 \\
\Rightarrow\ & 1\delta(\lceil \underline{S}, s\rceil \lceil \underline{X}, p\rceil \lceil \underline{S}, q\rceil)205 \lfloor X, \underline{p}\rfloor \lfloor S, \underline{s}\rfloor \lfloor S, \underline{s}\rfloor 1 \\
\Rightarrow\ & 1\delta(\lceil \underline{S}, s\rceil \lceil \underline{X}, p\rceil \lceil \underline{S}, q\rceil)20aa5 \lfloor S, \underline{q}\rfloor \lfloor X, \underline{p}\rfloor \lfloor X, \underline{p}\rfloor \lfloor S, \underline{s}\rfloor \lfloor S, \underline{s}\rfloor 1 \\
\Rightarrow\ & 1\delta(\lceil \underline{S}, s\rceil \lceil \underline{X}, p\rceil \lceil \underline{S}, q\rceil)20aabb302 \lfloor S, \underline{q}\rfloor \lfloor S, \underline{q}\rfloor \lfloor X, \underline{p}\rfloor \lfloor X, \underline{p}\rfloor \lfloor S, \underline{s}\rfloor \lfloor S, \underline{s}\rfloor 1
\end{aligned}
$$

According to the construction, the injection ι should handle $\mathrm{card}((V-T)\times(W-F))$ elements. Thus, for simple coding, k should be at least $\mathrm{card}((V-T)\times(W-F))+2$. In the second phase of this example, we need to code six pairs—(S,s), (S,p), (S,q), (X,s), (X,p), and (X,q). Take $k=8$. Next, we introduce ι for these pairs—that is,

$$
\begin{aligned}
\iota(Ss) &= 1031(10)^6 = \lceil \underline{S}, s\rceil & \iota(Xs) &= (103)^4 1(10)^3 = \lceil \underline{X}, s\rceil \\
\iota(Sp) &= (103)^2 1(10)^5 = \lceil \underline{S}, p\rceil & \iota(Xp) &= (103)^5 1(10)^2 = \lceil \underline{X}, p\rceil \\
\iota(Sq) &= (103)^3 1(10)^4 = \lceil \underline{S}, q\rceil & \iota(Xq) &= (103)^6 110 = \lceil \underline{X}, q\rceil \\
\kappa(Ss) &= (301)^6 030101 = \lfloor S, \underline{s}\rfloor & \kappa(Sq) &= (301)^4 0301(01)^3 q = \lfloor S, \underline{q}\rfloor \\
\kappa(Xp) &= (301)^2 0301(01)^5 = \lfloor X, \underline{p}\rfloor
\end{aligned}
$$

Now we illustrate an erasure in the second phase of the derivation with $y = aabb$ in G, which is similar to erasure in [6]:

$$
\begin{gathered}
1\delta(\lceil \underline{S}, s\rceil \lceil \underline{X}, p\rceil)\lceil \underline{S}, q\rceil (103)^3 1(10)^4\ 20y302\ (301)^4 0301(01)^3 \lfloor S, \underline{q}\rfloor \delta(\lfloor X, \underline{p}\rfloor \lfloor S, \underline{s}\rfloor)1 \\
\Rightarrow^8\ 1\delta(\lceil \underline{S}, s\rceil \lceil \underline{X}, p\rceil)(103)^3 1(10)^4\ 203y02\ (301)^4 0301(01)^3 \delta(\lfloor X, \underline{p}\rfloor \lfloor S, \underline{s}\rfloor)1 \\
\Rightarrow^8\ 1\lceil \underline{S}, s\rceil \lceil \underline{S}, s\rceil \lceil \underline{X}, p\rceil (103)^5 1(10)^2\ 203y02\ (301)^2 0301(01)^5 \lfloor X, \underline{p}\rfloor \lfloor S, \underline{s}\rfloor \lfloor S, \underline{s}\rfloor 1 \\
\Rightarrow^8\ 1\lceil \underline{S}, s\rceil \lceil \underline{S}, s\rceil (103)^5 1(10)^2\ 203y02\ (301)^2 0301(01)^5 \lfloor S, \underline{s}\rfloor \lfloor S, \underline{s}\rfloor 1 \\
\Rightarrow^8\ 1\lceil \underline{S}, s\rceil 1031(10)^6\ 203y02\ (301)^6 030101 \lfloor S, \underline{s}\rfloor 1 \\
1\ 1031(10)^6\ 203y02\ (301)^6 030101\ 1 \\
\Rightarrow^8\ 1\ 203y02\ 1 \\
\Rightarrow 2\ y\ 2 \\
\Rightarrow^2\ y
\end{gathered}
$$

Lemma 4. *Algorithm 1 is correct.*

The rigorous proof is due to the lengthiness included in the appendix.

Theorem 1. *Let L be a recursively enumerable language; then, there is a scattered context grammar $G = (N, T, P, S)$ such that (a) $L = L(G)$, (b) N has no more than six nonterminals, and (c) P has no more than one non-context-free production.*

Proof. Let us consider the algorithm based on the Algorithm 1 such as:

Algorithm 2. *Input: A left-extended queue grammar $Q = (V, T, W, F, s, R)$ in normal form 2.*
Output: A scattered context grammar $G = (N, T, P, 4)$ such that $L(G) = L(Q)$.
Method:

1. *Set $N = \{4, 5\} \cup D$.*
2. *Consider the definition of ι (see Definition 2) with $A = V - T$ and $B = W - F$. Based on A, B, and ι, consider specific definitions of κ, μ, ν, and δ (see Definitions 2, 4, and 5).*
3. *Initialize M with $\emptyset$. Perform (3i) through (3v), given next, to construct M.*
   - *(i) if $s = a_0q_0$, where $a_0 \in V - T$ and $q_0 \in W - F$, then add $4 \rightarrow 1\delta(u)4w1$ to M, for all $u \in \nu(a_0)$ and $w \in \mu(q_0)$;*
   - *(ii) if $(a, q, y, p) \in R$, where $a \in V - T$, $p, q \in W - F$, and $y \in (V - T)^*$, then add $4 \rightarrow \delta(u)4w$ to M, for all $u \in \nu(y)$ and $w \in \mu(p)\mu(q)$;*
   - *(iii) add $4 \rightarrow 205$ to M;*
   - *(iv) if $(a, q, y, p) \in R$, where $a \in V - T$, $p, q \in W - F$, $y \in T^*$, then add $5 \rightarrow y5w$ to M, for all $w \in \mu(p)\mu(q)$;*
   - *(v) if $(a, q, y, p) \in R$, where $a \in V - T$, $q \in W - F$, $y \in T^*$, and $p \in F$, then add $5 \rightarrow y302w$ to M, for all $w \in \mu(q)$.*
4. *Set $O = \{(1, 2, 0, 3, 0, 2, 1) \rightarrow (2, \varepsilon, \varepsilon, \varepsilon, \varepsilon, \varepsilon, 2),\ 2 \rightarrow \varepsilon\}$.*
5. *Set $P = M \cup O$.*

Lemma 5. *Algorithm 2 is correct.*

It allows two new subsets of derivations compared to Algorithm 1. Therefore, to show that a grammar from Algorithm 2 generates identical language as a grammar from Algorithm 1, we need to show that all new sets of derivations do not change the language. Therefore, we split the two new derivations in two Claims to prove Algorithm 2 is correct.

Claim. If a derivation of grammar G begins with the rule $4 \rightarrow 1\delta(u)4w1$ and there are n applications of the rule $4 \rightarrow 1\delta(u)4w1$, where $n \neq 1$, then it does not generate any words.

Proof. If there is n applications of the rule $4 \rightarrow 1\delta(u)4w1$ after the first derivation step with the rule $4 \rightarrow 1\delta(u)4w1$, where $n \geq 1$ then a sentential form is $(1\delta(u))^n1$ $\delta(u)41\delta(u)(w1)^n$. Therefore we would have to be able in the annihilation phase to eliminate more nonterminals 1 but we do not have enough nonterminals 0 to use the rule $(1, 2, 0, 3, 0, 2, 1) \rightarrow (2, \varepsilon, \varepsilon, \varepsilon, \varepsilon, \varepsilon, 2)$ which is only possible way to eliminate nonterminal 1. Therefore, this does not generate any words.

Claim. If a derivation of grammar G does not start with rule $4 \rightarrow 1\delta(u)4w1$, then it does not generate any words.

Proof. There is no rule to get rid of nonterminal 0 since the only possibility to get rid of 0 is rule $(1, 2, 0, 3, 0, 2, 1) \rightarrow (2, \varepsilon, \varepsilon, \varepsilon, \varepsilon, \varepsilon, 2)$, which is not possible because there cannot be a nonterminal 1 before a nonterminal 0. Or if nonterminals 1 are generated in different positions, then they interrupt the dependency between codes and anticodes and, in this case, do not generate any words. Therefore, the grammar does not generate any words. □

4 Conclusion

In conclusion, we would like to propose open problems. Firstly, is it possible to reduce the grammar further to five or fewer nonterminals? Secondly, we already know that two-nonterminal scattered context grammars are computationally complete (see [1]). So are scattered context grammars with a single non-context-free production (see [6]). Consider two-nonterminal scattered context grammars with one non-context-free production. Are they computationally complete, too? If not, then study, from a more general viewpoint, whether there exist constants n and m such that n-nonterminal scattered context grammars with m non-context-free productions are computationally complete.

Acknowledgements. This work was supported by Brno University of Technology grant FIT-S-23-8209.

References

1. Csuhaj-Varjú, E., Vaszil, G.: Scattered context grammars generate any recursively enumerable languages with two nonterminals. Inf. Process. Lett. **110**(20), 902–907 (2010)
2. Dassow, J., Stiebe, R.: Nonterminal complexity of some operations on context-free languages. Fund. Inform. **83**(1–2), 35–49 (2008). https://doi.org/10.3233/FUN-2008-831-205
3. Geffert, V.: Context-free-like forms for the phrase-structure grammars. In: Chytil, M.P., Koubek, V., Janiga, L. (eds.) MFCS 1988. LNCS, vol. 324, pp. 309–317. Springer, Heidelberg (1988). https://doi.org/10.1007/BFb0017154
4. Ginsburg, S.: Algebraic and automata-theoretic properties of formal languages. J. Symb. Log. **41**(4), 788–789 (1976). https://doi.org/10.2307/2272400
5. Kleijn, H., Rozenberg, G.: On the generative power of regular pattern grammars. Acta Informatica **20**(4), 391–411 (1983). https://doi.org/10.1007/BF00264281
6. Křivka, Z., Meduna, A.: Scattered context grammars with one non-context-free production are computationally complete. Fund. Inform. **179**(4), 361–384 (2021). https://doi.org/10.3233/FI-2021-2028
7. Maurer, H.A., Penttonen, M., Salomaa, A., Wood, D.: On non context-free grammar forms. Math. Syst. Theory **12**, 297–324 (1978)

8. Maurer, H.A., Salomaa, A., Wood, D.: EOL forms. Acta Informatica **8**, 75–96 (1977)
9. Meduna, A.: Automata and Languages: Theory and Applications. Springer, London (2000). https://doi.org/10.1007/978-1-4471-0501-5
10. Meduna, A.: Generative power of three-nonterminal scattered context grammars. Theoret. Comput. Sci. **246**(1), 279–284 (2000). https://doi.org/10.1016/S0304-3975(00)00153-5
11. Meduna, A., Techet, J.: Scattered Context Grammars and their Applications. WIT Press, UK, WIT Press (2010). https://www.fit.vut.cz/research/publication/c62000/
12. Meduna, A., Zemek, P.: Regulated Grammars and Automata. Springer, New York (2014). https://doi.org/10.1007/978-1-4939-0369-6
13. Rozenberg, G., Salomaa, A. (eds.): Handbook of Formal Languages, Vol. 1: Word, Language, Grammar. Springer, New York (1997). https://doi.org/10.1007/978-3-642-59136-5
14. Čulik, K., Maurer, H., Ottmann, T.: On two-symbol complete EOL forms. Theoret. Comput. Sci. **6**(1), 69–92 (1978). https://doi.org/10.1016/0304-3975(78)90005-1

Disjunctive Complexity

Nikita Ivanov[3], Alexander Rubtsov[2,3], and Mikhail Vyalyi[1,2,3](✉)

[1] Federal Research Center "Computer Science and Control", Russian Academy of Sciences, 42 Vavilov Street, 119333 Moscow, Russia
[2] Moscow Institute of Physics and Technology (National Research University), 1A, bld. 1, Kerchenskaya str, 117303 Moscow, Russia
[3] National Research University Higher School of Economics, 11 Pokrovsky Blvd, 109028 Moscow, Russia
vyalyi@gmail.com

Abstract. A recently introduced measure of Boolean functions complexity–disjunctive complexity (DC)–is compared with other complexity measures: the space complexity of streaming algorithms and the complexity of nondeterministic branching programs (NBP). We show that DC is incomparable with NBP. Specifically, we present a function that has low NBP but has subexponential DC. Conversely, we provide arguments based on computational complexity conjectures to show that DC can superpolynomially exceed NBP in certain cases. Additionally, we prove that the monotone version of NBP complexity is strictly weaker than DC.

We prove that the space complexity of one-pass streaming algorithms is strictly weaker than DC. Furthermore, we introduce a generalization of streaming algorithms that captures the full power of DC. This generalization can be expressed in terms of nondeterministic algorithms that irreversibly write 1 s to entries of a Boolean vector (i.e., changes from 1 to 0 are not allowed).

Finally, we discuss an unusual phenomenon in disjunctive complexity: the existence of *uniformly hard functions*. These functions exhibit the property that their disjunctive complexity is maximized, and this property extends to all functions dominated by them.

1 Introduction

In this paper, we study a novel complexity measure for Boolean functions, which we refer to as *disjunctive complexity*. A Boolean function f is represented succinctly by describing its accepting set $f^{-1}(1)$ through paths in a labeled directed graph. We call these graphs *transition graphs*. At first glance, this representation resembles the branching programs model (see, e.g., [9]). However, as we discuss in detail in Sect. 4, the two models are quite different. From another point of view, disjunctive complexity generalizes the space complexity of streaming algorithms (see [4,5,8,10]). In Sect. 3, we discuss this connection and propose several variants of disjunctive complexity to capture both the similarities and differences between the space complexity of streaming algorithms and our model.

Published by Springer Nature Switzerland AG 2025
A. Malcher and L. Prigioniero (Eds.): DCFS 2025, LNCS 15759, pp. 137–150, 2025.
https://doi.org/10.1007/978-3-031-97100-6_10

Disjunctive complexity was introduced in [11] as a tool for investigating the regular realizability problem in Formal Language Theory. In that work, the measure was defined for families of subsets of a finite set U. It is straightforward to observe that such families correspond naturally to Boolean functions: the indicator function of a subset is essentially a $(0, 1)$-assignment of Boolean variables indexed by U, therefore a family of subsets corresponds to a Boolean function.

In [11] several basic results on disjunctive complexity were obtained. Notably, lower bounds for this measure are relatively easy to prove, and an explicit class of functions with exponential disjunctive complexity was presented in the same work. Algorithmic properties of disjunctive complexity are counter-intuitive. It was proved in [11] that computing the value of a function represented by a transition graph is NP-complete while the accepting set $f^{-1}(1)$ can be generated with polynomial delay. For most of standard models of Boolean function complexity computing the function value is easy, while even the check $f^{-1}(1) \neq \varnothing$ (the satisfiability problem) is NP-complete. All these facts indicate that disjunctive complexity is worth to be studied. Our main motivation behind this work is to deepen our understanding of the relationships between disjunctive complexity and other complexity measures for Boolean functions. We anticipate that disjunctive complexity will find applications in Boolean functions analysis.

Our Contribution

We explore the relationship between streaming algorithms for computing Boolean functions and the representation of Boolean functions by transition graphs. The most important characteristic of a streaming algorithm is its space complexity. Lower bounds of the space complexity are well-elaborated. They are based on communication complexity, see e.g. [1,6,7,9], or on information-theoretic arguments, see [3,4].

In Sect. 3, we demonstrate that streaming algorithms can be viewed as a special case of the transition graph representation model for Boolean functions. This connection provides a pathway to prove lower bounds on the space complexity of streaming algorithms by establishing lower bounds on disjunctive complexity. In the latter case, combinatorial arguments can be employed. In [11], the separability property was used to derive such lower bounds. Here, we introduce a new tool based on the closure properties of the labeling functions in transition graphs. This tool yields subexponential lower bounds for very simple functions, such as the indicator function of P_3-free graphs (see Sect. 4 for the proof) or even simpler functions like the indicator function of cliques (see Sect. 5). These results suggest that transition graphs may serve as an useful tool for proving lower bounds on the space complexity of streaming algorithms.

Up to a polynomial blow-up, the transition graph representation model can be interpreted as a way of generating the accepting set $f^{-1}(1)$ of a Boolean function f using a non-deterministic algorithm that writes units to a Boolean vector entries irreversibly. Comparing this model with streaming algorithms leads to several restricted variants of disjunctive complexity, which we present in Sect. 3.

We prove two separation results for these restricted measures (see Theorems 1 and 2 in Sect. 3).

In Sect. 4, we compare branching program complexity and disjunctive complexity. Assuming the complexity-theoretic conjecture NP $\not\subseteq$ P/poly, these complexity measures appear to be incomparable. We provide corresponding examples in this section. In one direction the separation is unconditional.

In Sect. 5, we discuss an interesting phenomenon specific to disjunctive complexity. We prove that there exist functions f such that for all functions g dominated by f, the disjunctive complexity of g is maximized and equals the size of $g^{-1}(1)$. This phenomenon is specific to disjunctive complexity and has no known counterpart in other common complexity measures for Boolean functions.

2 Definitions and Initial Observations

In this paper we adopt the following notation concerning Boolean functions. Arguments of a Boolean function (assignments) are functions themselves of type $x\colon U \to \{0,1\}$, where U is the index set for Boolean variables. For $i \in U$ and an assignment x we use also a subscript notation $x_i = x(i)$. For an assignment x, we define the *unit set* $U_x = \{i \in U : x_i = 1\}$. In the notation of a Boolean function $f\colon \{0,1\}^U \to \{0,1\}$ the exponent U is always the set of variables. In particular, we replace the standard notation $f(x_1, \ldots, x_n)$ by $f\colon \{0,1\}^{[n]} \to \{0,1\}$.[1]

We allow directed graphs to have loops and multiple edges. For vertices x, y of a directed graph we denote by $E(x, y)$ the set of edges directed from the endpoint x to the endpoint y. A *transition graph* is a tuple $G = (V, s, t, E, \ell)$, where V is the set of vertices, E is the set of directed edges, s is the initial vertex, t is the terminal vertex, and $\ell\colon E \to 2^U$ is the labeling function, where U is a finite set. The size $|G|$ of a transition graph is defined as the number of edges. The set $\ell(e)$, $e \in E$, is called the *edge label*. The *label set* $S = \ell(P)$ of a path P is the union of all edge labels along the path. We also say that P *is marked* by S.

The Boolean function $f_G\colon \{0,1\}^U \to \{0,1\}$ described by G is defined as follows: $f_G(x) = 1$ if and only if $U_x = \ell(P)$, where P is a path from s to t (referred to as an (s,t)-path for brevity). See Fig. 1 for an example. We say that a transition graph G *represents* the function f_G. Graphs G' and G'' are called *equivalent* if $f_{G'} = f_{G''}$.

Our main concern are bounds on the sizes of transition graphs up to a polynomial blow-up. At this level of precision, it suffices to focus on specific classes of transition graphs. For instance, only vertices lying on (s,t)-paths affect f_G. Therefore, vertices that are unreachable from s or *dead* (defined as vertices from which t is unreachable) can be removed from the graph. This yields an equivalent transition graph without unreachable or dead vertices. Note that this transformation can be performed in time polynomial in the size of the transition graph.

Another example is restricting the labeling function to the empty label and *singletons* (1-element sets). An edge (u_0, u_n) marked by a nonempty set S of size

[1] Hereinafter we adopt notation $[n] = \{1, 2, \ldots, n\}$.

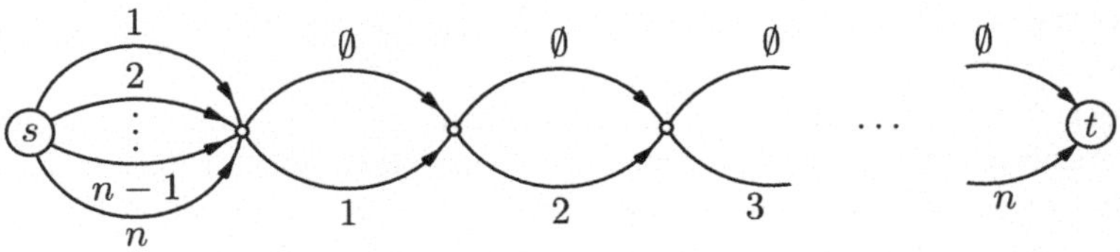

Fig. 1. A transition graph representing the disjunction $x_1 \vee \cdots \vee x_n$

n can be replaced by a path $u_0, u_1, \ldots, u_n$, where $u_1, \ldots, u_{n-1}$ are new vertices, and each edge (u_i, u_{i+1}) in the path is marked by a distinct singleton from S. It is clear that this transformation produces an equivalent transition graph and takes a time polynomial in $|U|$, $|G|$.

An important result from [11] is the following:

Proposition 1 ([11]). *For any transition graph G, there exists an equivalent directed acyclic graph (DAG) G', which can be constructed in time polynomial in $|U|$, $|G|$.*

Based on this proposition, we will henceforth assume that a transition graph is always a DAG. The *disjunctive complexity* $\Delta(f)$, where $f\colon \{0,1\}^U \to \{0,1\}$ (recall that U is a finite set), is the smallest size of a transition graph (DAG) representing f. It is easy to see that

$$\Delta(f) \leq |f^{-1}(1)|. \tag{1}$$

This bound is attained by constructing a transition graph with the set of edges $E = \{e_x : x \in f^{-1}(1),\ e_x \in E(s,t)\}$, and with the labeling function $\ell(e_x) = U_x$.

3 Disjunctive Complexity and Streaming Algorithms

In this section, we introduce several classes of labeling functions such that the corresponding transition graphs simulate computations performed by streaming algorithms. These classes give rise to restricted variants of disjunctive complexity.

In a streaming algorithm, input data is accessed in small portions that arrive sequentially, forming a "stream". The algorithm uses limited memory to compute a function of the input data. Boolean functions can be computed by such algorithms, where the most natural choice for a portion of input is a single bit. We are interested in the space complexity of streaming algorithms. Exact definitions of streaming algorithms varies in different papers. We combine our definition using definitions from [5,8,10]. In lecture notes [5] it is called the *basic setup*. Also we extend the definition to cover non-deterministic algorithms. In our settings a *non-deterministic one-pass streaming algorithm* $\mathcal{A}$ computing a Boolean function $f\colon \{0,1\}^{[n]} \to \{0,1\}$ in memory m, where m is an integer, is determined by a transition relation $\delta \subseteq Q \times Q \times \{0,1\}$, where Q is the state set, $|Q| = 2^m$, and by an accepting set $Q_a \subseteq Q$. The algorithm starts a run from the initial state

q_0. A valid run on the input $x\colon [n] \to \{0,1\}$ is a sequence of states $q_0, q_1, \ldots, q_n$, such that $(q_i, q_{i+1}, x_{i+1}) \in \delta$ for all $0 \leq i < n$. The value $f_{\mathcal{A}}(x)$ of the function computed by $\mathcal{A}$ is 1 if there exists a valid run $q_0, q_1, \ldots, q_n$ on the input x such that $q_n \in Q_a$. In this form, streaming algorithms resemble automata with 2^m states. However, for streaming algorithms, the memory size may depend on n.

We have described the simplest model of streaming algorithms. In more general models, multiple passes through the input data are allowed. In [4], a streaming algorithm chooses an order in which input data is read. Generalizing this approach, we consider algorithms such that the variable to be read at a particular moment is determined by the current state of the algorithm. Up to our knowledge this model is new. It appears that such algorithms correspond precisely to general transition graphs. Formally, a *generalized streaming algorithm* $\mathcal{A}$ is determined by the following data: the state set Q, the initial state s, the halting state t, the set of Boolean variables U, and the transition relation $\delta \subseteq Q \times Q \times (\{\emptyset\} \cup U)$.

The algorithm $\mathcal{A}$ operates on a Boolean assignment from $\{0,1\}^U$, which is initially zero. Configurations of $\mathcal{A}$ are pairs (q, x), where $q \in Q$, $x \in \{0,1\}^U$. The initial configuration is $(s, \mathbf{0})$; $\mathbf{0} = (0, \ldots, 0)$. A transition can change a configuration (q, x) to a configuration (q', x') as follows. A transition $(q, q', \emptyset) \in \delta$ preserves x (i.e., $x' = x$); a transition $(q, q', i) \in \delta$ sets i-th component to 1: i.e., $x'_i = 1$ while $x'_j = x_j$ for $j \neq i$. In a halting configuration (t, x), the algorithm stops, and we say that the resulting assignment x is *generated by* $\mathcal{A}$. The Boolean function $f_{\mathcal{A}}$ computed by $\mathcal{A}$ takes the value 1 at all assignments generated by the algorithm and 0 otherwise. Note that a one-pass streaming algorithms accepts words, while a generated streaming algorithms generate words. So, they are different types of algorithms.

The transition graph corresponding to the generalized streaming algorithm $\mathcal{A}$ is $G = (V, s, t, E, \ell)$, where

$$V = Q, \quad E = \{e_{q',q'',i} \in E(q', q'') : (q', q'', i) \in \delta\}, \quad \ell(e_{q',q'',i}) = i. \tag{2}$$

Restricted types of streaming algorithms are represented by transition graphs with restricted labeling functions. We consider three types of restricted disjunctive complexity:

A transition graph is *streaming* if $U = [n]$, edge labels are singletons or the empty label, and along any (s,t)-path non-empty labels form an increasing sequence. For $f\colon \{0,1\}^{[n]} \to \{0,1\}$ the *streaming disjunctive complexity* $\Delta_{\mathrm{s}}(f)$ is the smallest size of a streaming transition graph representing f.

A transition graph is *adaptively streaming* if there exists a linear order on U such that the graph is streaming if elements of U are numbered with respect to this order. For $f\colon \{0,1\}^U \to \{0,1\}$ the *adaptive streaming disjunctive complexity* $\Delta_{\mathrm{as}}(f)$ is the smallest size of an adaptively streaming transition graph representing f. Note that adaptively streaming algorithms correspond to the model considered in [4].

A transition graph is *write-once* if, along any (s,t)-path, each variable appears at most once. For $f\colon \{0,1\}^U \to \{0,1\}$ the *write-once disjunctive complexity* $\Delta_1(f)$ is the smallest size of a write-once transition graph representing

f. Note that verifying the write-once property of a transition graph can be done effciently, see Lemma 1 below.

It is clear from the definitions that $\Delta_{\mathrm{s}}(f) \geq \Delta_{\mathrm{as}}(f) \geq \Delta_1(f) \geq \Delta(f)$. We present below an exponential separation between Δ_{as} and Δ_{s}. We are able to prove a superpolynomial separation between Δ_1 and Δ under the conjecture NP $\not\subseteq$ P/poly. The value of a gap between $\Delta_1(f)$ and $\Delta_{\mathrm{as}}(f)$ remains open.

The separation Δ_{as} from Δ_{s} uses the well-known idea of deriving lower bounds for streaming space complexity by applying lower bounds from communication complexity. We adapt this idea to the case of disjunctive complexities.

3.1 Streaming Disjunctive Complexity

The conversion of a one-pass streaming algorithm to a streaming transition graph is straightforward.

Proposition 2. *If there exists a one-pass streaming algorithm computing a function* $f\colon \{0,1\}^{[n]} \to \{0,1\}$ *in memory* m, *then* $\Delta_{\mathrm{s}}(f) = O(n2^m)$.

Proof. To represent the operation of a one-pass streaming algorithm computing a Boolean function f, we use a streaming transition graph $G = (V, s, t, E, \ell)$ that differs from the definition for generalized streaming algorithms, see Eq. (2). Let Q be the state set of the algorithm, $|Q| = 2^m$. The vertex set V consists of pairs (q, i), where $q \in Q$ and $0 \leq i \leq n$, along with the terminal vertex t. The initial vertex is $s = (q_0, 0)$, where q_0 is the initial state of the algorithm. For each triple (q', q'', x) in the transition relation of the algorithm, there are edges in $E(G)$ in the form $e_{q',q'',i} \in E\big((q', i-1), (q'', i)\big)$ for all $1 \leq i \leq n$. The label of $e_{q',q'',i}$ is $\{i\}$ if $x = 1$, otherwise the label is the empty set. For each accepting state q, there exists an edge $e_q \in E((q, n), t)$ labeled by the empty set. Edges $e_{q',q'',i}$ and e_q form the edge set E of G.

This construction ensures that the label set of an (s,t)-path in G is exactly U_x for an assignment x such that $f(x) = 1$. Conversely, if $f(x) = 1$, the streaming computation on the input x produces an $(s, (q, n))$-path P, where q is an accepting state. This path can be extended to the (s,t)-path Pe, $e \in E((q, n), t)$, and the label set of this path is exactly the unit set of x. Thus, $f = f_G$ and $|G| = (n+1)|Q| = O(n2^m)$.

Using streaming algorithms and this proposition, we can immediately construct examples of functions with low disjunctive complexity.

Example 1. The simplest example is the parity function $\mathrm{XOR}_n\colon \{0,1\}^{[n]} \to \{0,1\}$. It takes the value 1 if the number of variables set to 1 is odd. To compute XOR_n by a streaming algorithm, only 1 bit of memory is needed to track the parity of 1 s encountered so far. Thus $\Delta_{\mathrm{s}}(\mathrm{XOR}_n) = O(n)$ due to Proposition 2. See Fig. 2 for an illustration.

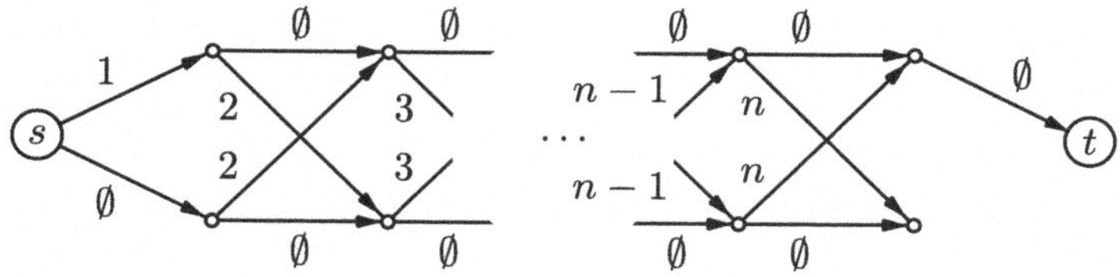

Fig. 2. A transition graph for XOR_n

Example 2. The threshold function $T_{n,k}\colon \{0,1\}^{[n]} \to \{0,1\}$ is equal to 1 if at least k variables are set to 1. The well-known majority function is a special case of the threshold function, namely, $T_{n,\lfloor n/2\rfloor+1}$. The slice function $S_{n,k}\colon \{0,1\}^{[n]} \to \{0,1\}$ is equal to 1 if exactly k variables are set to 1. Streaming algorithms for computing $T_{n,k}$ and $S_{n,k}$ store the count of 1s encountered so far and make a decision at the end of the stream. For this purpose they use a counter of encountered 1s of size $\lceil \log_2 n \rceil$. So, by Proposition 2, $\Delta_{\mathrm{s}}(T_{n,k}) = O(n^2)$ and $\Delta_{\mathrm{s}}(S_{n,k}) = O(n^2)$.

Example 3. More generally, counting the number of 1s suffices to compute any symmetric function. Thus, for any symmetric function $f\colon \{0,1\}^{[n]} \to \{0,1\}$, we have $\Delta_{\mathrm{s}}(f) = O(n^2)$.

For a transition graph $G = (V, s, t, E, \ell)$, we define the counting function $\#_1\colon V \to \mathbb{Z}$ as $\#_1(v) = \max(|\ell(P)| : P$ is an (s,v)-path$)$. Note that $\#_1(u) \le \#_1(v)$ for any edge $e = (u,v) \in E$.

Theorem 1. *There exists a sequence of Boolean functions f_n of $4n$ variables such that $\Delta_{\mathrm{as}}(f_n) = \mathrm{poly}(n)$ and $\Delta_{\mathrm{s}}(f_n) = 2^{\Omega(n)}$.*

Proof. The functions $\mathrm{Eq}_n\colon \{0,1\}^{[4n]} \to \{0,1\}$ are defined as follows. For an assignment $a\colon [4n] \to \{0,1\}$ of the variables, we define binary words x and y of length $2n$ by the rule: $x_i = a_i$, $y_i = a_{i+2n}$, $1 \le i \le 2n$. By definition, $\mathrm{Eq}_n(a) = 1$ iff the Hamming weight of x is n and $x = y$.

First, we prove that $\Delta_{\mathrm{as}}(\mathrm{Eq}_n) = \mathrm{poly}(n)$. Consider the linear order on $[4n]$: $1 < 1{+}2n < 2 < 2{+}2n < \dots < 2n < 2n{+}2n$. A streaming algorithm computing Eq_n with respect to this order is straightforward and uses $O(\log n)$ memory. The algorithm checks the conditions $x_i = y_i$ for all $1 \le i \le 2n$ (it requires $O(1)$ memory since the corresponding entries are neighbors), counts the number of 1s in x, and accepts if and only if all checks are successful and the total number of 1s in x is n. This algorithm can be converted into a streaming transition graph representing Eq_n. The size of the graph is $O(n^2)$ due to Proposition 2.

Next, we prove that $\Delta_{\mathrm{s}}(\mathrm{Eq}_n) = 2^{\Omega(n)}$. Let $G = (V, s, t, E, \ell)$ be a streaming transition graph representing Eq_n. Take an (s,t)-path P in G going through a vertex $v \in V$ such that $\#_1(v) = n$. Divide the path into two subpaths $P'P''$, where P' is an (s,v)-path and P'' is a (v,t)-path. From the definition of Eq_n we conclude that $\ell(P') \subset \{i : 1 \le i \le 2n\}$ and $i + 2n \in \ell(P'')$ iff $i \in \ell(P')$. Thus, $\ell(\widetilde{P}) = \ell(P')$ for any (s,v)-path $\widetilde{P}$. Since G represents Eq_n, there are $\binom{2n}{n}$

different values of $\ell(P')$, each corresponding to a different vertex in the graph. Therefore, $|G| \geq \binom{2n}{n} = 2^{\Omega(n)}$.

3.2 Write-Once Disjunctive Complexity

Lemma 1. *There exists a polynomial time algorithm that, given a transition graph G and an assignment $x\colon U \to \{0,1\}$, decides whether G is a write-once transition graph and, if so, computes $f_G(x)$.*

Proof. We assume that the graph $G = (V, s, t, E, \ell)$ is DAG and that the edge labels are either singletons or the empty label. The assumption is valid because the transformation to this form can be performed in polynomial time, as explained in Sect. 2.

To verify that G is write-once, the algorithm examines all pairs of edges e_1, e_2 such that $\ell(e_1) = \ell(e_2) \neq \varnothing$. For each such pair, the algorithm checks whether there exists no (s,t)-path that passes through both e_1 and e_2. This check is easily reduced to the reachability problem in a directed graph.

Let $S = x^{-1}(1)$. The algorithm removes all edges e in G such that $\ell(e) \nsubseteq S$, resulting in a modified graph $G' = (V, s, t, E', \ell)$. It follows immediately from the definitions that $f_G(x) = 1$ if and only if there exists an (s,t)-path in G' labeled by S. In terms of the counting function of G' it means that $\#_1(t) = |S|$. So, to compute $f_G(x)$, it suffices to compute $\#_1(t)$ in the graph G'.

Since G' remains write-once, the counting function satisfies a recurrence

$$
\begin{aligned}
&\#_1(s) = 0; \\
&\#_1(v) = \max_{u:(u,v)\in E'} \bigl(\#_1(u) + |\ell(u,v)|\bigr).
\end{aligned}
\tag{3}
$$

To solve this recurrence, the algorithm first computes a topological sorting of the vertices in G', which can be done in polynomial time. Then, it evaluates the recurrence using Eq. (3) in the order of the topological sorting, which also takes polynomial time.

Theorem 2. *Assuming* NP $\nsubseteq$ P/poly, *there exists a sequence of Boolean functions $f_n\colon \{0,1\}^{[\mathrm{poly}(n)]} \to \{0,1\}$ such that $\Delta(f_n) = \mathrm{poly}(n)$ and $\Delta_1(f_n)$ grows faster than any polynomial in n.*

Proof. It was proved in [11] that computation $f_G(x)$ for general transition graphs is NP-complete. Suppose that for any general transition graph G there exists an equivalent write-once transition graph of size poly($|G|$). It is well-known that P $\subset$ P/poly (see, e.g., [2, Th. 6.6]). From Lemma 1 we conclude that there exist circuits of polynomial size computing $f_G(x)$ for an arbitrary transition graph G. Due to the aforementioned theorem P $\subset$ P/poly, polynomial reductions can be converted to the circuits of polynomial size. Thus, we get the inclusion NP $\subseteq$ P/poly and come to a contradiction with the assumption made.

4 Disjunctive Complexity and Branching Programs

A (nondeterministic) branching program is a directed acyclic graph G having distinguished the initial vertex s and the terminal vertex t, whose edges are labeled by *literals* (variables and negations of variables). An assignment x of variables switches on edges labeled by literals that are true under x. Switched on edges form an *assignment graph* G_x. A Boolean function f computed by a branching program G takes the value 1 if there exists an (s,t)-path in G_x. The corresponding complexity measure $\mathrm{NBP}(f)$ is the minimum size of a branching program computing a Boolean function f. If all labels in a branching program are variables (i.e., no negations are used), then it is called *monotone*. For a monotone Boolean function f, another complexity measure $\mathrm{NBP}_+(f)$ is well-defined: it is the minimum size of a monotone branching program computing f.

For more details on branching programs, see, e.g., [9].

At first glance, branching programs look similar to transition graphs. However, these models are quite different. For instance, transition graphs use only variables (no negations) but can represent non-monotone functions (in fact, any function can be represented by a transition graph). Moreover, a monotone branching program can be simulated by a transition graph with only a polynomial blow-up in size.

Proposition 3. *Let G be a monotone branching program computing a function f. Then there exists a transition graph G' such that $f_{G'} = f$ and $|G'| \leq |G| + O(n)$, where n is the number of variables. Thus $\Delta(f) \leq \mathrm{NBP}_+(f) + O(n)$.*

Proof. We assume that variables of f are indexed by $[n]$. Replacing variables in G by their indices, we get a transition graph $G'' = (V, E, s, t, \ell)$, where V, E, s, t are the same as in G and $\ell(e) = i$ the edge e is labeled in the branching program G by a variable x_i. Now define the transition graph $G' = (V', E', s', t', \ell')$ as follows: $V' = V \cup \{w_i : 1 \leq i \leq n\}$; $E' = E \cup \{e_{i,\alpha} \in E(w_{i-1}, w_i)\}$, where $1 \leq i \leq n$, $\alpha \in \{0,1\}$; $\ell'(e) = \ell(e)$ for $e \in E$, $\ell'(e_{i,0}) = \varnothing$, $\ell'(e_{i,1}) = \{i\}$, $s' = s$, $t' = w_n$. For uniformity, we set $t = w_0$, where t is the terminal vertex in G'' (and in G). The construction ensures that for each assignment $x\colon [n] \to \{0,1\}$ there exists a (w_0, w_n)-path P such that $\ell(P) = x^{-1}(1)$.

If $f(x) = 1$, then there exist an (s,t)-path in G'' with edges labeled by i such that $x_i = 1$. The path can be extended by a suitable (v_0, v_n)-path to an (s',t')-path P' in G' such that $\ell'(P') = x^{-1}(1)$. Therefore $f_{G'}(x) = 1$.

If $f(x) = 0$, then for any an (s,t)-path P in G'', there exists an edge $e \in P$ such that $\ell(e) \notin x^{-1}(1)$. Thus, any (s',t')-path in G' contains an edge labeled by $i \notin x^{-1}(1)$. Therefore $f_{G'}(x) = 0$.

Given a (general) branching program G computing a function f, the value $f(x)$ can be computed in polynomial time by solving a reachability problem in the assignment graph G_x. Since computing a value of a function represented by a transition graph is NP-complete (see [11]), it leads to an analogue of Theorem 2.

Proposition 4. *Assuming* NP $\not\subseteq$ P/poly, *there exists a sequence of Boolean functions* $f_n\colon \{0,1\}^{[\mathrm{poly}(n)]} \to \{0,1\}$ *such that* $\Delta(f_n) = \mathrm{poly}(n)$ *and* $\mathrm{NBP}(f_n)$ *grows faster than any polynomial in* n.

The proof of this proposition repeats the proof of Theorem 2 with appropriate modifications.

In the opposite direction, we can prove unconditional separation of branching and disjunctive complexities. For this purpose, we introduce Boolean functions with variables indexed by unordered pairs of integers in $[n] = \{1, \ldots, n\}$. We denote the set of all these pairs by $\binom{[n]}{2}$. An assignment $x\colon \binom{[n]}{2} \to \{0,1\}$ is naturally interpreted as an undirected graph Γ_x on the vertex set $[n]$: edges of Γ_x are pairs $\{i,j\}$ such that $x_{ij} = 1$. To distinguish these graphs from transition graphs we call them *label graphs*. A Boolean function $f\colon \{0,1\}^{\binom{[n]}{2}} \to \{0,1\}$ is interpreted as a property of graphs on n vertices.

We now define functions that separate branching and disjunctive complexities. Let $\mathrm{P3f}_n$ be the indicator function of P_3-free graphs. That is, $U = \binom{[n]}{2}$ and $\mathrm{P3f}_n(x) = 1$ if Γ_x is a P_3-free graph, i.e., Γ_x does not contain an induced path on 3 vertices. It is well-known that P_3-free graphs are disjoint unions of complete graphs.

Proposition 5. $\mathrm{NBP}(\mathrm{P3f}_n) = O(n^3)$.

Proof. A graph is P_3-free if and only if, for any triple v_1, v_2, v_3 of its vertices, the induced subgraph does not contain exactly two edges. In other words, the existence of two edges between these vertices implies the existence of the third one. Since $(x \wedge y) \to z$ is equivalent to $\neg x \vee \neg y \vee z$, this condition is easily implemented in a branching program. We construct a branching program $G = (V, s, t, E, \ell)$ as follows. The input variables are unordered pairs $\{i,j\}$, $1 \le i \ne j \le n$. Let $[n]_3$ be the set of ordered arrangements of triples of integers in the range $[n]$, and $\nu\colon [N] \to [n]_3$ be an enumeration of $[n]_3$, here $N = n(n-1)(n-2)$. Set $V = \{0\} \cup [N]$, $s = 0$, $t = N$. For each $1 \le i \le N$ there are three edges $e_{i,\alpha}$ in $E(i-1, i)$, $\alpha \in \{1,2,3\}$. Their labels are $\ell(e_{i,1}) = \neg x_{\{p,q\}}$, $\ell(e_{i,2}) = \neg x_{\{q,r\}}$, $\ell(e_{i,3}) = x_{\{r,p\}}$, where $\nu(i) = (p,q,r)$. Here, we extend the labeling function to allow literals as labels. An (s,t)-path in the assignment graph G_x does exist if and only if $\neg x_{\{p,q\}} \vee \neg x_{\{q,r\}} \vee x_{\{r,p\}}$ is true for all p, q, r, which is equivalent to Γ_x being P_3-free. Thus, G computes $\mathrm{P3f}_n$.

To prove a lower bound for $\Delta(\mathrm{P3f}_n)$ we need to show that a restricted class of labeling functions is equivalent to the general case. Let $G = (V, s, t, E, \ell)$ be a transition graph. The *closure* $\bar{\ell}$ of the labeling function ℓ is defined as follows. For $e \in E(u,v) \subseteq E(G)$ the label set $\bar{\ell}(e)$ is the union of three sets: (1) the label set $\ell(e)$; (2) the set of $a \in U$ such that $a \in \ell(P)$ for any (s,u)-path P; (3) the set of $a \in U$ such that $a \in \ell(P)$ for any (v,t)-path P.

Lemma 2. *The closure of the labeling function yields an equivalent transition graph:* $f_{(V,s,t,E,\ell)} = f_{(V,s,t,E,\bar{\ell})}$.

Proof. Let P be an (s,t)-path. By definition, $\ell(e) \subseteq \bar{\ell}(e)$ for any edge e, so $\ell(P) \subseteq \bar{\ell}(P)$. Now we prove the opposite inclusion. Let $a \in \bar{\ell}(e)$, $e \in P$. The edge e divides P in three parts: $P = P'eP''$.

If $a \in \ell(e)$, then $a \in \ell(P)$. If $a \in \bar{\ell}(e) \setminus \ell(e)$, then, by definition, at least one of the following holds: $a \in \ell(P') \subseteq \ell(P)$ or $a \in \ell(P'') \subseteq \ell(P)$. Thus $\bar{\ell}(P) \subseteq \ell(P)$.

We have proved that $\bar{\ell}(P) = \ell(P)$, which implies that the two labeling functions yield equivalent transition graphs.

We say that the labeling function ℓ is closed if $\ell = \bar{\ell}$. From Lemma 2, we conclude that closed labeling functions determine the disjunctive complexity.

Lemma 3. *The closure operator is idempotent: the closure of the closure of ℓ is the closure of ℓ.*

Proof. Let $a \notin \bar{\ell}(e)$. It implies that $a \notin \ell(e)$, and there exists a path $P = P'eP''$ such that $a \notin \ell(P')$ and $a \notin \ell(P'')$. So $a \notin \bar{\ell}(e')$ for any edge e' of P, since e' divides P in three parts satisfying the same conditions. Therefore a does not belong to the closure of $\bar{\ell}$.

To get the desired lower bound, we need to establish several properties of transition graphs representing functions whose accepting sets are subsets of the set of P_3-free graphs. Fix a transition graph $G = (V, s, t, E, \ell)$ such that $U = \binom{[n]}{2}$ and $f_G(x) = 1$ implies that Γ_x is P_3-free. Due to Lemma 2, we assume w.l.o.g. that ℓ is closed.

Proposition 6. *For any $e \in E$ the label graph $\ell(e)$ is P_3-free.*

Proof. Suppose for contradiction that $\{i,k\} \in \ell(e)$, $\{j,k\} \in \ell(e)$, and $\{i,j\} \notin \ell(e)$. Since ℓ is closed, due to Lemma 3, there exists an (s,t)-path $P = P'eP''$ such that $\{i,j\} \notin \ell(P')$ and $\{i,j\} \notin \ell(P'')$. Thus the label graph $\ell(P)$ is not P_3-free, contradicting the assumption made.

Proposition 7. *For any (s,x)-path P, where $x \in V$, the label graph $\ell(P)$ is P_3-free. Moreover, for any (s,x)-path P in G and any edge $e \in E(x,y)$ the maximal cliques of $\ell(P)$ and $\ell(e)$ either do not intersect or are comparable under the inclusion relation.*

Proof. The induction on the length of P. The base case follows from Proposition 6.

The induction step. Let C_1 be a maximal clique in $\ell(P)$ and C_2 be a maximal clique in $\ell(e)$. Suppose for contradiction that $i \in C_1 \setminus C_2$, $j \in C_2 \setminus C_1$, and $k \in C_1 \cap C_2$. Then $\{i,j\} \notin \ell(P) \cup \ell(e)$. Thus, there exists a (y,t)-path P' such that $\{i,j\} \notin \ell(P')$ due to Lemma 3. Therefore, the label graph of the path PeP' is not P_3-free, since $\{i,j\} \notin \ell(PeP')$, while $\{i,k\} \in \ell(PeP')$ and $\{j,k\} \in \ell(PeP')$. We come to a contradiction to the assumption made.

Theorem 3. $\Delta(\mathrm{P3f}_n) = 2^{\Omega(n)}$.

Proof. Let $f_G = \mathrm{P3f}_n$. Without changing the number of edges in G, we assume that the labeling function is closed. From Proposition 7, we conclude that for any (s,t)-path P every maximal clique in $\ell(P)$ must be a clique in some $\ell(e)$ for an edge e in the path. Since the number of maximal cliques in any label graph $\ell(e)$ is at most n (since it is P_3-free), and there are 2^n possible cliques, the number of edges in G must be at least $2^n/n$.

Remark 1. It is easy to verify that that $\neg\,\mathrm{P3f}_n$ is represented by a transition graph of size polynomial in n. The corresponding generalized streaming algorithm nondetermistically guesses a triple i, j, k, writes $x_{ij} = 1$, $x_{jk} = 1$, and after that writes arbitrary values for the remaining edges in the label graph except $\{i, k\}$. Thus, we get an example of a function such that the gap between the disjunctive complexity of the function and its negation is (sub-)exponential.

5 Uniformly Hard Functions

A Boolean function f is *uniformly hard* with respect to the disjunctive complexity if $\Delta(g) = |g^{-1}(1)|$ for any function g such that $g^{-1}(1) \subseteq f^{-1}(1)$ (denoted as $g \leq f$). It means that the disjunctive complexity of f is the largest possible (see the bound (1)) and, moreover, the same holds for all functions that are dominated by f, i.e. $g(x) \leq f(x)$ for all x.

In [11] exponential lower bounds on the disjunctive complexity were proved for indicator functions of asymptotically good binary linear codes (AGLC functions). These functions are *almost uniformly hard.* It means that $|g^{-1}(1)| = \mathrm{poly}(\Delta(g))$ for all $g \leq f$. For AGLC functions, the known estimates of the degree of a polynomial in this bound depend on the relative code distance and are rather large.

Here we present an example of uniformly hard functions. A graph is called a *clique graph* if it is a disjoint union of a complete graph and a set of isolated vertices. The name reflects the fact that a clique graph is determined by its unique non-trivial clique, except in the case of the empty graph. The function $\mathcal{C}_n$ is the indicator function of clique graphs, i.e., $\mathcal{C}_n(x) = 1$ if Γ_x is a clique graph. By definition, $|\mathcal{C}_n^{-1}(1)| = 2^n$. A modification of the proof of Theorem 3 gives the matching lower bound.

Theorem 4. $\Delta(\mathcal{C}_n) = 2^n$.

Fix a transition graph $G = (V, s, t, E, \ell)$ such that $U = \binom{[n]}{2}$ and $f_G \leq \mathcal{C}_n$. W.l.o.g. we assume that ℓ is closed. The following two propositions are similar to Propositions 6, 7.

Proposition 8. *For any $e \in E$ the label graph $\ell(e)$ is a clique graph.*

Proof. If the label graph $\ell(e)$ is empty, we are done. Otherwise, let i, j be vertices of positive degree in the label graph $\ell(e)$. Specifically, let $\{i, i'\} \in \ell(e)$ and $\{j, j'\} \in \ell(e)$. We will prove that $\{i, j\} \in \ell(e)$. This implies the proposition, since in any graph that is not a clique graph, there exists a pair of non-adjacent vertices of positive degrees.

Suppose for contradiction that $\{i, j\} \notin \ell(e)$. Due to Lemma 3, there exists an (s, t)-path $P = P'eP''$ such that $\{i, j\} \notin \ell(P')$ and $\{i, j\} \notin \ell(P'')$. Thus, the label graph $\ell(P)$ is not a clique graph, since $\{i, i'\} \in \ell(P)$, $\{j, j'\} \in \ell(P)$. This contradicts the assumption $f_G \leq \mathcal{C}_n$.

Proposition 9. *For any (s, x)-path P in G, where $x \in V$, the label graph $\ell(P)$ is a clique graph. Moreover, for any (s, x)-path P in G and any edge $e \in E(x, y)$, the maximal cliques of $\ell(P)$ and $\ell(e)$ are comparable under the inclusion relation.*

Proof. The induction on the length of P. The base case follows from Proposition 8. For the induction step, if $\ell(P)$ or $\ell(e)$ are empty graphs, the claim follows from Proposition 8 or from the induction hypothesis. Otherwise, let $\ell(P)$ be a clique graph with a non-trivial clique A, where P is an (s, x)-path P, and $\ell(e)$ be a clique graph with a non-trivial clique B. Suppose for contradiction that A and B are incomparable under the inclusion relation. It means that there exist $i \in A \setminus B$ and $j \in B \setminus A$. Thus, $\{i, j\} \notin \ell(P) \cup \ell(e)$. Due to Lemma 3, there exists a (y, t)-path P' such that $\{i, j\} \notin \ell(P')$. Therefore, the label graph of the path PeP' is not a clique graph, since i, j are non-adjacent in the graph but both have positive degree. This contradicts to the assumption $f_G \leq \mathcal{C}_n$.

Proof (of Theorem 4). Let $f_G = \mathcal{C}_n$. Without changing the number of edges in G, we assume that the labeling function is closed. From Proposition 9, it follows that the label graph $\ell(P)$ of any (s, t)-path P coincides with the label graph of some edge in the path. Thus, the number of edges in G is at least the number of satisfying assignments of $\mathcal{C}_n$, i.e. 2^n.

The existence of (almost) uniformly hard functions looks specific for the disjunctive complexity. For example, it is open whether almost uniform hard functions exist with respect to circuit complexity.

Acknowledgements. The work of the second and third authors was done within the framework of the HSE University Basic Research Program. The third author was also partially supported by the state assignment topic no. FFNG-2024-0003.

Disclosure of Interests. The authors have no competing interests to declare that are relevant to the content of this article.

References

1. Alon, N., Matias, Y., Szegedy, M.: The space complexity of approximating the frequency moments. J. Comput. Syst. Sci. **58**(1), 137–147 (1999)
2. Arora, S., Barak, B.: Computational Complexity: A Modern Approach. Cambridge Univ, Press (2009)
3. Bar-Yossef, Z., Jayram, T., Kumar, R., Sivakumar, D.: Information statistics approach to data stream and communication complexity. J. Comput. Syst. Sci. **68**(4), 702–732 (2004)

4. Bar-Yossef, Z., Kumar R., Sivakumar, D.: Reductions in streaming algorithms, with an application to counting triangles in graphs. In: Proceedings of the Thirteenth Annual ACM-SIAM Symposium on Discrete Algorithms (SODA '02), pp. 623–632. Society for Industrial and Applied Mathematics, USA (2002)
5. Chakrabarti, A.: Data Stream Algorithms. Lecture Notes. https://www.cs.dartmouth.edu/~ac/Teach/data-streams-lecnotes.pdf Last update: March 7, 2024
6. Chou, C.-N., Golovnev, A., Velusamy, S.: Optimal streaming approximations for all Boolean Max-2CSPs and Max-$k$sat. In: 2020 IEEE 61st Annual Symposium on Foundations of Computer Science (FOCS), pp. 330–341. Durham, NC, USA (2020)
7. Gibbons, P., Trithapura, S.: Estimating simple functions on the union of data streams. In: SPAA01: 13th ACM Symposium on Parallel Algorithms and Architectures, pp. 281–290. Association for Computing Machinery, New York, NY, USA (2001)
8. Jain, R., Nayak, A.: The space complexity of recognizing well-parenthesized expressions in the streaming model: the index function revisited. IEEE Trans. Inf. Theory **60**(10), 6646–6668 (2010)
9. Jukna, S.: Boolean Function Complexity Advances and Frontiers. Springer-Verlag, Berlin Heidelberg (2012)
10. Muthukrishnan, S.: Data streams: algorithms and applications. Found. Trends® Theoret. Comput. Sci. **1**(2), 117–236 (2005)
11. Rubtsov, A.A., Vyalyi, M.N.: On universality of regular realizability problems. Probl. Inf. Transm. **60**(3), 209–232 (2024)

Two-Way Finite Automata with Translucent Input Letters

Martin Kutrib[1], Andreas Malcher[1], Carlo Mereghetti[2,3](✉), and Beatrice Palano[2,3]

[1] Institut für Informatik, Universität Giessen, Arndtstr. 2, 35392 Giessen, Germany
{kutrib,andreas.malcher}@informatik.uni-giessen.de
[2] Dipartimento di Informatica "G. Degli Antoni", Università degli Studi di Milano, via Celoria 18, 20133 Milan, Italy
{carlo.mereghetti,beatrice.palano}@unimi.it
[3] Gruppo Nazionale Calcolo Scientifico Istituto Nazionale di Alta Matematica (GNCS-INdAM), Rome, Italy

Abstract. Finite automata with translucent input letters can be obtained by equipping classical finite automata with a translucency function which, depending on the current state, establishes the set of invisible input symbols: such symbols are skipped in the current move and dealt with subsequently, while the first visible symbol from the current input head position is processed and consumed. These models can be returning, meaning that the input head is rewinded at each move after processing a visible symbol, or not. In their original definition by Mráz and Otto [13], translucent finite automata feature a one-way input head, i.e., the head always "looks to the right" to spot the next visible symbol. Here, we extend this definition in the deterministic case by allowing a two-way input head motion, meaning that the next visible symbol can be found by looking either to the left or to the right of the head. We also consider translucent sweeping finite automata, as the restricted version of two-way devices reverting input head direction at the endmarkers only. We prove that the sweeping restriction does not affect the recognition power in the returning mode, while the opposite holds for non-returning devices. We show that our devices are strictly more powerful than their one-way version, and that they are incomparable with translucent pushdown automata [9,14,17]. We investigate some closure properties for the families of languages recognized by translucent two-way and sweeping finite automata. In particular, while dealing with this latter topic, an open problem stated in [13] is addressed and solved.

Keywords: Translucent input letters · Finite automata · Two-way and Sweeping motion · Returning and non-returning computations · Closure Properties

A. Malcher and L. Prigioniero (Eds.): DCFS 2025, LNCS 15759, pp. 151–165, 2025.
https://doi.org/10.1007/978-3-031-97100-6_11

1 Introduction

Language recognition devices are typically thought of as parsing input strings from left to right, one symbol after the other, in a continuous fashion; they usually sweep the whole input and finally accept or reject, unless they get stuck in some kind of loop. This one-way input head motion, which can encompass the possibility of performing stationary or λ-moves, and/or accepting in the middle of the string, is basically the default for all the most famous and studied computational models such as Turing machines, finite automata of various kinds, pushdown automata, and so on (see, e.g., [1,4–6,8,12]). Naturally, alternative ways of processing input strings, such as rotating, sweeping and restarting modes, are well worth investigating; the reader is referred to, e.g., [2,5,7,11,21,23] for an overview of these and other input processing modes. In all these cases, meaningful differences in recognition and/or descriptional power are emphasized, stating that the way of acquiring input is truly a computational resource that can be used to tune device capabilities. Among others, here we focus on two parsing forms, central in the present contribution: *two-way* motion and *translucency*.

In a two-way device, the input head can choose to move backward or forward or stay at each move. In the realm of finite automata, it is well known that two-way motion does not increase the recognition power, but it may greatly affect the descriptional power, with deep implications in structural complexity. In particular, a relevant open problem is to establish the optimal state cost of deleting nondeterminism on two-way finite automata [24]. Showing the optimality of the known exponential size blow-up would immediately separate determinism from nondeterminism in logarithmic space bounded computations [3], together with P vs. NP, one of the main open questions in theoretical computer science. A positive (unfortunately, not decisive) answer is obtained by assuming the simulating two-way deterministic finite automata to be sweeping [25], which is a restricted form of two-way dynamic where head reversals may occur at the ends of the input tape only.

The notion of translucent input letters in the realm of finite automata is introduced by Nagy and Otto in [15]. The built-in key feature for translucent devices is a translucency function which, based on the current state, establishes translucent (invisible) input letters. At each move, the device skips (by looking through) the translucent portion of the input, from the current input head position rightward, up to the first non-translucent letter. From this point of view, such devices can be understood as being *one-way*, in the sense that they always "look to the right" in order to discover the next visible input symbol to be processed. After processing the non-translucent symbol, in the *returning mode* the input head returns to the left end of the input while, in the *non-returning mode*, the input head continues to process the input according to its updated current state and the corresponding translucent symbols. Also, in this latter mode, the input head returns to the left end when the right end of the input is reached, unless acceptance/rejection takes place. Deterministic and nondeterministic finite automata with translucent letters are deeply investigated in the literature (see, e.g., [13,16,17,20,22]). However, many questions are still open.

In this paper, we equip finite automata with *both* the two-way and the translucent paradigm, thus defining and investigating *two-way deterministic finite automata with translucent input letters*, as well as their *sweeping* restriction, in both returning and non-returning mode (these devices being abbreviated as 2DFAwtl, SDFAwtl, nr2DFAwtl, and nrSDFAwtl, respectively). Very roughly speaking, we equip a classical 2DFA or SDFA (sweeping 2DFA) with a translucency function. In a 2DFAwtl M, states are partitioned into sets Q_r and Q_l. At each move, if M is in a state in Q_r (resp., Q_l), then it must look to the right (resp., left) of the current head position in order to spot the next visible input symbol to be processed. From this point of view, our devices generalize one-way automata by Nagy and Otto [15], in that they can "look both ways" to spot the next visible symbol, whence the designation *two-way*. After consuming the spotted visible symbol, in the *returning mode* the input head gets back to the left or to the right end of the input, depending on whether the reached state belongs either to Q_r or to Q_l, respectively. Instead, in the *non-returning mode*, the input head continues to process the input toward the direction implied by the reached state. In any case, the direction switches on the endmarkers. An SDFAwtl is the restricted version of a 2DFAwtl, where the direction of the input head changes at the endmarkers only. Returning and non-returning modes work as for 2DFAwtl.

It should be noted that Nagy and Otto introduced and investigated in [18,19] *linear automata with translucent letters*, which are basically finite automata working with translucent letters that additionally have two heads starting at opposite ends and moving from left to right and from right to left, respectively. Such devices are in its deterministic variant equivalent to SDFAwtl in the returning mode. Hence, some positive and negative closure properties obtained in [18,19] carry over to returning SDFAwtl. On the other hand, some closure properties left open in [18,19] can now be solved in terms of returning SDFAwtl.

In Sect. 2, preliminary notions and notations are provided, and the formal definition of 2DFAwtl, SDFAwtl, and nr2DFAwtl, nrSDFAwtl is set forth, together with some working examples and basic relations among models.

In Sect. 3, we compare the recognition power of sweeping and general two-way translucent finite automata. We get that, in the returning mode, the sweeping dynamic does not lower the acceptance capability. To this aim, we show how to build an equivalent SDFAwtl from any given 2DFAwtl. Instead, this is not the case for the non-returning mode. In fact, we provide a language accepted by an nr2DFAwtl, and show that it cannot be accepted by any nrSDFAwtl.

In Sect. 4, we compare the power of two-way head movement vs. pushdown storage (abbreviated DPDAwtl and nrDPDAwtl [9,10]) in the translucent setting. From a recognition power viewpoint, we show that 2DFAwtl, nrSDFAwtl, and nr2DFAwtl are incomparable with DPDAwtl and nrDPDAwtl. This is obtained by designing suitable witness languages.

In Sect. 5, we graphically sketch the obtained recognition power results in a hierarchy, which also encompasses the recognition power of other translucent devices investigated in the literature.

In Sect. 6, we investigate some closure properties for the families of languages recognized by 2DFAwtl, nrSDFAwtl, and nr2DFAwtl. By providing suitable witness languages, we prove that all these families are not closed under union, intersection, concatenation, iteration, length-preserving and inverse non-erasing homomorphisms. Instead, they are all closed for reversal and complementation. The closure under this latter operation is obtained by showing how to detect and avoid loops on our two-way translucent devices.

While designing witness languages to settle recognition limits, we define a particular language, and prove it cannot be recognized by any nrSNFAwtl. This enables us to show that one-way translucent finite automata are not closed under intersection with regular languages, thus closing an open problem proposed by Mráz and Otto [13]. In addition, we point out that the above quoted non-closures under iteration and inverse homomorphism we obtain for SDFAwtl enable us to answer analogous closure questions left open in [18,19] for linear automata with translucent letters.

2 Preliminaries

Given a set S, we denote by 2^S its power set, and by $|S|$ its cardinality. We use $\subseteq$ for inclusions, and $\subset$ for proper inclusions. We denote by Σ^* the set of all words on the finite alphabet Σ, including the empty word λ, and let $\Sigma^+ = \Sigma^* \setminus \{\lambda\}$. For any word $w \in \Sigma^*$, we let $|w|$ denote its length, w^R its reversal, and $|w|_a$ the number of occurrences of the symbol $a \in \Sigma$ in w. Maximal factors of the form a^+ in w, where $a \in \Sigma$, are called a-blocks. A language on Σ is any subset $L \subseteq \Sigma^*$. The complement of L is the language $\overline{L} = \Sigma^* \setminus L$, its reversal is $L^R = \{\, w^R \mid w \in L \,\}$. Two language families $\mathscr{L}_1$ and $\mathscr{L}_2$ are said to be incomparable whenever $\mathscr{L}_1$ is not a subset of $\mathscr{L}_2$ and vice versa.

Two-way finite automata feature a single read-only input tape whose inscription is the input word between two endmarkers. The head of the automaton can move freely on the tape but not beyond the endmarkers. Finite automata with translucent letters are extensions of classical finite automata, which do not necessarily have to read the "next" input symbol. Instead, depending on the current state of such devices, some of the input letters may be translucent (invisible). Thus, a two-way finite automaton with translucent letters reads and processes the first input letter, visible in the direction of the head movement.

Formally, a *deterministic two-way finite automaton with translucent letters* (abbreviated as 2DFAwtl) is a system $M = \langle Q, \Sigma, q_0, \rhd, \lhd, \tau, \delta \rangle$, where Q is the finite set of *states* partitioned into the sets Q_l (states leading the input head leftward) and Q_r (states leading the input head rightward), Σ is the finite alphabet of *input symbols*, with $\Sigma \cap Q = \emptyset$, $q_0 \in Q_r$ is the *initial state*, $\rhd, \lhd \notin \Sigma$ are, respectively, the left and right *endmarkers*, $\tau \colon Q \to 2^\Sigma$ is the *translucency mapping*, and $\delta \colon Q \times (\Sigma \cup \{\rhd, \lhd\}) \to Q \cup \{\texttt{accept}\}$ is the *partial transition function*. The translucency mapping τ bears the following meaning: for any state $q \in Q$, the letters from the set $\tau(q)$ are *translucent (invisible) for* q. Therefore, whenever in q, the automaton M does not see these letters (or equivalently, M can see through such letters). Note that the endmarkers are always visible.

A *configuration* of M is represented: by $(\triangleright qw \triangleleft)$ if $q \in Q_r$, by $(\triangleright wq \triangleleft)$ if $q \in Q_l$, or by $\texttt{accept}$, where $q \in Q$ is the current state and $w \in \Sigma^*$ is the current tape inscription. The computation of M on input $w \in \Sigma^*$ starts from the *initial configuration* $(\triangleright q_0 w \triangleleft)$, and steps through a sequence of configurations as follows. Being in some configuration $(\triangleright qw \triangleleft)$, first M determines the next symbol to scan. To this end, it processes the first visible symbol in the direction of its input head motion. Precisely, if $q \in Q_r$ and $w\triangleleft = xy\triangleleft$ with $x \in \tau(q)^*$, $y \in \Sigma^*$, and $a \notin \tau(q)$ is the first symbol of $y\triangleleft$, then M processes a. Now, M halts and rejects whenever $\delta(q, a)$ is undefined, otherwise it enters state $p = \delta(q, a)$, and the successor configuration becomes either $(\triangleright pxy \triangleleft)$ if $p \in Q_r$, or $(\triangleright xyp \triangleleft)$ if $p \in Q_l$. The behavior of M being in the state $q \in Q_l$ is symmetric. Overall, M halts and accepts if and only if δ maps the current situation to $\texttt{accept}$. One step from a configuration to its successor configuration is denoted by $\vdash$. We let $\vdash^*$ (resp., $\vdash^+$) denote the reflexive and transitive (resp., transitive) closure of $\vdash$.

The language accepted by the 2DFAwtl M is defined to be the set $L(M)$ of those words in Σ^* on which the computation of M eventually halts accepting, namely, $L(M) = \{\, w \in \Sigma^* \mid (\triangleright q_0 w \triangleleft) \vdash^+ \texttt{accept} \,\}$. In order to exemplify the dynamics of 2DFAwtl, let us propose the following

Example 1. We design a 2DFAwtl $M = \langle Q, \{a, b, c\}, q_a, \triangleright, \triangleleft, \tau, \delta \rangle$ for the language $L = \{\, uc^{n-1} \mid u \in \{a, b\}^*, |u|_a = n = |u|_b, n > 0 \,\}$. We set $Q_r = \{q_a, q_b\}$, $Q_l = \{q_c\}$, and define τ and δ while elucidating the computation of M. At the beginning of the computation, M processes the first-from-the-left a (being in $q_a \in Q_r$), followed by processing the first-from-the-left b (being in $q_b \in Q_r$). This can be accomplished by setting translucency and transitions as

$$\tau(q_a) = \{b\}, \quad \delta(q_a, a) = q_b,$$
$$\tau(q_b) = \{a\}, \quad \delta(q_a, b) = q_c.$$

After such a double-processing, M enters the state $q_c \in Q_l$ and shifts on the rightmost input symbol, if any, verifying whether this symbol is c. If M sees an a or b, it rejects; if it sees the left endmarker, it accepts. This is implemented as

$$\tau(q_c) = \emptyset, \quad \delta(q_c, c) = q_a,$$
$$\delta(q_c, \triangleright) = \texttt{accept}.$$

If the input was uc^{n-1}, with $u \in \{a, b\}^*$, $|u|_a = n = |u|_b$ then, after this phase, the tape inscription would reduce to vc^{n-2}, with $v \in \{a, b\}^*$, $|v|_a = n - 1 = |v|_b$, and with a new iteration starting from $q_a \in Q_r$ on the leftmost input symbol. The reader may verify that M accepts L. ■

A sweeping finite automaton with translucent letters is a restricted version of a 2DFAwtl. While the direction of the head movement can be freely switched in the two-way case, it can and must be changed *on the endmarkers only* in the sweeping case. So, a *deterministic sweeping finite automaton with translucent letters* (abbreviated as SDFAwtl) is a 2DFAwtl $M = \langle Q, \Sigma, q_0, \rhd, \lhd, \tau, \delta \rangle$, where $q_0 \in Q_r$, and the transition function obeys the following restrictions:

$$\delta\colon Q_r \times \Sigma \to Q_r \cup \{\texttt{accept}\}, \quad \delta\colon Q_r \times \{\lhd\} \to Q_l \cup \{\texttt{accept}\},$$
$$\delta\colon Q_l \times \Sigma \to Q_l \cup \{\texttt{accept}\}, \quad \delta\colon Q_l \times \{\rhd\} \to Q_r \cup \{\texttt{accept}\}.$$

The following example shows an SDFAwtl in action.

Example 2. We design an SDFAwtl $M = \langle Q, \{a, b\}, q_0, \rhd, \lhd, \tau, \delta \rangle$ for the mirror language $L_{mi} = \{\, ww^R \mid w \in \{a, b\}^* \,\}$. We set $Q_r = \{q_0, q_a, q_b\}$, $Q_l = \{p_a, p_b, p_r\}$, and explain τ and δ while describing the computation of M. At the beginning of the computation, M reads the first letter of the input:

$$\begin{aligned} \tau(q_0) = \emptyset, \quad & \delta(q_0, \lhd) = \texttt{accept}, \\ & \delta(q_0, a) = q_a, \\ & \delta(q_0, b) = q_b. \end{aligned}$$

Note that, by these instructions, even the empty word is accepted. If the first input letter, i.e., the first symbol of w, is $x \in \{a, b\}$, then M enters the state q_x and remains at the left end. Then, M sweeps to the right end and enters the state p_x:

$$\begin{aligned} \tau(q_a) = \Sigma, \quad \delta(q_a, \lhd) = p_a, \\ \tau(q_b) = \Sigma, \quad \delta(q_b, \lhd) = p_b. \end{aligned}$$

Once at the right end, M tries to read the symbol x as the last letter of w^R. If the read letter does not match x, the computation gets stuck and rejects. Otherwise, it continues in the state p_r:

$$\begin{aligned} \tau(p_a) = \emptyset, \quad \delta(p_a, a) = p_r, \\ \tau(p_b) = \emptyset, \quad \delta(p_b, b) = p_r. \end{aligned}$$

If the input was $x_1 x_2 \cdots x_n x_n x_{n-1} \cdots x_1$, then the tape inscription reduces to $x_2 x_3 \cdots x_n x_n x_{n-1} \cdots x_2$, still to be tested. Clearly, the input has to be accepted if and only if this latter tape inscription belongs to L_{mi}. To this end, from the state p_r, M jumps back to the left end and enters state the q_0 again:

$$\tau(p_r) = \Sigma, \quad \delta(p_r, \rhd) = q_0.$$

■

In [13], a variant of (one-way) finite automata with translucent letters has been introduced, implementing the so-called non-returning mode. According to this paradigm, after processing a visible letter, the head of the automaton does not return to the left or right end of the input but it continues from the position of the letter just processed. So, we are now going to focus on *deterministic two-way finite automata with translucent letters working in the non-returning mode* (abbreviated as nr2DFAwtl). Basically, definitions and notations for 2DFAwtl apply to nr2DFAwtl as well.

Let $M = \langle Q, \Sigma, q_0, \rhd, \lhd, \tau, \delta \rangle$ be an nr2DFAwtl. Now, a configuration of M is represented by $(\rhd uqv \lhd)$ or accept, where $q \in Q$ is the current state, $uv \in \Sigma^*$ is the remaining part of the input with u to the left and v to the right of the input head. The successor configuration is now specified as follows. As before, M halts and accepts whenever δ maps the current situation to accept. Moreover, for $p \in Q$, $q \in Q_r$, $s \in Q_l$, $a \in \Sigma$, $x, u, v, w \in \Sigma^*$, we have

1. $(\rhd uqxay \lhd) \vdash (\rhd uxpy \lhd)$, if $x \in \tau(q)^*$, $a \notin \tau(q)$, and $p = \delta(q, a)$,
2. $(\rhd uqv \lhd) \vdash (\rhd uvp \lhd)$, if $v \in \tau(q)^*$ and $p = \delta(q, \lhd)$,
3. $(\rhd xaysv \lhd) \vdash (\rhd xpyv \lhd)$, if $y \in \tau(s)^*$, $a \notin \tau(s)$, and $p = \delta(s, a)$,
4. $(\rhd usv \lhd) \vdash (\rhd puv \lhd)$, if $u \in \tau(s)^*$ and $p = \delta(s, \rhd)$.

As for the returning mode, we also consider non-returning sweeping finite automata. So, a *deterministic sweeping finite automaton with translucent letters working in the non-returning mode* (abbreviated as nrSDFAwtl) is an nr2DFAwtl with transition function enjoying the same restrictions as for SDFAwtl.

Throughout the rest of the paper, we will be denoting by $\mathscr{L}(\mathsf{X})$ the family of all languages accepted by some device X.

2.1 Basic Observations and Known Results

The computational capabilities of one-way deterministic and nondeterministic finite automata with translucent input letters working in the returning and non-returning mode (abbreviated, respectively, as DFAwtl, NFAwtl, nrDFAwtl, nrNFAwtl) are deeply investigated in [13]. For instance, all the families of languages accepted by these devices are shown to properly include the family of regular languages. Moreover, the proper inclusions $\mathscr{L}(\mathsf{nrDFAwtl}) \subset \mathscr{L}(\mathsf{nrNFAwtl})$, $\mathscr{L}(\mathsf{NFAwtl}) \subset \mathscr{L}(\mathsf{nrNFAwtl})$, $\mathscr{L}(\mathsf{DFAwtl}) \subset \mathscr{L}(\mathsf{NFAwtl})$, and $\mathscr{L}(\mathsf{DFAwtl}) \subset \mathscr{L}(\mathsf{nrDFAwtl})$ are also pointed out. So, these results witness that the resources *nondeterminism* and *non-returning mode* impact the recognition power.

The computational power of deterministic pushdown automata with translucent input letters (abbreviated as DPDAwtl and nrDPDAwtl) is studied in [9]. In particular, the following proper hierarchy is shown, where DCFL (resp., DCSL) is the family of deterministic context-free (resp., context-sensitive) languages:

$$\mathsf{DCFL} = \mathscr{L}(\mathsf{DPDA}) \subset \mathscr{L}(\mathsf{DPDAwtl}) \subset \mathscr{L}(\mathsf{nrDPDAwtl}) \subset \mathsf{DCSL}.$$

Further comparisons among acceptance capabilities can be derived almost immediately by structural reasons and known results. For example, the deterministic context-free language $\{ w\varphi(w^R) \mid w \in \{a,b\}^*, \varphi(a) = c, \varphi(b) = d \}$ is not accepted by any nrNFAwtl [13]. Due to the above-recalled inclusions, the proper inclusions $\mathscr{L}(\mathsf{DFAwtl}) \subset \mathscr{L}(\mathsf{DPDAwtl})$ and $\mathscr{L}(\mathsf{nrDFAwtl}) \subset \mathscr{L}(\mathsf{nrDPDAwtl})$ easily follow. Moreover, we recall from [10], that the families $\mathscr{L}(\mathsf{DPDAwtl})$ and $\mathscr{L}(\mathsf{nrDFAwtl})$ are incomparable

Example 2 shows that the mirror language $\{ ww^R \mid w \in \{a,b\}^* \}$ is accepted by some SDFAwtl. A straightforward modification of the construction yields an SDFAwtl for the language $\{ w\varphi(w^R) \mid w \in \{a,b\}^*, \varphi(a) = c, \varphi(b) = d \}$. Since this latter language is not accepted by any nrNFAwtl [13], we obtain the proper inclusions $\mathscr{L}(\mathsf{DFAwtl}) \subset \mathscr{L}(\mathsf{SDFAwtl})$ and $\mathscr{L}(\mathsf{nrDFAwtl}) \subset \mathscr{L}(\mathsf{nrSDFAwtl})$.

The next proposition deals with the language $L_{aba} = \{ a^n b^n a^n \mid n \geq 0 \}$, whose membership in $\mathscr{L}(\mathsf{nrDFAwtl})$ is shown in [13]. On the contrary, we get

Proposition 3. $L_{aba} \notin \mathscr{L}(\mathit{SDFAwtl})$.

Proposition 3, the mentioned membership $L_{aba} \in \mathscr{L}(\mathsf{nrDFAwtl})$, and the fact $\{ w\varphi(w^R) \mid w \in \{a,b\}^*, \varphi(a) = c, \varphi(b) = d \} \in \mathscr{L}(\mathsf{SDFAwtl}) \backslash \mathscr{L}(\mathsf{nrDFAwtl})$, give

Corollary 4. *The families* $\mathscr{L}(\mathit{SDFAwtl})$ *and* $\mathscr{L}(\mathit{nrDFAwtl})$ *are incomparable.*

By the witness language L_{aba}, we are also able to obtain

Proposition 5. $\mathscr{L}(\mathit{SDFAwtl}) \subset \mathscr{L}(\mathit{nrSDFAwtl})$.

Proof. The inclusion follows by structural arguments. Moreover, since $L_{aba} \in \mathscr{L}(\mathsf{nrDFAwtl})$, we have $L_{aba} \in \mathscr{L}(\mathsf{nrSDFAwtl})$ as well. Finally, Proposition 3 proves $L_{aba} \notin \mathscr{L}(\mathsf{SDFAwtl})$, whence the result follows. □

These preliminary relationships between language families raise the natural question of how the resources *two-way head movement* and *sweeping* compare to each other and to the resource *pushdown store*. In what follows, we are going to explore these relationships, which are finally summarized in Fig. 1, Sect. 5.

3 Sweeping vs. Two-Way Head Movement

We have introduced two-way and sweeping finite automata with translucent letters. Model definition directly implies the inclusions $\mathscr{L}(\mathsf{SDFAwtl}) \subseteq \mathscr{L}(\mathsf{2DFAwtl})$ and $\mathscr{L}(\mathsf{nrSDFAwtl}) \subseteq \mathscr{L}(\mathsf{nr2DFAwtl})$. A natural question arises of whether two-way strictly outperforms sweeping, i.e., whether these inclusions are proper. Here, we are going to show that the answer depends on whether the returning or non-returning mode is assumed. Let us start with the returning mode.

Lemma 6. *For any given 2DFAwtl, an equivalent SDFAwtl can effectively be constructed.*

As a direct consequence of Lemma 6, we get

Theorem 7. $\mathscr{L}(\mathit{SDFAwtl}) = \mathscr{L}(\mathit{2DFAwtl})$.

The same comparison between non-returning devices leads to a completely different result. In order to separate non-returning devices, the following witness language $L_{ta} = \{ a^m \# a^{m+n} \# a^n \mid m, n \geq 0 \}$ will be considered. First, we show that L_{ta} does not belong to the sweeping family.

Theorem 8. $L_{ta} \notin \mathit{nrSDFAwtl}$.

Finally, we are left to prove that L_{ta} can be accepted by some nr2DFAwtl.

Lemma 9. $L_{ta} \in \mathscr{L}(\mathit{nr2DFAwtl})$.

Theorem 8 and Lemma 9 enable us to conclude with

Theorem 10. $\mathscr{L}(\mathit{nrSDFAwtl}) \subset \mathscr{L}(\mathit{nr2DFAwtl})$.

4 Two-Way Head Movement vs Pushdown Store

The translucency paradigm has been imposed in [9,14,17] to pushdown devices, leading to the definition of DPDAwtl and nrDPDAwtl. Here, we are going to compare the recognition power of these two latter devices with that of two-way and sweeping translucent finite automata. In other words, we investigate the impact of adding a pushdown store to translucent deterministic finite automata vs. adding two-way or sweeping input head movement.

To this end, we consider the language $L = \{ w \in \{a,b\}^+ \mid |w|_a = |w|_b \}$, which is accepted by DFAwtl [17]. Then, we intersect L with the regular language $R = \{aa, bb\}^*$, to obtain the language $L_{dab} = L \cap R$. For L_{dab}, we can prove

Theorem 11. $L_{dab} \notin$ *nr2DFAwtl.*

We are now ready to account for incomparability results:

Theorem 12. *Each of the families $\mathscr{L}$(nrDPDAwtl) and $\mathscr{L}$(DPDAwtl) is incomparable with each of the families $\mathscr{L}$(SDFAwtl), $\mathscr{L}$(nrSDFAwtl), $\mathscr{L}$(nr2DFAwtl).*

Proof. Being a deterministic context-free language, L_{dab} is accepted by some DPDAwtl and, thus, by some nrDPDAwtl as well. On the other hand, by Theorem 11, we have that L_{dab} is not accepted by any nr2DFAwtl and, thus, not by any nrSDFAwtl and, thus, not by any SDFAwtl.

In addition, the mirror language $\{ ww^R \mid w \in \{a,b\}^* \}$ is not accepted by any DPDAwtl or nrDPDAwtl. However, by Example 2, we get that the mirror language it is accepted by some SDFAwtl and, thus, by some nrSDFAwtl and, thus, by some nr2DFAwtl. □

5 The Final Language Scenario

The hierarchy here sketches the relationships among the recognition power of our two-way translucent automata and that of other known translucent devices.

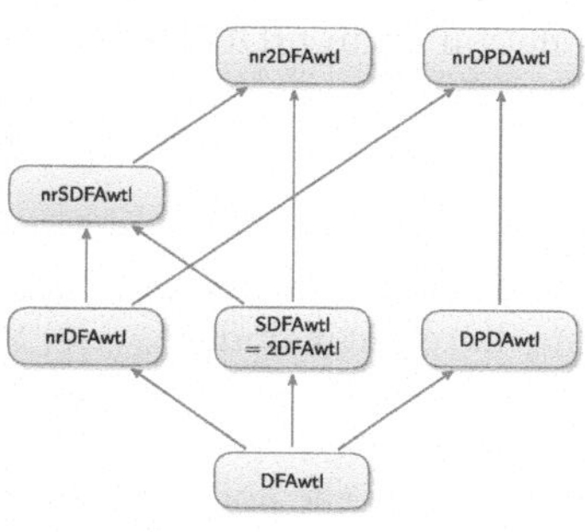

Fig. 1. Relationships between language families. An arrow between families indicates a strict inclusion. Families not connected by a path are incomparable.

6 Closure Properties

We investigate closure properties for the families $\mathscr{L}(\mathsf{SDFAwtl}) = \mathscr{L}(\mathsf{2DFAwtl})$, $\mathscr{L}(\mathsf{nrSDFAwtl})$, and $\mathscr{L}(\mathsf{nr2DFAwtl})$. Our results are collected at the end of this section in Table 1, page 13. While on this subject, we solve an open problem on nrDFAwtl and nrNFAwtl posed by Mráz and Otto in [13].

6.1 Boolean Operations

The following lemma proves that all families under consideration are closed under complementation:

Lemma 13. *From any given automaton of type $X \in \{\mathsf{SDFAwtl}, \mathsf{nrSDFAwtl}, \mathsf{nr2DFAwtl}\}$, an equivalent automaton of the same type can effectively be constructed, that halts on any input.*

The following proposition gives a complete account on closure under Boolean operations. We note that the results for the family $\mathscr{L}(\mathsf{SDFAwtl})$ have already been obtained in terms of linear automata with translucent letters [18,19].

Proposition 14. *The language families $\mathscr{L}(\mathsf{SDFAwtl})$, $\mathscr{L}(\mathsf{nrSDFAwtl})$, and $\mathscr{L}(\mathsf{nr2DFAwtl})$ are closed under complementation, but they are neither closed under union nor under intersection, even if the union or intersection are taken with a regular language.*

6.2 Solving an Open Problem

Before turning to further operations, we address an open problem posed by Mráz and Otto in [13]. The question is whether or not the language families nrDFAwtl and nrNFAwtl are closed under intersection with regular languages. We recall that an nrNFAwtl is a nondeterministic finite automaton with translucent input letters in the non-returning mode. As usual, nondeterminism is obtained by extending the transition function of an nrDFAwtl as

$$\delta\colon Q \times (\Sigma \cup \{\rhd, \lhd\}) \to 2^Q \cup \{\mathtt{accept}\}. \tag{1}$$

We answer the open question negatively. The witness language is again L_{dab}, used in Theorem 11 for deterministic devices, but here considered for nondeterminism. So, we cannot immediately conclude $L_{dab} \notin \mathscr{L}(\mathsf{nrNFAwtl})$ from known results, and a new proof is needed. In fact, we are going to show that $L_{dab} \notin \mathscr{L}(\mathsf{nrSNFAwtl})$, where an nrSNFAwtl is a nondeterministic sweeping finite automaton with translucent letters in the non-returning mode (roughly speaking, an nrSDFAwtl equipped with a nondeterministic dynamic as in (1)):

Theorem 15. *The language L_{dab} cannot be accepted by any nrSNFAwtl (and hence,* a fortiori*, by any nrNFAwtl as well).*

Proof. As in the proof of Theorem 11, we assume by contradiction an nrSNFAwtl $M = \langle Q, \Sigma, q_0, \rhd, \lhd, \tau, \delta \rangle$ for L_{dab}, and consider accepting computations on input words of the form $a^{x_1}bba^{x_2}b^y a^{x_3}bba^{x_4}$, where $y = x_1 + x_2 + x_3 + x_4 - 4$ and all x_i with $i \in \{1, 2, 3, 4\}$ are even and large enough. Let us focus on the computations on blocks. Even with M being an nrSNFAwtl, we get that more than $|Q|$ consecutive steps on a block without jumping would result in seeing the same input symbol in the same state twice. Thus, the input factor consumed in between could be deleted, still accepting, a contradiction. So, M must jump while processing a long block.

An accepting computation on some input $a^{x_1}bba^{x_2}b^y a^{x_3}bba^{x_4}$ begins in the configuration $(\rhd q_0 a^{x_1}bba^{x_2}b^y a^{x_3}bba^{x_4}\lhd)$, from which M starts processing the input prefix a^{x_1} and eventually jumps to the right, say, in the state q_1. For $\tau(q_1) = \{a, b\}$, the right end is reached with a jump. However, since the rightmost block of the input is also an a-block, in this case M continues to read a's. So, jumping from the left end to the right end and back can occur only finitely often, after which M has to jump to a b-block. Without loss of generality, we may assume that this jump shows up at the left end, say, in state q_2. So, we have $\tau(q_2) = \{a\}$, and obtain

$$\begin{aligned}(\rhd q_0 a^{x_1}bba^{x_2}b^y a^{x_3}bba^{x_4}\lhd) &\vdash^* (\rhd q_2 a^{x_1'}bba^{x_2}b^y a^{x_3}bba^{x_4'}\lhd)\\ &\vdash (\rhd a^{x_1'} q_3 ba^{x_2}b^y a^{x_3}bba^{x_4'}\lhd),\end{aligned}$$

where $x_1 \geq x_1'$ and $x_4 \geq x_4'$. From now on, we distinguish between two cases:

CASE 1: M continues the computation by reading the next input symbol b, and possibly some of the following input symbols a before jumping on the a-block to the right, say, in the state q_4. So, we have $a \in \tau(q_4)$. If $\tau(q_4) = \{a\}$, we get

$$\begin{aligned}(\rhd a^{x_1'} q_3 ba^{x_2}b^y a^{x_3}bba^{x_4'}\lhd) &\vdash^* (\rhd a^{x_1'} q_4 a^{x_2'}b^y a^{x_3}bba^{x_4'}\lhd)\\ &\vdash (\rhd a^{x_1'+x_2'} q_5 b^{y-1} a^{x_3}bba^{x_4'}\lhd),\end{aligned}$$

where $x_2 \geq x_2'$. If $\tau(q_4) = \{a, b\}$, we get

$$\begin{aligned}(\rhd a^{x_1'} q_3 ba^{x_2}b^y a^{x_3}bba^{x_4'}\lhd) &\vdash^* (\rhd a^{x_1'} q_4 a^{x_2'}b^y a^{x_3}bba^{x_4'}\lhd)\\ &\vdash (\rhd a^{x_1'+x_2'} b^y a^{x_3}bba^{x_4'} q_5\lhd).\end{aligned}$$

Therefore, also the computation

$$\begin{aligned}(\rhd q_0 a^{x_1+1}bba^{x_2-1}b^y a^{x_3}bba^{x_4}\lhd) &\vdash^* (\rhd a^{x_1'+1} q_3 ba^{x_2-1}b^y a^{x_3}bba^{x_4'}\lhd)\\ &\vdash^* (\rhd a^{x_1'+1} q_4 a^{x_2'-1}b^y a^{x_3}bba^{x_4'}\lhd)\\ &\vdash (\rhd a^{x_1'+x_2'} q_5 b^{y-1} a^{x_3}bba^{x_4'}\lhd)\end{aligned}$$

ends accepting. If $\tau(q_4) = \{a, b\}$, then the last configuration in the sub-computation is $(\rhd a^{x_1'+x_2'} b^y a^{x_3}bba^{x_4'} q_5\lhd)$. In both cases for $\tau(q_4)$, we have that the input $a^{x_1+1}bba^{x_2-1}b^y a^{x_3}bba^{x_4}$ is accepted. However, since x_1 and x_2 are even, $x_1 + 1$ and $x_2 - 1$ are odd, and the input cannot belong to L_{dab}, a contradiction.

CASE 2: M continues by jumping over the next input symbol b in the state q_3. If $\tau(q_3) = \{a, b\}$, then M will jump to the right end, and this case is treated below. So, we now assume $\tau(q_3) = \{b\}$, and obtain

$$(\rhd a^{x'_1} q_3 b a^{x_2} b^y a^{x_3} bba^{x'_4} \lhd) \vdash (\rhd a^{x'_1} b q_4 a^{x_2-1} b^y a^{x_3} bba^{x'_4} \lhd).$$

Next, M may read some a's from the factor a^{x_2}, then jump to the right end or to the factor b^y from which it may read some symbols, then jump to the right end or to the factor a^{x_3} from which it may read some symbols, then jump to the right end or to the factor bb. Assume that M jumps on the factor bb in the state p_6. Then, we have $\tau(p_6) = \{a\}$ and

$$(\rhd a^{x'_1} ba^{x'_2} b^{y'} p_6 a^{x'_3} bba^{x'_4} \lhd) \vdash (\rhd a^{x'_1} ba^{x'_2} b^{y'} a^{x'_3} p_7 ba^{x'_4} \lhd),$$

where $y \geq y'$ and $x_3 \geq x'_3$. Now, assume $b \notin \tau(p_7)$. Then, M reads the second b, some a's from the factor $a^{x'_4}$, and then jumps to the right end. This leads to a configuration $(\rhd a^{x'_1} ba^{x'_2} b^{y'} a^{x'_3+x''_4} p_8 \lhd)$. But then, also the computation

$$\begin{aligned}(\rhd q_0 a^{x_1} bba^{x_2} b^y a^{x_3+1} bba^{x_4-1} \lhd) &\vdash^* (\rhd a^{x'_1} ba^{x'_2} b^{y'} a^{x'_3+1} p_7 ba^{x'_4-1} \lhd)\\ &\vdash^* (\rhd a^{x'_1} ba^{x'_2} b^{y'} a^{x'_3+x''_4} p_8 \lhd)\end{aligned}$$

ends accepting, which is a contradiction since $x_3 + 1$ is odd. This contradiction implies that M cannot read the next b in state p_7. So, it directly jumps either to the right end by $\tau(p_7) = \{a, b\}$ or to the rightmost a-block by $\tau(p_7) = \{b\}$, and then to the right end.

Finally, the situation where M has reached the right end remains to be considered. Basically, we now have to distinguish between two types of configurations. The first type has the form $(\rhd a^\alpha ba^\beta b^\gamma a^\kappa bba^\sigma r_1 \lhd)$, while the second has the form $(\rhd a^\alpha ba^\beta b^\gamma a^\kappa ba^\sigma r_1 \lhd)$, with α, β, γ, κ, σ still being large enough. As observed, jumping from one end to the opposite end and back may occur only finitely often. So, M has to jump over the a-block to the adjacent b either from right or from left. This means, that either one b from the factor bb is read, or a single b. In the former case, we apply the same argument once more, obtaining that either the entire factor bb or the sole b is processed. Thus, we obtain the same contradiction as before, since either input $a^{x_1+1}bba^{x_2-1}b^y a^{x_3} bba^{x_4}$ or input $a^{x_1}bba^{x_2}b^y a^{x_3+1} bba^{x_4-1}$ is accepted, but none of them belongs to L_{dab}. □

A direct consequence of Theorem 15 is contained in the following corollary, which negatively answers the open problem in [13]:

Corollary 16. *None of the families $\mathscr{L}$(nrDFAwtl) and $\mathscr{L}$(nrNFAwtl) are not closed under intersection with regular languages.*

6.3 Concatenations and Homomorphisms

To assess closure under concatenation, iteration, and length-preserving homomorphisms, we already have all the ingredients.

Proposition 17. *The language families $\mathscr{L}$(SDFAwtl), $\mathscr{L}$(nrSDFAwtl), and $\mathscr{L}$(nr2DFAwtl) are neither closed under concatenation nor under iteration nor under length-preserving homomorphisms.*

To show non-closure under inverse homomorphism, we consider the language $L_{tb} = \{ b^n\#b^n\#b^n \mid n \geq 1 \}$.

Theorem 18. $L_{tb} \notin$ *nr2DFAwtl.*

This impossibility result qualifies L_{tb} as witnessing non-closure under inverse homomorphism. However, to this end, we need the following positive result on the language $L_{td} = \{ x\#y\#z \mid x, y, z \in \{a, b\}^+, |x|_a = |z|_a, |y|_b = |z|_b \}$.

Lemma 19. $L_{td} \in \mathscr{L}$*(SDFAwtl).*

In conclusion, we can state:

Proposition 20. *The language families $\mathscr{L}$(SDFAwtl), $\mathscr{L}$(nrSDFAwtl), and $\mathscr{L}$(nr2DFAwtl) are not closed under non-erasing inverse homomorphisms.*

As a final remark, we feel it worth noticing that, for the family $\mathscr{L}$(SDFAwtl), the non-closure under concatenation and length-preserving homomorphism is shown in [18,19] in terms of linear automata with translucent letters. However, the non-closure under iteration and inverse homomorphism is there stated as an open problem. The results in the present contribution clearly enable us to close such a problem.

The following table allows to grasp at a glance closure properties for several translucent devices.

Table 1. A summary of closure properties for the language families $\mathscr{L}$(DPDAwtl) and $\mathscr{L}$(nrDPDAwtl), as well as for $\mathscr{L}$(SDFAwtl) = $\mathscr{L}$(2DFAwtl), $\mathscr{L}$(nrSDFAwtl) and $\mathscr{L}$(nr2DFAwtl). The closure of the last three families under reversal (R) follows trivially. Non-closure properties marked '✖' solve some open questions raised in [18,19].

Language Family	—	$\cup$	$\cap$	$\cap_{\text{reg}}$	$\cdot$	$*$	$h_{\text{len.pres.}}$	h^{-1}	R
$\mathscr{L}$(DPDAwtl)	✓	✗	✗	✗	✗	✗	✗	✗	✗
$\mathscr{L}$(nrDPDAwtl)	✓	✗	✗	✗	✗	✗	✗	✗	✗
$\mathscr{L}$(SDFAwtl)	✓	✗	✗	✗	✗	✖	✗	✖	✓
$\mathscr{L}$(nrSDFAwtl)	✓	✗	✗	✗	✗	✗	✗	✗	✓
$\mathscr{L}$(nr2DFAwtl)	✓	✗	✗	✗	✗	✗	✗	✗	✓

Acknowledgements. The authors wish to thank the anonymous referees for their valuable and helpful comments.

References

1. Bednárová, Z., Geffert, V., Mereghetti, C., Palano, B.: Removing nondeterminism in constant height pushdown automata. Inform. Comput. **237**, 257–267 (2014). https://doi.org/10.1016/j.ic.2014.03.002
2. Bensch, S., Bordihn, H., Holzer, M., Kutrib, M.: On input-revolving deterministic and nondeterministic finite automata. Inform. Comput. **207**, 1140–1155 (2009). https://doi.org/10.1016/j.ic.2009.03.002
3. Berman, P., Lingas, A.: On the complexity of regular languages in terms of finite automata. Technical report 304, Polish Academy of Sciences (1977)
4. Geffert, V., Bednárová, Z., Mereghetti, C., Palano, B.: Boolean language operations on nondeterministic automata with a pushdown of constant height. In: Bulatov, A.A., Shur, A.M. (eds.) CSR 2013. LNCS, vol. 7913, pp. 100–111. Springer, Heidelberg (2013). https://doi.org/10.1007/978-3-642-38536-0_9
5. Hopcroft, J.E., Ullman, J.D.: Introduction to Automata Theory, Languages, and Computation. Addison-Wesley, Reading (1979)
6. Jakobi, S., Meckel, K., Mereghetti, C., Palano, B.: Queue automata of constant length. In: Jurgensen, H., Reis, R. (eds.) DCFS 2013. LNCS, vol. 8031, pp. 124–135. Springer, Heidelberg (2013). https://doi.org/10.1007/978-3-642-39310-5_13
7. Jančar, P., Mráz, F., Plátek, M., Vogel, J.: Restarting automata. In: Reichel, H. (ed.) FCT 1995. LNCS, vol. 965, pp. 283–292. Springer, Heidelberg (1995). https://doi.org/10.1007/3-540-60249-6_60
8. Kutrib, M., Malcher, A., Mereghetti, C., Palano, B.: Iterated uniform finite-state transducers on unary languages. Theoret. Comput. Sci. **969**, 114049 (2023). https://doi.org/10.1016/j.tcs.2023.114049
9. Kutrib, M., Malcher, A., Mereghetti, C., Palano, B., Raucci, P., Wendlandt, M.: Deterministic pushdown automata with translucent input letters. In: Day, J.D., Manea, F. (eds.) Developments in Language Theory (DLT 2024). LNCS, vol. 14791, pp. 203–217. Springer (2024). https://doi.org/10.1007/978-3-031-66159-4_15
10. Kutrib, M., Malcher, A., Mereghetti, C., Palano, B., Raucci, P., Wendlandt, M.: On properties of languages accepted by deterministic pushdown automata with translucent input letters. In: Fazekas, S.Z. (ed.) Implementation and Application of Automata (CIAA 2024). LNCS, vol. 15015, pp. 208–220. Springer (2024). https://doi.org/10.1007/978-3-031-71112-1_15
11. Malcher, A., Mereghetti, C., Palano, B.: Descriptional complexity of two-way pushdown automata with restricted head reversals. Theoret. Comput. Sci. **449**, 119–133 (2012). https://doi.org/10.1016/j.tcs.2012.04.007
12. Mereghetti, C., Palano, B.: Quantum automata for some multiperiodic languages. Theoret. Comput. Sci. **387**, 177–186 (2007)
13. Mráz, F., Otto, F.: Non-returning deterministic and nondeterministic finite automata with translucent letters. RAIRO Theor. Inform. Appl. **57**, 8 (2023). https://doi.org/10.1051/ita/2023009
14. Nagy, B., Otto, F.: CD-systems of stateless deterministic R(1)-automata governed by an external pushdown store. RAIRO Theor. Inform. Appl. **45**, 413–448 (2011). https://doi.org/10.1051/ITA/2011123
15. Nagy, B., Otto, F.: Finite-state acceptors with translucent letters. In: Bel-Enguix, G., Dahl, V., De La Puente, A. (eds.) International Workshop on AI Methods for Interdisciplinary Research in Language and Biology (BILC 2011), pp. 3–13. SciTePress (2011). https://doi.org/10.5220/0003272500030013

16. Nagy, B., Otto, F.: On CD-systems of stateless deterministic R-automata with window size one. J. Comput. Syst. Sci. **78**, 780–806 (2012). https://doi.org/10.1016/J.JCSS.2011.12.009
17. Nagy, B., Otto, F.: Deterministic pushdown-CD-systems of stateless deterministic R(1)-automata. Acta Inform. **50**, 229–255 (2013). https://doi.org/10.1007/S00236-012-0175-X
18. Nagy, B., Otto, F.: Two-head finite-state acceptors with translucent letters. In: Catania, B., Královič, R., Nawrocki, J., Pighizzini, G. (eds.) SOFSEM 2019. LNCS, vol. 11376, pp. 406–418. Springer, Cham (2019). https://doi.org/10.1007/978-3-030-10801-4_32
19. Nagy, B., Otto, F.: Linear automata with translucent letters and linear context-free trace languages. RAIRO Theor. Inform. Appl. **54**, 3 (2020). https://doi.org/10.1051/ita/2020002
20. Nagy, B., Otto, F.: Finite automata with sets of translucent words. In: Day, J.D., Manea, F. (eds.) Developments in Language Theory (DLT 2024). LNCS, vol. 14791, pp. 236–251. Springer (2024). https://doi.org/10.1007/978-3-031-66159-4_17
21. Otto, F.: Restarting automata and their relations to the Chomsky hierarchy. In: Ésik, Z., Fülöp, Z. (eds.) DLT 2003. LNCS, vol. 2710, pp. 55–74. Springer, Heidelberg (2003). https://doi.org/10.1007/3-540-45007-6_5
22. Otto, F.: A survey on automata with translucent letters. In: Nagy, B. (ed.) Implementation and Application of Automata (CIAA 2023). LNCS, vol. 14151, pp. 21–50. Springer (2023). https://doi.org/10.1007/978-3-031-40247-0_2
23. Otto, F.: Restarting Automata. Springer, Cham (2025). https://doi.org/10.1007/978-3-031-70094-1
24. Sakoda, W.J., Sipser, M.: Nondeterminism and the size of two way finite automata. In: ACM Symposium on Theory of Computing (STOC 1978), pp. 275–286. Association for Computing Machinery (1978). https://doi.org/10.1145/800133.804357
25. Sipser, M.: Lower bounds on the size of sweeping automata. J. Comput. Syst. Sci. **21**, 195–202 (1980). https://doi.org/10.1016/0022-0000(80)90034-3

Relative Densities of Formal Languages

J. Andres Montoya(✉)

Universidad Nacional de Colombia, Bogota, Colombia
jamontoyaa@unal.edu.co

Abstract. We study asymptotic densities and relative densities of formal languages. We show that the class of regular languages is, to some extent, the only class of formal languages for which those limit probabilities can be effectively computed.

1 Introduction

The study of asymptotic densities of regular and context-free languages has a long history that goes back to Chomsky and Miller; see [4]. There are many published works on this topic as there are many potential applications of those limit probabilities, including but not limited to: temporal planning, approximation of nonregular languages, and analytic proofs of inherent ambiguity; see [8] and the references therein. Let us introduce the asymptotic densities that we study in this work:

Definition 1. *Let $L, T \subset \Sigma^*$ be two languages.*

1. *Set* $\Pr_n(L) = \frac{|\Sigma^n \cap L|}{|\Sigma|^n}$. *Suppose that* $\lim_{n\to\infty} \Pr_n(L)$ *exists. We use* $\Pr(L)$ *to denote this limit. We say that* $\Pr(L)$ *is the asymptotic density of* L.
2. *Let* $\Pr_n(L \mid T)$ *be equal to* $\frac{|\Sigma^n \cap L \cap T|}{|\Sigma^n \cap T|}$. *Suppose that* $\lim_{n\to\infty} \Pr_n(L \mid T)$ *exists. We use* $\Pr(L \mid T)$ *to denote this limit. We say that* $\Pr(L \mid T)$ *is the conditional probability of* L *given* T *(also the relative density of* L *in* T*).*

Remark 1. Notice that $\Pr(L) = \Pr(L \mid \Sigma^*)$.

Relative densities of formal languages were first studied by Berstel; see [2]. It should be said that there are few works devoted to the study of those asymptotic densities (conditional probabilities); see [12,13] and the references therein. A reason for this could be that relative densities are uncomputable for most relevant classes of formal languages, see below. We study the problem of computing relative densities of formal languages. We show that this problem cannot be solved for most classes of languages; including the classes of linear deterministic context-free languages, one-counter languages, and the class of languages accepted by deterministic two-way reversal-bounded two-counter automata. On the other hand, we show that asymptotic densities and relative densities of regular languages can be effectively approximated. The complexity of approximating those limit probabilities depends on the way the input languages are represented.

Published by Springer Nature Switzerland AG 2025
A. Malcher and L. Prigioniero (Eds.): DCFS 2025, LNCS 15759, pp. 166–179, 2025.
https://doi.org/10.1007/978-3-031-97100-6_12

We prove that the problem is PSPACE-hard for most presentations of regular languages. And we prove that the problem can be solved in polynomial time for DFA's and unambiguous automata. We have to observe that the numerical calculations involved in these latter computations remain a grand challenge, and could be considered unfeasible. We explore some potential applications of asymptotic densities that involve nonregular languages.

Organization of the Work and Contributions. This work is organized into four section besides this introduction. In Sect. 2, we introduce the algorithmic problems that we study in this paper, and we show that those problems are undecidable for the classes of deterministic linear context-free languages, deterministic one-counter languages, and deterministic reversal-bounded two-counter automata. This leaves essentially one choice, namely: the class of deterministic one-way reversal-bounded counter automata. In Sect. 3, we focus on regular languages. We prove that for all L and T the limit probability $\Pr(L \mid T)$ can be effectively approximated. In Sect. 4, we study the complexity of approximating the relative densities of regular languages. We prove that the problem is PSPACE-hard for most presentations of regular languages. On the other hand, we prove that the problem can be solved in polynomial time when the input languages are represented by DFA's or by unambiguous NFA's. In Sect. 5.2, we study two classes of nonregular languages, namely: geodesic languages and hairpin languages. We prove a few results concerning those two classes of languages.

2 Relative Densities of Formal Languages

Let us introduce some of the algorithmic problems that we study in this paper:

Definition 2. *Let $\mathcal{C}$ be a class of languages.*

1. *We define $CLP(\mathcal{C})$ as the problem of deciding, given $L \in \mathcal{C}$, whether the limit probability* $\Pr(L)$ *exists and is different from zero.*
2. *We define $CCP(\mathcal{C})$ as the problem of deciding, given L and T in $\mathcal{C}$, whether the limit probability* $\Pr(L \mid T)$ *exists and is different from zero.*
3. *We define $CLP^1(\mathcal{C})$ as the problem of deciding, given $L \in \mathcal{C}$, whether the limit probability* $\Pr(L)$ *exists and equals* 1. *We define $CCP^1(\mathcal{C})$ accordingly.*

Asymptotic densities of context-free and multicounter languages have been previously studied; see [2,10], and the references therein. There are many deep results concerning the analytic behavior of those limit probabilities.

Definition 3. *Let $\mathcal{C}$ be a class of languages. Let $L \subseteq \Sigma^*$ be a language in $\mathcal{C}$, and let c be a fresh character not in Σ. We use the symbol L_c to denote the language $Lc(\Sigma \cup \{c\})^*$.*

Example 1. Let $L \subset \{0,1\}^*$ be equal to 1^*. The language L_c equals the language $\{1^k cw : k \geq 0 \text{ and } w \in \{0,1,c\}^*\}$. Notice that $\Pr(L_c)$ exists and is nonzero.

Suppose $L = \emptyset$. We get $Lc(\Sigma \cup \{c\})^* = \emptyset$. Now suppose $L \neq \emptyset$. The sequence $\frac{|(\Sigma \cup \{c\})^n \cap L|}{|\Sigma \cup \{c\}|^n}$ is bounded and monotone. Then, the limit $\Pr(L_c)$ exists. Let $w \in T \cap \Sigma^n$. The language $wc(\Sigma \cup \{c\})^*$ is included in L_c. We obtain that $\Pr(L_c)$ exists and is greater than $\frac{1}{(|\Sigma|+1)^{n+1}}$.

Definition 4. *Let $\mathcal{C}$ be a class of languages. We say that $\mathcal{C}$ is closed if and only if for all $L \in \mathcal{C}$ the language L_c also belongs to $\mathcal{C}$.*

Example 2. The following classes are closed: the class of regular languages, the class of context-free languages, the class of deterministic context-free languages, the class of unambiguous context-free languages, and the class of linear deterministic context-free languages.

Example 3. Let DCM(k, r) be the class of languages accepted by deterministic one-way k-counter automata such that each counter can make at most r reversals (turns); see [10]. The class DCM(k, r) is closed.

Remark 2. Let $\mathcal{REG}$ be the class of regular languages. Notice that for all $k \geq 0$ the class $\mathcal{REG}$ equals the classes DCM$(k, 0)$ and DCM$(0, k)$.

Theorem 1. *Suppose that $\mathcal{C}$ is closed. The following assertions hold.*

1. *The emptiness problem is reducible to the problem $CLP(\mathcal{C})$.*
2. *The universe problem is reducible to the problem $CLP^1(\mathcal{C})$.*
3. *The disjointedness problem is reducible to the problem $CCP(\mathcal{C})$.*
4. *The equivalence and the inclusion problems are reducible to $CCP^1(\mathcal{C})$.*

Proof. Let us proceed.

1. Notice that L is nonempty if and only if $\Pr(L_c) > 0$. This shows that the emptiness problem is reducible to $CLP(\mathcal{C})$.
2. Notice that L equals Σ^* if and only if $\Pr(L_c) = 1$. This shows that the universe problem is reducible to $CLP^1(\mathcal{C})$.
3. Let L and T be two languages. Notice that L intersects T if and only if the inequality
$$\Pr(L_c \mid T_c) > 0$$
holds. This shows that the disjointedness problem is reducible to the problem $CCP(\mathcal{C})$.
4. Let $L, T \subseteq \Sigma^*$ be two languages in $\mathcal{C}$. Notice that L is included in T if and only if the equality
$$\Pr(L_c \mid T_c) = 1$$
holds. We get that inclusion and the equivalence problems are reducible to $CCP^1(\mathcal{C})$.

Let $\mathcal{C}$ be a class of languages. The above theorem shows that the problem of computing asymptotic densities of languages in $\mathcal{C}$ is a very robust problem that subsumes most decision problems about this class, (all the F-problems). We use this to prove that $CCP(\mathcal{C})$ or $CCP^1(\mathcal{C})$ are undecidable for most $\mathcal{C}$'s.

Theorem 2. *The following assertions hold:*

1. *Let $\mathcal{LDCFL}$ be the class of linear deterministic context-free languages. The problem $CCP(\mathcal{LDCFL})$ is undecidable.*
2. *Let $\mathcal{OC}$ be the class of languages accepted by deterministic one-way one-counter automata. The problem $CCP^1(\mathcal{OC})$ is undecidable.*
3. *Let $2DCM(2,-)$ be the class of languages accepted by deterministic two-way reversal-bounded two-counter automata. The problem $CCP(2DCM(2,-))$ is undecidable.*
4. *Let $NCM(1,1)$ be the class of languages accepted by one-way nondeterministic one-counter one-reversal automata. The problem $CCP^1(NCM(1,1))$ is undecidable.*

Proof. Let us proceed:

1. The disjointedness problem for $\mathcal{LDCFL}$'s is undecidable. This is a folklore result. Let us sketch the proof of this result. Let $L \subset \{a\}^*$ be a language that is recursively enumerable but undecidable. Let $\mathcal{M}$ be a deterministic Turing machine that halts and accepts the strings in L, and which does not halt on the inputs that do not belong to L. Let Q be the set of states of $\mathcal{M}$, and let Γ be its work alphabet. We assume $a \in \Gamma$. Let $\#$ be a fresh character not in Γ. Let $L_{\mathcal{M},q} \subset (\Gamma \cup Q)^*$ be the regular language constituted by the set of instantaneous configurations of $\mathcal{M}$; see [11]. Let $ID_{0,q}$ be the string in $L_{\mathcal{M},q}$ that encodes the initial configuration with input a^q. Let us suppose that all the halting computations of $\mathcal{M}$ have even length, and that all those computations halt in the same final configuration c_∞. Let ID_F be the string in $L_{\mathcal{M},q}$ that encodes this final configuration. Let L_q be equal to the set of strings of the form
$$ID_{0,q}\#ID_2\#\cdots\#ID_{2n-2}\#ID_F\#\left(ID_{2n-1}\right)^R\#\cdots\#\left(ID_1\right)^R$$
and such that for all $1 \le i \le n$ the instantaneous configuration encoded by ID_{2i} is a legitimate successor of ID_{2i-1}. Let T_q be equal to the set of strings such that for all $0 \le i \le n-1$ the instantaneous configuration encoded by ID_{2i+1} is a legitimate successor of ID_{2i}. The languages L_q and T_q are LDCFL's. Moreover, we have that $\mathcal{M}$ accepts a^q if and only if $L_q \cap T_q$ is nonempty. We get that the disjointedness problem for LDCFL's is undecidable, and we also get that $CCP(\mathcal{LDCFL})$ is undecidable.
2. The inclusion problem for one-counter languages is undecidable; see [19].
3. The emptiness problem for the languages in the class 2DCM$(2,-)$ is undecidable; see [10].
4. The universe problem for the languages in the class NCM$(1,1)$ is undecidable; see [11].

It could be argued that the above theorem leaves open only one choice, namely: deterministic one-way reversal-bounded multicounter languages; see [10]. We focus on the class $\mathcal{REG}$.

Remark 3. Let $\mathcal{M}$ be a DFA of size n. Let $suf(\mathcal{M})$ be the language

$$\{u : \text{there exists } v \text{ such that } \mathcal{M} \text{ accepts } vu\}$$

This language is regular and can be easily accepted using a NFA of size n. Then, the asymptotic density of $suf(\mathcal{M})$ can be computed in time $2^{O(n)}$; see [3]. Now suppose that $\mathcal{M}$ is a deterministic one-way three-reversal one-counter automaton. Suppose we are asked to compute the asymptotic density of the language $suf(\mathcal{M})\, c\, (\Sigma \cup \{c\})^*$. This problem is uncomputable. This suggests that relative densities of languages in DCM(1, 3) are uncomputable. This also suggests that asymptotic reasoning beyond the class $\mathcal{REG}$ is unfeasible.

Remark 4. A reviewer pointed out that the first two facts in the statement of Theorem 1 were already known; see [15].

Kozik proved that the problem $CCP(\mathcal{REG})$ is decidable; see [12]. Bodirsky et al. proved that asymptotic densities of DFA's can be computed in cubic time; see [3]. We prove that there exist polynomial time approximation schemes for the relative densities of DFA's. This implies that $CCP^1(\mathcal{REG})$ and $CCP(\mathcal{REG})$ are both decidable.

3 Relative Densities of Regular Languages

There exist regular languages for which the limit probability $\Pr(L)$ does not exist. The language $(11)^*$ is an example of this. Observe that the sequence $\{\Pr_n((11)^*)\}$ oscillates between 0 and 1. Let us average. We get:

$$\lim_{n\to\infty}\left(\frac{1}{n}\sum_{i\leq n}\frac{|(11)^* \cap \{1\}^n|}{|\{1\}^n|}\right)=\frac{1}{2}$$

Definition 5. *Let L and T be two languages. We define the limit probabilities $\widetilde{\Pr}(L)$ and $\widetilde{\Pr}(L \mid T)$ as follows:*

$$\widetilde{\Pr}(L)=\lim_{n\to\infty}\left(\frac{1}{n}\sum_{i\leq n}\frac{|L\cap\Sigma^n|}{|\Sigma^n|}\right),$$

$$\widetilde{\Pr}(L \mid T)=\lim_{n\to\infty}\left(\frac{1}{n}\sum_{i\leq n}\frac{|L\cap T\cap\Sigma^n|}{|T\cap\Sigma^n|}\right)$$

We say that $\widetilde{\Pr}(L)$ is the Cesàro density of L, and we say that $\widetilde{\Pr}(L \mid T)$ is the Cesàro density of L in T.

We have:

Proposition 1. *If the limit probabilities* $\Pr(L)$ *and* $\Pr(L \mid T)$ *exist, the equalities*

$$\Pr(L) = \widetilde{\Pr}(L) \text{ and } \Pr(L \mid T) = \widetilde{\Pr}(L \mid T)$$

hold.

Moreover, we have:

Theorem 3. *Let L and T be two regular languages, the limit probabilities* $\widetilde{\Pr}(L)$ *and* $\widetilde{\Pr}(L \mid T)$ *exist.*

Proof. Lynch proved that for all regular language L the limit probability $\widetilde{\Pr}(L)$ exists; see [17]. We prove that for all L and T the limit probability $\widetilde{\Pr}(L \mid T)$ also exists. Let $\mathcal{M}$ and $\mathcal{N}$ be two minimal DFA's accepting the languages $L \cap T$ and T. Let $T(\mathcal{M})$ be the transition matrix of $\mathcal{M}$, and let $\lambda_1, ..., \lambda_m$ be the eigenvalues of this matrix. There exist polynomials

$$p_1(n), \ldots, p_m(n) \in \mathbb{Q}[n]$$

such that for all n, the equality

$$|L \cap T \cap \Sigma^n| = p_1(n)\lambda_1^n + \cdots + p_m(n)\lambda_m^n$$

holds; see [8]. Let $\xi_1, \ldots, \xi_r$ be the eigenvalues of $T(\mathcal{N})$, and let

$$q_1(n), \ldots, q_r(n) \in \mathbb{Q}[n]$$

be the corresponding polynomials. The Perron-Frobenius Theorem ensures the existence of a period M such that the powers $\lambda_1^M, ..., \lambda_1^M$ and $\xi_1^M, ..., \xi_r^M$ are non-negative real numbers; see [17]. We have:

$$\begin{aligned} \widetilde{\Pr}(L_{\mathcal{M}} \mid L_{\mathcal{N}}) &= \lim_{n\to\infty} \frac{\Sigma_{i\le n} \left|L \cap T \cap \Sigma^i\right|}{\Sigma_{i\le n} \left|T \cap \Sigma^i\right|} \\ &= \lim_{n\to\infty} \frac{p_1(nM)\lambda_1^{nM} + \cdots + p_m(nM)\lambda_m^{nM}}{q_1(nM)\xi_1^{nM} + \cdots + q_r(nM)\xi_r^{nM}} \end{aligned}$$

Let $\lambda_M = \max\left\{\lambda_i^M : i \le m\right\}$, and let $\xi_M = \max\left\{\lambda_i^M : i \le r\right\}$. We get

$$|L \cap T \cap \Sigma^{nM}| = p(nM)\lambda_M^{nM} + \sum_{\lambda \ne \lambda_M} \lambda^{nM} p_\lambda(nM),$$

and

$$|T \cap \Sigma^{nM}| = q(nM)\xi_M^{nM} + \sum_{\xi \ne \xi_M} \xi^{nM} q_\xi(nM)$$

The inequality $\lambda_M \le \xi_M$ holds since $L \cap T$ cannot grow faster than T. Moreover, if the equality $\lambda_M = \xi_M$ holds, the inequality $\deg(p(n)) \le \deg(q(n))$ has to hold. We have that $\lim_{n\to\infty} \frac{p(n)}{q(n)}$ exists. And we have that $\widetilde{\Pr}(L_{\mathcal{M}} \mid L_{\mathcal{N}})$ equals $\lim_{n\to\infty} \frac{p(n)}{q(n)}$. The theorem is proved.

The variety of aperiodic languages is the maximum variety of regular languages such that for all L in this variety the limit probability $\Pr(L)$ exists. The variety **UL** (star-free unambiguous languages [18]) is the maximum variety of regular languages such that for all L and T in this variety the limit probability $\Pr(L \mid T)$ exists. It could be conjectured that $\mathcal{REG}$ is the maximum *robust* class of formal languages such that for all L in this class the limit probability $\widetilde{\Pr}(L)$ exists. We have to observe that there exist large classes of languages for which those Cesàro densities always exist. The class of linear context-free languages is an example of this. It is important to observe that this latter class is not closed under intersection. Let L and T be linear context-free languages. Does the limit probability $\widetilde{\Pr}(L \mid T)$ exist?

4 Computing Relative Densities of Regular Languages

Let L and T be regular languages. How do we compute the limit probability $\widetilde{\Pr}(L \mid T)$? We use the symbol $\#CCP(\mathcal{REG})$ to denote the problem of computing the relative densities of regular languages.

Definition 6. *An approximation scheme for $\#CCP(\mathcal{REG})$ is an algorithm $\mathcal{M}$ that computes, on input (L, T, n), a rational number $q_{L,T} \in [0,1]$ such that the inequalities*

$$\left(1 - \frac{1}{2^n}\right) \widetilde{\Pr}(L \mid T) \leq q_{L,T} \leq \left(1 + \frac{1}{2^n}\right) \widetilde{\Pr}(L \mid T)$$

both hold.

We have:

Theorem 4. *There exist approximation schemes for the problem $\#CCP(\mathcal{REG})$.*

Proof. Let L and T be two regular languages. Let $\mathcal{M}$ and $\mathcal{N}$ be minimal DFA's accepting the languages $L \cap T$ and T. The equalities

$$|L \cap T \cap \Sigma^n| = p_1(n)\lambda_1^n + \cdots + p_m(n)\lambda_m^n$$
$$|T \cap \Sigma^n| = q_1(n)\xi_1^n + \cdots + q_r(n)\xi_r^n$$

hold. Let us assume that the inequalities

$$|\lambda_2|, \ldots, |\lambda_m| < \lambda_1 \text{ and } |\xi_2|, \ldots, |\xi_r| < \xi_1$$

all hold. The inequality $\lambda_1 \leq \xi_1$ must hold. Let

$$p_1(n) = a_k\lambda_1^k + \cdots + a_0 \text{ and } q_1(n) = b_t\xi_1^t + \cdots + b_0$$

Suppose $a_k, b_t \neq 0$. Observe that

$$\widetilde{\Pr}(L \mid T) = \begin{cases} 0, \text{ if } \lambda_1 < \xi_1 \\ 0, \text{ if } \lambda_1 = \xi_1 \text{ and } k < t \\ \frac{a_k}{b_k}, \text{ if } \lambda_1 = \xi_1 \text{ and } k = t \end{cases}$$

Then, the problem of computing $\widetilde{\Pr}(L \mid T)$ reduces to the problem of computing $\lambda_1, \xi_1, k, t, a_k$ and b_t. Those six real numbers can be easily approximated (computed) from the Jordan canonical forms of $T(\mathcal{M})$ and $T(\mathcal{N})$. Let us suppose that the spectra of $T(\mathcal{M})$ and $T(\mathcal{N})$ contain irrational eigenvalues. Notice that, in this case, we cannot exactly compute the aforementioned canonical forms. We observe that:

1. λ_1 and ξ_1 can be computed with arbitrary high precision, and it can be determined whether these eigenvalues are equal.
2. The positive integers k and t are completely determined by the combinatorial structure of the Jordan canonical forms of $T(\mathcal{M})$ and $T(\mathcal{N})$, and this combinatorial structure can be computed in polynomial time using symbolic computing; see [16].
3. The coefficients a_k and b_t can be suitably approximated using symbolic computing; see [9].

Let (L, T, n) be an instance of the problem $\#CCP(\mathcal{REG})$. We can compute a rational number $q_{L,T}$ that approximates $\widetilde{\Pr}(L \mid T)$ within the range $\frac{1}{2^n}$. The theorem is proved.

How hard is to approximate the conditional probabilities of regular languages? The complexity of this problem depends on the way the input languages are represented.

Definition 7. *Let $\mathcal{M}$ be a NFA, we say that $\mathcal{M}$ is an unambiguous automaton, (UFA, for short), if and only if for all w the number of accepting computations of $\mathcal{M}$, on w, cannot be greater than one.*

Let us remark that the notion of unambiguous computation has played a major role in automata theory; [5]. The class of unambiguous automata is a relevant class of NFA's that is almost as tractable as the class of DFA's: the universe, the equivalence, and the inclusion problems can be solved in polynomial for UFA's and DFA's. Moreover, the class of UFA's is exponentially more succinct than the class of DFA's.

Theorem 5. *Let L be a regular language, and suppose that L requires n states to be accepted by DFA's. Let L^R be the reverse of L. This language requires $2^{\Omega(n)}$ states to be accepted by DFA's, and it requires $O(n)$ states to be accepted by UFA's.*

Proof. We construct a sequence $\{L_n\}_{n\geq 1}$ such that L_n is accepted by a DFA of size $O(n)$, and such that L_n^R requires $2^{\Omega(n)}$ states to be accepted by DFA's. The sequence $\left\{\{0,1\}^n 1 \{0,1\}^*\right\}_{n\geq 1}$ works. The language $\{0,1\}^n 1 \{0,1\}^*$ can be easily accepted with $O(n)$ states, and the reverse language $\{0,1\}^* 1 \{0,1\}^n$ requires $2^{\Omega(n)}$ states to be accepted by DFA's.

Let L be a regular language. Let $\mathcal{M}$ be a DFA that accepts L. The language L^R can be accepted by a NFA with the same set of states, simply by reversing the transition relation of $\mathcal{M}$. This automaton is unambiguous.

We have:

Theorem 6. *The following assertions hold:*

1. *Suppose that the input languages L and T are represented by NFA's. We use the symbol* $\#CCP\,(\mathcal{REG}, NFA)$ *to denote this problem. We have that* $\#CCP\,(\mathcal{REG}, NFA)$ *is hard for PSPACE.*
2. *The problem* $\#CCP\,(\mathcal{REG}, REGEX)$ *is hard for PSPACE.*
3. *The problem* $\#CCP\,(\mathcal{REG}, 2DFA)$ *is hard for PSPACE.*
4. *The problem* $\#CCP\,(\mathcal{REG}, UFA)$ *can be approximated in polynomial time. This means that there exists an approximation scheme that runs in polynomial time with respect to* $|\mathcal{M}|$, $|\mathcal{N}|$ *and* n.

Proof. Let us proceed.

1. The universe problem for NFA's is hard for PSPACE; see [14]. Moreover, if we are given a NFA for the language L, we can compute in polynomial time a NFA for the language $Lc\,(\Sigma \cup \{c\})^*$.
2. We proceed similarly to the previous item. The universe problem for 2DFA's and regular expressions are hard for PSPACE.

Remark 5. The limit probabilities of NFA's, regular expressions and 2DFA's are hard to approximate.

3. Let $\mathcal{M}$ be a UFA. Let $\lambda_1, ..., \lambda_m$ be the spectrum of $T\,(\mathcal{M})$, and let

$$p_1\,(n)\,, ..., p_m\,(n) \in \mathbb{Q}\,[n]$$

be the corresponding polynomials. For all $n \geq 1$, the equality

$$|L \cap \Sigma^n| = p_1\,(n)\,\lambda_1^n + \cdots + p_m\,(n)\,\lambda_m^n$$

holds. The Jordan canonical form of $T\,(\mathcal{M})$ can be approximated, within the range $\frac{1}{2^n}$, in polynomial time in $|\mathcal{M}|$ and n; see [9] and see [16]. The limit probability $\Pr\,(L_{\mathcal{M}} \mid L_{\mathcal{N}})$ can be easily computed from the Jordan canonical forms of $T\,(\mathcal{M})$ and $T\,(\mathcal{N})$.

Let us observe that:

1. The limit probabilities of regular languages can be effectively approximated. The computability of those limit probabilities does not depend on the way the input languages are represented.
2. The complexity of approximating the limit probabilities of regular languages depends on the way those languages are represented. This problem is intractable for most presentations of regular languages. The problem becomes tractable when the input languages are represented by DFA's or UFA's.

5 Coping with Nonregular Languages

We showed that relative densities of regular languages can be effectively approximated. The same task cannot be accomplished for most language classes. The class of reversal-bounded languages seems to be the last loophole through which a little tractability could slip through. We know a few things about the asymptotic densities of those languages:

1. Asymptotic densities of unambiguous reversal-bounded (finite-turn) context-free languages are effectively computable; see [1]. The relative densities of those languages are uncomputable.
2. Asymptotic densities of unambiguous reversal-bounded one-counter languages are effectively computable. We do not know whether the relative densities of those languages are computable.

5.1 Reversal Bounded One-Counter Automata

Let G be a finitely generated group, and let X be a spanning set for G. Let $R_X = X \cup \{g^{-1} : g \in X\}$. Let $\mathcal{K}(G, R_X)$ be the *Cayley graph* of (G, R_X); see [7]. Notice that $\mathcal{K}(G, R_X)$ is a directed graph all whose edges hold labels from the set R_X. Let e_G be the identity of G, and let $\mathcal{G}(G, R_X)$ be the set of *geodesic paths* that start at e_G. Let $\mathcal{L}(G, R_X)$ be the language

$$\mathcal{L}(G, R_X) = \{w \in R_X^* : w \text{ labels a path in } \mathcal{G}(G, R_X)\}$$

This is the *geodesic language* of the pair (G, R_X).

Example 4. Let $G = \mathbb{Z} \times \mathbb{Z}$, and let $X = \{(1,0), (0,1)\}$. Let us use the letters N, S, E, W to encode the elements of R_X, i.e. $N = (0,1)$, $S = (0,-1)$, $E = (1,0)$, and $W = (-1,0)$. The equality

$$\mathcal{L}(\mathbb{Z} \times \mathbb{Z}, R_X) = \{N, E\}^* \cup \{N, W\}^* \cup \{S, E\}^* \cup \{S, W\}^*$$

holds. Notice that $\mathcal{L}(\mathbb{Z} \times \mathbb{Z}, R_X)$ is a regular language.

The notion of geodesic language lead us to consider a potential application of our research work. Let a be an agent that moves over $\mathcal{K}(G, R_X)$. Suppose a starts all its trips at e_G. Suppose we can only see the labels of the paths traversed by a. Can we measure the distance from a to the ideal itinerary represented by $\mathcal{L}(G, R_X)$? It depends on G and R_X. If the word problem for (G, R_X) is unsolvable, the language $\mathcal{L}(G, R_X)$ is undecidable. Let $\mathcal{R}$ be the class of finitely generated groups for which there exists X such that $\mathcal{L}(G, R_X)$ is a regular language. It is a remarkable fact that $\mathcal{R}$ is a large class that contains the class of virtually Abelian groups, the class of hyperbolic groups, as well as many other classes of groups. Let $G \in \mathcal{R}$, and let X be a generating set of G such that $\mathcal{L}(G, R_X)$ is regular. We can compute the conditional probability $\Pr(co\text{-}\mathcal{L}(G, R_X) \cap L_{\mathcal{M}} \mid L_{\mathcal{M}})$, and use it to measure the distance from a to $\mathcal{L}(G, R_X)$. There exist *natural* groups with solvable word problem, and such that all their geodesic languages are nonregular.

Example 5. Let

$$G_0 = \left\langle a, b, t \mid ab = ba;\ t^2 = 1;\ \text{and } tat = b \right\rangle$$

Let $c = a^2$, and let $d = ab$. Let $X = \{a, c, d, t\}$. It can be proved that

$$\mathcal{L}(G_0, R_X) \cap c^* t c^* t = \{c^n t c^m t : m < n\}$$

This implies that $\mathcal{L}(G_0, R_X)$ is not regular.

Let us observe that $\{c^n t c^m t : m < n\}$ is accepted by a deterministic one-reversal one-counter automaton. It can be checked that the language $\mathcal{L}(G_0, R_X)$ is a deterministic one-way reversal-bounded one-counter language. Thus, suppose $\mathcal{L}(G, R_X)$ is a linear unambiguous one-counter language. Can we measure the distance from a to the ideal itinerary represented by $\mathcal{L}(G, R_X)$? We have:

Theorem 7. *Let $\mathcal{M}$ be a linear unambiguous one-counter automaton, and let L be a regular language. It can be decided whether the limit probability $\Pr(L_{\mathcal{M}} \cap L \mid L)$ exists and is different from zero.*

Proof. Let $\mathcal{M}^*$ be a linear unambiguous one-counter automaton that accepts the language $L_{\mathcal{M}} \cap L$. We use $\mathcal{M}^*$ to compute an unambiguous linear context-free grammar generating this language $L_{\mathcal{M}} \cap L$. Let $G = (V, T, S, R)$ be this grammar. Let us suppose $V = \{X_1, ... X_m\}$ and $S = X_1$. Let $i \leq m$ and let

$$X_i \to a_{i_1} X_{i_1} \mid \cdots \mid a_{i_p} X_{i_p} \mid X_{j_1} a_{j_1} \mid \cdots \mid X_{j_r} a_{j_r} \mid a_{k_1} \mid \cdots \mid a_{k_l}$$

be the set of production rules associated to the nonterminal symbol X_i. We apply Chomsky-Schützenberger method to compute, from that set of

$$X_i(x) = x \left(\sum_{s=1}^{p} X_{i_s}(x) + \sum_{s=1}^{r} X_{j_s}(x) \right) + \ell x + \varepsilon_i$$

where $\varepsilon_i = 1$ if and only if $X_i \to \varepsilon$ is a production rule. We do the same with all the terminal symbols in V. We obtain a system

$$\overrightarrow{X} = (I - xA)^{-1} \left(x\Delta + \overrightarrow{\varepsilon} \right).$$

The solution of this system is a rational function that can be effectively computed. We use this to compute a rational function $m(x)$ which is the generating function of $L_{\mathcal{M}} \cap L$. We can also compute a rational generating function for the regular language L. Let $n(x)$ be this function. Then, we can use *Kozik's criterion* to decide whether $\Pr(L_{\mathcal{M}} \cap L_{\mathcal{N}} \mid L)$ exists and is different from zero; see [12]. The theorem is proved.

5.2 Hairpin Languages

Let us introduce an operation on regular languages that comes from computational genetics and DNA computing. We are referring to hairpin completions; see [6].

Definition 8. *Let L and T be two regular languages and let $k \geq 0$. The hairpin completion $\mathcal{H}_k(L,T)$ is the language*

$$\left\{uvwv^Ru^R : \left(uvwv^R \in L \vee vwv^Ru^R \in T\right) \text{ and } |v| = k\right\}$$

We say that $\mathcal{H}_k(L,T)$ is a hairpin language.

The computation of limit probabilities of hairpin languages seems to be of interest in DNA computing and bioinformatics; see [6]. Most hairpin languages are nonregular. It can be proved that hairpin languages are linear unambiguous context-free languages; see [6]. This yields a polynomial time algorithm for computing the census function of $\mathcal{H}_k(L,T)$, as well as an algorithm for computing the asymptotic densities of those languages; see [13]. Let us observe that the densities of most hairpin languages are equal to zero. What could be of interest is the computation of relative densities between hairpin languages. We cannot use that Hairpin languages are LUCFL's since the relative densities of these latter languages are uncomputable. We have:

Theorem 8. *Let $k \geq 0$. Let $L_1 \subseteq L_2$ and $T_1 \subseteq T_2$ be four regular languages. There exist regular languages $g_k(L_1,T_1)$ and $g_k(L_2,T_2)$ such that:*

1. *For $i = 1, 2$, and for all $n \geq 1$ the equality $c_{g_k(L_i,T_i)}(n) = c_{\mathcal{H}_k(L_i,T_i)}(n)$ holds.*
2. *The condition $g_k(L_1,T_1) \subseteq g_k(L_2,T_2)$ holds.*
3. *If we are given two DFA's of size n accepting the languages L and T, we can compute a 2NFA of size $O(n)$ accepting the language $g_k(L,T)$.*

Proof. Let us focus on the case $k = 0$.

1. Let c be a fresh character not in Σ. Let $u \in \Sigma^n$. We use the symbol u_c to denote the string $u[1]c \cdots cu[n]c$. We use the symbol $g(L,T)$ to denote the language

$$\left\{\begin{array}{c} u_cw : \text{if } |w| \geq 2 \text{ the condition } w[1] \neq w[|w|] \text{ holds,} \\ \text{and there exists } i \leq |u| \text{ such that} \\ uwu[|u|]\,u[|u|-1] \cdots u[i] \in L \text{ or} \\ u[i] \cdots u[|u|]\,wu^R \in T \end{array}\right\}$$

   Let $uwu^R \in \Sigma$. We can assume that either $|w| \leq 1$ or $w[1] \neq w[2]$. Notice that uwu^R belongs to $\mathcal{H}_0(L,T)$ if and only if $u_cw \in g(L,T)$. Moreover, the equality $\left|uwu^R\right| = |u_cw|$ holds.
2. It is easy to check that for all $L_1 \subset T_1$ and $L_2 \subset T_2$ the condition $g(L_1,T_1) \subseteq g(L_2,T_2)$ holds. Let us then focus on proving the third item.

3. Let $\mathcal{M}$ be a DFA that accepts L, and let $\mathcal{N}$ be a DFA that accepts T. Let $\mathcal{N}^R$ the reverse automaton that accepts T^R. Notice that $\mathcal{N}^R$ is an UFA of size $O(n)$. We use these two automata to construct a 2NFA $\mathcal{G}$ that accepts the language $g(L, T)$. Automaton works, on input $u_c w$, as follows:
   (a) Automaton $\mathcal{G}$ checks the L-condition. If this condition is not fulfilled, then $\mathcal{G}$ checks the T-condition. If this second condition is not fulfilled the automaton rejects the input.
   Let us first focus on checking the L-condition.
   (b) Automaton $\mathcal{G}$ scans u_c from left to right while simulating the computation of $\mathcal{M}$, on input u. Automaton $\mathcal{G}$ checks that the prefix u_c satisfies the pattern $(\Sigma c)^*$.
   (c) When the input head of $\mathcal{G}$ reaches the right end of the input, it moves leftward until it finds the first occurrence of the letter c. Then, automaton $\mathcal{G}$ scans u, from right to left, resuming the simulation of the computation of $\mathcal{M}$, on input uwu^R.
   (d) Suppose that the input head of $\mathcal{G}$ reaches the cell occupied by $u[i]$. Notice that $\mathcal{G}$ has simulated the computation of $\mathcal{M}$, on input
   $$uwu[|u|]\,u[|u|-1]\cdots u[i]$$
   If this simulation reaches an accepting state of $\mathcal{M}$, the automaton $\mathcal{G}$ halts and accepts the input. Otherwise, it continues until such an i is found or the input head reaches the left end of the input. In the first case the automaton accepts its input, in the second it goes to the next step.
   (e) Automaton $\mathcal{G}$ checks whether there exists $i \leq |u|$ such that
   $$uw^R u[|u|]\,u[|u|-1]\cdots u[i]$$
   belongs to T. To this end, $\mathcal{G}$ simulates the computation of $\mathcal{N}^R$.

   It can be checked that $\mathcal{G}$ accepts the language $g(L, T)$. Notice that $\mathcal{G}$ has size $O(n)$.

Let us finish this work formulating a question that deserves further investigation: are the relative densities of deterministic one-way reversal-bounded multicounter automata computable?

Acknowledgement. This author thanks Centro de Investigaciones Antonio Sanchez de Cozar, Vereda los Egidos, San Gil Colombia. Most of this work was written while this author was visiting this charming research center.

References

1. Baron, G., Kuich, W.: The characterization of nonexpansive grammars by rational power series. Inf. Control **48**(2), 109–118 (1981)
2. Berstel, J.: Sur la densité asymptotique de langages formels. In: ICALP 1972, pp. 345–358 (1972)

3. Bodirsky, M., Gärtner, T., Oertzen, T.V., Schwinghammer, J.: Efficiently computing the density of regular languages. In: Proceedings of LATIN 2004, pp. 262–270
4. Chomsky, N., Miller, G.: Finite state languages. Inf. Control **1**(2), 91–112 (1958)
5. Colcombet, T.: Unambiguity in automata theory. In: DCFS 2015, pp. 3–18
6. Diekert, V., Kopecki, S.: Complexity results and the growths of hairpin completions of regular languages. In: CIAA 2010, pp. 105–114
7. Elder, M.: A context-free and a 1-counter geodesic language for a Baumslag–Solitar group. Theor. Comput. Sci. **339**(2–3), 344–371 (2005)
8. Flajolet, P., Sedgewick, R.: Analytic Combinatorics. Princenton University Press, Boston (2009)
9. Giesbrecht, M.: Nearly optimal algorithms for canonical matrix forms. SIAM J. Comp. **24**, 948–969 (1995)
10. Ibarra, O.: Reversal-bounded multicounter machines and their decision problems. J. ACM **25**(1), 116–133 (1978)
11. Ibarra, O.: Restricted one-counter machines with undecidable universe problems. Math. Syst. Theory **13**, 181–186 (1979)
12. Kozik, J.: Conditional densities of regular languages. In: Proceedings of CLA 2004, pp. 67–79 (2004)
13. Kozik, J.: Undecidable problems concerning densities of languages. In: Proceedings of CLA 2005, pp. 69–76 (2005)
14. Krötzsch, M., Masopust, T., Thomazo, M.: Complexity of universality and related problems for partially ordered NFAs. Inf. Comput. **255**, 177–192 (2017)
15. Nakamura, Y.: Computational complexity of several extensions of Kleene algebra. PhD. Thesis, Tokyo Institute of Technology (2019)
16. Li, T., Zhang, Z., Wang, T.: Determining the structure of the Jordan normal form of a matrix by symbolic computation. Linear Algebra Appl. **252**, 221–259 (1997)
17. Lynch, J.: Convergence laws for random words. Australasyan J. Comb. **7**, 145–156 (1993)
18. Schützenberger, M.: Sur le produit de concatenation non ambigu. Semigroup Forum **13**, 47–75 (1976). https://doi.org/10.1007/BF02194921
19. Valiant, L., Paterson, M.: Deterministic one-counter automata. J. Comput. Syst. Sci. **10**(3), 340–350 (1975)

On A Measure for The Descriptional Complexity of Finite Automata with Translucent Words

František Mráz[1(✉)] and Friedrich Otto[2]

[1] Charles University, Faculty of Mathematics and Physics, Department of Computer Science, Malostranské nám. 25, CZ-118 00 Praha 1, Prague, Czech Republic
frantisek.mraz@mff.cuni.cz

[2] Universität Kassel, Fachbereich Elektrotechnik/Informatik, D-34109, Kassel, Germany
f.otto@uni-kassel.de

Abstract. We propose two parameters that should be incorporated into the measure for the descriptional complexity of deterministic and nondeterministic finite automata with translucent words: the maximal length of a translucent word and the maximal cardinality of a set of translucent words. We illustrate the influence of these two parameters on the expressive capacity of finite automata with translucent words, where we concentrate, in particular, on automata over a binary alphabet. We establish that the restrictions for the length of the longest word in any set of translucent words and the restriction for the cardinality of the admitted sets of translucent words yield a two-dimensional infinite hierarchy of classes of binary languages.

Keywords: Finite automaton · static complexity measure · translucent word · length-restriction · cardinality-restriction · hierarchy

1 Introduction

The size of the description of a finite automaton, be it deterministic or nondeterministic, is closely related to the number of its states and the cardinality of the underlying alphabet. In fact, if $A = (Q, \Sigma, q_0, F, \delta)$ is a complete deterministic finite automaton (a DFA) with a set of states Q, an input alphabet Σ, an initial state $q_0 \in Q$, a set of final states $F \subseteq Q$, and a transition function $\delta : Q \times \Sigma \to Q$, then δ contains $|Q| \cdot |\Sigma|$ many transitions. Accordingly, a description of A, which is essentially an encoding of the transition function δ, needs space $O(|Q| \cdot |\Sigma|)$. Moreover, if A is a nondeterministic finite automaton (an NFA), then $\delta(q, a)$ may contain up to $|Q|$ many states for each pair $(q, a) \in Q \times \Sigma$, and therefore, a description of A may need space $O(|Q|^2 \cdot |\Sigma|)$.

In [3] (see also [8]), the finite automaton was generalized to the finite automaton with translucent letters. Such an automaton is equipped with a translucency mapping that assigns a set of translucent letters to each state of the automaton.

Published by Springer Nature Switzerland AG 2025
A. Malcher and L. Prigioniero (Eds.): DCFS 2025, LNCS 15759, pp. 180–195, 2025.
https://doi.org/10.1007/978-3-031-97100-6_13

Accordingly, in each step, the automaton just reads and deletes the first letter from the left end of its tape, which is not translucent for its current state. It turned out that the NFA with translucent letters (the NFAwtl) is quite interesting, as it accepts a class of semi-linear languages that includes all rational trace languages [1,2]. However, the class of languages that are accepted by deterministic finite automata with translucent letters (the DFAwtl) is incomparable to the rational trace languages with respect to inclusion [4,5].

As the set of translucent letters assigned to a state of an NFAwtl is a subset of the underlying input alphabet, the encoding of the translucency sets of an NFAwtl needs space $O(|Q| \cdot |\Sigma|)$. This means that the description of a DFAwtl or an NFAwtl needs asymptotically the same space as that of a DFA or an NFA, respectively.

Finally, in [6], the finite automaton with translucent letters was generalized even further by extending the sets of translucent letters to sets of translucent words, which yields the *finite automaton with translucent words* or *NFAwtw*. An NFAwtw reads (and deletes) the first letter from the left that is only preceded by a prefix that is a product of words that are translucent for the current state. This gives the automaton more control over the structure of the prefix ignored in a transition than for an NFAwtl.

In order to guarantee that the resulting computation relation of an NFAwtw A can be computed efficiently, it is required in [6] that, for each state q, the set of translucent words $\tau(q)$ is a finite prefix code such that no word in this set begins with a letter that A can read in state q. As it turned out, there are languages that are accepted by deterministic finite automata with translucent words (that is, by DFAwtws), but that are not even accepted by any nondeterministic finite automaton with translucent letters.

For a complete description of a deterministic finite automaton with translucent words, we need to encode the transition function together with all the sets of translucent words. To limit the size of the latter, the following two parameters have been introduced:

(a) An NFAwtw A is *k-cardinality-restricted* for some integer $k \geq 1$, if each set of translucent words of A contains at most k elements.
(b) An NFAwtw A is *ℓ-length-restricted* for some integer $\ell \geq 1$, if no set of translucent words of A contains a word of length larger than ℓ.

Obviously, the 1-length-restricted NFAwtw is just the NFAwtl. A description of a DFAwtw that is k-cardinality-restricted and ℓ-length-restricted needs space $O(|Q| \cdot (|\Sigma| + k \cdot \ell))$, while for the description of a corresponding NFAwtw, space $O(|Q| \cdot (|Q| \cdot |\Sigma| + k \cdot \ell))$ is needed. Accordingly, we propose the quadruple $(|Q|, |\Sigma|, k, \ell)$ as a measure for the descriptional complexity of an NFAwtw $A = (Q, \Sigma, \lhd, \tau, I, F, \delta)$. We present DFAwtws that illustrate the range for the parameters k and ℓ, and we recall from [7] that the two parameters above induce an infinite two-dimensional hierarchy of language classes.

Then, we abstract from the influence that the cardinality of the input alphabet has on the descriptional complexity of an NFAwtw by considering the above measure for finite automata with translucent words that work with a fixed finite alphabet. In fact, we concentrate on the binary alphabet $\Sigma_2 = \{a, b\}$.

For each $\ell \geq 2$, we present a language $L^{(2)}_{\ell-1}$ over Σ_2 that is accepted by an ℓ-length-restricted DFAwtw, but that is not accepted by any $(\ell - 1)$-length-restricted NFAwtw. In addition, for each $k \geq 2$, we present a language $L^{(3)}_{k-1}$ on Σ_2 that is accepted by a k-cardinality-restricted DFAwtw, but not by any $(k-1)$-cardinality-restricted NFAwtw. Thus, the degree of length-restriction and the degree of cardinality-restriction both induce infinite strictly ascending hierarchies of language classes for DFAwtws and for NFAwtws that just have a binary alphabet. Moreover, we shall see that the degree ℓ of length-restriction induces the exponential upper bound of $2^{\ell-1}$ for the degree of cardinality-restriction for NFAwtws with the alphabet Σ_2. In fact, for each given degree ℓ of length-restriction, we establish a finite hierarchy of language classes over Σ_2 that is based on the degree of cardinality-restriction. In addition, we present a family of binary languages such that their degrees of cardinality-restriction grow exponentially with their degrees of length-restriction.

This paper is structured as follows. In Sect. 2, we present the necessary definitions related to the NFAwtw. Based on some simple example languages, we then illustrate the proposed complexity measure, establishing, in particular, the aforementioned upper bound for the degree of cardinality-restriction. In the next section, based on the results of [6] and [7], we show that the degrees of length-restriction and of cardinality-restriction induce an infinite strictly ascending two-dimensional hierarchy of language classes that are specified through DFAwtws and NFAwtws. Then, in Sect. 4, we present the announced examples over the binary alphabet Σ_2. In the concluding section, we provide some open problems for future studies.

2 Finite Automata with Sets of Translucent Words

The finite automaton with translucent words is defined as follows.

Definition 1 ([6]). *An* NFAwtw *is defined as a 7-tuple* $A = (Q, \Sigma, \lhd, \tau, I, F, \delta)$, *where* Q *is a finite set of states,* Σ *is a finite input alphabet,* $\lhd \notin \Sigma$ *is a sentinel that is used to mark the end of the tape,* $I \subseteq Q$ *is a set of initial states, and* $F \subseteq Q$ *is a set of final (or accepting) states. The function* $\tau : Q \to \mathcal{P}_{\text{fin}}(\Sigma^+)$ *is a* translucency mapping *and* $\delta : Q \times \Sigma \to \mathcal{P}(Q)$ *is a transition function. For each state* $q \in Q$, *let*

$$\Sigma^{(A)}_q = \{\, a \in \Sigma \mid \delta(q, a) \neq \emptyset \,\},$$

that is, $\Sigma^{(A)}_q$ *contains those letters that* A *can read in state* q. *It is required that, for each state* $q \in Q$, *if* $\tau(q) \neq \emptyset$, *then* $\tau(q)$ *is a finite prefix code that does not contain any word that begins with a letter from the set* $\Sigma^{(A)}_q$. *Actually, this means that the set* $\tau(q) \cup \Sigma^{(A)}_q$ *is a finite prefix code.*

The computation relation $\vdash_A^*$ *that* A *induces on its set of configurations*

$$Q \cdot \Sigma^* \cdot \{\lhd\} \cup \{\mathsf{Accept}, \mathsf{Reject}\}$$

is the reflexive and transitive closure of the following single-step computation relation, where $q \in Q$ *and* $w \in \Sigma^*$*:*

$$qw \cdot \lhd \vdash_A \begin{cases} q'uv \cdot \lhd, & \text{if } w = uav, u \in (\tau(q))^*, a \in \Sigma_q^{(A)}, v \in \Sigma^*, \text{ and } q' \in \delta(q,a), \\ \mathsf{Reject}, & \text{if } w = uav, u \in (\tau(q))^*, a \in \Sigma \setminus \Sigma_q^{(A)}, v \in \Sigma^*, \\ & \text{and } av \notin \tau(q) \cdot \Sigma^*, \\ \mathsf{Accept}, & \text{if } w \in (\tau(q))^* \text{ and } q \in F, \\ \mathsf{Reject}, & \text{if } w \in (\tau(q))^* \text{ and } q \notin F. \end{cases}$$

A word $w \in \Sigma^*$ *is* accepted by A *if there exist an initial state* $q_0 \in I$ *and a computation* $q_0 w \cdot \lhd \vdash_A^*$ Accept. *Now,* $L(A)$ *denotes the* language *that consists of all words* accepted by A, *and* $\mathcal{L}(\mathsf{NFAwtw})$ *denotes the class of all languages that are accepted by NFAwtws.*

An NFAwtw $A = (Q, \Sigma, \lhd, \tau, I, F, \delta)$ *is* deterministic *(or a* DFAwtw*) if* $|I| = 1$ *and* $|\delta(q,a)| \leq 1$ *for each* $q \in Q$ *and* $a \in \Sigma$. *Then* $\mathcal{L}(\mathsf{DFAwtw})$ *denotes the class of all languages that are accepted by DFAwtws.*

As $\tau(q)$ is a prefix code for each state q, the factorization $w = uav$, where $u \in (\tau(q))^*$, $a \in \Sigma$, $v \in \Sigma^*$, and $av \notin \tau(q) \cdot \Sigma^*$, is uniquely determined. This is not the case without the requirement that $\tau(q)$ is a prefix code, as shown in [6]. Moreover, the additional requirement that, for each state q of an NFAwtw A, no word from the set $\tau(q)$ begins with a letter that A can read in state q implies that, in each step, the next letter to be read and deleted by A can simply be identified by scanning the current tape contents letter by letter from left to right. From the definition of the single-step computation relation of an NFAwtw, we immediately obtain the following useful property.

Lemma 1 ([6]). *Let* $A = (Q, \Sigma, \lhd, \tau, I, F, \delta)$ *be an NFAwtw and assume that* $quav \cdot \lhd \vdash_A puv \cdot \lhd$, *where* $q, p \in Q$, $u \in (\tau(q))^*$, $a \in \Sigma_q^{(A)}$, *and* $v \in \Sigma^*$. *Then* $quavz \cdot \lhd \vdash_A puvz \cdot \lhd$ *for each word* $z \in \Sigma^*$ *and* $qaw \cdot \lhd \vdash_A pw \cdot \lhd$.

Assume that the NFAwtw $A = (Q, \Sigma, \lhd, \tau, I, F, \delta)$ contains a state $q \in Q$ such that $\Sigma_q^{(A)} = \emptyset$, that is, A cannot read any letter when it is in state q. Thus, the NFAwtw A halts immediately once it reaches a configuration of the form $qz \cdot \lhd$, and it accepts if and only if q is a final state and $z \in (\tau(q))^*$. If q is not final, then we can simply replace this state by a trap state in which the automaton reads all letters. On the other hand, if q is final, then we can replace this state with the initial state of a DFA for the language $(\tau(q))^*$. In this way, we obtain the following normalization.

Lemma 2. *For each NFAwtw* A, *there exists an equivalent NFAwtw* B *such that, for each state* q *of* B, *the set* $\Sigma_q^{(B)}$ *is non-empty. If* A *is deterministic, then so is* B.

Since no word in the prefix code $\tau_B(q)$ begins with a letter that B can read in state q, the lemma above implies in particular that, for each state q of B, there exists at least one letter such that no word in the set $\tau(q)$ begins with that letter. Next, we formally introduce the two parameters for NFAwtws mentioned before.

Definition 2. (a) *An NFAwtw $A = (Q, \Sigma, \triangleleft, \tau, I, F, \delta)$ is called* k-cardinality-restricted *(or simply* k-restricted *or a* k-rNFAwtw*) for some $k \geq 1$, if $|\tau(q)| \leq k$ for each state $q \in Q$, that is, for each state of A, there are at most k translucent words. If A is deterministic, it is called a* k-rDFAwtw.

(b) *An NFAwtw $A = (Q, \Sigma, \triangleleft, \tau, I, F, \delta)$ is called* ℓ-length-restricted *(or an* ℓ-lr-NFAwtw*) for some $\ell \geq 1$, if the longest word in any set of translucent words of A is of length at most ℓ. If A is deterministic, it is called an* ℓ-lr-DFAwtw.

The 1-lr-DFAwtw is just the DFAwtl, and the 1-lr-NFAwtw is the NFAwtl from [3]. In addition, if $A = (Q, \Sigma, \triangleleft, \tau, I, F, \delta)$ is an NFAwtw, then A is ℓ-length-restricted and k-cardinality-restricted for

$$\ell = \max\{\, |u| \mid \exists q \in Q : u \in \tau(q)\,\} \text{ and } k = \max\{\, |\tau(q)| \mid q \in Q\,\},$$

that is, it is an ℓ-lr-k-rNFAwtw. It follows that, for all $\ell \geq 1$ and all $k \geq 1$,

$$\mathcal{L}(\ell\text{-lr-NFAwtw}) = \bigcup_{s \geq 1} \mathcal{L}(\ell\text{-lr-}s\text{-rNFAwtw}),\ \mathcal{L}(k\text{-rNFAwtw}) = \bigcup_{t \geq 1} \mathcal{L}(t\text{-lr-}k\text{-rNFAwtw}),$$

and

$$\mathcal{L}(\mathsf{NFAwtw}) = \bigcup_{\ell \geq 1} \mathcal{L}(\ell\text{-lr-NFAwtw}) = \bigcup_{k \geq 1} \mathcal{L}(k\text{-rNFAwtw}) = \bigcup_{k,\ell \geq 1} \mathcal{L}(\ell\text{-lr-}k\text{rNFAwtw}),$$

and a corresponding statement holds for the deterministic classes. This observation implies that the degree ℓ of length-restriction and the degree k of cardinality-restriction are well suited to classify finite automata with translucent words.

To describe a DFAwtw $A = (Q, \Sigma, \triangleleft, \tau, q_0, F, \delta)$, we need to encode the translucency mapping $\tau : Q \to \mathcal{P}_{\text{fin}}(\Sigma^+)$ and the transition function $\delta : Q \times \Sigma \to Q$. The latter takes space $O(|Q| \cdot |\Sigma|)$ as for a DFA, and the former takes space $O(|Q| \cdot k \cdot \ell)$, if A is ℓ-length-restricted and k-cardinality-restricted. This yields an upper bound of $O(|Q| \cdot (|\Sigma| + k \cdot \ell))$. In the nondeterministic case, the encoding of the transition function may need space $O(|Q|^2 \cdot |\Sigma|)$ as for an NFA, which then yields the upper bound of $O(|Q| \cdot (|Q| \cdot |\Sigma| + k \cdot \ell))$ for the space needed to encode an ℓ-lr-k-rNFAwtw. Accordingly, we propose to take the 4-tuple $(|Q|, |\Sigma|, k, \ell)$ as the measure for the descriptional complexity of an NFAwtw.

Let $D_1 \subseteq \{a, b\}^*$ be the semi-Dyck language over $\Sigma_2 = \{a, b\}$, that is, D_1 is the language that is generated by the context-free grammar

$$G = (\{S\}, \Sigma_2, S, \{S \to \lambda, S \to SS, S \to aSb\}).$$

Furthermore, let $\Gamma = \{a, b, c\}$, let $\varphi : \Sigma_2^* \to \Gamma^*$ be the morphism that is defined through $a \mapsto ab$ and $b \mapsto c$, and let $L_1 = \varphi(D_1)$. It is shown in [6] that L_1 is accepted by a DFAwtw that is 2-length-restricted and 1-cardinality restricted, but not by any NFAwtl.

For $s \geq 2$, let $\Gamma_s = \{a_1, a_2, \ldots, a_s\}$ be an alphabet of cardinality s. Moreover, let $\ell \geq 2$ and let $\psi_{s,\ell} : \{a, b\} \to \mathcal{P}(\Gamma_s^+)$ be the substitution that is defined through

$$a \mapsto \{\, a_i u \mid 1 \leq i \leq s-1, u \in \Gamma_s^{\ell-1} \,\} \text{ and } b \mapsto \{a_s\}.$$

Then we take $L_{s,\ell} = \psi_{s,\ell}(D_1)$. This language is easily seen to be accepted by the DFAwtw $A_{s,\ell} = (Q, \Gamma_s, \triangleleft, \tau, q_0, \{q_0\}, \delta)$ that is defined through $Q = \{q_0, q_1, q_2, \ldots, q_\ell\}$ and the functions τ and δ that are specified as follows:

$$\begin{aligned} \tau(q_i) &= \emptyset \text{ for } 0 \leq i \leq \ell-1, \quad \tau(q_\ell) = \{\, a_i u \mid 1 \leq i \leq s-1, u \in \Gamma_s^{\ell-1} \,\}, \\ \delta(q_0, a_i) &= q_1 \text{ for } 1 \leq i \leq s-1, \ \delta(q_i, x) = q_{i+1} \text{ for } 1 \leq i \leq \ell-1 \text{ and } x \in \Gamma_s, \\ \delta(q_\ell, a_s) &= q_0, \end{aligned}$$

where δ is undefined for all other pairs from $Q \times \Gamma_s$. As the set $\tau(q_\ell)$ contains $(s-1) \cdot s^{\ell-1}$ words of length ℓ, we see that the DFAwtw $A_{s,\ell}$ is ℓ-length-restricted and $((s-1) \cdot s^{\ell-1})$-cardinality-restricted.

Now let $k \geq 1$ be an integer such that $k < (s-1)s^{\ell-1}$, let V_k be a subset of $(\Gamma_s \setminus \{a_s\}) \cdot \Gamma_s^{\ell-1}$ of cardinality k, let $\psi_{s,\ell,V_k} : \{a, b\} \to \mathcal{P}(\Gamma_s^+)$ be the substitution that is defined through

$$a \mapsto \{u \mid u \in V_k\} \text{ and } b \mapsto \{a_s\},$$

and let $L_{s,\ell,V_k} = \psi_{s,\ell,V_k}(D_1)$. By adjusting the definition of the DFAwtw $A_{s,\ell}$ accordingly, we obtain a DFAwtw A_{s,ℓ,V_k} for the language L_{s,ℓ,V_k} that is ℓ-length-restricted and k-cardinality-restricted. Hence, we have the following result.

Theorem 1. *For all integers $s, \ell \geq 2$ and $k \in \{1, 2, \ldots, (s-1) \cdot s^{\ell-1}\}$, there exists a DFAwtw with an alphabet of cardinality s such that this DFAwtw is ℓ-length-restricted and k-cardinality-restricted.*

In fact, the value $(s-1) \cdot s^{\ell-1}$ for the degree of cardinality-restriction is a sharp upper bound for ℓ-length-restricted NFAwtws with an alphabet of cardinality s. There are only s^ℓ words of length ℓ over Γ_s. As observed above, we can assume without loss of generality that an NFAwtw A can read some letter no matter which state it is in. Accordingly, for each state q of A, there exists a letter x such that no word in the set $\tau(q)$ begins with the letter x. Thus, $\tau(q)$ is a prefix code that is a subset of $(\Gamma_s \setminus \{x\}) \cdot \Gamma_s^{\leq \ell-1}$. The set $(\Gamma_s \setminus \{x\}) \cdot \Gamma_s^{\ell-1}$ is the largest prefix code with this property, and it is of cardinality $(s-1) \cdot s^{\ell-1}$.

We have seen above that the cardinality of the alphabet and the degree of length-restriction together induce an exponential upper bound for the degree of cardinality-restriction of an NFAwtw, that is, the four components $(|Q|, |\Sigma|, k, \ell)$ of our measure for the size of an NFAwtw are not independent of each other. Nevertheless, as the upper bound for the degree of cardinality-restriction is exponential in the degree of length-restriction and the cardinality of the alphabet, we consider it worthwhile to include the degree of cardinality-restriction in our measure. Theorem 1 illustrates that, for all possible degrees of length-restriction and cardinality-restriction, there are corresponding DFAwtws.

Finally, let

$$L_\vee = \{\, w \in \Sigma_2^* \mid \exists n \geq 0 : |w|_a = n \text{ and } |w|_b \in \{n, 2n\} \,\},$$

where $\Sigma_2 = \{a, b\}$. The language $L_\vee$ is a rational trace language, which is accepted by a 1-cardinality-restricted NFAwtl, but it is not even accepted by any DFAwtw [7]. Hence, we see that all nondeterministic classes considered above strictly contain the corresponding deterministic classes.

3 An Infinite Two-Dimensional Hierarchy

The parameters ℓ of length-restriction and k of cardinality-restriction yield an infinite two-dimensional hierarchy of DFAwtws, and this fact is easily extended to NFAwtws. Is there a corresponding two-dimensional hierarchy for languages that are accepted by DFAwtws or by NFAwtws? As demonstrated in [6] and [7], this is indeed the case.

In [6], the language class $\mathcal{L}(\ell\text{-lr-DFAwtw})$ is separated from the class $\mathcal{L}((\ell-1)\text{-lr-NFAwtw})$ by generalizing the idea of the construction of the example language L_1 above.

Let $\ell \geq 2$, let $\Gamma_\ell = \{a, b, e_2, e_3, \ldots, e_{\ell-1}, c\}$, let $\varphi_\ell : \Sigma^* \to \Gamma_\ell^*$ be the morphism that is defined through $a \mapsto abe_2e_3 \cdots e_{\ell-1}$ and $b \mapsto c$, and let $L_{\ell-1} = \varphi_\ell(D_1)$. For $\ell = 2$, we just get the above language L_1, which belongs to $\mathcal{L}(2\text{-lr-DFAwtw}) \smallsetminus \mathcal{L}(1\text{-lr-NFAwtw})$. It is established in [6] that the language $L_{\ell-1}$ is accepted by the ℓ-length-restricted DFAwtw $A_\ell = (Q_\ell, \Gamma_\ell, \lhd, \tau_\ell, q_0, \{q_0\}, \delta_\ell)$ that is obtained by taking $Q_\ell = \{q_0, q_1, q_2, \ldots, q_\ell\}$ and by defining the functions τ_ℓ and δ_ℓ as follows:

$$\begin{array}{lll} \tau_\ell(q_i) &= \emptyset \text{ for all } 0 \leq i \leq \ell-1, \ \tau_\ell(q_\ell) &= \{abe_2e_3 \cdots e_{\ell-1}\}, \\ \delta_\ell(q_0, a) = q_1, \ \delta_\ell(q_1, b) = q_2, & & \delta_\ell(q_i, e_i) = q_{i+1} \text{ for all } 2 \leq i \leq \ell-1, \\ \delta_\ell(q_\ell, c) &= q_0, & \end{array}$$

where δ_ℓ is undefined for all other pairs from $Q_\ell \times \Gamma_\ell$. Moreover, it is proved in [6] that $L_{\ell-1}$ is not accepted by any $(\ell-1)$-length-restricted NFAwtw. This establishes the following results.

Corollary 1 ([6]). *For all* $\ell \geq 2$, (a) $\mathcal{L}((\ell-1)\text{-lr-DFAwtw}) \subsetneq \mathcal{L}(\ell\text{-lr-DFAwtw})$.
(b) $\mathcal{L}((\ell-1)\text{-lr-NFAwtw}) \subsetneq \mathcal{L}(\ell\text{-lr-NFAwtw})$.

In [7], this result is extended into a two-dimensional hierarchy, where the second dimension is obtained by restricting the cardinality of the sets of translucent words. Let $k, \ell \geq 2$, let

$$\Gamma_{k,\ell} = \{\, a_{i,j} \mid 1 \leq i \leq k, 1 \leq j \leq \ell \,\} \cup \{c\},$$

let $\psi_{k,\ell} : \Sigma^* \to \mathcal{P}(\Gamma_{k,\ell}^*)$ be the substitution that is defined through

$$a \mapsto \{ a_{i,1}a_{i,2} \cdots a_{i,\ell} \mid i = 1, 2, \ldots, k \} \text{ and } b \mapsto \{c\},$$

and let $L_{ck,\ell}$ denote the language $L_{ck,\ell} = \psi_{k,\ell}(D_1)$.

Theorem 2 ([7]). *For all $k, \ell \geq 2$,*

$$L_{ck,\ell} \in \mathcal{L}(\ell\text{-lr-}k\text{-rDFAwtw}) \smallsetminus (\mathcal{L}((\ell-1)\text{-lr-NFAwtw}) \cup \mathcal{L}((k-1)\text{-rNFAwtw})).$$

Thus, based on the degrees of length-restriction and cardinality-restriction, there exists an infinite strictly ascending two-dimensional hierarchy of language classes for the deterministic and the nondeterministic finite automaton with translucent words. This means that these two parameters are useful for classifying classes of languages that are accepted by finite automata with translucent words.

4 NFAwtws with a Binary Alphabet

The example language $L_{\ell-1}$ is defined over the alphabet $\Gamma_\ell = \{a, b, e_2, e_3, \ldots, e_{\ell-1}, c\}$, which is of cardinality $\ell + 1$, and the language $L_{ck,\ell}$ is defined over the alphabet $\Gamma_{k,\ell} = \{ a_{i,j} \mid 1 \leq i \leq k, 1 \leq j \leq \ell \} \cup \{c\}$, which is of cardinality $k \cdot \ell + 1$. Hence, in these examples, the cardinality of the alphabet grows with the degree of length-restriction and the degree of cardinality restriction. Here we shall show that corresponding hierarchical results can be obtained even when example languages are considered that are specified over an alphabet of a fixed finite cardinality. In fact, our example languages are defined over the binary alphabet $\Sigma_2 = \{a, b\}$.

Definition 3. *Let $\ell \geq 2$, let $\varphi_\ell^{(2)} : \{a,b\}^* \to \{a,b\}^*$ be the morphism that is defined through $a \mapsto a^\ell$ and $b \mapsto b$, and let $L_{\ell-1}^{(2)}$ be the language $L_{\ell-1}^{(2)} = \varphi_\ell^{(2)}(D_1)$.*

Then $L_{\ell-1}^{(2)}$ is a binary language that satisfies the following separation result.

Theorem 3. *For all $\ell \geq 2$, $L_{\ell-1}^{(2)} \in \mathcal{L}(\ell\text{-lr-DFAwtw}) \smallsetminus \mathcal{L}((\ell-1)\text{-lr-NFAwtw})$.*

Proof. Let $\ell \geq 2$. We first show that $L_{\ell-1}^{(2)}$ is accepted by an ℓ-length-restricted DFAwtw. Let $B_\ell = (Q_\ell, \Sigma_2, \triangleleft, \tau_\ell, q_0, F_\ell, \delta_\ell)$ be the DFAwtw that is defined by taking $Q_\ell = \{q_0, q_1, \ldots, q_\ell\}$ and $F_\ell = \{q_0\}$ and by defining the functions τ_ℓ and δ_ℓ as follows:

$$\begin{aligned} \tau_\ell(q_i) &= \emptyset \quad \text{for all } 0 \leq i \leq \ell - 1,\ \tau_\ell(q_\ell) = \{a^\ell\}, \\ \delta_\ell(q_i, a) &= q_{i+1} \text{ for all } 0 \leq i \leq \ell - 1,\ \delta_\ell(q_\ell, b) = q_0, \end{aligned}$$

where δ_ℓ is undefined for all other pairs from $Q_\ell \times \Sigma_2$. Then it is easily checked that $L(B_\ell) = L_{\ell-1}^{(2)}$ holds.

It remains to prove that $L^{(2)}_{\ell-1}$ is not accepted by any $(\ell-1)$-length-restricted NFAwtw. Assume to the contrary that $A = (Q, \Sigma_2, \lhd, \tau, I, F, \delta)$ is an NFAwtw such that $L(A) = L^{(2)}_{\ell-1}$ and A is $(\ell-1)$-length-restricted. Hence, for each state $q \in Q$, the set $\tau(q)$ is a subset of $\Sigma_2^{\leq \ell-1}$.

For each integer $n \geq 0$, the word $w_n = a^{\ell \cdot n} b^n = \varphi^{(2)}_{\ell}(a^n b^n)$ belongs to the language $L^{(2)}_{\ell-1}$. Hence, A has an accepting computation for the input w_n, which necessarily looks as follows, since we may assume, without loss of generality, that A reads and deletes its input completely in each of its accepting computations:

$$q_0 w_n \cdot \lhd = q_0 a^{\ell \cdot n} b^n \cdot \lhd \vdash_A q_1 z_1 \cdot \lhd \vdash_A q_2 z_2 \cdot \lhd \vdash_A \cdots \vdash_A q_t z_t \cdot \lhd = q_t \cdot \lhd \vdash_A \mathsf{Accept},$$

where $t = \ell \cdot (n+1)$, $q_0 \in I$, $q_1, q_2, \ldots, q_{t-1} \in Q$, $q_t \in F$, and the word z_i is obtained from the input w_n by deleting i letters for all $i = 1, 2, \ldots, t$.

Assume that $n \geq |Q|$. Then the NFAwtw A cannot simply read (and delete) the word w_n from left to right, as, in this case, pumping arguments could be used to show that, together with $w_n = a^{\ell \cdot n} b^n$, A would also accept a word of the form $a^{\ell \cdot n + r} b^n$ for some integer $1 \leq r \leq |Q|$. Thus, after a finite number of steps in which a prefix w' of w_n of length at most $|Q|$ is read and deleted, a transition of the following form is applied:

$$p_1 u x v \cdot \lhd \vdash_A p_2 u v \cdot \lhd,$$

where $p_1, p_2 \in Q$, $x \in \Sigma_2$, $u, v \in \Sigma_2^*$, $p_2 \in \delta(p_1, x)$, and $u \in (\tau(p_1))^+$. Thus, the accepting computation of A on input w_n has the following form:

$$q_0 w_n \cdot \lhd = q_0 w' u x v \cdot \lhd \vdash_A^{|w'|} p_1 u x v \cdot \lhd \vdash_A p_2 u v \cdot \lhd \vdash_A^* q_t \cdot \lhd \vdash_A \mathsf{Accept}.$$

As $|w'| \leq |Q| \leq n < \ell \cdot n$, the word uxv has a prefix of the form a^m for some $m \geq 1$. Hence, the set $\tau(p_1)$ contains a word that begins with the letter a, which implies that $\delta(p_1, a)$ is undefined. It follows that $x = b$.

As $u \neq \lambda$, we have $u = yz$ for some word $y \in (\tau(p_1))^*$ and a non-empty word $z \in \tau(p_1)$. However, in this situation, A can also execute the following computation:

$$q_0 w' y x z v \cdot \lhd \vdash_A^{|w'|} p_1 y x z v \cdot \lhd \vdash_A p_2 y z v \cdot \lhd = p_2 u v \cdot \lhd \vdash_A^* q_t \cdot \lhd \vdash_A \mathsf{Accept}.$$

Thus, A accepts the word $w' y x z v$ that is obtained from $w_n = w' u x v = w' y z x v$ by commuting the factor $z \in \tau(p_1)$ and the letter $x \in \Sigma^{(A)}_{p_1}$. Since $z \in \tau(p_1)$, $1 \leq |z| \leq \ell - 1$ and $x = b$ does not coincide with the first letter of z, which must be an a. Furthermore, $yzxv$ is a suffix of w_n of length $n \cdot (\ell+1) - |w'| \geq \ell \cdot n$. However, by performing a commutation of the above form on a suffix of w_n that does not only consist of occurrences of the letter b, we obtain a word in which the last block of letters a is of length shorter than ℓ. Hence, the word does not belong to the language $L^{(2)}_{\ell-1}$. Thus, $w' y x z v \notin L^{(2)}_{\ell-1}$, contradicting our choice of the NFAwtw A. Hence, $L^{(2)}_{\ell-1}$ is not accepted by any $(\ell-1)$-lr-NFAwtw. □

This result yields the following consequence.

Corollary 2. *The degree of length-restriction induces strictly ascending infinite hierarchies of language classes for DFAwtws and for NFAwtws with a binary alphabet.*

The language $L_{ck,\ell}$ of Theorem 2 is defined over the alphabet $\Gamma_{k,\ell}$ of cardinality $(k \cdot \ell) + 1$. Are there corresponding example languages over an alphabet of a fixed finite cardinality?

Actually, that is not possible in general, since, as observed above, an ℓ-length-restricted NFAwtw with an alphabet of cardinality s is necessarily cardinality-restricted of degree $(s-1) \cdot s^{\ell-1}$. However, we may ask whether, for fixed values of s and ℓ, there are corresponding example languages for all values of k between 2 and $(s-1) \cdot s^{\ell-1}$. Furthermore, we may just consider the degree k of cardinality-restriction for NFAwtws and DFAwtws over a finite alphabet of small cardinality without any regard for length-restriction. Do we obtain infinite strictly ascending hierarchies based on k for a binary alphabet?

To answer this question in the affirmative, we proceed as follows. As before, let $\Sigma_2 = \{a, b\}$, let $k \geq 2$ be an integer, let $\psi_k : \{a, b\}^* \to \mathcal{P}_{\text{fin}}(\{a, b\}^*)$ be the substitution that is defined through

$$a \mapsto \{ a^i b^{k+1-i} \mid 1 \leq i \leq k \} \text{ and } b \mapsto \{b\},$$

and let $L^{(3)}_{k-1} = \psi_k(D_1)$. For the language $L^{(3)}_{k-1}$, we have the following result.

Theorem 4. *For all $k \geq 2$, $L^{(3)}_{k-1} \in \mathcal{L}(k\text{-rDFAwtw}) \smallsetminus \mathcal{L}((k-1)\text{-rNFAwtw})$.*

Proof. Let $k \geq 2$ and let $A_k = (Q_k, \Sigma_2, \lhd, \tau_k, q_0, \{q_0\}, \delta_k)$ be the k-rDFAwtw that is defined by taking $Q_k = \{q_0, q_1, \ldots, q_k, p_2, p_3, \ldots, p_{k+1}\}$ and by defining the functions τ_k and δ_k as follows:

$$\begin{array}{lll}
\tau_k(q_i) & = \emptyset & \text{for all } i = 0, 1, \ldots, k, \\
\tau_k(p_i) & = \emptyset & \text{for all } i = 2, 3, \ldots, k, \\
\tau_k(p_{k+1}) & = \{ a^i b^{k+1-i} \mid 1 \leq i \leq k \} = \psi_k(a), & \\
\delta_k(q_0, a) & = q_1, \quad \delta_k(q_i, a) = q_{i+1}, \delta_k(q_i, b) = p_{i+1} & \text{for all } i = 1, 2, \ldots, k-1, \\
\delta_k(q_k, b) & = p_{k+1}, & \\
\delta_k(p_i, b) & = p_{i+1} \quad \text{for all } i = 2, 3, \ldots, k, \ \delta_k(p_{k+1}, b) = q_0, &
\end{array}$$

where δ_k is undefined for all other pairs from $Q_k \times \Sigma_2$. Then it is easily seen that $L(A_k) = L^{(3)}_{k-1}$. Observe that the DFAwtw A_k is k-cardinality-restricted and $(k+1)$-length-restricted.

It remains to prove that the language $L^{(3)}_{k-1}$ is not accepted by any NFAwtw that is $(k-1)$-cardinality-restricted. Assume to the contrary that $B = (Q, \Sigma_2, \lhd, \tau, I, F, \delta)$ is a $(k-1)$-cardinality-restricted NFAwtw such that $L(B) = L^{(3)}_{k-1}$. For each integer n, the word

$$w_n = (a^k b)^n (a^{k-1} b^2)^n \cdots (ab^k)^n b^{k \cdot n} \in \psi_k(a^{k \cdot n} b^{k \cdot n})$$

belongs to the language $L^{(3)}_{k-1}$, and hence, B has an accepting computation for the input w_n. As we may assume that B reads and deletes its input completely in each of its accepting computations, each accepting computation of B on the input w_n looks as follows:

$$q_0 w_n \cdot \lhd \vdash_B q_1 z_1 \cdot \lhd \vdash_B q_2 z_2 \cdot \lhd \vdash_B \cdots \vdash_B q_t \cdot \lhd \vdash_B \mathsf{Accept},$$

where $q_0 \in I$, $q_1, q_2, \ldots, q_{t-1} \in Q$, $q_t \in F$, and $z_i \in \Sigma_2^*$ is obtained from w_n by deleting i letters for all $i = 1, 2, \ldots, t$. Accordingly, $t = (k+2) \cdot k \cdot n$. We assume that the integer n is sufficiently large.

Claim. If during the first r steps in the above computation, B just reads and deletes the first r letters from left to right, then $r < |Q|$.

Proof. Let the first r steps of the above computation look as follows:

$$\begin{array}{rcl} q_0 w_n \cdot \lhd & = & q_0 (a^k b)^n (a^{k-1} b^2)^n \cdots (ab^k)^n b^{k \cdot n} \cdot \lhd \\ & \vdash_B & q_1 a^{k-1} b (a^k b)^{n-1} (a^{k-1} b^2)^n \cdots (ab^k)^n b^{k \cdot n} \cdot \lhd \\ & \vdash_B & q_2 a^{k-2} b (a^k b)^{n-1} (a^{k-1} b^2)^n \cdots (ab^k)^n b^{k \cdot n} \cdot \lhd \\ & \vdash_B^{r-2} & q_r v (a^k b)^{n-i} (a^{k-1} b^2)^n \cdots (ab^k)^n b^{k \cdot n} \cdot \lhd, \end{array}$$

where $i \geq 1$ such that $(i-1) \cdot (k+1) < r \leq i \cdot (k+1)$, and v is the suffix of $(a^k b)^i$ of length $(k+1) \cdot i - r$. If $r \geq |Q|$, then within the above prefix of the accepting computation of B considered, some state q of B is used twice, that is, there are indices $0 \leq \alpha < \beta \leq |Q|$ such that $q_\alpha = q_\beta$. During the steps $\alpha + 1$ to β, a factor of length $\beta - \alpha$ is deleted from $(a^k b)^i$. If we now insert another copy of this factor into w_n, then B will also accept this new word, which, however, cannot possibly be an element of the language $L^{(3)}_{k-1}$. This contradicts our assumption on B. Accordingly, it follows that $r < |Q|$. □

Hence, in the above computation of B on the input w_n, a transition of the following form is executed after r, $r < |Q|$, many steps:

$$p_1 u x v \cdot \lhd \vdash_B p_2 u v \cdot \lhd,$$

where $p_1, p_2 \in Q$, $x \in \Sigma_2$, $u, v \in \Sigma_2^*$ such that uxv is the suffix of w_n of length $(k+2) \cdot k \cdot n - r$, $p_2 \in \delta(p_1, x)$, and $u \in (\tau(p_1))^+$.

By analyzing the various possibilities for this transitional step, it can now be shown that B either accepts a word that does not belong to the language $L^{(3)}_{k-1}$ or B is not $(k-1)$-cardinality-restricted, contradicting our choice of B. It follows that the language $L^{(3)}_{k-1}$ is not accepted by any NFAwtw that is $(k-1)$-cardinality-restricted. □

Thus, we obtain the following consequence.

Corollary 3. *The degree of cardinality-restriction induces strictly ascending infinite hierarchies of language classes for DFAwtws and for NFAwtws with a binary alphabet.*

The DFAwtw for the language $L^{(3)}_{k-1}$ presented in the proof of Theorem 4 is k-cardinality-restricted and $(k+1)$-length-restricted. When we replace the set $\psi_k(a)$ with a proper subset of itself of cardinality m, then we obtain a language that is m-cardinality-restricted and $(k+1)$-length-restricted. That is, for each value of k, we obtain a finite hierarchy of classes of languages that are accepted by $(k+1)$-length-restricted DFAwtws that is based on the degree of cardinality-restriction. For a fixed value of k, this hierarchy consists of k levels, one for each value of m between 1 and k. Accordingly, we see that the degree ℓ of length-restriction and the degree k of cardinality-restriction yield the following finite hierarchies of classes of binary languages, where $\mathsf{DFAwtw}(2)$ denotes the class of DFWwtws with an alphabet of cardinality two, and analogously for the NFAwtws.

Corollary 4. *For all $\ell \geq 2$,*

$$\mathcal{L}(\ell\text{-lr-1-rDFAwtw}(2)) \subsetneq \mathcal{L}(\ell\text{-lr-2-rDFAwtw}(2)) \subsetneq \cdots \subsetneq \mathcal{L}(\ell\text{-lr-}(\ell-1)\text{-rDFAwtw}(2))$$

and

$$\mathcal{L}(\ell\text{-lr-1-rNFAwtw}(2)) \subsetneq \mathcal{L}(\ell\text{-lr-2-rNFAwtw}(2)) \subsetneq \cdots \subsetneq \mathcal{L}(\ell\text{-lr-}(\ell-1)\text{-rNFAwtw}(2)).$$

In addition, as $L_\vee$ is a binary language that is accepted by a 1-lr-1-rNFAwtw, but not by any DFAwtw, we see that, for each of the above classes, the deterministic class is properly contained in the corresponding nondeterministic class. Finally, we show that there is a family of binary languages such that the degree of cardinality-restriction grows exponentially with the degree of length-restriction.

Definition 4. *Let $\ell \geq 1$, let $\varphi^{(4)}_\ell : \{a,b\}^* \to \{a,b\}^*$ be the substitution that is defined through $a \mapsto \{aw \mid w \in \{a,bb\}^+ \text{ and } |w| = \ell - 1\}$ and $b \mapsto \{b\}$, and let $L^{(4)}_\ell$ be the language $L^{(4)}_\ell = \varphi^{(4)}_\ell(D_1)$.*

For an integer $\ell \geq 1$, let $C'_\ell = \{\, w \in \{a,bb\}^+ \mid |w| = \ell - 1 \,\}$. The set C'_ℓ consists of those words from $\Sigma_2^{\ell-1} = \{a,b\}^{\ell-1}$ for which each block of letters b is of even length. Evidently, $C'_1 = \{\lambda\}$, $C'_2 = \{a\}$, $C'_3 = \{aa, bb\}$, and $C'_4 = \{aaa, abb, bba\}$. Observe that, for $\ell \geq 3$, each word in the set C'_ℓ either starts with an a followed by a word from $C'_{\ell-1}$ or starts with a factor bb followed by a word from $C'_{\ell-2}$. Hence, $|C'_\ell| = |C'_{\ell-1}| + |C'_{\ell-2}|$, $|C'_1| = 1$, $|C'_2| = 1$, and the number of words in C'_ℓ and $\varphi^{(4)}_\ell(a)$ is the ℓ-th Fibonacci number $F_\ell = \frac{\phi^\ell - (1-\phi)^\ell}{\sqrt{5}}$, where $\phi = \frac{1+\sqrt{5}}{2}$.

Theorem 5. *For each integer $\ell \geq 3$,*

$$L^{(4)}_\ell \in \mathcal{L}(\ell\text{-lr-}F_\ell\text{-rDFAwtw}) \setminus \mathcal{L}(\ell\text{-lr-}(F_\ell - 1)\text{-rNFAwtw}).$$

Proof. Let $\ell \geq 3$ be an integer. Since $\varphi^{(4)}_\ell(a)$ is a finite language, there exists a DFA $A^{\mathrm{C}}_\ell = (Q^{\mathrm{C}}_\ell, \Sigma_2, q^{\mathrm{C}}_0, F^{\mathrm{C}}_\ell, \delta^{\mathrm{C}}_\ell)$ for the language $\varphi^{(4)}_\ell(a)$ such that $q^{\mathrm{C}}_0 \notin F^{\mathrm{C}}_\ell$.

The language $L_\ell^{(4)}$ is accepted by the following ℓ-lr-F_ℓ-rDFAwtw $A_\ell^{(4)} = (Q_\ell^{\mathrm{C}}, \Sigma_2, \lhd, \tau_\ell, q_0^{\mathrm{C}}, F_\ell^{\mathrm{C}}, \delta_\ell)$, where the functions τ_ℓ and δ_ℓ are defined as follows:

$$\begin{array}{lll} \tau_\ell(q) & = \emptyset & \text{for all } q \in (Q_\ell^{\mathrm{C}} \smallsetminus F_\ell^{\mathrm{C}}), \\ \tau_\ell(q) & = \varphi_\ell^{(4)}(a) & \text{for all } q \in F_\ell^{\mathrm{C}}, \\ \delta_\ell(q,x) & = \delta_\ell^{\mathrm{C}}(q,x) & \text{for all } q \in (Q_\ell^{\mathrm{C}} \smallsetminus F_\ell^{\mathrm{C}}) \text{ and } x \in \{a,b\}, \\ \delta_\ell(q,b) & = q_0^{\mathrm{C}}, & \text{for all } q \in F_\ell^{\mathrm{C}}. \end{array}$$

Next, we prove that, for all integers $\ell \geq 3$, each ℓ-lr-NFAwtw for the language $L_\ell^{(4)} = \varphi_\ell^{(4)}(D_1)$ has a state with a translucency set of cardinality at least F_ℓ.

Let us explain the idea of the proof. We shall show that any ℓ-length-restricted NFAwtw, on a sufficiently long input word w from $\varphi_\ell^{(4)}(a^n b^n)$, must delete an occurrence of the letter b that is obtained as $\varphi_\ell^{(4)}(b)$ after a 'small' number of steps. To do that, a long factor from $\varphi_\ell^{(4)}(a^n)$ must be translucent for the current state p. We shall show that $\tau_\ell(p)$ is of cardinality at least F_ℓ.

We only consider the case that $\ell \geq 3$ is an odd integer. The case of even ℓ can be dealt with similarly.

Let $B = (Q, \Sigma_2, \lhd, \tau, I, F, \delta)$ be an NFAwtw that is ℓ-length-restricted and $L(B) = L_\ell^{(4)} = \varphi_\ell^{(4)}(D_1)$. Let $z_1, z_2, \ldots, z_{F_\ell}$ be the lexicographically ordered sequence of words from $\varphi_\ell^{(4)}(a)$. Then $z_1 = a^\ell$ and $z_{F_\ell} = ab^{\ell-1}$. For each integer n, the word

$$w_n = (z_1)^n z_{F_\ell} z_{F_\ell-1} z_{F_\ell} z_{F_\ell-2} z_{F_\ell} \cdots z_{F_\ell} z_2 z_{F_\ell} z_1 z_{F_\ell} z_1 b^{n+2F_\ell}$$

belongs to the set $\varphi_\ell^{(4)}\left(a^{n+2F_\ell} b^{n+2F_\ell}\right)$, which is a subset of the language $L_\ell^{(4)}$, and hence, B has an accepting computation for the input w_n. As we may assume that B reads and deletes its input completely in each of its accepting computations, each accepting computation of B on the input w_n looks as follows:

$$q_0 w_n \cdot \lhd \vdash_B q_1 \alpha_1 \cdot \lhd \vdash_B q_2 \alpha_2 \cdot \lhd \vdash_B \cdots \vdash_B q_t \cdot \lhd \vdash_B \mathsf{Accept},$$

where $q_0 \in I$, $q_1, q_2, \ldots, q_{t-1} \in Q$, $q_t \in F$, and $\alpha_i \in \Sigma_2^*$ is obtained from w_n by deleting i letters for all $i = 1, 2, \ldots, t-1$. Accordingly, $t = (n + 2F_\ell) \cdot (\ell + 1)$. We assume that the integer n is sufficiently large.

Claim. If during the first r steps in the above computation, B just reads and deletes the first r letters from left to right, then $r < |Q|$.

Proof. Let the first r steps of the above computation look as follows:

$$\begin{array}{rl} q_0 w_n \cdot \lhd = & q_0 a^{n\ell} z_{F_\ell} z_{F_\ell-1} z_{F_\ell} z_{F_\ell-2} \cdots z_{F_\ell} z_1 z_{F_\ell} z_1 b^{n+2F_\ell} \cdot \lhd \\ \vdash_B & q_1 a^{n\ell-1} z_{F_\ell} z_{F_\ell-1} z_{F_\ell} z_{F_\ell-2} \cdots z_{F_\ell} z_1 z_{F_\ell} z_1 b^{n+2F_\ell} \cdot \lhd \\ \vdash_B & q_2 a^{n\ell-2} z_{F_\ell} z_{F_\ell-1} z_{F_\ell} z_{F_\ell-2} \cdots z_{F_\ell} z_1 z_{F_\ell} z_1 b^{n+2F_\ell} \cdot \lhd \\ \vdash_B^{r-2} & q_r a^{n\ell-r} z_{F_\ell} z_{F_\ell-1} z_{F_\ell} z_{F_\ell-2} \cdots z_{F_\ell} z_1 z_{F_\ell} z_1 b^{n+2F_\ell} \cdot \lhd. \end{array}$$

For a contradiction, let us assume that $r \geq |Q|$. Then, within the above prefix of the accepting computation of B considered, some state q appears at least twice, and there exist indices i_1, i_2, $0 \leq i_1 < i_2 \leq |Q|$, such that $q_{i_1} = q_{i_2}$. Between steps i_1 and i_2, $i_2 - i_1$ occurrences of the letter a are deleted from the prefix of w_n. If we remove this factor from w_n, we obtain a word that does not belong to the language $L_\ell^{(4)}$, but B will accept it anyway – a contradiction. Accordingly, it follows that $r < |Q|$. □

Hence, in the above computation of B on the input w_n, a transition of the following form is executed after r, $r < |Q|$, many steps:

$$q_r uxv \cdot \lhd \vdash_B q_{r+1} uv \cdot \lhd,$$

where $q_r, q_{r+1} \in Q$, $x \in \Sigma_2$, and $u, v \in \Sigma_2^*$ such that uxv is the suffix of w_n of length $(n + 2F_\ell) \cdot (\ell + 1) - r$, $q_{r+1} \in \delta(q_r, x)$, and $u \in (\tau(q_r))^+$.

As n is sufficiently large, u starts with the letter a, therefore, $x = b$ and all words in the set $\tau(q_r)$ start with an a. Evidently, when we commute x and u, we obtain an accepting computation

$$\begin{aligned} q_0 a^r xuv \cdot \lhd \vdash_B^r q_r xuv \cdot \lhd \vdash_B q_{r+1} uv \cdot \lhd = q_{r+1} \alpha_{r+1} \cdot \lhd \\ \vdash_B \cdots \vdash_B q_t \cdot \lhd \vdash_B \mathsf{Accept}. \end{aligned} \tag{1}$$

Assume that $|v| > n + 2F_\ell$. In this case, $x = b$ is a letter that was originally in the prefix of w_n belonging to $\varphi_\ell^{(4)}(a^{n+2F_\ell})$. As (1) is an accepting computation, the automaton B accepts the word $a^r ba^{n\ell - r} \beta b^{n+2F_\ell}$, where the word β is obtained from the word $z_{F_\ell} z_{F_\ell - 1} z_{F_\ell} z_{F_\ell - 2} \cdots z_{F_\ell} z_1 z_{F_\ell} z_1$ by deleting a single occurrence of the letter b. But then β contains a block of letters b of odd length, that is, $a^r ba^{n\ell - r} \beta b^{n+2F_\ell}$ is not in $L_\ell^{(4)}$. Therefore, the letter x is from the suffix b^{n+2F_ℓ} of w_n and there exists some $s \geq 0$ such that

$$u = a^{n\ell - r} z_{F_\ell} z_{F_\ell - 1} z_{F_\ell} z_{F_\ell - 2} \cdots z_{F_\ell} z_1 z_{F_\ell} z_1 b^s$$

is in $(\tau(q_r))^*$.

Since all words in $\tau(q_r)$ start with an a and are of length at most ℓ, the word $z_{F_\ell} = ab^{\ell - 1} \in \varphi_\ell^{(4)}(a)$ must be in $\tau(q_r)$. As $\tau(q_r)$ is prefix-free, no prefix of the word $ab^{\ell - 1}$ is contained in $\tau(q_r)$. In particular, a is not in $\tau(q_r)$.

For each $i = 1, 2, \ldots, F_\ell - 1$, the word u contains a factor of the form

$$z_{F_\ell} \cdot z_i \cdot z_{F_\ell} = ab^{\ell - 1} \cdot z_i \cdot ab^{\ell - 1}.$$

The length of the words in $\tau(q_r)$ is limited by ℓ. Thus, both occurrences of z_{F_ℓ} in this factor must be 'covered' with the word z_{F_ℓ} from $\tau(q_r)$ and, hence, z_i belongs to $(\tau(q_r))^+$.

Recall that z_i can contain blocks of letters b of even length only. Let z_i contain just a single block of letters b of length $\ell - 3$. There are only three such words in $\varphi_\ell^{(4)}(a)$, namely $ab^{\ell-3}aa$, $aab^{\ell-3}a$ and $aaab^{\ell-3}$. The words a and $ab^{\ell-3}$ are prefixes of z_{F_ℓ} from $\tau(q_r)$. Therefore, $ab^{\ell-3}aa$, $aab^{\ell-3}a$, and $aaab^{\ell-3}$ must all be in $\tau(q_r)$. Additionally, the prefixes aa and aaa of $aaab^{\ell-3}$ cannot be in $\tau(q_r)$.

Let z_i contain the factor $b^{\ell-5}$. There are only five such words (assuming $\ell \geq 7$) in $\varphi_\ell^{(4)}(a)$, namely $ab^{\ell-5}a^4$, $aab^{\ell-5}a^3$, $a^3b^{\ell-5}a^2$, $a^4b^{\ell-5}a$, and $a^5b^{\ell-5}$.

These words are in $(\tau(q_r))^+$, but the words a, aa, aaa, $ab^{\ell-5}$, $aab^{\ell-5}$, and $aaab^{\ell-5}$ are all prefixes of words from $\tau(q_r)$. Therefore, the words $ab^{\ell-5}a^4$, $aab^{\ell-5}a^3$, $a^3b^{\ell-5}a^2$, $a^4b^{\ell-5}a$, and $a^5b^{\ell-5}$ must all be in $\tau(q_r)$.

By induction on the length j of a block of letters b, for $j = \ell-1, \ell-3, \ldots, 2$, we can show that all words from $\varphi_\ell^{(4)}(a)$ that contain a single block of letters b are in $\tau(q_r)$ and none of their prefixes is in $\tau(q_r)$.

Furthermore, we can show that, for $i = 2, 3, \ldots, \ell-1$, if z_i contains two blocks of letters b, then z_i is in $\tau(q_r)$. Assume that $z_i = a^{i_1}b^{2j_1}a^{i_2}b^{2j_2}a^{i_3}$ for some integers $i_1, i_2, j_1, j_2 \geq 1$, $i_3 \geq 0$, and $i_1 + 2j_1 + i_2 + 2j_2 + i_3 = \ell$. As $z_i \in (\tau(q_r))^+$ and $a^{i_1}b^{2j_1}a^{i_2}$ is a prefix of some word in $\tau(q_r)$ containing a single block of letters b, the word $a^{i_1}b^{2j_1}a^{i_2}b^{2j_2}$ must be a prefix of a word from $\tau(q_r)$. If $i_1 + 2j_1 + i_2 + 2j_2 = \ell$, then $a^{i_1}b^{2j_1}a^{i_2}b^{2j_2} = z_i$ must be in $\tau(q_r)$. Otherwise, $i_3 > 0$ and $a, a^2, \ldots, a^{i_3}$ are prefixes of $a^{\ell-2}bb$ already proved to be in $\tau(q_r)$. Therefore, also in this case, z_i must be in $\tau(q_r)$.

Similarly, we can show that all z_i containing at least one block of letters b must belong to $\tau(q_r)$. Finally, as $a^{\ell-2}bb$ is in $\tau(q_r)$ and u starts with a long prefix containing just letters a, $\tau(q_r)$ cannot contain any word a^y where $y \leq \ell-2$. Thus, $\tau(q_r)$ must contain a word of the form a^y for some integer $y > \ell-2$ and $z_1 = a^\ell$ is in $(\tau(q_r))^*$, that is, z_1 must be in $\tau(q_r)$.

Altogether, we have shown that all words from $\varphi_\ell^{(4)}(a)$ are in $\tau(q_r)$ and, hence, the degree of cardinality-restriction of the automaton B is at least $|\varphi_\ell^{(4)}(a)| = F_\ell$. This completes the proof in the case $\ell \geq 3$ is odd. □

5 Conclusion

We have shown that the degree ℓ of length-restriction and the degree k of cardinality-restriction induce an infinite two-dimensional hierarchy for (deterministic and nondeterministic) finite automata with translucent words. In addition, the parameter ℓ induces a strictly ascending hierarchy of $\ell-1$ levels of classes of binary languages for each value $\ell \geq 2$. However, the theoretical upper bound of $2^{\ell-1}$ for the degree of cardinality-restriction of an ℓ-length-restricted finite automaton with translucent words over a binary alphabet has not yet been attained. It remains the question of whether we can actually derive a finer hierarchy with respect to the degree of cardinality-restriction for classes of binary languages that are specified by ℓ-length-restricted finite automata with translucent words, a hierarchy with more than just a linear number of levels. Moreover, what is the number of levels we can actually obtain for the corresponding hierarchies when we employ a ternary alphabet?

References

1. Aalbersberg, I.J., Rozenberg, G.: Theory of traces. Theoret. Comput. Sci. **60**, 1–82 (1988). https://doi.org/10.1016/0304-3975(88)90051-5

2. Diekert, V., Rozenberg, G.: The Book of Traces. World Scientific, Singapore (1995). https://doi.org/10.1142/2563
3. Nagy, B., Otto, F.: Finite-state acceptors with translucent letters. In: Bel-Enguix, G., Dahl, V., De La Puente, A.O. (eds.) BILC 2011: AI Methods for Interdisciplinary Research in Language and Biology, Proc., pp. 3–13. SciTePress, Portugal (2011)
4. Nagy, B., Otto, F.: Globally deterministic CD-systems of stateless R(1)-automata. In: Dediu, A.H., Inenaga, S., Martín-Vide, C. (eds.) Language and Automata Theory and Applications, LATA 2011, Proc., Lecture Notes in Computer Science, vol. 6638, pp. 390–401. Springer, Berlin (2011). https://doi.org/10.1007/978-3-642-21254-3_31
5. Nagy, B., Otto, F.: Globally deterministic CD-systems of stateless R-automata with window size 1. Int. J. Comput. Math. **90**, 1254–1277 (2013). https://doi.org/10.1080/00207160.2012.688820
6. Nagy, B., Otto, F.: Finite automata with sets of translucent words. In: Day, J.D., Manea, F. (eds.) DLT 2024, Proc., pp. 236–251. Lecture Notes in Computer Science 14791, Springer, Cham, Switzerland (2024). https://doi.org/10.1007/978-3-031-66159-4_17
7. Nagy, B., Otto, F.: A two-dimensional infinite hierarchy for finite automata with translucent words (2024). submitted
8. Otto, F.: Restarting Automata – Extensions and Generalizations. Theory and Applications of Computability, Springer, Cham, Switzerland (2025). https://doi.org/10.1007/978-3-031-78701-0

What is the Most Natural Generalized Pumping Lemma beyond Regular and Context-Free Languages?

Tomoyuki Yamakami(✉)

Faculty of Engineering, University of Fukui, 3-9-1 Bunkyo, Fukui 910-8507, Japan
tomoyukiyamakami@gmail.com

Abstract. One of the most useful properties of regular and context-free languages is the well-known pumping lemmas of Bar-Hillel, Perles, Shamir [1] in 1961. In this work, we consider their most natural generalization for languages beyond regular and context-free languages. In fact, we prove that languages recognized by one-way nondeterministic depth-k storage automata (or k-sna's) satisfy such a generalization for every positive integer k. As a direct application of this generalized pumping lemma, we demonstrate a separation of the complexity classes of languages recognized by k-sna's for different positive integers k. This result instantly implies that those complexity classes form truly infinite hierarchies.

Keywords: pumping lemma · context-free language · storage automata · depth-bounded · kSNA

1 A Historical Account and an Overview of Contributions

1.1 Pumping Properties of Regular and Context-Free Languages and Their Natural Generalizations

The extra use of *memory devices* is a key to empower the functionality of finite automata. A (pushdown) stack is a classic memory device for storing data necessary for an underlying automaton to perform its complex computation. Such a machine is known as a *pushdown automaton* and its nondeterministic variant characterizes a *context-free language*. We write CFL for the collection of all context-free languages. One of the most important and useful properties of context-free languages is the property known as the *pumping lemma for CFL*, proven first by Bar-Hillel, Perles, Shamir [1] in 1961, in which we can "pump" two correlated portions of any given input string simultaneously any number of times with preserving the membership of the resulting string to a target language. This pumping property is a useful technical tool in proving the non-context-freeness of various languages. The notation ε denotes the empty string.

[Pumping Lemma for CFL] Given an infinite language L in CFL, there exists a constant $c > 0$ (known as the *pumping length*) that satisfies the following statement: for any input w in L of length more than c, there exists a series of

Published by Springer Nature Switzerland AG 2025
A. Malcher and L. Prigioniero (Eds.): DCFS 2025, LNCS 15759, pp. 196–210, 2025.
https://doi.org/10.1007/978-3-031-97100-6_14

strings x, y, z, u, v such that (1) $w = xyzuv$, (2) $yu \neq \varepsilon$, (3) $|yzu| \leq c$, and (4) for any integer $i \geq 0$, the string $w^{(i)} = xy^i zu^i v$ also belongs to L.

A similar but weak form of pumping lemma also holds for the class REG of all *regular languages* derived by finite automata.

[Pumping Lemma for REG] Given an infinite language L in REG, there exists a constant $c > 0$ that satisfies the following statement: for any input w in L of length more than c, there exists a series of strings x, y, z such that (1) $w = xyz$, (2) $y \neq \varepsilon$, (3) $|xy| \leq c$, and (4) for any integer $i \geq 0$, the string $w^{(i)} = xy^i z$ also belongs to L.

Let us seek for a natural generalization of the above two pumping lemmas for REG and CFL. In the first lemma, two correlated substrings, y and u, of an input string w are pumped; in the second lemma, one substring, y, of w is pumped. It thus seems quite natural for us to expand the number of iterated substrings of w in (2) and (4) from "two strings" in the first lemma and "one string" in the second lemma to more general "k strings" for any fixed integer $k \geq 2$. Associated with such a number k, we denote by $\mathcal{C}_k$ an appropriately chosen class of languages beyond context-free languages. The generalized pumping property for $\mathcal{C}_k$ is then stated as follows. Let $[k] = \{1, 2, \ldots, k\}$ for any integer $k \geq 1$.

[Generalized Pumping Property for $\mathcal{C}_k$] Given an infinite language L in $\mathcal{C}_k$, there exists a constant $c > 0$ that satisfies the following statement: for any input w in L of length more than c, there exists a series of strings $z_1, z_2, \ldots, z_k, y_1, y_2, \ldots, y_{k+1}$ such that (1) $w = y_1 z_1 y_2 z_2 y_3 \ldots, y_k z_k y_{k+1}$, (2) $z_1 z_2 \cdots z_k \neq \varepsilon$, (3) $|z_j y_{j+1} z_{j+1}| \leq c$ for an appropriate index $j \in [k-1]$, and (4) for any integer $i \geq 0$, the string $w^{(i)} = y_1 z_1^i y_2 z_2^i y_3 \ldots, y_k z_k^i y_{k+1}$ also belongs to L. (When $k = 1$, we should set $j = 0$ and $z_j = \varepsilon$.)

In the above generalized pumping property, nonetheless, unknown is the exact description of the complexity class $\mathcal{C}_k$. When $k = 1, 2$, in particular, $\mathcal{C}_1$ and $\mathcal{C}_2$ can be replaced by REG and CFL because the generalized pumping properties for $\mathcal{C}_1$ and $\mathcal{C}_2$ are identical to the pumping lemmas for REG and CFL, respectively. From this fact, we wish to raise the following crucial question.

Open Problem 1. What kind of a complexity class $\mathcal{C}_k$ satisfies the above generalized pumping property?

As an answer to this natural and also important question, we wish to look into the recently introduced machine model of so-called *storage automata* [11–13].

1.2 Depth-Bounded Storage Automata as a Solution

Lately, depth-bounded *storage automata* have been studied in [11–13] as a natural extension of pushdown automata and Hibbard's limited automata [5] and also as a reasonable modification of stack automata [3,4]. Each storage automaton is equipped with a one-way read-only input tape and a two-way rewritable storage tape. On this storage tape, however, its tape head should revise the content of each tape cell during the first k visits but the tape cell must be *frozen blank* forever after the k visits. Such a machine is said to have *depth k*. This specific machine may model a physical abrasion of a hard disc by frequent access to data stored in each disc cell. Deterministic depth-k storage automata (or k-sda's, for short) were discussed in [11] and nondeterministic ones (or k-sna's) were studied in [12,13] in connection to a new circuit model called *cascading circuits*. A recent progress is found in [14].

Although k-sna's resemble to Hibbard's limited automata, the computational power of k-sna's are significantly higher than that of the limited automata. This partly comes from the fact that Hibbard's nondeterministic k-limited automata are merely as powerful as one-way nondeterministic pushdown automata (or 1npda's) but k-sna's can recognize non-context-free languages if $k \geq 3$. Various restrictions have been introduced to control the changes of input-tape heads and inner states. A *depth-susceptible* k-sda cannot move its input-tape head while reading any storage symbols that have been already revised at least $k-1$ times and, in particular, when reading the frozen blank symbol, inner states of the k-sna cannot be altered. It was proven that the language family characterized by k-sda's, denoted kSDA, is contained in SC^k (i.e., the kth level of Steve's class) [11] and, furthermore, its nondeterministic variant, denoted kSNA, is contained in NSC^k (i.e., the nondeterministic variant of SC^k) [13].

For a small number k, it was shown in [11] that 1SDA and 2SDA respectively coincide with REG and DCFL (deterministic context-free language class), provided that underlying 2-sda's are depth-susceptible. This result was updated in [13] to the case where underlying 2-sda's are frozen blank sensitive, where a *frozen blank sensitive* k-sda cannot move its input-tape head while reading the frozen blank symbol. Similarly, restricted to frozen blank sensitive k-sna's, 1SNA and 2SNA respectively match REG and CFL. These facts instantly suggest that kSNA is a natural generalization of REG and CFL.

Here is our solution to Open Problem 1.

(Our Solution) The complexity class $\mathcal{C}_k$ given in the generalized pumping property is replaceable by kSNA, provided that underlying k-sna's are all frozen blank sensitive.

For clarity, hereafter, we explicitly write $k\mathrm{SDA}_{FBS}$ and $k\mathrm{SNA}_{FBS}$ when underlying k-sda's and k-sna's are assumed to be frozen blank sensitive. Moreover, the notations $\omega\mathrm{SDA}_{FBS}$ and $\omega\mathrm{SNA}_{FBS}$ denote the infinite unions $\bigcup_{k\geq 1} k\mathrm{SDA}_{FBS}$ and $\bigcup_{k\geq 1} k\mathrm{SNA}_{FBS}$, respectively.

We further seek direct applications of the generalized pumping property for $\mathcal{C}_k = k$SNA. This property further leads to a new result in Sect. 3 on the difference between kSNA and $(k+1)$SNA for each positive number $k \geq 1$. Figure 1 summarizes the main results of this work.

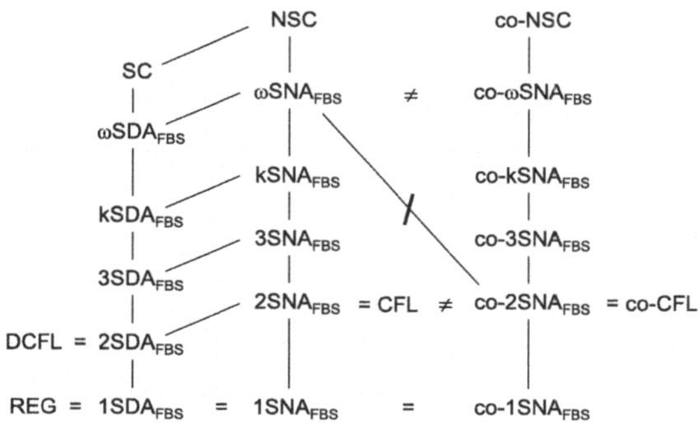

Fig. 1. Three infinite hierarchies of complexity classes of languages recognized by k-sna's and k-sda's, where k stands for an arbitrary positive integer. Each solid line indicates a proper inclusion of a lower class by an upper class whereas $\not\subseteq$ indicates the non-inclusion relationship.

2 Fundamental Notions and Notation

2.1 Numbers, Alphabets, and Languages

For natural numbers (including 0), we use the notation $\mathbb{N}$ to denote the set of all such numbers. When we are interested only in positive numbers, we use the notation $\mathbb{N}^+$, namely, $\mathbb{N}^+ = \mathbb{N} - \{0\}$. Given two integers m, n with $m \leq n$, the notation $[m, n]_{\mathbb{Z}}$ expresses the *integer interval* $\{m, m+1, m+2, \ldots, n\}$. As a special case of $n \geq 1$, $[1, n]_{\mathbb{Z}}$ is abbreviated as $[n]$. Given a set S, the notation $\mathcal{P}(S)$ denotes the *power set* of S.

We write ε for the *empty string* of length 0. For a nonempty string u and a number $j \in [|u|]$, the notation $u[j]$ denotes the jth symbol of u. Given strings u and w, u is called a *substring* of w, denoted $u \sqsubseteq w$, if there are two strings z_1 and z_2 for which $w = z_1 u z_2$. Given a string u, the notation u^R stands for the *reverse* of u.

2.2 Depth-k Storage Automata

We review the existing terminology of [11–13]. A *depth-k nondeterministic storage automaton* (abbreviated as a *k-sna*) is a octuple $(Q, \Sigma, \{\triangleright, \triangleleft\}, \{\Gamma^{(e)}\}_{e \in [0,k]_{\mathbb{Z}}}, q_0, \delta, Q_{acc}, Q_{rej})$, where Q is a finite set of inner states, Σ is an alphabet, $\Gamma^{(e)}$ is a storage alphabet of depth e with $\Gamma^{(0)} = \{\Box\}$ and $\Gamma^{(k)} = \{\triangleright, B\}$, $\Box$ is the initial blank symbol, B is the *frozen blank symbol*, $\triangleright$ and $\triangleleft$ are designated endmarkers, q_0 is the initial (inner) state, δ is a transition function, Q_{acc} and Q_{rej} are sets of accepting (inner) states and rejecting (inner) states, respectively. We demand that $\Gamma^{(e)} \cap \Gamma^{(f)} = \varnothing$ for any distinct pair $e, f \in [0, k]_{\mathbb{Z}}$. Initially, an input tape contains $\triangleright x \triangleleft$, where x is a given input string over Σ to process. A *storage tape* is a semi-infinite tape whose cells are indexed by natural numbers, starting with $\triangleright$ in the leftmost cell indexed 0. Initially, the storage tape consists of $\Box$ in all other tape cells.

The *transition function* δ maps $(Q - Q_{halt}) \times \check{\Sigma} \times \Gamma$ to $\mathcal{P}(Q \times \Gamma \times D_1 \times D_2)$, where $Q_{halt} = Q_{acc} \cup Q_{rej}$, $\check{\Sigma} = \Sigma \cup \{\triangleright, \triangleleft\}$, $\Gamma = \bigcup_{e \in [0,k]_{\mathbb{Z}}} \Gamma^{(e)}$, $D_1 = \{0, +1\}$, and $D_2 = \{-1, 0, +1\}$. A transition $(p, \xi, d_1, d_2) \in \delta(q, \sigma, \tau)$ means that, when M reads σ on the input tape and τ on the storage tape in state q, M changes q to p, replace τ with ξ, and move its input-tape head and storage-tape head in directions d_1 and d_2, respectively, where "-1" and "$+1$" respectively indicate "move to the left" and "move to the right", and "0" does "stay still" (or "make a stationary move"). It is useful to distinguish between two kinds of stationary moves of the storage-tape head. When the storage-tape head has moved to the current tape cell and stays still at the next step, we call this last move an *intrinsic stationary move.* On the contrary, the storage-tape head has stayed still and further makes a stationary move, we call the last move an *extrinsic stationary move.*

A *left turn* (resp., a *right turn*) of a tape head at tape cell t means the following consecutive moves of the tape head: it moves to cell t from the left (resp., the right) and it then moves from cell t to the left (resp., the right). A *turn* refers to either a left turn or a right turn. A *frozen blank turn* indicates a turn while reading the frozen blank symbol B.

Each k-sna M must satisfy the following two requirements.

(i) (depth-k requirement) when $e < k$, if M makes a turn, then M should replace τ with another symbol $\xi \in \Gamma^{(\min\{e+2,k\})}$; in contrast, if M moves forward to a neighboring tape cell, then M should change τ to $\xi \in \Gamma^{(\min\{e+1,k\})}$.

(ii) (stationary-move requirement) when $e < k$ and $d_2 = 0$, if M makes an intrinsic stationary move, then it should replace the content of tape cell from τ to a symbol ξ in $\Gamma^{(\min\{e+1,k\})}$; in contrast, if M makes an extrinsic stationary move, then M should maintain τ on the current tape cell.

We say that M *accepts* (resp., *rejects*) x if M starts with $\triangleright x \triangleleft$ on the input tape and halts in accepting states (resp., rejecting states) on at least one computation path (resp., on all computation paths) of M on x. Two machines M and N are said to be *computationally equivalent* if (i) M and N have the same input alphabet and (ii) for any input x, M accepts (resp., rejects) x iff N accepts (resp., rejects) x. For convenience, we write $L(M)$ for the set of all input strings accepted by M.

A k-sna M is said to be *frozen blank sensitive* if, while reading the frozen blank symbol B on a storage tape, M's input-tape head does not move (i.e., makes an input-stationary move). In what follows, the notation $k\mathrm{SNA}_{FBS}$ denotes the collection of all languages recognized by frozen-blank-sensitive k-sna's. A k-sna M is *weakly depth-susceptible* if the input-tape head cannot move while reading any symbol in $\Gamma^{(k)}$ and inner states do not alter while reading B. A k-sna M is said to be *right-turn restricted* if, for any input x and on any computation path of M on x, M makes right turns no more than once at each storage-tape cell.

Lemma 2. [13, Lemmas 2.5 & 3.5] *If a k-sna M is frozen blank sensitive, then there exists another k-sna N such that N is computationally equivalent to M, is weakly depth-susceptible, makes no frozen blank turn, and is right-turn restricted.*

The deterministic variants of k-sna's and kSNA are succinctly called "k-sda's" and kSDA. See [11] for their basic properties. The notation $\omega\mathrm{SNA}_{FBS}$ denotes the infinite union $\bigcup_{k\geq 1} k\mathrm{SNA}_{FBS}$. Similarly, $\omega\mathrm{SDA}_{FBS}$ is defined.

3 Generalized Pumping Lemma for $k\mathrm{SNA}_{FBS}$ and Its Quick Applications

We resolve Open Problem 1 by proving the generalized pumping property for $\mathcal{C}_k = k\mathrm{SNA}_{FBS}$. Hereafter, we fix k in $\mathbb{N}^+$.

Theorem 3. *For each $k \in \mathbb{N}^+$, the generalized pumping property holds for $\mathcal{C}_k = k\mathrm{SNA}_{FBS}$.*

Before proving this theorem, we plan to demonstrate how to apply it in the context of kSDA and kSNA.

Theorem 4. *For each number $k \geq 1$, $(k+1)\mathrm{SDA}_{FBS} \nsubseteq k\mathrm{SNA}_{FBS}$ holds.*

To verify Theorem 4, let us consider the set of flipped strings (or the set of "marked" even-length palindromes), $2\text{-}FLIP = \{w\#w^R \mid w \in \{0,1\}^*\}$. Obviously, $2\text{-}FLIP$ belongs to DCFL. Since $2\mathrm{SDA}_{FBS} = \mathrm{DCFL}$ [13], $2\text{-}FLIP$ is also in $2\mathrm{SDA}_{FBS}$. Next, we wish to expand $2\text{-}FLIP$ to $k\text{-}FLIP$ for every number $k \geq 2$. Given a string w and a number $k \in \mathbb{N}$, the notation $w_{[k]}$ expresses the string of the form $(w\#w^R\#)^l w$ if $k = 2l+1$ and $(w\#w^R\#)^l w\#w^R$ if $k = 2l+2$. For instance, we obtain $w_{[1]} = w$, $w_{[2]} = w\#w^R$, $w_{[3]} = w\#w^R\#w$, $w_{[4]} = w\#w^R\#w\#w^R$, and $w_{[5]} = w\#w^R\#w\#w^R\#w$.

k-Flipped Strings Problem ($k\text{-}FLIP$)

○ **instance:** a string $x \in \{0,1,\#\}^*$.
○ **question:** is it true that x has the form $w_{[k]}$ for an appropriate string w?

Proof Sketch of Theorem 4. The case of $k = 1$ follows from the fact that $1\mathrm{SNA}_{FBS} = \mathrm{REG}$ and $2\mathrm{SDA}_{FBS} = \mathrm{DCFL}$ [13]. In what follows, we thus fix $k \geq 2$ and consider $(k+1)\text{-}FLIP$. Since $(k+1)\text{-}FLIP \in (k+1)\mathrm{SDA}_{FBS}$, it suffices to prove that no k-sna recognizes $(k+1)\text{-}FLIP$. Assuming otherwise, we take a string s of the form 0^c1^c and define w to be $s_{[k+1]}$.

By Theorem 3, there are a pumping length $c > 0$ and a series of substrings $z_1, z_2, \ldots, z_k, y_1, y_2, \ldots, y_{k+1}$ of w satisfying Conditions (1)–(4) of the generalized pumping property with $w = y_1z_1y_2z_2\ldots, y_kz_ky_{k+1}$ in $(k+1)\text{-}FLIP$. Note that, for every number $i \in \mathbb{N}$, $w^{(i)} = y_1z_1^iy_2z_2^i\ldots, y_kz_k^iy_{k+1}$ always belongs to $(k+1)\text{-}FLIP$. Because of the presence of $\#$ in $(k+1)\text{-}FLIP$, no z_j contains $\#$. Hence, for each index $i \in [k]$, either $z_i \sqsubseteq s$ or $z_i \sqsubseteq s^R$ holds. This implies that at least one of the segments (either s or s^R) of $s_{[k+1]}$ contains none of z_j's because there are $k+1$ segments in $(k+1)\text{-}FLIP$. However, this is a contradiction with $w^{(i)} \in (k+1)\text{-}FLIP$. Therefore, $(k+1)\text{-}FLIP$ cannot belong to $k\mathrm{SNA}_{FBS}$.

Theorem 5. co-CFL $\nsubseteq \omega$SNA$_{FBS}$.

Proof Sketch. We succinctly write ω-$FLIP$ for the infinite unions of k-$FLIP$ for all $k \in \mathbb{N}^+$. Firstly, we prove that ω-$FLIP$ is in co-CFL. Consider the following machine. For any input x, we assume that x is of the form $u_1\#u_2\#\cdots\#u_n$ for binary strings $u_1, u_2, \ldots, u_n$. The checking of this form can be done by an appropriate finite automaton. We then universally choose u_i and u_{i+1} for all $i \in [n-1]$ and check if $u_{i+1} = u_i^R$ using a stack. If all computation paths terminate in accepting states, then we accept x; otherwise, we reject it. This machine determines whether x is in ω-$FLIP$. Hence, ω-$FLIP$ belongs to co-CFL.

It thus suffices to verify that ω-$FLIP \notin k$SNA for all numbers $k \geq 1$. It is rather easy to show that ω-$FLIP \notin$ REG ($=$ 1SNA$_{FBS}$), and thus we assume that $k \geq 2$. Toward a contradiction, we assume that ω-$FLIP \in k$SNA$_{FBS}$ for a certain index $k \geq 2$. Take a k-sna M such that $L(M) = \omega$-$FLIP$. We define $C = \{z_1\#z_2\#\cdots\#z_{k+1} \mid, z_1, z_2, \ldots, z_{k+1} \in \{0,1\}^*\}$. It follows that $(k+1)$-$FLIP = L(M) \cap C$. Since $C \in$ REG, there is another k-sna N satisfying $L(N) = L(M) \cap C$. This implies that $(k+1)$-$FLIP$ belongs to kSNA$_{FBS}$, a contradiction. Therefore, we conclude that ω-$FLIP \notin \omega$SNA$_{FBS}$.

Corollary 6. *For every* $k \geq 1$, kSDA$_{FBS} \neq (k+1)$SDA$_{FBS}$ *and* kSNA$_{FBS} \neq (k+1)$SNA$_{FBS}$ *hold.*

Proof Sketch. Since ωSDA$_{FBS} \subseteq \omega$SNA$_{FBS}$, if ωSDA$_{FBS} = \omega$SNA$_{FBS}$, then we obtain ωSNA$_{FBS} = \omega$SDA$_{FBS} =$ co-ωSDA$_{FBS} \subseteq$ co-ωSNA$_{FBS}$. This implies ωSNA$_{FBS} \subseteq$ co-ωSNA$_{FBS}$, which is equivalent to co-ωSNA$_{FBS} \subseteq \omega$SNA$_{FBS}$. It then follows that co-CFL $\subseteq \omega$SNA$_{FBS}$ because of co-CFL $\subseteq$ co-ωSNA$_{FBS}$. This is a contradiction with Theorem 5. We thus conclude that ωSDA$_{FBS} \neq \omega$SNA$_{FBS}$.

4 Proof of the Generalized Pumping Lemma for kSNA$_{FBS}$

A standard proof of the pumping lemma for CFL is carried out by the exclusive use of context-free grammars (see textbooks, e.g., [6]). Unlike CFL, no formal grammars are known at present to characterize languages in kSNA, and therefore the intended proof of Theorem 3 requires a completely different strategy.

4.1 Normal Form

We first transform each k-sna into a specified form, called *normal form*. For this purpose, let us recall Lemma 2 and then enforce an additional condition to this lemma. A k-sna M is said to be *one-turn restricted* if, along every computation path of M on each input, M must make at most one turn at any tape cell.

Lemma 7. *If a k-sna is frozen blank sensitive, then there exists another k-sna N such that N is computationally equivalent to M, is weakly depth-susceptible, makes no frozen blank turn, and is one-turn restricted.*

Proof Sketch. We expand the proof of Lemma 2, which is given in [13]. Let M denote any frozen-blank-sensitive k-sna. Our starting point is a modification of this k-sna by applying Lemma 2 to another one, say, M', which is weakly depth-susceptible, makes no frozen blank turn, and is right-turn restricted. We further modify M' to the desired k-sna N by keeping all these properties and by additionally enforcing the one-turn restriction. A basic idea is to transform each tape cell c of M to a "block" $(c', c_k, c_{k-1}, \ldots, c_1)$ of $k+1$ tape cells of N in the way that cell c' records the symbol modified when the storage-tape head makes a left turn at cell c and each cell c_i records the symbol modified by the tape head when it passes through or makes a right turn. Using N's inner states, it is possible to identify each block of $k+1$ cells on the storage tape by repeatedly counting from 1 to $k+1$ internally.

More precisely, let us consider the case where M's storage-tape head visits cell c for the ith time ($i \in [2, k-3]_{\mathbb{Z}}$) from the left and overwrites τ. When M makes a left turn, N (i) visits tape cell c', (ii) overwrites τ, and (iii) makes a left turn to the adjacent block. Although cells $c_k, \ldots, c_1$ are not altered, this does not affect the result of the entire computation. In contrast, when M passes through cell c, N (i′) visits $c', c_k, c_{k-1}, \ldots, c_1$ in this order, (ii′) overwrites τ on cells $c', c_k, c_{k-1}, \ldots, c_{i+1}$ and Bs on cells $c_i, c_{i-1}, \ldots, c_1$, and (iii′) moves rightward to the next block.

Next, let us consider the case where M's storage-tape head visits cell c for the ith time from the right and writes τ over $\sigma \in \Gamma^{(i)}$. We examine two subcases: (a) M makes a right turn at this cell and (b) M passes through the cell. The behaviors of N is in essence similar to the previous case.

Finally, we examine the case where M's storage-tape head visits a cell for the first time. Assume that M visits cell c holding the initial blank symbol $\Box$ and changes it to σ. When M further makes a left turn, N visits cell c', changes $\Box$ to σ, and makes a left turn. On the contrary, when M passes through cell c to the next initially blank cell, then N changes the content of cells $c', c_k, c_{k-1}, \ldots, c_1$ in this order from $\Box$ to σ and then moves to the next block.

For convenience, we succinctly say that a k-sna M is *in normal form* whenever M satisfies the three conditions of Lemma 7. By adding extra steps of moving the storage-tape head back and forth between the leftmost tape cell and the rightmost non-$\Box$ tape cell, we can force each k-sna to make all storage-tape cells (except for the leftmost and the rightmost ones) frozen blank without violating the normal form condition. We refer to this additional frozen-blank requirement as "halting with frozen-blank cells".

4.2 Necessary Terminology for the Proof

Before starting the actual proof, we intend to describe various terminology necessary to use in the proof. Our k-sna's are a generalization of 1npda's, and thus we wish to adapt the existing terminology, which is introduced and discussed in [7,8,10] to analyze the behaviors of 1npda's and their deterministic counterparts. Let $M = (Q, \Sigma, \{\triangleright, \triangleleft\}, \{\Gamma^{(e)}\}_{e\in[0,k]_{\mathbb{Z}}}, q_0, \delta, Q_{acc}, Q_{rej})$ be any k-sna.

A single application of δ induces a single step of M. For later convenience, we visualize each step of M as a sequence of the following four consecutive actions: (i) firstly, changing the content of the currently scanned storage-tape cell, (ii) secondly, updating the current inner state, (iii) thirdly, either moving the storage-tape head or making it stay still, and (iv) lastly, either moving the input-tape head or making it stay still.

To make our intended proof simpler, we intend to treat "ε" as a special input symbol, which expresses the "absence" of symbols. Formally, we set Σ_ε to be the *extended alphabet* $\Sigma \cup \{\varepsilon\}$. An *$\varepsilon$-enhanced string* is a string over Σ_ε. The notation $|x|_\varepsilon$ is used to express the *length* of such an ε-enhanced string x, whereas $|x|$ denotes the length of the string x after deleting all ε's from x. An *ε-enhanced k-sna* (or an ε-k-sna, for short) is a k-sna working over Σ_ε. The use of such an ε-enhanced string makes an ε-k-sna "one way" with no stationary moves of the input-tape head.

Lemma 8. *For any k-sna M, there exists a one-way ε-k-sna N with no input stationary move such that, for any input string x, there is an appropriate ε-enhanced string $\hat{x}$ for which (1) x is obtainable by deleting all ε's from $\hat{x}$ and (2) M accepts (resp., rejects) x iff N accepts (resp., rejects) $\hat{x}$. Moreover, $\hat{x}$ is uniquely determined from x, M, and a specified computation path of M on x. In this case, $\hat{x}$ is said to be induced from x and M.*

In what follows, we consider a one-way ε-k-sna M.

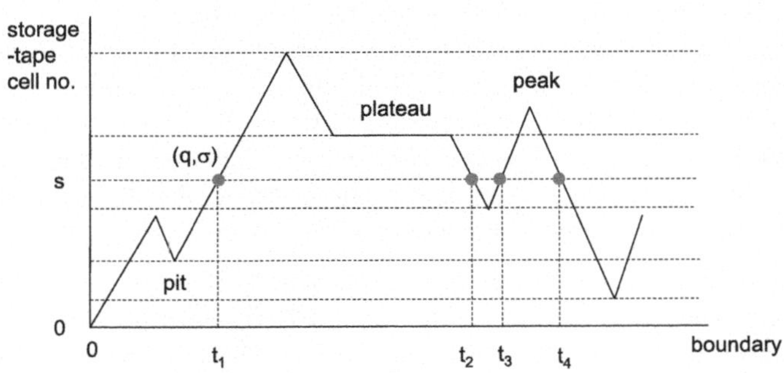

Fig. 2. An example of a transition history of a fixed computation path of M on input w. The point (s, t_1) in the graph has state-storage pair (q, σ) as its value (or its "label"). The numbers t_1, t_2, t_3, t_4 are hitting positions at s.

A *boundary* indicates a borderline between two adjacent tape cells (except for the leftmost tape cell). Boundary 0 is the left borderline of the leftmost input-tape cell (i.e., cell 0) and boundary $t + 1$ ($t \geq 0$) is located between cell t and cell $t+1$. A *boundary block* between two boundaries t_1 and t_2 with $t_1 < t_2$, denoted $[t_1, t_2]$, is a sequence of consecutive boundaries from t_1 to t_2, including t_1 and t_2. The term "(t_1, t_2)-region" refers to a tape area composed of all consecutive input-tape cells located in the boundary block $[t_1, t_2]$. When a string x is currently written in this (t_1, t_2)-region, x is called the (t_1, t_2)-*regional string* as long as x is clear from the context.

Since an ε-k-sna moves its input-tape head to the right without stopping, it is possible to identify "time" with the "location" of the input-tape head. A *transition history* of a computation path is a sequence of the storage-tape head locations according to "time". We draw a transition history as a single (zigzag) line in the xy-coordinated plain of points (s, t), where x and y axes indicate boundaries and storage-tape cell numbers, respectively.

A *peak* (resp., a *pit*) is a point (s, t) of a transition history for which the storage-tape head makes a left turn (resp., a right turn) at cell s without any stationary moves and the input-tape head crosses boundary t. A *plateau* between two boundaries t_1, t_2 is a consecutive sequence of points (s, t) of a transition history, where $t_1 \le t \le t_2$. The *height* of a peak (s, t) is s. Similarly, the heights of a pit and a plateau are defined.

A *state-storage pair* is an element of the set $Q \times \Gamma$. We assign such a pair (q, σ) to each point (s, t) of a transition history as its value (or its label). We can treat every computation path as a sequence of state-storage pairs.

Figure 2 illustrates the aforementioned concepts.

4.3 Useful and Supportive Lemmas

We fix a string w over Σ in L and fix an accepting computation path of M on w. *Line* s refers to the horizontal straight line consisting of all points of the form (s, t) for any $t \in [0, |w|_\varepsilon + 1]_\mathbb{Z}$. When s is specified, we can determine the points $t_1, t_2, \ldots, t_m$ of a given transition history that lie on line s when the tape head moves, from left to right, passing this line. We call these values $t_1, t_2, \ldots, t_m$ as *hitting positions at* s. See Fig. 2.

Given a transition history, an ℓ-*line segment* is a single (zigzag) line whose points (s, t) have labels of the form (q, σ) for inner state $q \in Q$ and tape symbol $\sigma \in \Gamma^{(\ell)}$. Such an ℓ-line segment is *maximum* if it cannot be properly contained in another ℓ-line segment. For each ℓ-line segment seg, we define the set $\{s \mid \exists t\, [seg \text{ contains points } (s, t)]\}$, which is called the *cell-number projection*.

Lemma 9. *Fix a maximum $(k-1)$-line segment seg with its cell-number projection $[s_1, s_2]_\mathbb{Z}$ and take hitting positions t_1, t_2 of lines s_1, s_2, respectively. There is no plateau, peak, or pit in the square $[s_1, s_2]_\mathbb{Z} \times [t_1, t_2]_\mathbb{Z}$.*

We introduce a key notion of smooth base. Let us consider a $(2k+2)$-tuple $(s_1, s_2, t_1, t_2, \ldots, t_{2k})$. Such a tuple is said to be a *smooth base* if (1) $1 \le s_1 < s_2 \le |w|_\varepsilon + 1$ and $t_1, t_2, \ldots, t_{2k}$ are hitting positions at s enumerated from left to right (with $1 \le t_1 < t_{2k} \le |w|_\varepsilon + 1$), (2) for any odd number j in $[k]$, two corner points $(s_1, t_{2j-1}), (s_2, t_{2j})$ in the square $[s_1, s_2]_\mathbb{Z} \times [t_{2j-1}, t_{2j}]_\mathbb{Z}$

have state-storage pairs, (3) for any even number j in $[k]$, two corner points $(s_2, t_{2j-1}), (s_1, t_{2j})$ in the square $[s_1, s_2]_{\mathbb{Z}} \times [t_{2j-1}, t_{2j}]_{\mathbb{Z}}$ have state-storage pairs, (4) there is a single connected (zigzag) line between two corners of (2)–(3) as long as $j < k$, (5) between t_{2k-1} and t_{2k}, if k is even (resp., odd), then all pits below s_2 (resp., all peaks above s_1) are present in this square, and (6) for any $j \in [k-1]$, $[s_1, s_2]_{\mathbb{Z}} \times [t_{2j}, t_{2j+1}]_{\mathbb{Z}}$ has no points of the transition history. Two simple examples are presented in Fig. 3(a) and Fig. 4.

A pair (s_1, s_2) of natural numbers is said to be *eligible* if there exist $2k$ elements $t_1, t_2, \ldots, t_{2k} \in \mathbb{N}$ for which $(s_1, s_2, t_1, t_2, \ldots, t_{2k})$ is a smooth base. Such eligible pairs are obtainable from ℓ-line segments.

Lemma 10. *For any maximum $(k-1)$-line segment whose cell-number projection is $[s_1, s_2]_{\mathbb{Z}}$ for two s_1, s_2 with $s_1 < s_2$ and for any $s'_1, s'_2 \in [s_1, s_2]_{\mathbb{Z}}$, if $s'_1 < s'_2$, then the pair (s'_1, s'_2) is eligible.*

A smooth base is further called an *iterative base* if two corners of each square associated with this smooth base have the same state-storage pair. See Fig. 3(a) and Fig. 4 for iterative bases when $k = 2, 3$.

We then introduce another notion of effective set. Assume that $(s_1, s_2, t_1, t_2, \ldots, s_{2k})$ is a smooth base. We say that a subset S of $[s_1, s_2]_{\mathbb{Z}}$ is called *effective* for the set $[s_1, s_2]_{\mathbb{Z}} \times [t_1, t_2]_{\mathbb{Z}} \times [t_3, t_4]_{\mathbb{Z}} \times \cdots \times [t_{2k-1}, t_{2k}]_{\mathbb{Z}}$ if no value $s' \in S$ (excluding the corner points) satisfies the following condition: there exist an index $j \in [k]$ and both a peak v_1 and a pit v_2 in $[s_1, s_2]_{\mathbb{Z}} \times [t_{2j-1}, t_{2j}]_{\mathbb{Z}}$ for which line s' crosses between any line between v_1 and v_2.

In Lemma 11, we consider only two simple situations. (1) There is no peak or pit. (2) A consecutive series of pit heights is increasing (when k is odd) and a series of peak heights is decreasing (when k is even).

Lemma 11. *Fix a consecutive series of maximum $(k-1)$-line segments and assume that their cell-number projections are all included in $[s_1, s_2]_{\mathbb{Z}}$ with $s_1 < s_2$. Assume that $(s_1, s_2, t_1, t_2, \ldots, t_{2k})$ is a smooth base for appropriate positions $t_1, t_2, \ldots, t_{2k}$. Let S denote the maximum effective set for $[s_1, s_2]_{\mathbb{Z}} \times [t_1, t_2]_{\mathbb{Z}} \times \cdots \times [t_{2k-1}, t_{2k}]_{\mathbb{Z}}$ and let $m = |S|$. The following properties then hold. (1) When $k = 1$, if $m > |Q||\Gamma|$, then there are values s'_1, s'_2, t'_1, t'_2 such that $s_1 \leq s'_1 < s'_2 \leq s_2$, $t_1 \leq t'_1 < t'_2 \leq t_2$, and (s'_1, s'_2, t'_1, t'_2) is an iterative base. (2) When $k = 2$, if $m > (|Q||\Gamma|)^2$, then there are values $s'_1, s'_2, t'_1, t'_2, t'_3, t'_4$ such that $s_1 \leq s'_1 < s'_2 \leq s_2$, $t_1 \leq t'_1 < t'_2 \leq t_2$, $t_3 \leq t'_3 < t'_4 \leq t_4$, and $(s'_1, s'_2, t'_1, t'_2, t'_3, t'_4)$ is an iterative base. (3) If $m > (|Q||\Gamma|)^k$, then there are values $s'_1, s'_2, t'_1, t'_2, \ldots, t'_{2k}$ such that $s_1 \leq s'_1 < s'_2 \leq s_2$, $t_{2j-1} \leq t'_{2j-1} < t'_{2j} \leq t_{2j}$ for any $j \in [k]$, and $(s'_1, s'_2, t'_1, t'_2, \ldots, t'_{2k})$ is an iterative base.*

Lemma 12. *If an iterative base exists, then there exists an iterative base $(s_1, s_2, t_1, t_2, \ldots, t_{2k})$ and an index $j \in [k-1]$ satisfying $|t_{2j+1} - t_{2j}| \leq c$.*

4.4 Proof of Theorem 3

The proof of Theorem 3 proceeds by induction on k (≥ 1). Take any infinite language L in $k\mathrm{SNA}_{FBS}$ and a k-sna M that recognizes L. By Lemma 7, we can assume that M is in normal form, halting with frozen-blank cells (defined in Sect. 2.2). We further modify the last part of M's behavior so that M halts on the start cell (when k is odd) and the rightmost cell (when k is even). Furthermore, the input-tape head must move to $\lhd$ before halting. Meanwhile, we set $c = (|Q||\Gamma|)^k$. Later, we will explain why the desired pumping length must be c^2. We arbitrarily take a string w in L of length more than c^2. In what follows, we intend to show that Conditions (1)–(3) of the generalized pumping property for $\mathcal{C}_k$ in Sect. 1.1 indeed hold.

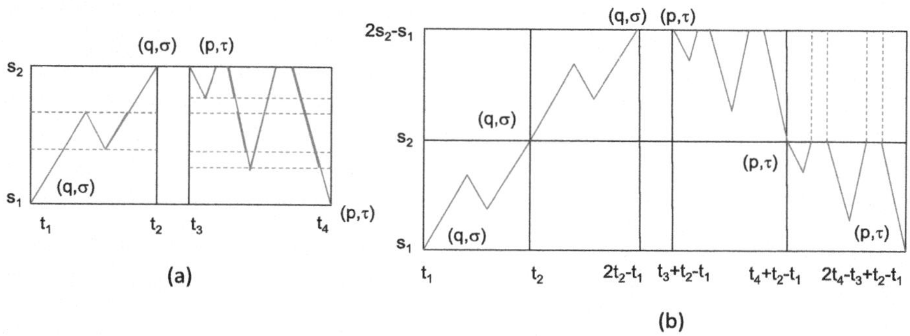

Fig. 3. (a) An example of iterative base when $k = 2$. This graph depicts a transition history of a particular computation path of a 2-sna, restricted to two squares $[s_1, s_2]_{\mathbb{Z}} \times [t_1, t_2]_{\mathbb{Z}}$ and $[s_1, s_2]_{\mathbb{Z}} \times [t_3, t_4]_{\mathbb{Z}}$. The solid red lines as well as the small red circle indicate tape cells are already frozen blank. (b) Here, the squares of (a) is expanded. This corresponds to the iteration of (t_1, t_2)-regional string and (t_3, t_4)-regional strings. The green dotted lines are additional moves of the storage-tape head while reading Bs.

We begin with the base cases of $k = 1, 2$. In these cases, Theorem 3 is identical to the standard pumping lemmas for REG and CFL because $1\mathrm{SNA}_{FBS}$ and $2\mathrm{SNA}_{FBS}$ respectively equal REG and CFL. Nevertheless, we try to describe the detailed proof for the case of $k = 2$ because this case exemplifies an underlying idea of the proof for a more general case of $k \geq 3$. We also remark that this actually provides an alternative proof of the standard pumping lemma for CFL.

Case of $k = 2$: Since $w \in L$, we hereafter fix an accepting computation path of M on w and further fix its associated transition history. Meanwhile, for the ease of the proof description, we assume that there is no plateaus; instead, there are only peaks and pits.

(1) Firstly, we discuss the case where there exists an iterative base $(s_1, s_2, t_1, t_2, t_3, t_4)$. We partition the input string w into $y_1 z_1 y_2 z_2 y_3$ using (t_1, t_2)-regional string z_1, (t_2, t_3)-regional string y_2, and (t_3, t_4)-regional string z_2. Here, the transition history restricted to z_1 corresponds to $[s_1, s_2]_{\mathbb{Z}} \times [t_1, t_2]_{\mathbb{Z}}$. Similarly, the transition history restricted to y_2 and z_2 correspond to $[s_1, s_2]_{\mathbb{Z}} \times [t_2, t_3]_{\mathbb{Z}}$ and $[s_1, s_2]_{\mathbb{Z}} \times [t_3, t_4]_{\mathbb{Z}}$, respectively. As shown in Fig. 3(b), this iterative base can be

expanded into another one $(s_1, 2s_2 - s_1, t_1, 2t_2 - t_1, t_3 + t_2 - t_1, 2t_4 - t_3 + t_2 - t_1)$. This fact shows the following.

Claim 13. *For each number $i \in \mathbb{N}$, $w^{(i)}$ is accepted by M.*

We next claim that $z_1 z_2 \neq \varepsilon$. If $z_1 z_2 = \varepsilon$, then the string $w^{(i)} = y_1 z_1^i y_2 z_2^i y_3$ is equal to $y_1 y_2 y_3$, independent of i, for every number $i \in \mathbb{N}$. However, the runtime of M increases as i grows. This is absurd. Thus, $z_1 z_2 \neq \varepsilon$ follows.

(2) Next, we discuss the case where no iterative base exists. We wish to evaluate the number of symbols in $\Gamma^{(1)}$ produced during the computation of M. We first claim that M does not continuously write more than c symbols in $\Gamma^{(1)}$. To show this, we introduce the notion of "session". Generally, for an even number k, a *session* refers to a period of time when the storage-tape head moves from one pit (by treating the starting point $(0, 0)$ as a "pit") to the next pit. In other words, a session is a series of consecutive moves by which the storage-tape head moves to the right, makes a left turn, and then moves to the left. The behavior of the storage-tape head can be described as a sequence of sessions.

Claim 14. *On every session, M writes at most c non-blank symbols before making a left turn.*

We are now concerned with the amount of symbols in $\Gamma^{(1)}$ remaining on the storage tape at each moment. Even if M writes no more than c symbols in $\Gamma^{(1)}$ (Claim 14) and turns some of them to Bs, the total amount of symbols in $\Gamma^{(1)}$ on the tape may increase according to "time". This case happens when pit heights are always increasing.

Claim 15. *Any sequence of consecutive pits whose heights are always increasing has length at most c.*

We intend to simulate M using only "depth-1" storage tape. Since M writes only a few non-blank symbols before writing Bs, it is possible to simplify M as follows. Whenever the storage-tape head moves to the area of $\Box$s and writes a non-blank string of length $< c$, we remember the string using inner states and write Bs instead. Whenever the storage-tape head modifies symbols in $\Gamma^{(1)}$ to Bs (from right to left) and then moves the tape head rightward, we discard the information on the written symbols stored inside inner states.

Consider the period when M produces a series of consecutive pits whose heights are increasing. The number of pits in that period is at most c (Claim 15) in each session and the number of strings during that period is at most c (Claim 14). After that period, M's pit height goes below the previously lowest height. This means that we delete all stored symbols (except for some of the firstly stored symbols). Thus, we need only to remember at most c^2 symbols at any moment.

Unfortunately, we may need to simulate a left turn while reading the newly written Bs. Since we cannot move the input-tape head (because of the frozen blank sensitivity), instead, we always pre-scan c^2 input symbols and use them to determine appropriate moves without actually moving the input-tape head.

This new 1-sna can simulate the behavior of M, and thus it can recognize L. To complete the case of $k = 2$, we then apply to L the pumping lemma for $1\mathrm{SNA}_{FBS}$ (= REG). To make the above simulation to work, nonetheless, we need to define the desired pumping length to be c^2.

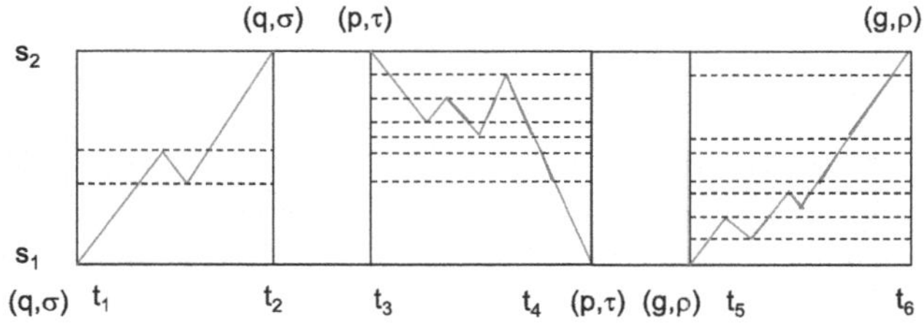

Fig. 4. An example of an iterative base when $k = 3$. The above figure depicts a transition history of a computation path of a 3-sna, restricted to three squares $[s_1, s_2]_{\mathbb{Z}} \times [t_1, t_2]_{\mathbb{Z}}$, $[s_1, s_2]_{\mathbb{Z}} \times [t_3, t_4]_{\mathbb{Z}}$, and $[s_1, s_2]_{\mathbb{Z}} \times [t_5, t_6]_{\mathbb{Z}}$. The red lines indicate tape cells are already frozen blank.

Case of $k \geq 3$: Next, we consider the general case of $k \geq 3$. In essence, the proof is a generalization of the cases of $k = 1, 2$. A key of the proof is to focus on $(k-1)$-line segments.

In the case where an iterative base exists, similarly to Claim 13, we can prove that, for each number $i \in \mathbb{N}$, $w^{(i)}$ is accepted by M. In the other case where there is no iterative base, it is important to remark that no $(k-1)$-line segment whose cell-number projection has more than c elements because, otherwise, Lemma 11 leads to the existence of an iterative base. We can show two claims similar to Claims 14–15. These properties make it possible to simulate M using only depth-$(k-1)$ storage tape, and thus L belongs to $(k-1)\mathrm{SNA}_{FBS}$. Hence, we can apply to L the generalized pumping lemma for $(k-1)\mathrm{SNA}_{FBS}$.

5 Summary and Open Problems

We have sought a most natural generalization of the well-known pumping lemmas for REG and CFL [1]. In this work, we have claimed that depth-bounded storage automata, which had been discussed in [11–13], are good candidates for such a generalized pumping property. In fact, we have proven that the complexity class $k\mathrm{SNA}_{FBS}$ composed of all languages recognized by nondeterministic depth-k storage automata (or k-sna's) with frozen blank sensitiveness indeed satisfies the generalized pumping property. With the use of this property, we have obtained the new result that $\{k\mathrm{SDA}_{FBS} \mid k \geq 1\}$ and $\{k\mathrm{SNA}_{FBS} \mid k \geq 1\}$ form truly infinite hierarchies. Moreover, we have shown that co-CFL $\nsubseteq \omega\mathrm{SNA}_{FBS}$, where $\omega\mathrm{SNA}_{FBS}$ is the infinite union of all $k\mathrm{SNA}_{FBS}$ over $k \geq 1$. This implies the separations among $\omega\mathrm{SNA}_{FBS}$, co-$\omega\mathrm{SNA}_{FBS}$, and $\omega\mathrm{SDA}_{FBS}$ (i.e., the deterministic variant). See Fig. 1 to recapitulate.

There still remain numerous unsolved questions. Does SC contain $\omega\mathrm{SNA}_{FBS}$? Does NSC contain co-$\omega\mathrm{SNA}_{FBS}$? Other known properties of REG and CFL include the *swapping lemmas* for REG [7, Lemma 3.1] and for CFL [7, Lemma 4.1] and [8, Corollary 4.2]. Does $k\mathrm{SNA}_{FBS}$ satisfy their natural generalization? We expect that the solutions to these questions help promote our understandings of kSDA and kSNA.

References

1. Bar-Hillel, Y., Perles, M., Shamir, E.: On formal properties of simple phrase-structure grammars. Zeitschrift für Phonetik, Sprachwissenschaft, und Kommunikationsforschung **14**, 143–172 (1961)
2. Cook, S.A.: Characterizations of pushdown machines in terms of time-bounded computers. J. Assoc. Comput. Mach. **18**, 4–18 (1971)
3. Ginsburg, S., Greibach, S., Harrison, M.A.: Stack automata and compiling. J. Assoc. Comput. Mach. **14**, 172–201 (1967)
4. Ginsburg, S., Greibach, S., Harrison, M.A.: One-way stack automata. J. Assoc. Comput. Mach. **14**, 389–418 (1967)
5. Hibbard, T.N.: A generalization of context-free determinism. Inf. Control **11**, 196–238 (1967)
6. Hopcroft, J.E., Ullman, J.D.: Introduction to Automata Theory. Addison-Wesley Publishing Company, Languages and Computation (1979)
7. Yamakami, T.: Swapping lemmas for regular and context-free languages. Manuscript. arXiv: 0808.4122 (2008)
8. Yamakami, T.: Pseudorandom generators against advised context-free languages. Theoret. Comput. Sci. **613**, 1–27 (2016)
9. Yamakami, T.: Intersection and union hierarchies of deterministic context-free languages and pumping lemmas. In: Leporati, A., Martín-Vide, C., Shapira, D., Zandron, C. (eds.) LATA 2020. LNCS, vol. 12038, pp. 341–353. Springer, Cham (2020). https://doi.org/10.1007/978-3-030-40608-0_24
10. Yamakami, T.: Intersection and union hierarchies of deterministic context-free languages and pumping lemmas. This is an extended and corrected version of [9] (2021). arXiv:2112.09383
11. Yamakami, T.: Between SC and LOGDCFL: families of languages accepted by logarithmic-space deterministic auxiliary depth-k storage automata. Int. J. Comput. Math. Comput. Syst. Theory **8**, 1–31 (2023). In: A Preliminary Report Appeared In The Proceedings of COCOON 2021, LNCS, vol. 13025, pp. 164–175, Springer (2021). https://doi.org/10.1007/978-3-030-89543-3_14
12. Yamakami, T.: Nondeterministic auxiliary depth-bounded storage automata and semi-unbounded fan-in cascading circuits (extended abstract). In: Proceedings of the 28th International Conference on Computing and Combinatorics (COCOON 2022), LNCS, vol. 13595, pp. 61–69, Springer (2022). https://doi.org/10.1007/978-3-031-22105-7_6
13. Yamakami, T.: Nondeterministic auxiliary depth-bounded storage automata and semi-unbounded fan-in cascading circuits. This is a complete, corrected version of [12] (2024). arXiv:2412.09186 (2024)
14. Yamakami, T.: Alternation-bounded semi-unbounded fan-in cascading circuits and the complementation closure property. In: To appear in the Proceedings of the 21st Conference on Computability in Europe (CiE 2025), LNCS, vol. 15764. Springer (2025). https://doi.org/10.1007/978-3-031-95908-0_35

Small Balanced Vertex Separators in NFA to Regular Expression Conversion

Derek Youngman(✉) and Kai Salomaa

School of Computing, Queen's University, Kingston, ON K7L 3N6, Canada
{youngman.derek,salomaa}@queensu.ca

Abstract. We explore small balanced vertex separators in NFA to regular expression conversion. We show that any class of finite automata whose underlying class of graphs admits "strongly sublinear separators" also admits shorter regular expressions. We propose a new state elimination ordering heuristic, called the "gate score" heuristic, which is a variant of the weight heuristic of Delgado and Morais. Empirically, we find that both the weight heuristic and the gate score heuristic perform better than directly exploiting vertex separators despite having no provable performance guarantee. We also provide some theoretical support for the weight heuristic of Delgado and Morais in finite automata with dense transition structures.

1 Introduction

There are some classical algorithms for conversion between regular expressions and various types of finite automata. Conversion from regular expression to ε-NFA is straightforward in the sense that for a regular expression r of size n, $\frac{22}{15}n$ states are sufficient for an ε-NFA describing $L(r)$ [9]. However, the opposite direction can incur an exponential blow-up in size: if A is an n-state ε-NFA (or NFA/DFA) over alphabet Σ, then, in the worst case, size $|\Sigma| \cdot 2^{\Theta(n)}$ is sufficient and necessary for a regular expression describing $L(A)$ [9]. Still, in many cases, smaller regular expressions exist. Yet, the known algorithms for ε-NFA to regular expression conversion often produce much larger regular expressions than necessary, and the problem of finding an equivalent minimal regular expression is PSPACE-complete [13]. The typical conversion algorithm is the state elimination technique, which works by iteratively "eliminating" each state. The order in which one eliminates states greatly affects the size of the resulting regular expression.

In the present work, building on the work of [6] and [8], we examine the idea of choosing an elimination order by computing small balanced vertex separators. The idea, which we call the *separator technique*, is to eliminate states in the leaves of the separator first, recursively computing small balanced vertex separators within the leaves. Using a proof technique similar to Gruber and Holzer [8], we prove that every class of finite automata whose underlying class of graphs has "strongly sublinear separators" also has corresponding regular expressions of

Published by Springer Nature Switzerland AG 2025
A. Malcher and L. Prigioniero (Eds.): DCFS 2025, LNCS 15759, pp. 211–223, 2025.
https://doi.org/10.1007/978-3-031-97100-6_15

sizes $|\Sigma| \cdot 2^{o(n)}$. We also revisit the weight heuristic of Delgado and Morais [4]. In particular, we provide theoretical support for the weight heuristic in automata with dense transition structures. Furthermore, the weight heuristic and the separator technique inspire a new heuristic, which we call the "gate score" heuristic. We conclude with statistically significant empirical results which suggest that, while the separator technique is useful, the weight heuristic and the gate score heuristic are better on average. These results also show that the new gate score heuristic improves relative to the weight heuristic as n and $|\Sigma|$ grow. When, for example, $n = 50$ and $20 \leq |\Sigma| \leq 50$, the gate score heuristic is better on average.

2 Preliminaries

We assume the reader is familiar with the basic notions of formal languages, regular expressions, and finite automata. Otherwise, refer to, e.g., [16].

As a size measure for regular expressions, we use the alphabetic width. The *alphabetic width* of a regular expression r is the number of alphabet symbols in r, counted with multiplicity. We also call this the *size* of r and denote it by $|r|$. For example, if $r = aa^* + bc + \varepsilon + \emptyset$, then $|r| = |\{a_1, a_2, b_1, c_1\}| = 4$.

Let $A = (Q, \Sigma, \delta, q_0, F)$ be an ε-NFA. We call A *initially-connected* if, for every state $q \in Q$, there exists $w \in \Sigma^*$ such that $q \in \delta(q_0, w)$. We call A *useful* if, for every state $q \in Q$, there exists $w \in \Sigma^*$ and $f \in F$ such that $f \in \delta(q, w)$. We call A *trim* if it is initially-connected and useful. If A is a DFA with $|\delta(q, a)| = 1$ for all $q \in Q$ and $a \in \Sigma$, we call A *complete*. We abbreviate "complete, initially-connected DFA" by ICDFA. A *generalized nondeterministic finite automaton* (GNFA) [12] is a quintuple (Q, Σ, T, q_0, F) where $T : Q \times Q \to R(\Sigma)$ is the *transition function* and $R(\Sigma)$ denotes the set of all regular expressions over Σ. Every ε-NFA can be seen as a GNFA. Let A be a regular expression or GNFA, and let A' be a regular expression or GNFA. We say that A and A' are *equivalent* if $L(A) = L(A')$ and write $A \cong A'$. Finally, for a state $q \in Q$ of a GFNA, we denote $\text{In}(q) = |\{j \in Q \backslash \{q\} \mid T(j, q) \neq \emptyset\}|$ as the number of incoming transitions and $\text{Out}(q) = |\{k \in Q \backslash \{q\} \mid T(q, k) \neq \emptyset\}|$ as the number of outgoing transitions.

We briefly introduce the necessary notions of graph theory. For a thorough introduction to graph theory, refer to, e.g., [3]. A *(directed) graph* (digraph) is a pair $G = (V, E)$, where V is the set of *vertices* and $E \subseteq V \times V$ is the set of *edges*. A *(directed) subgraph* of G is a digraph $G' = (V', E')$ where $V' \subseteq V$ and $E' \subseteq (V' \times V') \cap E$. We say G' is the subgraph *induced* by V' if $E' = (V' \times V') \cap E$. We define the *underlying digraph* of a GNFA $A = (Q, \Sigma, T, q_0, F)$ by $G(A) = (Q, E)$ where $(j, k) \in E$ if and only if $T(j, k) \neq \emptyset$. A *(vertex) separator* of a digraph $G = (V, E)$ is a partition (B, S, C) of V such that $(B \times C) \cap E = \emptyset$ and $(C \times B) \cap E = \emptyset$. We call B and C the *leaves* of (B, S, C). For a real number $\alpha \in (0, 1)$, a separator (B, S, C) of a digraph $G = (V, E)$ is *α-balanced* if $\max\{|B|, |C|\} \leq \alpha |V|$. Moreover, (B, S, C) is *balanced* if it is $\frac{2}{3}$-balanced. The choice of $\frac{2}{3}$ is customary but arbitrary. The *size* of a separator (B, S, C) is $|S|$.

Finally, we briefly describe the standard algorithm for conversion from finite automata to regular expressions, called the *state elimination technique*. There are other algorithms, such as the *McNaughton-Yamada algorithm*, but almost all known algorithms are roughly equivalent to the state elimination technique [9]. Let us briefly describe the state elimination technique. As input, we have a GNFA $A = (Q, \Sigma, T, q_0, F)$. As preprocessing, we *normalize* A: if there is more than 1 final state or the initial state is final, we add a new state f, make f the only final state, and add an ε-transition from each state of F to f. Let $A = (\{q_0, q_1, \ldots, q_{n-1}\}, \Sigma, T, q_0, \{q_{n-1}\})$ be a normalized GNFA and let $Q = \{q_1, \ldots q_{n-2}\}$. We call a bijection $\sigma : [|Q|] \to Q$ an *elimination order* (where $[m] = \{0, 1, \ldots, m-1\}$ for any $m \in \mathbb{N}$). We denote the set of elimination orders by E_Q. Let $\sigma \in E_Q$ and $U \subseteq Q$ be such that $\{\sigma(i) \mid 0 \leq i < |U|\} = U$. We say that such a subset $U \subseteq Q$ is *eliminated first* by σ. Let $j, k \in \{q_0, q_1, \ldots, q_{n-1}\} \backslash U$. We write $r^U_{j,k,\sigma}$ to denote a regular expression that describes the set of words w such that k is reachable from j on w only going through states in U. The exact regular expression will be determined by σ, but $r^U_{j,k,\sigma} \cong r^U_{j,k,\tau}$ for all $\tau \in E_Q$ eliminating U first. If the initial state has no self-loop nor incoming transition and the final state has no outgoing transition nor self-loop, we have $A \cong r^Q_{q_0,f,\sigma}$. More generally,

$$A \cong \left(r^Q_{q_0,q_0,\sigma}\right)^* r^Q_{q_0,f,\sigma} \left(r^Q_{f,f,\sigma} + r^Q_{f,q_0,\sigma} \left(r^Q_{q_0,q_0,\sigma}\right)^* r^Q_{q_0,f,\sigma}\right)^*.$$

The state elimination algorithm starts with $U = \emptyset$ and iteratively "eliminates" each state by adding each state from Q to U until $U = Q$. We compute $r^U_{j,k,\sigma}$ inductively as follows: $r^\emptyset_{j,k,\sigma} = T(j,k)$ and

$$r^{U \cup \{q\}}_{j,k,\sigma} = r^U_{j,k,\sigma} + r^U_{j,q,\sigma} \left(r^U_{q,q,\sigma}\right)^* r^U_{q,k,\sigma}$$

where $q = \sigma(|U|)$. For convenience, when $r^U_{j,q,\sigma} = \emptyset$ or $r^U_{q,k,\sigma} = \emptyset$, we say that $r^U_{j,q,\sigma} \left(r^U_{q,q,\sigma}\right)^* r^U_{q,k,\sigma} = \emptyset$ and $r^{U \cup \{q\}}_{j,k,\sigma} = r^U_{j,k,\sigma}$. Throughout the state elimination, $r^U_{j,k,\sigma}$ yields an equivalent GNFA $A^U_\sigma = (\{q_0, q_1, \ldots, q_n\} \setminus U, \Sigma, T^U_\sigma, q_0, \{q_n\})$ where $T^U_\sigma(j,k) = r^U_{j,k,\sigma}$. We denote the regular expression obtained from A with elimination order σ by $\mathscr{S}(A, \sigma)$. The following is a generalized restatement of an established result [8,9].

Theorem 1. *For any $n \geq 2$, let $A = (Q, \Sigma, T, q_0, \{f\})$ be a normalized n-state GNFA and let $M = \max\{|T(j,k)| \mid j, k \in Q\}$. Then, for any elimination order σ, we have $|\mathscr{S}(A, \sigma)| \leq 6M \cdot 4^{n-2}$. In particular, if A is an ε-NFA, then $|\mathscr{S}(A, \sigma)| \leq 6 \cdot |\Sigma| \cdot 4^{n-2}$.*

We provide a proof in the appendix. This bound is tight when $|T(j,k)| = M$ for all $j, k \in Q$.

3 Related Work

A known fact is that the elimination order can greatly affect the size of the resulting regular expression. There are some established heuristics for choosing a good elimination order. Delgado and Morais [4] present a simple yet effective greedy heuristic. Let $A = (Q, \Sigma, T, q_0, \{f\})$ be a normalized GNFA. For $q \in Q \setminus \{q_0, f\}$, we define the *weight* of q by

$$W(q) = \mathrm{In}(q) \cdot |T(q,q)| \cdot \mathrm{Out}(q) + \sum_{j \in Q \setminus \{q\}} |T(j,q)| \cdot \mathrm{Out}(q) + \sum_{k \in Q \setminus \{q\}} \mathrm{In}(q) \cdot |T(q,k)|.$$

Delgado and Morais propose eliminating lower-weight states first. One variant of this is to compute the weight of each state of the input automaton once and then eliminate states in order of least to greatest weight. Computing this elimination order takes $\mathcal{O}(n^2)$ time for an ε-NFA. A second variant is to recompute the weight of each state at each stage of the state elimination and eliminate a state with minimal weight. The runtime in the second variant is slightly more difficult to determine because the arithmetic operations become costly. In this paper, we consider only the second variant. This heuristic has no known provable performance guarantee but performs very well empirically [10,15]. Moreira *et al.* [15] also propose a heuristic of a similar nature, counting the number of cycles passing through each state and eliminating states with fewer cycles earlier. Empirically, the weight heuristic performs better on average than the cycle heuristic on ICDFAs chosen uniformly at random, but not in all cases.

Han and Wood [11] introduce the notion of a bridge state. Later redefined by Ahn and Han [1], a state q of a finite automaton is called a *bridge state* if

(1) The state q is neither initial nor final;
(2) Every accepting path passes through q; and
(3) The state q does not participate in any cycle except for possibly a self-loop on q.

Han and Wood prove that the optimal elimination order must eliminate bridge states last.

4 Theoretical Results

Intuitively, bridge states are useful because they decompose the automaton into two separate pieces. This idea can be generalized. Gruber and Holzer [8] provide the framework for a divide-and-conquer strategy using separators.

Lemma 2. Let $A = (Q, \Sigma, T, q_0, \{f\})$ be a normalized GNFA and let (B, S, C) be a vertex separator of the underlying digraph of A such that $q_0, f \in S$. Then, for any elimination orders $\sigma, \tau, \pi \in E_Q$ such that σ eliminates $B \cup C$ first, τ eliminates B first, and π eliminates C first, we have

(1) $r^{B\cup C}_{j,k,\sigma} \cong r^{B}_{j,k,\tau} + r^{C}_{j,k,\pi}$ *for all* $j, k \in S$*; and*
(2) If σ *eliminates* B *in the same order as* τ *and* σ *eliminates* C *in the same order as* π*, then* $|r^{B\cup C}_{j,k,\sigma}| \leq |r^{B}_{j,k,\tau}| + |r^{C}_{j,k,\pi}|$ *for all* $j, k \in S$.

This lemma shows that if we eliminate B and C first (before S), we can compute an elimination order within B independently of an elimination order within C. Gruber and Holzer provide the proof of (1). We provide a proof of (2) very similar to the proof of (1) in the appendix.

In finite automaton to regular expression conversion, vertex separators were first exploited for planar graphs (graphs that can be drawn with no edge crossings). A well-known result from Lipton and Tarjan [14] is that every n-vertex planar graph has a balanced separator of size at most $\sqrt{8n}$. This yields the following result [9].

Theorem 3. *Let A be an n-state planar NFA over alphabet Σ. Then, size $|\Sigma| \cdot 2^{\mathcal{O}(\sqrt{n})}$ is sufficient for a regular expression describing $L(A)$. Such a regular expression can be constructed by state elimination.*

The key observation here is that every subgraph of a planar subgraph is planar, so finding small balanced separators can be employed recursively on B and C. We generalize this approach as follows. For real numbers $c, \omega > 0$, let $\mathscr{G}_{c,\omega}$ denote the class of graphs G such that each subgraph $H = (V', E')$ of G has a balanced separator of size at most $c|V'|^{1-\omega}$. A class $\mathscr{G}$ of graphs is said to have *strongly sublinear separators* if $\mathscr{G} \subseteq \mathscr{G}_{c,\omega}$ for some $c, \omega > 0$ [5]. We show that every class of finite automata whose underlying class of graphs has strongly sublinear separators also has corresponding regular expressions of sizes $|\Sigma| \cdot 2^{o(n)}$. We establish some terminology first.

Let $A = (Q, \Sigma, \delta, q_0, F)$ be an ε-NFA. For a subset $U \subseteq Q$, let δ_U denote the transition function of A restricted to U. More precisely, $\delta_U : U \times (\Sigma \cup \{\varepsilon\}) \to \mathcal{P}(U)$ is defined by $(q, a) \mapsto \delta(q, a) \cap U$.

Definition 4. *Let Q be a finite set and let $\delta : Q \times (\Sigma \cup \{\varepsilon\}) \to \mathcal{P}(Q)$ be a transition function. The graph of (Q, δ) is the graph $G(Q, \delta) = (Q, E)$ where*

$$E = \{(j, k) \mid k \in \delta(j, a) \text{ for some } a \in \Sigma \cup \{\varepsilon\}\}.$$

Moreover, we say that a normalized ε-NFA $A = (Q^+, \Sigma, \delta^+, q_0, \{f\})$ extends (Q, δ) if

(1) $Q \cap \{q_0, f\} = \emptyset$;
(2) $Q^+ = Q \cup \{q_0, f\}$; and
(3) $\delta^+_Q = \delta$.

Observe that, for any normalized ε-NFA A, there exists a unique (Q, δ) such that A extends (Q, δ).

Definition 5. *Let $c, \omega \in \mathbb{R}_{>0}$. A graph $G = (V, E)$ is said to have (c, ω)-separators if, for all subgraphs $G' = (V', E')$ of G, G' has a balanced separator of size at most $c|V'|^{1-\omega}$. Moreover, for a finite set Q and transition function $\delta : Q \times (\Sigma \cup \{\varepsilon\}) \to \mathcal{P}(Q)$, if $G(Q, \delta)$ has (c, ω)-separators, we say that (Q, δ) has (c, ω)-separators. Finally, for a normalized ε-NFA A, when (Q, δ) has (c, ω)-separators and A extends (Q, δ), we say that A has (c, ω)-separators.*

Theorem 6. *Let $c, \omega \in \mathbb{R}_{>0}$, let $n \in \mathbb{N}$, and let A be a normalized ε-NFA over alphabet Σ with $n+2$ states and (c, ω)-*separators. Then, size $|\Sigma| \cdot 2^{\mathcal{O}(n^{1-\omega})}$ *(where c and ω are constant) is sufficient for a regular expression describing $L(A)$. Such a regular expression can be constructed by state elimination.*

Proof. Let $c, \omega \in \mathbb{R}_{>0}$, let $n \in \mathbb{N}$, and let Σ be an alphabet. Let $F(n, \Sigma)$ be the smallest nonnegative integer such that, for all sets Q and transition functions $\delta : Q \times (\Sigma \cup \{\varepsilon\}) \to \mathcal{P}(Q)$ where $|Q| = n$ and (Q, δ) has (c, ω)-separators, there exists an elimination order $\sigma \in E_Q$ such that, for all normalized ε-NFAs A extending (Q, δ), we have $|\mathscr{S}(A, \varsigma)| \leq F(n, \Sigma)$. If $n \leq c^{1/\omega}$, then by Theorem 1 we have

$$F(n, \Sigma) \leq 6 \cdot |\Sigma| \cdot 4^{c^{1/\omega}}.$$

Suppose $n > c^{1/\omega}$ (i.e., $cn^{1-\omega} < n$). Let Q be such that $|Q| = n$ and let $\delta : Q \times (\Sigma \cup \{\varepsilon\}) \to \mathcal{P}(Q)$. Suppose (Q, δ) has (c, ω)-separators. Let (B, S, C) be a balanced separator of $G(Q, \delta)$ of size at most $cn^{1-\omega}$. Choose $\tau \in E_Q$ eliminating B first such that, for all normalized ε-NFAs A_B extending (B, δ_B), we have $|\mathscr{S}(A_B, \tau)| \leq F(|B|, \Sigma)$. Similarly, choose $\pi \in E_Q$ eliminating C first such that, for all normalized ε-NFAs A_C extending (C, δ_C), we have $|\mathscr{S}(A_C, \pi)| \leq F(|C|, \Sigma)$. Choose $\sigma \in E_Q$ eliminating $B \cup C$ first such that σ eliminates B in the same order as τ and σ eliminates C in the same order as π. Now let A be an ε-NFA extending (Q, δ) with initial state q_0 and final state f. For $j, k \in S \cup \{q_0, f\}$, we have

$$|r^B_{j,k,\tau}| \leq F(|B|, \Sigma) \leq F\left(\lfloor \frac{2}{3} n \rfloor, \Sigma\right)$$

and

$$|r^C_{j,k,\pi}| \leq F(|C|, \Sigma) \leq F\left(\lfloor \frac{2}{3} n \rfloor, \Sigma\right).$$

Therefore, Lemma 2 establishes that size $2 \cdot F\left(\lfloor \frac{2}{3} n \rfloor, \Sigma\right)$ is sufficient for $r^{B \cup C}_{j,k,\sigma}$. By Theorem 1, it follows that

$$F(n, \Sigma) \leq 6 \cdot 2 \cdot F\left(\lfloor \frac{2}{3} n \rfloor, \Sigma\right) \cdot 4^{cn^{1-\omega}}.$$

This recurrence relation has solution

$$F(n, \Sigma) \leq |\Sigma| \cdot 2^{\mathcal{O}(n^{1-\omega})}.$$

□

The idea here is to eliminate B and C before S while employing the same technique recursively to eliminate B and C. Our empirical study will examine this technique on more general automata (automata not necessarily admitting small balanced vertex separators). Notice that this technique only specifies a partial order. For instance, we are still free to decide the elimination order of S.

In the proof of Theorem 6, to show that such a regular expression can be constructed strictly by state elimination, we must be careful to show that there exists one specific elimination order $\sigma \in E_Q$ that bounds $|r^{B \cup C}_{j,k,\sigma}|$ for all $j, k \in S \cup \{q_0, f\}$. However, in practice, we could choose a different elimination order for each j, k. We examine this idea in our empirical study.

Note that the existence of strongly sublinear separators is a sufficient condition to permit this approach, but it is not necessary. Given a separator (B, S, C), we need the subgraphs induced by B and C to also admit small balanced separators. Still, we do not require the subgraph induced by S to admit a small balanced separator. This idea suggests that, in practice, we might want to find separators such that the structure of S is in some sense as complex as possible. This is consistent with, for example, the weight heuristic of Delgado and Morais.

Also, given the undirected nature of separators, some automata are without small balanced vertex separators but still with very small regular expressions. For example, consider the family of NFAs given by $B_n = ([n], \{a\}, \delta, 0, \{n-1\})$ where $\delta(j, a) = \{k \in [n] \mid k > j\}$ for all $j \in [n]$. There does not exist $c, \omega \in \mathbb{R}_{>0}$ such that, for all $n \in \mathbb{N}_{>0}$, B_n has (c, ω)-separators. However, the family still admits regular expressions of sizes $\mathcal{O}(n^3)$.

One observation is that dense digraphs (digraphs with many edges) aren't likely to contain small balanced separators. A supporting observation is that the elimination order of a dense automaton often does not matter as much. Let us consider the most extreme case of a dense automaton. We call an automaton *fully connected* if $T(j, k) \neq \emptyset$ for all states j, k. Obviously, a fully connected automaton with some constant M such that $|T(j, k)| = M$ for all states j, k yields the same size regular expression no matter the elimination order. Furthermore, the regular expression obtained by state elimination from such an automaton can be very well described regardless of the number of states. We present a proposition to characterize this. Before the proposition, let us establish some notation. For any $a \in \Sigma$ and any regular expression r over alphabet Σ, we define $c(a, r)$ as the number of occurrences of a in r and then define $p(a, r) = \frac{c(a,r)}{|r|}$.

Proposition 7. For $n \geq 3$, let $A_n = ([n], [n] \times [n], T, 0, \{n-1\})$ be a GNFA satisfying $T(j, k) = (j, k)$ for all $j, k \in [n]$. Let $\sigma \in E_{\{1,2,\ldots n-2\}}$ be defined by $m \to m + 1$ and let $r_n = \mathscr{S}(A_n, \sigma)$. Then, for all $1 \leq j, k \leq n-2$, we have

(1) $p((j, k), r_n) = 2^{-(j+k)}$*;*
(2) $p((0, j), r_n) = \frac{1}{3} \cdot 2^{-(n+j-3)}$*;*
(3) $p((j, 0), r_n) = p((j, n-1), r_n) = 2^{-(n+j-1)}$*;*
(4) $p((n-1, j), r_n) = \frac{1}{3} \cdot 2^{-(n+j-2)}$*;*
(5) $p((0, 0), r_n) = p((0, n-1), r_n) = \frac{1}{3} \cdot 4^{-(n-2)}$*; and*
(6) $p((n-1, 0), r_n) = p((n-1, n-1), r_n) = \frac{1}{6} \cdot 4^{-(n-2)}$*.*

Notice that (1) does not depend on n. Also, notice that the equation $p((1, 1), r_n) = 2^{-(1+1)} = \frac{1}{4}$ is immediate. In fact, after eliminating state 1, the alphabet symbol $(1, 1)$ is 1 of 4 symbols in each remaining transition. The proof of the remaining equations is by induction, as after eliminating state 1, the remaining automaton is essentially A_{n-1}. We give a full proof in the appendix.

If we consider each transition of A_n to be labelled by an arbitrary regular expression instead, this supports the intuition of the weight heuristic of Delgado and Morais. Note that the more states we eliminate, the closer an automaton becomes to being fully connected. It seems plausible that, for example, given any automaton chosen uniformly at random, after eliminating some number of states, there remains a (nearly) fully connected automaton with high probability. Our empirical results later support this possibility. This is strong evidence in favour of the weight heuristic.

5 New Heuristic: "Gate Score"

One case where the separator technique outperforms the weight heuristic is when there is a "bottleneck" in the structure of the automaton, but where the states that make up the "bottleneck" have relatively little weight. To make this clear, we consider two extreme examples of 50-state NFAs over a five-letter alphabet. Let $S = \{0, 1, \ldots, 10\} \cup \{49\}$, $B = \{11, 12, \ldots, 29\}$, and $C = \{30, 31, \ldots, 48\}$. First, consider a GNFA $A = (\{0, \ldots, 49\}, \{a, b, c, d, e\}, T, 0, \{49\})$ satisfying

- $T(j, k) = \emptyset$ for all $j \in B$ and $k \in C$;
- $T(j, k) = \emptyset$ for all $j \in C$ and $k \in B$;
- $T(j, k) = a$ for all $j, k \in B$;
- $T(j, k) = a$ for all $j, k \in C$; and
- $T(j, k) = a$ for all $j, k \in \{0, \ldots, 49\}$ with $j \in S$ or $k \in S$.

That is, every possible transition, except for transitions between B and C, is nonempty and labelled by a. Observe that (B, S, C) is a vertex separator of $G(A)$. Here, the weight heuristic agrees with the separator technique, and we obtain the same size regular expression from each strategy. Now, consider a GNFA $A' = (\{0, \ldots, 49\}, \{a, b, c, d, e\}, T', 0, \{49\})$ satisfying

- $T'(j, k) = \emptyset$ for all $j \in B$ and $k \in C$;
- $T'(j, k) = \emptyset$ for all $j \in C$ and $k \in B$;
- $T'(j, k) = a + b + c + d + e$ for all $j, k \in B$;
- $T'(j, k) = a + b + c + d + e$ for all $j, k \in C$; and
- $T'(j, k) = a$ for all $j, k \in \{0, \ldots, 49\}$ with $j \in S$ or $k \in S$.

The transitions in A' to/from states in S are now labelled by smaller regular expressions than the other transitions so that the weight of each state in S is lower than the weight of each state in $B \cup C$. If we use the weight heuristic on A', we obtain a regular expression approximately 27,487,913,902 times larger than if we eliminate B and C before $S \setminus \{0, 49\}$. We propose a new heuristic to capture this phenomenon in more general automata. Let $A = (Q, \Sigma, T, q_0, \{f\})$ be a normalized GNFA. For a state $q \in Q \setminus \{q_0, f\}$, define the set

$$\mathcal{X}(q) = \{(q_0, q_1) \in Q \times Q \mid T(q_0, q_1) = \emptyset \wedge T(q_0, q) \neq \emptyset \wedge T(q, q_1) \neq \emptyset\}.$$

That is, $\mathcal{X}(q)$ consists of all state pairs (q_0, q_1) for which there is no transition from q_0 to q_1, but such that a transition would appear should we eliminate q. We define

$$\mathcal{G}(q) = \sum_{(q_0,q_1)\in\mathcal{X}(q)} (|T(q_0,q)| + |T(q,q)| + |T(q,q_1)|)$$

and call this the *gate score* of q. Notice that if $\mathcal{X}(q) = (Q\setminus\{q\})\times(Q\setminus\{q\})$ (which will almost never happen), then $\mathcal{G}(q) = W(q)$. As a heuristic, we eliminate states with lower gate scores earlier. When more than one state has a minimal gate score, the weight heuristic is a reasonable tiebreaker. Ties may happen often. In fact, for example, in a fully connected automaton, we have $\mathcal{G}(q) = 0$ for all $q \in Q$.

In both examples above, the gate score heuristic (with any tiebreaker) agrees with the separator technique.

6 Experiments

We now support our theoretical discussion with some empirical results. For a fixed n, state set $[n]$, alphabet Σ, initial state 0, and final states $\{n-1\}$, we generate uniform random ICDFAs using the method of [2], as implemented in FAdo [7]. Let $A = ([n], \Sigma, \delta, 0, \{n-1\})$ be such a randomly generated DFA. Let (B, S, C) be a vertex separator of the underlying digraph of A with $0, n-1 \in S$. We compute such a vertex separator using a simple integer linear program which attempts to minimize $|S|$ while obtaining $|B| = |C|$. This integer linear program is at least reasonably effective in practice; it almost always obtains $|B| = |C|$ and produces reasonably small separators. For instance, when $|\Sigma| = 2$, we obtain separators of size approximately $\frac{n}{5}$ for $n = 20, 40, 50$. In the appendix, Table ?? shows the average values of $|S|$ and $||B| - |C||$. Now, we consider the following methods of computing a regular expression describing $L(A)$:

- (M0) Choose an elimination order uniformly at random.
- (M1) Use the weight heuristic of Delgado and Morais.
- (M2) Use the separator technique (possibly recursively on B and C) and complete the partial order uniformly at random.
- (M3) Use the separator technique (possibly recursively on B and C) and complete the partial order using the weight heuristic.
- (M4) Use the gate score heuristic with the weight heuristic as a tiebreaker.
- (M5) First, compute a vertex separator of (B_B, S_B, C_B) of the subgraph induced by B (note that B_B and C_B could be empty). Apply M5 recursively to eliminate B_B and C_B. Then, for each $j, k \in S$, update the transition between j and k with the regular expression $r^{S_B}_{j,k,\sigma}$ where $\sigma = \sigma(j,k)$ is an elimination order eliminating S_B first that minimizes $|r^{S_B}_{j,k,\sigma}|$. Eliminate C using the same recursive method. Then, eliminate $S\setminus\{0, n-1\}$ using the weight heuristic.

(M6) Let $X \subseteq \{1, 2, \ldots, n-1\}$ be a set of size $\max\{|B|, |C|\}$ such that $\sum_{q \in X} W(q)$ is minimized. For each $j, k \in [n] \setminus X$, update the transition between j and k with the regular expression $r^X_{j,k,\sigma}$ where $\sigma = \sigma(j,k)$ is an elimination order eliminating X first that minimizes $|r^X_{j,k,\sigma}|$. With X eliminated, use the same method for some set $Y \subseteq \{1, 2, \ldots, n-2\} \setminus X$ of size $\min\{|B|, |C|\}$ such that $\sum_{q \in Y} W(q)$ is minimized (where the weights correspond the GNFA with X eliminated). Finally, eliminate $\{1, 2, \ldots, n-2\} \setminus (X \cup Y)$ using the weight heuristic.

Table 1. Average regular expression sizes relative to M1 in ratio.

$\|\Sigma\|$	n	M0	M1	M2	M3	M4	M5	M6	MB
2	20	38.71	1.00	5.09	1.66	1.08	1.57	-	0.90
	40	22830.66	1.00	79.33	4.90	1.27	4.33	-	0.85
	50	737847.78	1.00	310.38	9.05	1.32	7.77	-	0.82
5	20	394.95	1.00	18.72	2.31	1.39	1.93	1.49	0.73
	40	5705583.57	1.00	552.90	13.84	1.42	11.76	-	0.64
	50	600837780.48	1.00	3730.53	37.51	1.41	31.11	-	0.58
$n/2$	20	140.05	1.00	10.60	1.88	1.35	1.64	1.56	0.69
	40	4626.27	1.00	57.68	4.43	1.08	3.51	5.47	0.54
	50	13001.93	1.00	88.95	5.15	0.95	3.94	11.68	0.50
n	20	23.98	1.00	5.96	1.33	1.20	1.27	1.31	0.74
	40	121.58	1.00	15.13	1.94	0.99	1.78	1.96	0.60
	50	203.21	1.00	17.22	2.08	0.92	1.86	3.05	0.58

For various values of n and $|\Sigma|$, we report the average regular expression size from each method in Table 1 over 10,000 trials. The averages are relative to the weight heuristic in ratio. For example, if, on average, M1 and M2 yield regular expression sizes of 100 and 107, respectively, then we report a relative average of 1.07 for M2. The last column, labelled "MB", is the average of taking the minimum result of each method (per trial). Table 2 reports, for each method, the number of trials where it was the best method. We do not count ties, and hence, the row sum can be less than 10,000.

For smaller alphabets, the transition structure is usually sparse, so B and C are large. When B and C are large, M6 is too slow, so we omit M6 for smaller alphabets. In such cases, we compute vertex separators recursively on B and C and stop the recursion when we reach a subgraph of size 3 or less. These cases correspond to all rows of the tables for which we omit M6.

For larger alphabets, we include M6 and don't compute vertex separators recursively since B and C are already small. These cases correspond to all rows of the tables for which we include M6.

Table 2. Frequencies as the best performing method.

$\lvert\Sigma\rvert$	n	M0	M1	M2	M3	M4	M5	M6
2	20	22	4042	33	23	3139	1413	-
	40	0	6138	2	22	2892	828	-
	50	0	6347	0	14	2971	622	-
5	20	1	3443	1	46	1615	1921	2841
	40	0	5734	0	36	3556	666	-
	50	0	5602	0	23	3973	399	-
$n/2$	20	0	3083	2	54	2090	2009	2509
	40	0	3712	0	61	3996	927	1258
	50	0	3662	0	56	4598	817	821
n	20	0	1666	0	37	2555	1821	1559
	40	0	2749	0	72	3720	1387	1720
	50	0	2891	0	75	4210	1352	1197

First of all, the results show that all methods M1-M6 are generally much better than computing an elimination order at random. Method M2 is mostly ineffective. Method M3 is reasonably effective but usually not as good as most of the others. Method M5 is considerably more effective than M3. Conversely, M6 is less effective than M1. Thus, this strategy of choosing a different elimination order for different pairs of states appears more well-suited to the vertex separator strategy. Stated more generally, if we have some small set of states that we know we want to eliminate first, this strategy should yield an improvement, but if not, then this strategy is perhaps not helpful on average. Overall, the methods M5 and M6, while useful fairly frequently, may often be too expensive to consider. Some variations of M5 or M6 could be worth considering. Methods M1 and M4 are the most effective, despite having no known provable performance guarantee. Further experiments show that it is often worthwhile to try both M1 and M4 and take the smaller result of the two. For instance, for $n = 40$ and $5 \leq |\Sigma| \leq 35$, the weight heuristic is always better on average over 10,000 trials, but taking the best result of the weight heuristic and gate score heuristic per trial, we obtain an average 30–40% (depending on the value of $|\Sigma|$) improvement compared to only using the weight heuristic. Further experiments also show that, as n and $|\Sigma|$ grow, the gate score heuristic appears to gain an advantage over the weight heuristic. For $n = 50$ and $20 \leq |\Sigma| \leq 50$, the gate score heuristic is 1–9% (depending on the value of $|\Sigma|$) better than the weight heuristic on average.

We now consider another experiment to support Proposition 7. For fixed n and a fixed positive integer $\ell \leq n - 2$:

(1) Generate a random n-state NFA over a unary alphabet with initial state 0 and final state $n - 1$, by including each possible transition with probability $p = 0.5$. Repeat this until we obtain a trim NFA.
(2) Select a subset $U \subseteq \{1, 2, \ldots, n - 2\}$ of size ℓ uniformly at random.

Table 3. Values of $\overline{\rho}$ and P.

ℓ	n	$\overline{\rho}$	P	ℓ	n	$\overline{\rho}$	P
5	20	0.963	2883	15	20	1.000	9995
	30		1338		30		9996
	50		320		50		9973
	100		11		100		9959
	200		0		200		9869
10	20	0.999	9809	20	30	1.000	10000
	30		9597		50		10000
	50		9263		100		9998
	100		8374		200		9999
	200		6800		500		9991

(3) Eliminate all states from U (in any order).
(4) After eliminating U, let t be the number of pairs of (not necessarily distinct) states $j, k \in [n] \setminus U$ such that there is a (non-empty) transition from state j to state k.
(5) Let $\rho = \frac{t}{(n-\ell)^2}$ and record the value of ρ.

Notice that the restriction to a unary alphabet is not limiting for the sake of this experiment; we are only concerned with the transition structure. For various fixed values of n, ℓ, we conducted 10,000 trials of this experiment, recording both the average value of ρ (call this $\overline{\rho}$) and the number of trials where ρ was exactly 1 (call this P). The results are shown in Table 3. Unsurprisingly, for a fixed value of ℓ, the value of $\overline{\rho}$ does not depend on n (to three decimal places).

The results suggest we do not need to eliminate many states until the automaton becomes fully connected. Therefore, Proposition 7 suggests that the weight heuristic is generally an excellent method for computing an elimination order for the remaining states after eliminating the first few states. Notably, this supports the weight heuristic as a tiebreaker for the gate score heuristic.

7 Conclusion

We have shown that any class of finite automata whose underlying class of graphs admits strongly sublinear separators also admits shorter regular expressions. We proposed a new heuristic, inspired by vertex separators, called the gate score heuristic. Empirically, we found that the weight heuristic and the gate score heuristic perform better than the separator technique on average, but not in all cases. Future work could attempt to characterize when each method is best. We also provided some theoretical support for the weight heuristic in finite automata with dense transition structures. Subsequently, we showed empirically that after eliminating a small number of states from a randomly generated automaton, the remaining transition structure is likely to be dense. Therefore, the weight heuristic should be generally effective after eliminating the first few states. On the other hand, it is still generally unclear how one should eliminate the first few states.

References

1. Ahn, J.H., Han, Y.S.: Implementation of state elimination using heuristics. In: Maneth, S. (ed.) Implementation and Application of Automata, pp. 178–187. Springer, Berlin Heidelberg, Berlin, Heidelberg (2009)
2. Almeida, M., Moreira, N., Reis, R.: Enumeration and generation with a string automata representation. Theor. Comput. Sci. **387**(2), 93–102 (2007). descriptional Complexity of Formal Systems
3. Cioabă, S., Murty, M.: A First Course in Graph Theory and Combinatorics. Springer Singapore (2022)
4. Delgado, M., Morais, J.: Approximation to the smallest regular expression for a given regular language. In: Domaratzki, M., Okhotin, A., Salomaa, K., Yu, S. (eds.) Implementation and Application of Automata, pp. 312–314. Springer, Berlin Heidelberg, Berlin, Heidelberg (2005)
5. Dvořák, Z.: On classes of graphs with strongly sublinear separators. Eur. J. Comb. **71**, 1–11 (2018)
6. Ellul, K., Krawetz, B., Shallit, J., Wang, M.W.: Regular expressions: new results and open problems. J. Autom. Lang. Comb. **9**(2–3), 233–256 (2004)
7. FAdo. https://fado.dcc.fc.up.pt/. Accessed 03 Feb 2025
8. Gruber, H., Holzer, M.: Provably shorter regular expressions from finite automata. Int. J. Found. Comput. Sci. **24**(08), 1255–1279 (2013)
9. Gruber, H., Holzer, M.: From finite automata to regular expressions and back–a summary on descriptional complexity. Int. J. Found. Comput. Sci. **26**(08), 1009–1040 (2015)
10. Gruber, H., Holzer, M., Tautschnig, M.: Short regular expressions from finite automata: empirical results. In: Maneth, S. (ed.) Implementation and Application of Automata, pp. 188–197. Springer, Berlin Heidelberg, Berlin, Heidelberg (2009)
11. Han, Y.S., Wood, D.: Obtaining shorter regular expressions from finite-state automata. Theoret. Comput. Sci. **370**(1), 110–120 (2007)
12. Han, Y.S., Wood, D.: The generalization of generalized automata: expression automata. In: Domaratzki, M., Okhotin, A., Salomaa, K., Yu, S. (eds.) Implementation and Application of Automata, pp. 156–166. Springer, Heidelberg (2005)
13. Jiang, T., Ravikumar, B.: Minimal NFA problems are hard. SIAM J. Comput. **22**(6), 1117–1141 (1993)
14. Lipton, R., Tarjan, R.: A separator theorem for planar graphs. SIAM J. Appl. Math. **36**(2), 177–189 (1979)
15. Moreira, N., Nabais, D., Reis, R.: State elimination ordering strategies: some experimental results. In: McQuillan, I., Pighizzini, G. (eds.). In: Proceedings Twelfth Annual Workshop on Descriptional Complexity of Formal Systems, DCFS 2010, Saskatoon, Canada, 8-10th August 2010. EPTCS, vol. 31, pp. 139–148 (2010)
16. Shallit, J.: A Second Course in Formal Languages and Automata Theory. Cambridge University Press (2008)

Author Index

Published by Springer Nature Switzerland AG 2025
A. Malcher and L. Prigioniero (Eds.): DCFS 2025, LNCS 15759, p. 225, 2025.
https://doi.org/10.1007/978-3-031-97100-6

The manufacturer's authorised representative in the EU is Springer Nature Customer Service Centre GmbH, Europaplatz 3, 69115 Heidelberg, Germany. If you have any concerns regarding our products, please contact ProductSafety@springernature.com

Printed and bound by CPI Group (UK) Ltd, Croydon, CR0 4YY
30/09/2026
02225560-0006